Handbook of
Student Financial Aid

*Programs, Procedures,
and Policies*

Robert H. Fenske
Robert P. Huff
and Associates

Foreword by John Brademas

Handbook of
Student Financial Aid

Jossey-Bass Publishers
San Francisco • Washington • London • 1983

HANDBOOK OF STUDENT FINANCIAL AID
Programs, Procedures, and Policies
by Robert H. Fenske, Robert P. Huff, and Associates

Copyright © 1983 by: Jossey-Bass Inc., Publishers
433 California Street
San Francisco, California 94104
&
Jossey-Bass Limited
28 Banner Street
London EC1Y 8QE

Library of Congress Cataloging in Publication Data
Main entry under title:

Handbook of student financial aid.

Bibliography: p. 471
Includes index.
1. Student financial aid administration—United States
—Addresses, essays, lectures. 2. Student aid—United
States—Addresses, essays, lectures. I. Fenske, Robert H.
II. Huff, Robert P.
LB2340.5.H36   1983   378'.3'0973   83-11336
ISBN 0-87589-571-9

Manufactured in the United States of America

The paper in this book meets the guidelines for
permanence and durability of the Committee on
Production Guidelines for Book Longevity of the
Council on Library Resources.

JACKET DESIGN BY WILLI BAUM

FIRST EDITION

Code 8318

*The Jossey-Bass
Higher Education Series*

Foreword

In 1643 Lady Anne Mowlson presented Harvard College with an endowment of 100 pounds, the income to be used to help a needy student. She thereby established the first scholarship fund in America.

By 1981, this book tells us, financial aid from all sources, private and public, to students in postsecondary institutions totaled $16 billion. Federal programs generated nearly $12 billion of that amount, aiding four and a half million students attending 6,700 institutions across the country.

In the financing of higher education, the nearly three and a half centuries that separate Lady Mowlson's act of generosity and Uncle Sam's current multibillion-dollar investment have not been ones of orderly evolution. As Robert H. Fenske tells us, the expansion of resources to help students pay the costs of college or graduate school is a recent development in our national history. The almost explosive growth in student financial aid has come only in the last twenty years with the entrance into the picture of the federal government.

Indeed, these were the years of my own service in Congress, where, as a member of the House Committee on Education and Labor, I took part in writing most of the legislation enacted during that time to support schools, colleges, universities, and other institutions of learning and culture in our country. Just what, in fashioning federal education programs, did my colleagues and I seek to accomplish during those years? Clearly, we made a number of commitments: to encourage educational research and development; to support the arts and humanities, libraries and museums; to strengthen international studies. But the central focus of our efforts—and I speak here of representatives and senators and presidents of both parties—was to make sure that education would be accessible to those likely to be excluded either by economic or physical disadvantage.

The conviction that an opportunity for a good education must be open to all with the talent and motivation for it was certainly a driving force in my own attitude as a legislator. When I was still very young, my father, a Greek immigrant, told me, "John, I'll probably not leave much money to my children but I will leave you all a first-class education"—and he did. That the son of an immigrant father and an Indiana schoolteacher should have been able to study at the finest universities in the world impressed deeply on me the importance of education, especially as a ladder of social and economic advance.

Moreover, I was first elected to Congress in 1958, the year after the Soviets launched the first *Sputnik* and shocked Americans into a reevaluation of the state of our educational system, and I felt strongly that the time had come for the federal government to provide greater support for education in our country. Over the next two decades, my colleagues and I worked hard to broaden access to higher education. Following the National Defense Education Act of 1958, we designed—through the Higher Education Act of 1965; the Education Amendments of 1972, 1976, and 1980; and the Middle Income Student Assistance Act of 1978—a structure of grants, loans, and work-study jobs to make it possible for young men and women of ability and desire who needed financial assistance to go to college.

Now I am president of a major urban university that is dedicated to educational opportunity. The founders of New York University launched, a century and a half ago, an institution whose doors would be open to all—not just the children of the rich but the sons and daughters of the middle and working classes, including the children of the thousands of immigrants then making their way to our shores. For the past 150 years, New York University has remained faithful to that goal.

My new responsibility—as head of the largest private university in the nation, with over 40,000 students enrolled in fourteen schools and divisions and an annual operating budget of over half a billion dollars—has enabled me to see the institutional side of the student aid coin. I now deal daily with the impact of the legislative programs I helped write.

From these dual perspectives—that of public policy maker and now campus administrator—I offer three observations. First, the issue of student aid, whether as an item on a legislative agenda or in the operation of a college or university, cannot be dealt with in isolation from other objectives. At an individual institution, for example, questions of financial aid intersect with a range of concerns: admissions, fund raising, student services, public relations. On the national level, educational financing policies have always been meshed, either explicitly or implicitly, with broad policy goals such as national security, civil rights, or technological advancement. Those who think seriously about student aid must delve into a thicket of related issues and questions.

My second point is that over the next decade the fate of federal student aid and that of the nation's colleges and universities will become still more closely intertwined. Government decisions on funds for student assistance will be crucial for thousands of students and will be critical as well to the health and viability of many institutions of higher learning.

My third point is this: As we endure a period of cuts in government spending for education, declining enrollments, and a sputtering economy, decision makers in Washington and the state governments and administrators of colleges and universities must be increasingly creative and flexible. Certainly university officials must utilize the resources of their institutions as efficiently as possible. But public leaders, on both the federal and state levels, must also pay attention to the intimate connection between adequately supporting education (including financial aid) and meeting the nation's economic and defense needs.

As a starting point for such considerations, I commend this survey of the landscape of student financial assistance. The authors trace the roots of our student aid policies, review their current state and future prospects, and offer practical advice on the nuts and bolts of administration.

This volume comes at a moment when federal student aid measures are under seemingly systematic assault by the current administration in Washington. As educators—as citizens—we must not lose sight of the original purpose of the commitment to student aid: to open the doors of opportunity to young men and women who lack the resources but have the talent and motivation to pursue a college education. More and more, however, Americans are realizing that student aid serves two other purposes as well: our economic vitality and our national security.

By helping us translate the aims of educational access into effective programs of assistance, the editors and the contributing authors to this volume have given us the right book at the right time.

New York, New York   John Brademas
June 1983   *President*
                                        New York University

Preface

Student financial aid emerged as a vital force in financing American higher education during the 1970s, when the Education Amendments of 1972 authorized a massive expansion of funding and also established a program to encourage the states to become involved or to do more in assisting their students with their educational costs. Today a large proportion of the tuition and fees that support the operating budgets of most public colleges and universities derives from the various forms of student aid. For example, at Arizona State University total financial aid provided to students to support their college education in the 1981–82 academic year equaled 36.3 percent of the institutional operating budget. Many private colleges and universities depend even more heavily on such funds because of their reliance on much higher tuition and fees. Students at Stanford University, for instance, received aid for 1981–82 in an amount equal to 43.7 percent of the operating budget. Well over half of all students in higher education today rely on one or more forms of financial aid during their academic careers. The College Scholarship Service has estimated that, in 1980–81, more than $16 billion was available from all sources (other than parents or the student's own earnings and savings) to help students meet their costs of higher education. As costs of attendance rise, so do the needs of these students for financial aid.

Policy makers and administrators are just beginning to realize how important student aid is to their institution and its students. Some administrators view student aid's newly important financial impact as a rationale to place the function in the business affairs area; others see it as an opportunity to expand student services. From nearly all perspectives, student aid is an area of critical concern and urgent importance to all colleges and universities. The substantial contribution it makes to institutional operational budgets has already been mentioned. But apart from considerations of finance, student aid is significant as a means of achieving enrollment goals and ensuring diversity in the composition of the student body, which in turn enriches the educational experience for all participants. It also helps to address such societal concerns as the need for an educated citizenry, the advancement of knowledge and technology, and equal educational opportunity.

The purpose of this book is to provide a comprehensive source of timely information on the basic functions, roles, problems, and prospects of student financial aid within the college or university. Because the field of financial aid administration is continuing to evolve rapidly, there is an urgent need for in-service professional development for practitioners and for description and analysis of student aid for the benefit of institutional administrators, including those at decision-making as well as functional levels in academic affairs, financial administration, and, of course, student services.

This book is intended for use at colleges and universities of varying enrollment size, both public and private, whether they are two-year, four-year, or beyond. Every effort has been made in the preparation of the book to seek a balance among policy, administrative, and technical matters. Considerable detail is offered in order to help the reader deal with the day-to-day issues that confront an educational institution as it seeks to operate an efficient student aid program and to use available resources to further its goals. However, our authors have also provided coverage of important financial aid policy issues that should be of interest to administrators at the highest levels of responsibility because they greatly affect enrollment planning, budgeting, student services, and fiscal accountability. With this book higher education now has a ready reference that should be helpful for decisions concerning student aid. It should also provide a general orientation for presidents, vice presidents for academic affairs, deans, business officers, directors of development, and admissions personnel, who do not work directly in the field but need to become quickly knowledgeable. As such, it fills the wide gap between currently available treatises on state and federal issues and studies of the financing of higher education, on the one hand, and various technical and operating manuals distributed by government agencies and the need analysis services to practitioners, on the other.

After having determined the need for a financial aid handbook, we agreed early in our planning that foremost experts in the field should be invited to contribute chapters. A book comprised of such material is authoritative by virtue of the background, credentials, and experience of the contributors. However, in commissioning each chapter, editors planning the book can (and should) offer to such authors only general suggestions about content. (The alternative to this approach is to emphasize internal construction of the book and restrict selection of authors only to those who are willing to write to detailed and somewhat inflexible directions.) We believe that the approach taken in this book achieves a satisfying combination of highly authoritative contributors and a comprehensive, logical plan of contents. Just as an effort has been made to balance the content of the handbook, so too authors with different backgrounds and experiences have been selected to balance opinions and perspectives. The authors selected to write each of the chapters include college and university administrators in financial aid and other areas, such as the president's office, student services, and legal affairs; educational consultants; key staff officers of the College Board and the National Association of Student Financial Aid Administrators; federal and state officials; and academic researchers. They all have an important attribute in common: each has achieved a leadership role and is highly regarded for his or her contribution to the field of student financial aid administration or scholarship. The authors were most diligent in providing high-quality, responsible material for this handbook, and we are grateful to each of them for accommodating our writing assignments to their busy schedules.

Obviously, there are some limitations in assembling a collection of original chapters by experienced professionals. Since each chapter is an independent, complete statement, there is some repetition in content. Our editing efforts were aimed at keeping such repetition to a minimum. Also, there are areas relating to financial aid administration on which consensus is lacking and differences of opinion abound. While we might ourselves take issue with some of the opinions presented, we encouraged independence of both thought and expression.

We did, however, suggest certain guidelines to our authors beyond a general identification of the topic to be covered. In order to avoid any possible conflict of interest and appearance of endorsement, we requested that they refrain as much as possible from identifying by name any commercially available products, software systems, and consulting firms. We also pointed out that, while descriptions of model student aid programs and exemplary case studies can provide highly useful illustrations, by the time most readers see these descriptions, the actual "models" have often deteriorated or ceased to exist at the places named, or the persons identified in the case studies have moved to other institutions. Similarly, we suggested that the authors make reference to the student aid "tradebooks" that purport to guide students toward available aid funds only if they are certain that such books do not, as is often the case, contain erroneous or badly outdated information.

Part One, "Development, Scope, and Purposes of Student Aid," focuses on the nature, sources, and objectives of student financial aid. Historical evolution is a central theme of this section, since such an approach often reveals not only objectives but also future directions. In the initial chapter, Robert Fenske considers the background, development, and current dimensions of student aid. The next three chapters then examine in depth federal, state, and institutional/private aid. The author of the chapter on federal aid, James Moore, discusses the purposes and provisions of the major programs administered by the Department of Education and offers useful information on a number of critical issues and problems. The variety of loan and grant programs now functioning in the states and their various objectives are explored by Arthur Marmaduke in Chapter Three. Robert Huff, in Chapter Four, discusses the sources and uses of institutional student support, with particular emphasis on how institutional and private aid can be increased in an era of diminishing public funding.

At the very center of the student aid function is the delivery of assistance in its various forms to students. The steps in this process are presented by the authors of Part Two, "Delivering Aid to Students on Campus." In Chapter Five Norman Beck discusses the dissemination of information to students about application procedures and the awarding policies applicable to all types of aid. The information that should be required of students and their parents in an aid application is also detailed. Joe Paul Case, in Chapter Six, presents the theoretical foundations of and the actual procedural steps in the determination of financial need. In the following chapter, on the packaging of aid, Shirley Binder considers generally accepted principles of awarding aid and suggests ways in which an institution can determine what its awarding policy might appropriately be. Part Two concludes with a chapter by Donald Ryan, who addresses the procedures for disbursing aid to the students and the various fiscal controls that must be maintained to ensure the proper use of resources.

Optimizing the effectiveness of the student aid program is the central theme of Part Three, "Ensuring Effectiveness in Administering Aid Programs." It begins with a chapter by Donald Ryan treating financial aid office staffing formulas and describing the training that is essential to maintaining a capable and efficient staff. In Chapter Ten Merle Lange examines the various considerations that influence the decision on how the student aid office should be organized. Where the aid office should be situated within the institutional structure and what expectations senior managers should have of its director are considered in the chapter by D. Bruce Johnstone and Robert Huff. The ways in which a college or university's student aid program can be evaluated are discussed by Dallas Martin in Chapter Twelve. This concluding chapter for Part Three also suggests how the aid program evaluation can improve effectiveness and efficiency.

Part Four, "Importance of Aid in Meeting Student Needs and Institutional Goals," addresses the numerous ways in which student aid can be used to foster institutional objectives. The initial chapter, by James Nelson and Robert Fenske, stresses the importance of applied research and suggests how aid administrators can forecast the amount and nature of required aid resources. The next two chapters are devoted to the critical topic of how best to employ financial aid to achieve and maintain desired enrollment goals. The first, by Joseph Boyd and George Henning, focuses on the impact of student aid on marketing and admissions. A wide range of strategies on using student aid to meet enrollment goals are offered by these authors. The second, by Leonard Wenc, discusses the interaction between attrition problems and institutional student aid policies. Resort to litigation in financial aid matters occurs with increasing frequency, and the chapter by Bruce Richardson is devoted to considering some of the more prevalent issues and problems. In Chapter Seventeen we summarize what seem to us to be several of the more significant findings contained in the preceding chapters. This effort to highlight and synthesize certain conclusions scarcely does justice to the vast array of information presented by our authors, but it should provide a focus for readers seeking at least a general familiarity with the nature and delivery of student aid and some indication of how it can be harnessed efficiently and responsibly to achieve institutional goals and objectives. In the concluding chapter of Part Four, Lawrence Gladieux, a knowledgeable and highly regarded observer of the student aid scene, discusses the directions in which student aid is likely to go in the future and alerts administrators to the trends to look for in their planning.

An annotated bibliography—culled by Robert Fenske, Louis Attinasi, and Richard Voorhees from a thorough review of the financial aid literature—follows Part Four. This bibliography—complementing the bibliographical notes that conclude each chapter except Chapter Seventeen—suggests several general works that should be included in every college or university financial aid library and discusses the content and utility of a number of sources that bear specifically on the topics of the book's four parts.

We gratefully acknowledge the enthusiastic interest and support of many leaders in the field of student aid. They were unanimous in their encouragement of our developing this handbook, and nearly all indicated that it was long overdue and would be highly useful. Such support was invaluable when our enthusiasm and stamina were tested during the many months involved in planning, preparing, writing, and editing.

We thank John Brademas, president of New York University and former key congressional leader of initiatives in student aid, for agreeing to provide the Foreword. His contribution adds a unique and invaluable perspective.

We are grateful to our families for their patient tolerance and support throughout the project. Robert Fenske thanks the board and staff of Luther Park Camp near Danbury, Wisconsin, for use of a cloistered cabin for a brief but intensive period of writing and editing.

June 1983
Robert H. Fenske
Tempe, Arizona

Robert P. Huff
Stanford, California

Contents

Presents a comprehensive background on the historical purposes and forms of student financial aid and how it became an integral part of the financing of higher education in the United States. Traces the growth of aid programs, principally during the era of major expansion starting in the late 1950s. Also reviews the impact of aid on students, especially minority and disadvantaged.

   of Financial Aid Awards   149
   Shirley F. Binder

   Explains how scholarships, loans, and jobs may be combined
   in an equitable manner to meet the particular needs of each
   student. Presents several proven methods for awarding aid
   to students.

8. Disbursing and Controlling Aid Funds   169
   Donald R. Ryan

   Discusses how the various forms of student aid are paid to
   recipients. Provides guidance on the ways in which postsecondary institutions are expected to be accountable to public and private donors for the appropriate use of student aid
   resources.

   **Part Three: Ensuring Effectiveness in
   Administering Aid Programs**   **191**

9. Staffing the Aid Office and Improving
   Professional Expertise   194
   Donald R. Ryan

   Provides information on the appropriate levels of professional and support staff for student aid programs of varying
   sizes and natures. Suggests ways in which the financial aid
   staff can improve its effectiveness through training and other opportunities to increase knowledge and capability.

10. Factors in Organizing an Effective
    Student Aid Office   221
    Merle L. Lange

    Describes some of the accepted patterns for organizing in-
    stitutional aid offices to achieve maximum efficiency and
    responsiveness to student needs. Treats various technical
    support functions that can enhance programs.

11. Relationship of Student Aid to Other
    College Programs and Services   237
    D. Bruce Johnstone, Robert P. Huff

    Examines typical reporting structures for institutional aid
    administrators and the relationship of the program to other
    functions that bear on how financial aid policy should be
    developed.

Discusses the various ways in which institutions may determine how well their student aid programs are serving their
purposes. Suggests various corrective measures that may be
taken when results and goals do not coincide.

Describes several models that can be used by aid offices in
colleges and universities to determine and disseminate information about the impact of student aid on institutional
goals and operations. Suggests ways in which institutions
can anticipate and prepare for changes in student demo-
graphics and support levels.

Presents various ways in which student financial aid can be
used to maintain and increase enrollment, even with the
anticipated drop in the size and quality of the traditional
applicant pool. Relatively small amounts of aid can be cre-
atively packaged to selectively increase enrollment of specific types of students.

Describes why, in terms of cost-effective means of maintaining and increasing enrollment, successful retention efforts
are more efficient than typical recruiting efforts. Presents
the latest research findings on preventing drop-outs and
strategies for using student aid as part of institution-wide
programs to retain students to graduation.

Contents

Tables, Figures, and Exhibits

Chapter Three

Chapter Six

Chapter Thirteen

Chapter Eighteen

Chapter Thirteen

Chapter Eighteen

The Authors

Robert H. Fenske is professor of higher education in the Department of Higher and Adult Education, Arizona State University. He received the B.A. degree in history (1957), the M.S. degree in history and education (1959), and the Ph.D. degree in higher education and educational psychology (1965), all from the University of Wisconsin at Madison. His professional responsibilities have included research and administration at the University of Wisconsin and teaching and institutional research at the University of Minnesota. He was director of research for the Illinois Board of Higher Education before his appointment in 1969 as senior research psychologist and director of the Research Institute at the American College Testing Program. He joined the faculty at Arizona State University in 1974.

Student financial aid has been prominent among Fenske's research interests over the years, beginning with statewide studies in Wisconsin of how family financial resources affected college-going in the late 1950s. He directed a systemwide survey of student income and expenditures at the University of Minnesota in 1966, and in 1968 he began a series of statewide studies of Illinois State Scholarship Commission monetary award recipients, which extended through 1980. Recent research activities include a 1980 statewide study of training needs for student financial aid practitioners in Arizona. Fenske is currently completing a three-year project with the Fund for the Improvement of Postsecondary Education, the aim of which is to develop a computer optimization model for improving the financial aid delivery system for disadvantaged students. Fenske's recent publications in the field of student aid include *Renewing and Developing the Partnership: Federal/State/Campus Cooperation in Student Financial Aid,* published by the American College Testing Program (1981), and *State Need-Based College Scholarship and Grant Programs: A Study of Their Development, 1969–1980* (with Joseph D. Boyd), published by the College Board (1981). Fenske currently serves on the editorial board of the *Journal of Student Financial Aid.*

Robert P. Huff is director of financial aids at Stanford University. He received the B.A. degree in history (1948), the M.A. degree in political science (1949), and the Ph.D. degree in political science (1966), all from Stanford. He is editor of the *Journal of Student Financial Aid,* past-president of the National Association of Student Financial Aid Administrators, and past-chairman of the College Scholarship Services Council and Assembly. He has served as a consultant on student financial aid matters to the U.S. Office of Education and the states of California and New York and has been a trustee of the College Board. He also chaired the U.S. Commissioner of Education's Panel of Experts on the Federal Student Aid Funding Process.

In addition to his administrative responsibilities, Huff is a lecturer in the School of Education at Stanford and has taught summer school courses in student aid administration and in the financing of higher education at Loyola-Marymount University in Los Angeles and the University of Hawaii at Manoa. He has authored journal articles, chapters in collected works, and other publications on student aid.

Louis C. Attinasi, Jr., is a doctoral candidate in the Department of Higher and Adult Education, Arizona State University, Tempe.

Norman E. Beck is director of employee relations and auxiliary services, Ball State University, Muncie, Indiana.

Shirley F. Binder is assistant vice president for student affairs and director of admissions, University of Texas at Austin.

Joseph D. Boyd is a consultant in higher education, Deerfield, Illinois.

Joe Paul Case is dean of financial aid, Amherst College, Massachusetts.

Lawrence E. Gladieux is executive director of the Washington, D.C., office of the College Board.

George E. Henning is president of George Henning and Associates, Inc., consultants to higher education, Rock Island, Illinois.

D. Bruce Johnstone is president of the State University of New York College at Buffalo.

Merle L. Lange is director of student financial assistance at Glendale Community College, Glendale, Arizona.

Arthur S. Marmaduke is director of the California Student Aid Commission, Sacramento.

A. Dallas Martin, Jr., is executive director of the National Association of Student Financial Aid Administrators, Washington, D.C.

James W. Moore has recently retired as director of student financial assistance programs, U.S. Department of Education, Washington, D.C.

James E. Nelson is former vice president for program planning and research and current program manager for new technology, the College Board, New York City.

Bruce M. Richardson is associate general counsel, California State University at Long Beach.

Donald R. Ryan is director of financial aid, California State University at San Jose.

Richard A. Voorhees is a graduate associate in the Department of Higher and Adult Education, Arizona State University, Tempe.

Leonard M. Wenc is director of financial aid, Carleton College, Northfield, Minnesota.

Handbook of
Student Financial Aid

*Programs, Procedures,
and Policies*

Part One

Development, Scope, and Purposes of Student Aid

Because there is so much technical detail and emphasis on mechanics in the field of student financial aid, one can lose sight of its nature and purposes. Therefore, a general orientation to student financial aid—that is, an overview of the history and development of the field and a description of federal, state, and institutional/private student aid programs—seems the best way to begin a comprehensive handbook.

In Chapter One Robert Fenske reveals that the concept of student financial aid has roots that lie deep in the long history of American higher education. Using the analogy of a twenty-four-hour day as the comparative time frame, he highlights the fact that large-scale governmental programs, particularly at the federal level, are very recent entries to the field. He

1

also points out that, historically, academic ability was regarded as the sine qua non of student aid. Although the President's Commission on Higher Education (1947) recommended that a full 40 percent of high school graduates should be provided access to college through financial aid and other means, that figure was meant to estimate the proportion who had the "ability to benefit" academically from the higher learning. The Great Society egalitarian surges led first to the Higher Education Act of 1965, with its emphasis on gaining equal opportunity for racial minorities and the economically disadvantaged; then to the "entitlement" philosophy of the 1972 amendments, which attempt to guarantee the right to a floor of support for postsecondary education to all who are interested, with minimal attention given to prior academic achievement or tested ability. Fenske reviews recent reports on how well minorities and others have been served by the new programs, and his chapter concludes with a discussion of problems and prospects that face student aid as the 1980s unfold. He underscores the continuing lack of coordination in the field and points out that the serious economic and political challenges now developing will be difficult to meet on a piecemeal, uncoordinated basis.

Since the lion's share of student financial aid today is provided by the federal government, it seems only reasonable as the sources of student aid are reviewed to commence with a description of its current dimensions. Chapter Two is authored by James Moore, who has had a major role in implementing federal student aid programs for over twenty years. He describes the provisions and purposes of each of the major student aid programs currently administered by the Department of Education. Moore's description of the development and current provisions of the major loan and grant programs is thoroughly authoritative, because he was an early participant in formulating and implementing regulations for most of them and, until his recent retirement, held a key leadership position in the Department of Education. The chapter treats the following programs: National Direct Student Loans, College Work-Study, Supplemental Educational Opportunity Grants, State Student Incentive Grants, Basic Educational Opportunity Grants (now renamed Pell Grants), and

Guaranteed Student Loans. Each of the descriptions reviews the origin and present status of the program.

Moore also offers a thorough discussion of important aspects of general program administration, including student eligibility, establishment of financial need criteria, allocation of campus-based aid to institutions, administrative expense allowance, institutional audits and program reviews, and sources of funds. The chapter concludes with an annotated list of official documents and reports. To the best of our knowledge, this list is unique in its comprehensiveness and, as such, is invaluable for any person interested in further study of the federal presence in student aid.

Arthur Marmaduke, the author of Chapter Three, has had one of the longest tenures among directors of a major state student aid agency. As director of the California agency since the 1950s and an early president of the National Association of State Scholarship and Grant Programs, he is admirably suited to review the stages of state student aid growth in the United States. He reminds the reader that the states' role in student aid predates the federal presence by several decades. Marmaduke traces the significant growth of student support programs at the state level and summarizes the various state governance structures for student aid. He then deals in considerable depth with the main types of loan and grant programs now functioning in every state of the union. He discusses the indexes available to measure the extent of the various states' support to students and the particular issue of student aid in the private sector. Marmaduke also includes recommendations on how individual campus aid officers can influence and interact with the state aid agency policies and operations.

The concluding chapter in Part One surveys the institutional and private sources of student aid. Robert Huff writes from his perspective as long-time director of student aid at a leading independent university and former president of the National Association of Student Financial Aid Administrators. He is able to draw on his general knowledge of the field to treat the need for and role of institutional financial aid as a supplement to federal and state support, which never seems adequate

and is currently threatened and also—since "most public funds
are awarded in response to the strict demonstration of financial
need"—does not allow institutions "to recognize and promote
the enrollment of students with exceptional academic accomplishments and promise or with other qualifications held in
high regard by the academic community." He discusses the
sources and uses of institutional support—distinguishing between restricted funds and unrestricted funds—and suggests how
these funds can be secured and increased. In the last part of the
chapter, Huff counsels the reader about ways in which over one
billion dollars in potential private student aid resources can be
identified and harnessed to assist in achieving institutional goals.

1

Student Aid
Past and Present

Robert H. Fenske

From a modest beginning early in the history of higher education, student financial aid has become in the early 1980s a most significant part of the financing of American higher education. In most colleges and universities, a significant portion of the institutional operating budget derives from the various forms of student aid, much of it brought to the campus from federal and state sources independent of influence by the institution. About half of all students in higher education use one or more forms of financial aid at some time during their undergraduate careers. Despite its size and significance, student financial aid has a continuing identity crisis as a professional field and also as a function within institutions of higher education.

If one were to cast the historical panorama of student financial aid in the metaphor of a single twenty-four-hour day representing the three and a half centuries of American higher education, the institutional role occupies the picture alone from the beginning of the day at midnight through early-morning hours, the forenoon, the afternoon, and the early evening. That is, throughout this early period, institutions themselves raised and administered scholarship funds from external private sources or in a few cases from internal sources, such as the reallocation of income from tuition. At this point, three fourths of the way through the hypothetical day, direct student aid involved a few million dollars and a few thousand students nationally. About 7:30 in the evening, state programs enter the picture as New York begins the first large-scale comprehensive program. Late in the evening, state efforts grow more significant as California and Illinois also establish programs. Less than an hour and a half before the end of the hypothetical day, the federal government enters the picture: the GI Bill is passed at the end of World War II and, just thirty-five minutes before midnight, the Basic Educational Opportunity Grant (BEOG) program is funded. Yet, as midnight strikes to signal the end of the hypothetical day, the proportions among the federal, state, and institutional sectors are most unequal. According to the Carnegie Council on Policy Studies in Higher Education (1979, p. 4), "Student aid is now 90 percent from public sources, as compared with 65 percent ten years ago; it was nearly zero percent from public sources before World War II." Of the current share from public sources, the states provide about 10 percent and the federal government provides 90 percent. The private and institutional sources remain significant; however, they are relatively small scale compared to the total of public sources.

A Historical Perspective

Most of the colonial colleges were supported by government appropriations or by land grants, lotteries, toll fees, and the like. In the context of the monolithic theocracies that comprised the early colonies, there simply was no distinction between the public good and private higher education, whether in support for institutions or for needy and/or talented students (Rudolph, 1962, pp. 185-187). "The period between the establishing of Harvard College and the Civil War is generally referred to as the first epoch of student financial aid. Within this period unquestioned evidence exists regarding the commitment to make higher education available to the economically poor student. Individuals, organizations, and state governments recognized the need for scholarship aid to the impoverished aspiring youth" (Meade, 1972, p. 41).

In 1862 the states aided students somewhat more directly by participating in the federal government's Land-Grant Act (the Morrill Act): "The low cost, to student and family, of attendance at these public institutions represented the first organized student financial aid program" (Godzicki, 1975, p. 18). This pattern was to be repeated a century later, when, largely in response to the recommendations of the 1946 Truman Commission, hundreds of low- or no-tuition community colleges for commuters were built to reduce the financial cost of college attendance.

Through the nineteenth century, however, direct student aid remained a private and institutional province; state and federal government participation is a twentieth-century phenomenon. Only a small percentage of the age group (less than 10 percent) enrolled in colleges and universities through the 1800s, and nearly all of these were young men from families of considerable means. The colleges used ingenuity to attract the brightest and most talented students, whether needy or not. One popular technique was the perpetual scholarship. Under this arrangement a donor could guarantee tuition-free enrollment of one or more of his descendants "in perpetuity," a practice that the colleges sometimes found disastrously expensive as costs rose and a seemingly never-ending succession of family scions appeared on the campus decade after decade. It was also during the 1800s that private colleges made "probably the greatest discovery in the development of student aid" (Moon, 1975, p. 4)— the discovery that a college did not need scholarship money in order to give scholarships. Reducing costs to needy students by waiving some or all tuition and fees and naming the reduction a scholarship was all that was needed. The reduction was funded by a sort of "Robin Hood" technique: Tuition was set somewhat higher than actually needed for the operating budget. A portion of the tuition income was skimmed from those students who paid full tuition and diverted to needy students in tuition waivers called "scholarships." This practice has continued, and to this day it is difficult to disentangle "real" scholarships—those funded from external gifts and grants—from what might be called "creative accounting."

State Student Aid. While there is general agreement about several landmarks in the development of state-funded programs of student aid, there is little clarity about the origins of the movement. The first program is variously reported as occurring in Connecticut in 1909 (Meade, 1972, p. 42), in the "mid-nineteenth century" in Maryland (Boyd, 1975, p. 120), in the Massachusetts Bay Colony in 1653 (Giddens, 1970, p. 39), and in New York in 1919 (Godzicki, 1975, p. 18). The era previous to the 1819 *Dartmouth College* decision can be discounted because the "state" interests were thoroughly intermingled with "private" college governance and financing. (In that decision the U.S. Supreme Court ruled [17Y.S518] that state governments could not control or influence the governance of colleges chartered as private foundations, effectively severing the private colleges from state support.) The direct student aid programs that appeared during the nineteenth century were highly targeted categorical programs that were generally short-lived (Giddens, 1970). The first comprehensive program, then, apparently did originate in New York in 1919. (A scholarship program begun in 1913 focused on honorary recognition of academically talented youth rather than the awarding of financial aid.) Over the next several decades, few states followed New York's lead. Meade (1972, p. 42) reports that only four state-funded programs existed by 1936; Giddens (1970, p. 37) states that three existed in 1954.

The proliferation of "open-door" two-year community and other types of colleges greatly increased the proportion of high school graduates going to college. As another means of ensuring access, tuition was kept low at practically all public institutions and was nonexistent at most two-year colleges. Consequently, by 1950 enrollments in the public sector equaled the enrollments in the historically predominant private sector for the first time and threatened to permanently surpass them. Out of concern for the continued viability of the private sector, a number of state student aid agencies were set up in the decades of the 1950s and 1960s and calibrated their awards to the higher tuition of the private institutions. "Maintenance of choice" was the catchword for these programs.

In the mid-1950s, many states established study groups to devise strategies for dealing with the impending enrollment bulge in the 1960s. Also, in response to the Truman Commission's recommendations and later civil rights initiatives, these study groups addressed the need to remove financial, racial, and ethnic barriers to higher education. Several more states, including California (1956) and Illinois (1958), established agencies to administer state aid programs. During this post-*Sputnik* era, most aid was tied to scholastic promise, as well as need, in a search for talent to upgrade the nation's scientific capacity. In the 1960s, however, the goals of student aid shifted: monetary awards now were given primarily to allow any interested student to have access to any college that would grant admission.

Boyd (1975, pp. 118-119) lists in more or less chronological order the purposes for which monetary awards were given to students by state agencies over their history to date:

1. Manpower needs—that is, to recruit future teachers or nurses.
2. Veterans' benefits (dating back to the Civil War).
3. Assistance to the physically handicapped for vocational training.
4. Recognition of academic achievement and potential.
5. Inclusion of financial need along with academic ability.
6. Emphasis on financial need, rather than ability, as main criterion.
7. Elimination of categorical programs, with specific targeted recipients subsumed in large comprehensive programs.
8. Provision for use of scholarship and grant awards at private colleges and universities.
9. Appropriation of funds to meet matching requirements of federal student aid programs.

Federal Role in Student Aid. Beginning with the passage of the Northwest Ordinance of 1787 and through the first half of the twentieth century, federal policy in support of higher education was limited to addressing specific national problems, usually precipitated by a crisis. Examples include the pivotal Morrill Act of 1862, which created the land-grant colleges to provide "practical" education in mechanical arts and agriculture; the National Defense Act of 1916, creating the federal Reserve Officers' Training Corps; the numerous programs under the New Deal's federal Emergency Relief Administration, which not only assisted institutions but enabled students to remain in college and therefore off the relief roles during the 1930s; the famous GI Bill, or Serviceman's Readjustment Act of 1944, which enabled tens of thousands of returning World War II veterans to enroll in higher education; and, of course, the National Defense Education Act of 1958, which was a response to the Russian launching of *Sputnik I* and *II* and signaled a major federal commitment to higher education through a dramatic increase in federal funding.

Few attempts have been made, however, to formulate a comprehensive federal policy toward higher education. The most noteworthy attempt to date was made by the historic President's Commission on Higher Education (the Truman Commission) in 1946. The Truman Commission, composed of twenty-eight national leaders, examined higher education in America with a thoroughness that was unprecedented prior to 1946 and was not approached again—not even by President Eisenhower's Committee on Education Beyond the High School or by the National Commission on the Financing of Postsecondary Education (1973) or the Carnegie Council on Policy Studies in Higher Education (1980). After studying almost every conceivable aspect of higher education, the Truman Commission made some extremely bold and sweeping recommendations for policy formulation (see President's Commission on Higher Education, 1947). For example, higher education had historically involved only a small minority of America's youth, but the commission (vol. 1, p. 101) contended that American colleges and universities "can no longer consider themselves merely the instrument for producing an intellectual elite; they must become the means by which every citizen, youth and adult, is enabled and encouraged to carry his education, formal and informal, as far as his native capacities permit." The commission also urged that all racial, ethnic, and sex discrimination barriers be struck down and that economic barriers be reduced or eliminated by two means: (1) by greatly increased expansion of low- or no-tuition commuter institutions, especially community colleges; and (2) by student financial aid in the form of loans, grants, and sponsored employment. In the Truman Commission's reports, one can find the germinal ideas for all of the major federal and many of the state student aid programs eventually enacted.

The key recommendations of the Truman Commission, however, even when viewed as an aggregate of the federal programs eventually enacted, never comprised a coherent national policy. Rather, a patchwork quilt of programs was developed through a rapid series of legislative initiatives beginning in the early 1960s—among them the Higher Education Facilities Act of 1963, which provided federal funds to institutions of higher education for the construction of academic facilities; the Economic Opportunity Act of 1964, which created the College Work-Study program and began to implement the federal policy of both institutional and direct student support for higher education; the Health Professions Educational Assistance Act of 1963; and the Nurse Training Act of 1964.

The passage of the Higher Education Act of 1965 marked the first planks of a federal platform of support to higher education as recommended by the Truman Commission. The act embodied a dual approach toward federal support of higher education in that it proposed to help both the institutions and the students. Specifically, it provided federal support to the states and their institutions in such areas as construction of academic facilities, educational institutions, and libraries; support for developing institutions; and community service and continuing education. Equally, and perhaps more important, Title IV of the act established a need-based student aid delivery system through the Educational Opportunity Grant (EOG) program, the College Work-Study (CWS) program, and the Guaranteed Student Loan (GSL) program. The Higher Education Act of 1965 was truly a historic legislative landmark. It recognized the need for federal support of higher education institutions, as well as the need for equal access to higher education for all Americans, regardless of an individual's economic status.

By 1972 Congress and the administration clearly swung toward student aid and away from institutional aid. The Education Amendments of 1972 (amendments to the Higher Education Act of 1965) greatly expanded support for student assistance. The Basic Educational Opportunity Grant (BEOG) program (renamed Pell Grants in 1980) was instituted as a direct way of entitling access to higher education for all potential students. The state role in student financial assistance was also expanded with creation of the State Student Incentive Grant (SSIG) program and increased incentives provided to states under the Guaranteed Student Loan program. The 1972 amendments signaled a heavy emphasis on student access and choice, and subsequent appropriations further reflected this emphasis. Federal appropriations for student aid programs, *including* Social Security benefits to students, increased from $55.7 million in 1965 to $2.5 billion in 1975. The Education Amendments of 1976 and 1980 and the Middle Income Student Assistance Act of 1978 increased this emphasis even more by authorizing $12.8 billion in expenditures for student assistance programs in 1985.

To assist in promoting student access and choice, the amendments created state and institutional programs such as the Educational Information Center Program (which became part of the Title I Educational Outreach program in the Education Amendments of 1980), the Trio programs (designed to provide special assistance to minority and economically disadvantaged youth), and the Student Financial Assistance Training Program.

The House Committee on Education and Labor (1979, pp. 4-5), in submitting its report on HB 5192 (the 1980 amendments) to the full House, stated that the overriding goal of the legislation as federal policy was to achieve equal educational opportunity for all persons, and to do so primarily through student assistance. The 1980 amendments, signed into law by President Carter in October of 1980, provided the legislative basis and funding levels in place in 1983, despite strenuous and partially successful efforts by the Reagan administration to reduce funding drastically and to eliminate a number of programs.

Current Impact of Student Aid

Student aid touches all aspects of higher education in America. Indeed, it reaches into the very core of the system that largely determines who gets ahead in society, who is allowed to keep pace, and who falls by the wayside. For all its importance, however, student financial aid was never founded on a coherent philosophical base. At the governmental level, it has always comprised disjointed, transitory programs targeted at momentarily popular national social goals. Student aid is a classic example of the American political genius for "muddling through" to some mixed, but generally effective, results.

Some of the basic societal and political issues reflected in student aid go to the very core of higher education's role in America:

• Student financial aid is now the main means by which the federal government supports higher education. It is among the least coordinated and consistent of all government programs. Ironically, it is also one of the most heavily and closely regulated. It is as far from the original federal involvement in higher education (the 1862 Morrill Land-Grant Act, which gave almost unrestricted support directly to institutions) as can possibly be imagined.

• Student financial aid is now the main determinant of participation rates in higher education, and higher education is the main determinant of economic status. This role will probably increase as every conceivable career and profession is certified by higher education.

• Student financial aid controls the balance between the public and private sectors of higher education. For a large proportion—perhaps even a majority—of private colleges, it determines their viability.

• Present aid programs and systems affect the traditional role of parental sacrifice for their children's higher education as a means to upward social and economic mobility. Consequently, many other facets of parent-child relationships in the family are affected.

• Student financial aid is directly involved in the issue of societal versus individual benefits of higher education. The Carnegie Commission on Higher Education (1973) phrased this issue as "Who Benefits? Who Pays?"

• Student financial aid drives the "market model" of the financing of higher education. The impact of student consumerism on curriculum and other basic matters is beginning to be felt. Basic problems arose when the proportion of aid-eligible students moved from about one third to over half. Before, the two thirds not eligible forced private colleges to lower costs to remain competitive and provided no incentive for increasing public tuitions. But now there is every incentive for both sectors to raise prices and to support student aid as a substitute for family contributions and state subsidies, respectively. What happens to institutional autonomy in the process?

The current impact of student aid may be considered from several perspectives. First, a large number of students are now conditioned to expect some financial assistance. Student aid has become part of the system as seen by students, and means of coping with it and using it have become as much a part of college life as making it through registration each term and dealing with the system of grades and credits. Thus, attitudes of the student-consumer have changed from gratitude to expectation, and the tolerance level for delays and seeming incompetence by aid administrators has fallen drastically.

From the point of view of the institution-wide administrator, student aid has evolved from a minor function affecting few people to a crucial part of the entire financial system of the institution. The fact that, for example, student aid may account for $25 million of a $100-million-dollar annual operating budget is only *part* of the picture. Consider that the availability of student aid may be the critical factor in a student's decision to enroll at a college. For public institutions this "enticement factor" also brings in other state funds to support the cost of instruction. For example, say the average in-state student at a public college is awarded $1,200 in federal and state grants and loans for tuition and fees, and the cost per student is $5,000. The state supplies an additional $3,800 per student to support the operating budget. If, as in many cases, the percentage of students receiving aid exceeds 40 or even 50 percent, it can be seen that *student* aid triggers massive amounts of *institutional* aid. For private colleges, whose dependence on student tuition is much greater, the institutional aid aspect of student aid is even more manifest.

Impact on Minority Students

The issue of continued emphasis on access to higher education for disadvantaged youth, many of whom are members of racial and ethnic minorities, is perhaps the thorniest issue that will confront student aid during the rest of the 1980s. This problem is discussed in considerable depth in Chapter Eighteen. However, in this consideration of contemporary student aid problems, the following quotation is relevant:

> Despite the explosion of student aid during the past decade, young people from low-income families are still less than half as likely to enroll in college as their counterparts from high-income families. The reasons for this disparity are obviously many and complex. Students from low-income families are often ill prepared for college educationally as well as financially, and they may be reluctant to apply for college even when they qualify. Another important factor that may impede educational access and opportunity for low-income and minority students is the complexity of the student financial aid system itself. Faced with intimidating application forms and procedures, and inadequate counseling, many needy students may not be receiving the assistance intended for them [College Entrance Examination Board, Washington Office, 1981b, p. 10].

The goals of the Truman Commission for removal of financial and other artificial barriers to higher education apparently remain unfulfilled. In fact, there may well be danger of retreat from the attack on the problem. Such a retreat would fuel social problems, particularly since ethnic and racial minorities (traditionally low-income and educationally disadvantaged) will become a much larger proportion of the college-age cohort over the next twenty years.

Even though complete equality in participation rates in higher education has not been achieved, recent studies indicate that much progress has been made (Astin, 1982; Green, 1982; Stampen, 1983). Measurement of goal attainment in student aid is difficult because no clear and consistent goals have been enunciated. However, as Green points out, minorities "have been the implicit if not the specific beneficiaries of a range of government programs intended to help the disadvantaged participate in higher education" (p. 9). Although "minority students are not the statutory beneficiaries" of some of these programs —for instance, the financial aid programs—the "disproportionately high minority participation in these programs provides clear evidence of their significance to minority group goals and interests" (p. 39).

How clear is the evidence of high participation rates for minorities? Until very recently there was little evidence of any kind, clear or otherwise. In 1978 the Commission on the Higher Education of Minorities initiated a large-scale study to document and analyze minority participation rates. The research staff found that 83 percent of the white age cohort graduated from high school, compared with 72 percent of black youth (Astin, 1982, p. 175). The graduation rate for Chicanos, Puerto Ricans, and American Indians was 55 percent. Thirty-eight percent of the white youth entered college. The percentage for blacks was lower (29), and even lower for Chicanos (22), Puerto Ricans (25), and American Indians (17). The inequity between whites and the minority groups widened even more drastically at the pay-off point. Nearly a quarter (23 percent) of all white youth graduated from college, but only about half as many blacks graduated (12 percent). And the graduation rate for other minorities was only about half of that for blacks (7 percent for Chicanos and Puerto Ricans; 6 percent for American Indians).

Yet, as depressed and inequitable as these participation

rates for minorities are, "Minority representation among entering college freshmen increased by 50 to 100 percent from the mid-1960s to the mid-1970s" (Astin, 1982, p. 87). In a research report based on the commission's studies, Green (1982, p. 25) concluded that "federal initiatives and incentives, particularly financial aid programs, have been responsible for much of the movement of minority students into public colleges." The findings from Stampen's (1983) national study of student aid expenditures in public higher education seem to corroborate Green's conclusion: "Student aid programs do what they were originally intended to do. They distribute dollars—mostly federal—to students who would otherwise have difficulty financing a college education" (Stampen, 1983, p. i). More specifically, "lower-income students received somewhat more aid" (p. ii), and "over half—55 percent—of all need-based student aid recipients were women. About one third were members of minority groups" (p. iii). These findings are consistent with more fragmentary ones from state and institutional student aid levels. For example, as a participant at a recent student aid conference reported, "the number of black female applicants to the Illinois State Scholarship Commission continues to mushroom. Over the past ten years, two thirds of the Illinois black American applicants have been women" (quoted in Fenske, 1981, p. 39). Similarly, at Glendale Community College, a large public institution in Arizona, "student aid is received by a larger proportion of minority students than is present in the general full-time student body . . . 18.9 percent of the total full-time student population is nonwhite while 51.3 percent of the campus-based aid recipients are. Note, too, that among racial groups, Hispanic students represent only 13.2 percent of the total full-time students but 41.4 percent of the financial aid recipients under examination" (Wilson, 1981, pp. 5-6).

Later, in Chapter Eighteen, Gladieux discusses the special case of continuing low college-going rates of Hispanics, who will comprise the fastest-growing segment of the college-age cohort for the 1980s and beyond. According to De los Santos and his colleagues (1980, p. 115), "Enrollment of Hispanics at the undergraduate level [in public colleges] in both California and Texas would have to be increased by more than 40 percent if Hispanic enrollment at this level were to be proportional to Hispanic representation in the total population in the two states. [At the national level,] at both the two-year and four-year institutions, Hispanics have significantly higher attrition rates and lower completion rates than do non-Hispanics." Olivas (1981) studied a national data set on Hispanic students and found that the neediest received more aid than those from middle- and high-income families: "The distribution system evidently is working, if the index is that lower-income students are to receive larger aid awards" (p. 16). He points out, however, that equitable need-based distribution is not the only important criterion. Student choice of college and human capital investment are also significant premises. Unrestricted choice of college and reasonable chances for successful completion of programs at those colleges remain as persistent challenges to all minorities.

If one is content to define equalization of opportunity merely as access to some postsecondary institution, that goal has been at least partially achieved, thanks to massive infusions of student aid dollars: "If institutions were roughly equivalent in their resources and offerings, this definition would probably be acceptable. However, institutions are by no means equivalent, and a minority student's future may depend as much on the *kind* of institution attended as on attendance in itself. With the proliferation of public community colleges and the substantial financial aid now available to needy students, the real issue of access is not who goes to college, but who goes to *which* college" (Astin, 1982, pp. 129-130). Minorities are more likely to attend public colleges than private ones, and "students from all minorities . . . tend to be concentrated in two-year public colleges" (p. 132).

> Different types of students are by no means randomly distributed among different types of institutions. The community colleges, which represent the bottom of the institutional hierarchy within public systems, have a disproportionate share of minority students, underprepared students, and

students from poor and relatively uneducated families. The universities, in contrast, have relatively few minority students and a high concentration of well-prepared students and students from well-educated and affluent families. The four-year colleges within public systems fall about midway between the two-year colleges and the universities with respect to these various freshman characteristics. An identical pattern exists within the private sector, with the differences within the hierarchy even more pronounced than is the case in the public sector [Astin, 1982, p. 141].

When these patterns are related to the fact that only about half as many minority students as white students persist to graduation, the success of student aid programs in equalizing opportunity remains questionable indeed. Nor should completion rates be regarded as meaningful in and of themselves. What is important is *not* mere persistence until a degree of some sort is finally awarded. The achievement is meaningful when significant academic learning has occurred and marketable skills have been attained. Early in this section, I indicated that failure to press on toward goals of equal opportunity could "fuel social problems." Perhaps the comments of one of the more astute and candid participants at a recent conference on student aid (by agreement, remarks published in the proceedings were not attributed) will serve well to summarize the problems yet remaining for minorities in higher education:

A lot of minorities have been persuaded that their only hope for either future economic power or self-realization is through what student aid has produced since the late 1960s. There has been a dramatic increase in the number of minorities who have been brought into the system. That may eventually backfire in terms of the quality of experience they are getting. The country responded in the early 1970s to be sure that the doors are not shut to anyone. Now these "new students" want to be assured of more than just an education. They need the skills to utilize the educational experiences provided to them. They need to know how to find and hold a job. The nation is going to wake up someday to the realization that providing access to these "new students" implies more than just traditional opportunity to traditional students. Unless higher education meets their high expectations by helping them succeed, there may be a big social problem still ahead in this country. The number of minority applicants is still increasing, and one gets the feeling they are being counseled: "This is the only path for your future." They now have clear access, but what about their skills at graduation? Someday they are going to react if they find they lack marketable skills [quoted in Fenske, 1981, p. 39].

These are large policy issues that will emerge and be dealt with on the national level. But each institution will confront the balance between open access versus academic quality with increasing urgency over the next fifteen years. For some institutions the issue will take on a different, more gut-level perspective: In order to cope with the coming crises linked with low enrollments and shrinking financial resources, must the institution choose between survival, on one hand, or cutting back the admission of minority students, who typically need much more costly student services and academic remediation, on the other? Unless state and federal governments can greatly expand (rather than reduce) funding for special services to minority students, that is exactly the dilemma to be faced by many colleges.

Student aid will play an important role in institutional decision strategies in meeting the challenges ahead. Like any instrument, it can be used for a variety of purposes. Certainly, the strategic uses will be on a more sophisticated plane than before. Only recently have top-level institutional administrators come to realize the vital importance of student aid, not only as infusion of tuition dollars and enrollment stabilization but also to basic institutional philosophy and operating policies. To be more specific, student marketing and retention plans, as outlined in Chapters Fourteen and Fifteen in this book, can draw on increasingly sophisticated projections and institutional research findings, such as those referred to in Chapter Thirteen.

As a concrete example, the Office of Management Planning and Analysis at Arizona State University has developed a computer program that tracks student aid dollars from various sources to each college, school, *and department* in the university. As more becomes known about the differing characteristics, academic performance, and need for special services of aid recipients with differing "packages" of aid (balance among work, grants, and loans), appropriate strategies can be developed. Slow enrollment growth in certain academic areas could be remedied by diversion of relatively more institutional, private, and campus-based aid funds. Colleges and departments that attract more students needing special services can now be identified. Aid dollars and sophisticated tracking systems are neutral, but the power they bring to institutional decision makers is not. The dollars and managerial information will be used to build policy toward one goal or another. A single campus in a public multicampus system could choose to become more or less selective of students who, for example, bring more aid dollars to the operating budget but less need for expensive special services. Or the institution could choose to focus on attracting more disadvantaged students. In the case of public institutions, survival is not usually at stake, but strong cases must be made to governing boards and legislatures for funding strategic shifts in student mix, whether the shifts serve large public goals or merely serve to improve the institution's competitive position for further funding or academic prestige. Private colleges that are facing survival or demise will be forced to make their decisions on a stricter basis; social goals may be relegated to secondary consideration. In any case, student aid funds will be increasingly recognized as crucial to institutional decision making.

Problems and Prospects

On the campus problems tend to revolve around the delivery system and its impact on student enrollment and, consequently, institutional financing. But these types of concerns are the result of more basic problems involving the question of who shall pay the higher education bill: private organizations and individuals or the states or the federal government? With the advent of the Reagan administration, the abrupt downturn in political support from the federal sector has thrown the private and state sectors into extreme conditions of uncertainty. All states are uncertain about the immediate and long-term impact of such massive federal programs as BEOG (renamed Pell Grants) on their own gift aid programs. Federal student aid has never developed under consistent policies; consequently, congressional initiatives have been unpredictable, maintenance of programs has been uncertain, and regulations have been somewhat arbitrarily and inconsistently interpreted and enforced. Furthermore, no effective coordinating mechanism or governance structure is likely to be set up in the near future (see Fenske, 1981, especially pp. 13–21).

As the 1980s continue, no one really knows what balance among student aid sources—gift aid, loans, self-help (student savings and employment), and parental support—the federal government will want through the decade. Whatever balance among these sources is struck through the next ten years will undoubtedly affect the states' student aid policies as significantly as it has through the past decade. For example, because of the emphasis through the late 1970s on noncompetitive need-based grants provided by the federal government and many of the states, many parents have been weaned away from the expectation of family sacrifice to send sons and daughters to college. Any significant retrenchment from the present high levels of gift aid will cause considerable political problems for the state student aid agencies. Cutbacks in Pell Grants could throw intolerable burdens on state student grant programs.

All states, whatever their level of involvement in funding student aid, are directly affected by federal initiatives. States with only small-scale "emerging" programs are almost entirely at the mercy of the federal decisions. Many such states now only match federal SSIG funds and sponsor a Guaranteed Student Loan agency. Cutbacks or reductions in federal funding of either of these programs would decimate these states' new efforts and cause political reactions all out of proportion to the money actually spent by the states.

States with long-established programs and large expenditures are also affected by federal initiatives. For example, the rapid growth of BEOG/Pell Grants encouraged many states to deemphasize their own grant programs, under the assumption that the goal of access would be reached by the federal grants. Consequently, some of these states shifted their funding to support the goal of choice by diverting proportionately more money to private college students. A cutback in the Pell Grant program would require these states either to pick up the slack in grant aid to public college students or to retrench from present support levels and ignore the shortfall in grant aid for public college students, many of whom have exceptional financial need and are often members of racial or ethnic minorities. The only other choice would be to shift support from the private sector to the public. The result of this shift in many states would be the financial failure of a number of private colleges now existing on the edge of solvency. Whatever the choice, the states will inherit problems they neither wanted nor anticipated.

Inflation, increasing at the current level, will in many states cause significant increases in tuition at both public and private institutions. State scholarship/grant funds will no doubt be unable to "keep up" with inflationary costs. Furthermore, the 1980s will see additional increases in part-time and older adult enrollment. Each state will be under pressure to extend its funding and eligibility criteria to include this type of student.

As college costs soar, each state will carefully look at ways it can assist in meeting the cost of grants, guaranteed loans, and work-study programs. To maximize limited dollars, a few states may soon be requiring packages of state funds that include all three of these parts. In such a package, grants and scholarships would be available only in combination with a required loan and a job paid by work-study funds. This change will be sharply different from operations over the past several years. Many states have for years given needy students their unrestricted choice of grant, loan, or employment aid. However, some states will now see the "required package" approach as a way to meet student aid needs with limited dollars. There may also be a return to heavy reliance on parental support.

The recent growth of state-funded student grants has helped preserve strong public and private colleges in many states. This purpose will be under new stress in the years ahead. Some will argue that additional dollars should go directly to faculty salaries (operating budgets), to keep the best-qualified people in the teaching profession. Others will plead for a dramatic expansion of funds for consortia programs, to encourage more colleges to do more things together, to serve students better, and to save dollars. Others will decide that public tuitions should significantly increase for all students and that additional state grant dollars must be provided first to financially needy students. Students from affluent homes will be expected to pay the higher public tuitions.

Regardless of how each state elects to use its higher education dollars in the years ahead, the most significant impact on state student aid programs will be the decisions made by the federal government—especially in the BEOG or Pell Grant program and the Guaranteed Student Loan program. One strategy, controversial in nature, may be a dramatic increase by the state in academic awards, not based on need, with an expressed desire to reward excellence and keep high-ability students enrolled in their own states. This effort would be strongly opposed by those who believe that higher education should be an "open door" to all, regardless of their measured abilities or high school grade performance, and who fear that dollars for the average student will decline as academic awards increase.

Both public and private institutions need to be aware of the scope of student aid and the continually changing balance among private (and intrainstitutional), state, and federal sources. The need for close working relationships and coordination among these three sources is essential in the 1980s. The prospect of such harmony and efficiency is much less certain.

The importance of student aid to institutions and to students has far outstripped the administrative capabilities of the state, federal, and institutional programs that supply and regulate the funds. Institutional administrators need to realize that the external student aid agencies and programs are likely to exist in chaotic conditions through the rest of the 1980s. Those colleges and universities that can operate smoothly and efficiently in student aid despite these conditions will prosper; those that compound external chaos with internal chaos will lose both student aid funds and, more important, enrollments to their more efficient competitors.

Bibliographical Note

In this chapter I drew heavily on two recent monographs. The first (Fenske, 1981) deals with the problems of coordination and cooperation. It contains two position papers on the subject and an edited discussion by national student aid leaders. I am grateful to the publisher, the American College Testing Program, for kindly extending permission to include portions of that monograph in this chapter. The second monograph (Fenske and Boyd, 1981) was a research report commissioned by the College Scholarship Service and published by the College Entrance Examination Board (CEEB). It is discussed in the bibliographical note in Chapter Three, but I wish to acknowledge here the kind permission of the publisher to include portions of the report in this chapter. I am also grateful to my coauthor of the report, Joseph D. Boyd, for allowing me to quote freely and without separate attribution.

In 1975 CEEB published one of the first general treatments of student aid, and it is still one of the best. Its ten chapters provide a treatment of many of the same topics in this book, and several of its chapter authors are also contributors to this book. The lead chapter on the history of institutional aid by Rexford Moon is the best discussion of that subject to date.

The most important recent book on student aid is, of course, the report of the Carnegie Council on Policy Studies in Higher Education (1979). It is primarily a commentary on, and recommendations for, political action on student aid. The council's staff (principally Margaret S. Gordon and Martin Kramer) also provide the most comprehensive set of data analyses available anywhere. The title of the report, *Next Steps for the 1980s in Student Financial Aid,* indicates the main thrust of the book.

Public Policy and Private Higher Education (Breneman

and Finn, 1978) contains several excellent chapters stressing the critical importance of student aid to private colleges and universities. The chapters by Susan C. Nelson and Robert W. Hartman are especially recommended, along with the first and last chapters, contributed by the coeditors, David W. Breneman and Chester E. Finn, Jr.

The best book on the competition between Congress and the Executive branch for control of federal student aid programs is *Congress and the Colleges* (Gladieux and Wolanin, 1976). Gladieux, currently director of the Washington, D.C., Office of CEEB (and author of Chapter Eighteen in this book), oversees a steady stream of excellent topical monographs on various timely subjects in student aid. These constitute important literature resources for the field, as do certain issues of the Jossey-Bass *New Directions* sourcebook series. Two recent examples are *Responding to Changes in Financial Aid Programs* (Binder, 1980b) and *The Impact of Student Financial Aid on Institutions* (Henry, 1980).

Finally, I am grateful to Kenneth C. Green for permission to review and quote from his prepublication manuscript of an important research report on minority participation in higher education (Green, 1982). Also, Jacob O. Stampen kindly sent me an early copy of the progress report on his national study of the distribution of student aid in public colleges and universities (Stampen, 1983). Astin's (1982) work for the Commission on the Higher Education of Minorities provided much helpful interpretive information on large data sets.

2

Purposes and Provisions of Federal Programs

James W. Moore

Student financial aid is largely a government enterprise. During the 1930s a college employment program was operated by the National Youth Administration as part of the Roosevelt administration's anti-Depression program. During 1942-43 a wartime student loan program, while not large, identified some operating principles to be followed in the next decade. And, beginning with the Serviceman's Readjustment Act of 1944 (the GI Bill), a succession of GI Bills have been directed toward the support of veterans of the armed forces who elected to pursue training beyond high school.

The GI Bill, while outside the current definition of need-based student aid, was financial assistance written large. It was also the intellectual and political wedge that provided an opening for a governmental role in financing college students, since it made the notion of governmental assistance acceptable to the public and, ultimately, essential to the institutions. By the mid-1950s, however, the impact of the GI Bill was diminished as the

surge of World War II veterans completed their educational objectives and moved into the employment marketplace; and, because of low birthrates in the Depression of the 1930s, there
were comparatively few college-age students to take the place
of these veterans. Colleges were using limited aid funds competitively to secure the most capable students in a market of
scarcity. The competition for students was intense, and student
aid administration needed principles and mechanisms to achieve
equity and economy.

In 1954 the College Scholarship Service (CSS)—an adjunct of the College Entrance Examination Board—was organized to provide the principles, administrative mechanisms, and
enforcement procedures for participating institutions and agencies to bring order out of a chaotic situation. CSS developed objectives and procedures of student aid administration that permitted institutions to allocate their funds more rationally, to
increase opportunity, and to serve students more effectively.
The policies and procedures that evolved were revolutionary for
those times but seem conventional by today's standards. For
example, the parents of aid applicants were expected to furnish
a common set of family income and assets data, which were
evaluated by standard criteria to determine an expected contribution toward college costs. CSS proved to be both a stimulant
and a model for a burst of federal and state aid legislation for
the next decade, and the concepts of standardized need analysis
and (eventually) packaging which it pioneered were adopted exclusively and implicitly in government programs.

With the passage of the National Defense Education Act
in 1958, federal participation in contemporary student financial
aid began. The opening sentences of the act made national policy explicit: "The Congress hereby finds and declares that the
security of the Nation requires the fullest development of the
mental resources and technical skills of its young men and wom-
en. The present emergency demands that additional and more
adequate education opportunities be made available. . . . We
must increase our efforts to identify and educate more of the
talent of our Nation. This requires programs that will give assurance that no student of ability will be denied an opportunity

for higher education because of financial need" (Public Law 85-864, Sept. 2, 1958).

This act established the National Defense (now Direct) Student Loan (NDSL) program by providing funds for loans, with the institutions choosing the recipients and determining the amounts of loans within federal limits. The legislation spelled out few administrative procedures and left the responsibility for carrying out the intent of the legislation primarily with the institutions.

The Higher Education Act of 1965 created the Educational Opportunity Grant (EOG) program. It also authorized the Guaranteed Student Loan (GSL) program and made a number of specific changes in the previously authorized loan and work programs. The policy of widening the access to higher education was affirmed and expanded. In submitting the legislation to Congress, President Lyndon Johnson stated: "I propose that we declare a national goal of full educational opportunity. . . . Every child must be encouraged to get as much education as he has the ability to take. . . . We want this not only for his sake —but for the nation's sake. Nothing matters more to the future of our country; not our military preparedness—for armed might is worthless if we lack the brainpower to build a world of peace; not our productive economy—for we cannot sustain growth without trained manpower; not our democratic system of government—for freedom is fragile if citizens are ignorant" (Presidential policy paper, Nov. 1964).

The language of this act was considerably more detailed than that of earlier student aid legislation and established additional mandatory requirements not subject to "discretion" by institutions. The Office of Education was assigned more responsibility for supervising the use that institutions made of funds allotted to them. This may have been a reflection of the belief that many colleges, in their use of student aid funds, were concerned primarily with their own self-interest and made public policy and social goals a secondary consideration.

In the 1972 amendments to the Higher Education Act, Congress established the Basic Educational Opportunity Grant (BEOG) program, as a national foundation for all student aid programs. All other federal, state, and institutional aid was to be built on a secure and known foundation. The grants were to be awarded directly to students, who would be qualified solely on the basis of their family income; colleges would have little or no part in their selection. Family contributions were to be determined from a means test developed by the Department of Health, Education and Welfare. The Educational Opportunity Grant program was recast as the Supplemental Educational Opportunity Grant (SEOG) program, and the State Student Incentive Grant (SSIG) program (to match state funds with federal dollars under specific eligibility criteria) was established.

With the passage of time, Congress has been much more specific and detailed in its language, and the provisions of the programs are more mandatory than they were earlier. In addition, considerably more responsibility and authority is vested in the secretary of education to manage the federal student aid programs. All this represents a major shift in the role of the federal government.

The partnership of institutions of higher education with the federal government in the establishment and operation of a series of student aid programs is one of the most significant events to occur in the post–World War II era of higher education in the United States. The initial program established under the National Defense Education Act of 1958 provided approximately $10 million in loans to some 25,000 students during the 1958–59 school year. In contrast, during 1980–81 the federal programs discussed in this chapter provided nearly $12 billion in direct student aid to an estimated four and a half million students. Approximately 1,100 colleges and universities elected to participate in the initial National Defense Student Loan program. Currently, some 6,700 institutions have signed agreements to participate in one or more federal programs. Included are virtually every college, university, and community college in this nation, as well as some 3,300 vocational, technical, and health-related institutions, many of them proprietary or for-profit private enterprises.

In addition to this broad pattern of institutional activity, fifty state loan guarantee agencies have been created, largely under federal initiatives, as well as fifty state grant or scholarship agencies, whose efforts augment those of institutions in providing eligible students with financial aid for their educational expenses.

National Direct Student Loans

Originally established as Title II of the National Defense Education Act of 1958, NDSL has been in existence continuously since the 1958-59 academic year. The statute provided for a long-term, extended repayment and low-interest loan program on each campus. The federal government contributed nine dollars to this loan fund for every dollar provided by the institution. Also, all repayments of loan principal and interest were to be deposited in the fund for future loans.

NDSL was the first of the federal programs to require a test of financial need in order to establish eligibility for a loan. It was also the first program to require a direct contract or terms of agreement between the participating institution and the federal government. To be eligible, students originally were required to be enrolled full time in a program leading to a degree or certificate. The students were also required to demonstrate financial need for the loan and to maintain good standing during the time they were enrolled. The 1958 statute also provided for preferred eligibility for students enrolled in programs of science, mathematics, teaching, or modern foreign language. This provision was withdrawn in later amendments to the program.

Each year, from amounts appropriated by Congress, new federal capital is allocated to each participating institution for deposit in its loan fund. The new funds and collections from prior loans are the main sources of capital for the program.

The terms and conditions of NDSL loans have been modified in some detail over the years but remain basically the same as they were in the original legislation. It is significant that the 3 percent simple interest rate remained unchanged from 1958 until 1980, when it was increased to 4 percent and then to 5 percent on October 1, 1981. Forgiveness of a part or all of the loan may be secured by a borrower who teaches the handicapped or in elementary or secondary schools with a high concentration of low-income students. At one time in the 1960s, cancellation existed for military service as well as for teaching in nearly any type of educational institution from kindergarten through graduate school. These categories of loan cancellation were rescinded during the 1970s.

By 1980 the total amount of NDSL capital extant in the loan funds managed by some 3,600 institutions amounted to more than $5 billion. Repayments to institutions in that year by prior borrowers amounted to slightly more than $400 million.

As the program has matured over the years, the most persistent problem plaguing most, but not all, participating institutions has been the rate of student default. Currently, the overall institutional default rate in the program is about 12 percent. This level actually represents a reduction from prior years and has been achieved in part through more vigorous collection efforts by the institutions and in part through assignment of uncollectible loans by the Department of Education to outside agencies. An entire loan-servicing industry has developed in the private sector during the last fifteen years to provide institutions with essential billing and collection services in those instances where the institutions elect not to develop their own collection capabilities. Congress has increased the institutional administrative allowance for actual operation of the program from 1 percent in the 1960s to 5 percent currently of each year's new loan volume.

At present, considering the high risk of young student borrowers in the commercial consumer credit market, there is general agreement that a default rate at or below 10 percent is acceptable. Nearly 40 percent of the participating institutions are currently able to operate at or below that level. It should also be pointed out that until the late 1970s there was no provision for an institution to write off or otherwise eliminate from its portfolio those loans that were by any measure absolutely uncollectible. Instead, the uncollectible loans, even though relatively few in number, accumulated from one year to the next and made up a rather alarming total by the time the program was twenty years old. Despite the success of a large number of institutions in managing the program properly, there are still far too many whose default rates are in excess of 10 or even 25 percent.

The amount of money available from NDSL repayments continues to increase modestly each year and will probably approximate $430 million by 1982–83. Amounts canceled for teaching service have been returned to the loan fund by the federal government since the program became the National Direct Student Loan program in 1972; consequently, the prior drain on the fund from the old National Defense Student Loans has been eliminated.

College Work-Study

College Work-Study (CWS) was originally created as Title I–Part C of the Economic Opportunity Act of August 1964. President Johnson, in his message on the "War on Poverty" earlier in that same year, directed that the program be assigned for administration to the Office of Economic Opportunity. The 1965 Higher Education Act transferred it to the Office of Education. As originally established, the program provided part-time employment—either at a postsecondary institution or, by contract, at a public or nonprofit agency—for students from low-income families. Wages, rates, work assignments, supervision, and the general management of the program were made the responsibility of the participating institutions. At the outset students were limited to employment of fifteen hours a week; however, they could be employed full time during periods of vacation or at other times when classes were not in session. In the program's first year, 1964–65, approximately 115,000 students were employed in 1,095 institutions. Nearly $33 million in payroll checks was disbursed to the students. By 1981–82 the total payroll had expanded to nearly $670 million (including the 80 percent federal share and 20 percent institutional share). Approximately 900,000 students at 4,100 postsecondary institutions were provided employment in that year.

Student eligibility for CWS, as stipulated in the original

legislation, included low income, enrollment in an eligible institution, and satisfactory academic progress. The low-income requirement was modified in 1965 to a preference, thus making the work assignment available to any student who showed need for financial assistance.

The College Work-Study program has been modified somewhat in its operational aspects during its nineteen years of existence. Eligibility related to income was expanded, as was the number of hours of work allowed each week. These and other restrictions have been relaxed to provide greater operational flexibility.

Also, new features added in recent years have been helpful in expanding the uses to which program funds can be put. For example, the Job Locator Program allows the use of up to 10 percent of an institution's total CWS allocation to promote off-campus job opportunities for all students without regard to their financial need. The Community Service Learning Program through student jobs provides services such as health care, education, public safety, and recreation for low-income individuals and families.

Generally, institutions expend about 80–85 percent of the total work-study payroll in employment within the institution. Types of employment include nearly every activity found on a college or university campus. By law, employment may not impair existing contracts for services, displace employed workers, or involve the operation of any facility used for sectarian instruction. Also, use of CWS for employment in political activities has been forbidden. The remaining 15–20 percent of the funds is used in contracting with public and private nonprofit agencies for employment of students. Since 1980 there has been a standard requirement to pay the existing minimum wage. However, maximum wages are within the province of the institution to establish, as long as they are in accordance with similar jobs and pay scales already in existence.

The College Work-Study program has been remarkably well managed by participating institutions. This splendid record includes not only the oversight and supervision of on-campus employment but the arrangements with community agencies, units of government, and other eligible public and private non-profit groups for which students work.

Supplemental Educational Opportunity Grants

The SEOG program was first established as the Educational Opportunity Grant (EOG) program under the 1965 Higher Education Act. Its appearance culminated several years of effort on the part of successive administrations to establish a federal undergraduate grant program. Congress wished to ensure that these grants would be awarded only to low-income students and that the amount of the grant would not exceed half of the aid provided to each recipient. Institutions were required to use a uniform system for measuring student need for grant assistance. It was therefore necessary for participating institutions to target funds on students from the lowest-income families and to make certain that students prepared for college attendance through such developmental programs as Upward Bound. The EOG program, perhaps more than any other, generated extensive efforts by colleges and universities to recruit minority and economically disadvantaged students during the latter part of the 1960s. These efforts led to marked increases in minority enrollments in all sectors of postsecondary education.

Funds appropriated for the program were allocated to institutions through a state allotment formula system and then on the basis of institutional application for funds. By 1967 institutions could apply for EOG and NDSL funds under a single application.

Eligibility for EOG funds was originally directed toward students from low-income backgrounds who could not enter and continue college without grant assistance. The original requirement of full-time enrollment was later modified to include half-time enrollment, and a requirement for satisfactory academic progress was also included.

In the 1972 amendments to the Higher Education Act, the EOG program was somewhat modified and retitled Supplemental Educational Opportunity Grants (SEOG)—primarily to distinguish it from the new Basic Educational Opportunity Grant program established in that year. Because the SEOG, CWS, and NDSL programs required administration at the institutional level, they became collectively referred to as the "campus-based" programs. In 1980 the amount of SEOG award that could be made to a student in any given year was increased to $2,000. The earlier rigid targeting of the award to the most needy and disadvantaged student was relaxed to become more sensitive to escalating student costs, especially in the private sector. In 1981–82 the program was supported at about $355 million, which provided grants for 586,000 students at 3,800 institutions.

State Student Incentive Grants

The State Student Incentive Grant program (SSIG) was enacted as part of the Education Amendments of 1972. Its purpose was to augment state scholarship and grant programs in states where they already existed or, conversely, to cause states that had no such program to create them. The incentive concept was built around the allocation of federal funds to provide up to half of each grant awarded by the state agency within the state. Basically, the statute provided for an annual allocation of appropriated grant funds to a state based on its higher education population as a proportion of the national enrollment of students in higher education. Awards are based on need and are available for use in any accredited institution within the state. The federal share is limited to no more than half, and the state is to provide the remainder. The grants are renewable only for the years required to earn the first baccalaureate degree.

For 1981–82, as well as for each of the previous three years, Congress has annually appropriated about $76 million to be allocated among the fifty states. The amounts granted to the states in relation to their share of the national enrollment ranged from a low of $128,000 in the state of Wyoming to a high of $11 million in California.

The total expenditure of all states for student aid from their own funds is now in excess of $800 million, exclusive of the federal SSIG share. Eight states account for the majority of state-appropriated student grant or scholarship funds. In the fiscal 1982 budget, the administration proposed termination of the SSIG program in the 1983 fiscal year, since the original purpose of the program had been achieved. That is, a state grant or scholarship agency is now in operation in each of the fifty states, as well as in the territories.

Basic Educational Opportunity Grants

The Basic Educational Opportunity Grant (BEOG) program was first authorized under the Education Amendments of 1972 and introduced several new concepts into the existing pattern of federal student aid programs. Foremost among these was the notion of grant entitlement. Under BEOG, grants were to be made to every student who was determined eligible under a formula that assessed the family's ability to contribute toward the student's cost of education. Previously such awards had been contingent on the availability of federal funds applied for and received by an institution, or, in the case of the SSIG program, matching funds provided by a state. Second, by law Congress established certain controls over the eligibility criteria to be used in the program and therefore made certain that the selection system was to a large extent insulated from change by successive administrations. Finally, the grant itself represented a direct transaction between the student applicant and the commissioner of education in the former Office of Education, or the secretary in the current Department of Education. The role of the institution of higher education was limited to disbursing grant funds to the student after computing the award amount against a preestablished payment schedule and the student's educational budget.

The student is afforded the opportunity of applying the grant to the cost of education at any accredited collegiate or vocational-technical institution in the United States. Thus, some 6,000 institutions at the postsecondary level enroll students who hold a BEOG.

Insofar as the student is concerned, the program is quite

simple. The student and his or her parents complete an application that requests data about the family size, income level, unusual expenses, and assets. Information from this application is processed by a central application facility under contract to the Department of Education, and a student eligibility report is issued which stipulates the amount of money the family is expected to contribute from its resources for the student's education. Consequently, a grant eligibility figure is subject to revision only by virtue of the cost of education at the school selected by the student. No grant may exceed half of the cost of education.

This program became successful only after information about it was available in every secondary school in the United States. Even though the first grants were made in 1973, an additional two years were required for the information to be totally absorbed by the secondary school network as well as all other agencies involved with eligible adult learners who might be interested in enrolling in a course of study if grant assistance were available.

In 1978 the Carter administration elected to use BEOG as its major counter to proposals for tuition tax credits. Its efforts resulted in the Middle Income Student Assistance Act, which materially expanded the number of families eligible for basic grant support. The amount of the grant available to a family was also increased, since the tax rate on discretionary income which determines the eligibility index was dropped from 20-30 percent at the upper income levels to a low of 10.5 percent. The cost of the program then escalated to approximately $2.5 billion per year, and awards were made to about 2.5 million students annually.

This rapid expansion of grant availability triggered an increase in the number of applicants who declared themselves as independent students (that is, not dependent on family income) and whose award calculations were based on their own income rather than that of their parents. Inasmuch as this program has functioned on an entitlement basis, it is regarded as the foundation program to which other forms of aid may be added in order to provide the student with enough money to meet the costs of education in the school of the student's choice.

Through contract arrangements with the large financial need assessment processing organizations—namely, the College Scholarship Service, the American College Testing Program, and the Pennsylvania Higher Education Assistance Agency—it became possible for a student to fill out a single application that provides data not only to the BEOG program but to state and institutional financial aid programs as well. This process, known as multiple data entry, has provided a much-needed alternative to the requirement that families fill out two, three, or more forms in order to apply for financial assistance from various sources. The obvious next step is to replace the paper application documents with an electronic data processing network that serves both institutions and governmental agencies.

As part of the Education Amendments of 1980, the program was renamed the Pell Grant program in honor of Senator Claiborne Pell of Rhode Island, who was largely responsible for the program's creation in 1972.

Guaranteed Student Loans

In the entire array of federal student financial aid programs, the Guaranteed Student Loan (GSL) program over the years has accounted for the largest provision of support for students and, consequently, revenue for colleges and universities. It has also proved to be the most expensive student aid activity conducted by the federal government.

This program was first authorized by the Higher Education Act of 1965. At that time the statute provided that a state or a private nonprofit agency could function as a guarantor of student loans made by commercial lenders. The guarantee was established through the encumbrance in a guarantee fund of an amount equal to approximately 10 percent of the face value of the loans. The fund was to protect the lender against loss through default, death, or disability of the borrower. The interest rate originally was 6 percent per annum, and the federal government provided the lender with an interest subsidy equal to 6 percent for the period of time the student was in school and 3 percent during the repayment period, which commenced nine months to a year after the student completed his or her course of study.

Under these provisions the borrower was liable for payment of the other 3 percent.

The interest subsidy was available to any student whose family income was at or below $15,000 per year. Students from income levels above that subsidy limit were eligible for nonsubsidized loans. Until 1977 about 96 percent of all loans carried the interest subsidy.

In addition, the federal government provided the states with deposits of guarantee funds, known as "seed money," which were to be utilized either to establish a guarantee fund or to augment the fund in states where the guaranteed loan program had existed prior to 1965. The "seed money" concept was employed because it was envisioned that at some future time these funds would be replaced by state appropriations. On loans amounting to more than $2,000, a student had ten years to repay the obligation. On loans amounting to less than $2,000, a shorter period of time could be arranged between the student and the lender.

The first guarantee programs for commercial student loans were established in Massachusetts, New York, and a few other states in the late 1950s. The concept of bank loans for college students was not new. There was, however, little evidence of interest subsidy payments in the early state programs, with the exception of New York, which adopted a partial subsidy program in the years following 1958.

Two major problems caused concern on the part of the lenders (banks, savings and loan associations, credit unions, and other regulated lenders) from the outset of the program. The first was the matter of liquidity, because each student loan was in fact a long-term obligation as a result of the extended statutory payback period following completion of the borrower's educational program. The second was the fact that the 6 percent interest rate by 1968 represented an inadequate return to the lender, since interest rates had generally begun a slow but persistent upward climb. A concurrent problem, which also plagued the program, resulted from the general lack of enthusiasm among most states for appropriation of additional state funds to expand the loan guarantee activity. In the event that an adequate loan guarantee program did not exist in a state, the federal government would—as stipulated in the federal statute—provide direct insurance for loans issued by eligible lenders within that state. By 1968 approximately twenty states were operating a guarantee program, and the remaining thirty were under programs of direct federal insurance, operated by the Office of Education.

In 1968 the concept of reinsurance was introduced. This was simply a melding of existing state guarantee funds and federal insurance, with the federal government providing 80 percent of the total; that is, the federal government assumed responsibility for 80 percent of a state's losses resulting from default, death, or disability. Later the federal government assumed all of a state's losses, thereby keeping the guarantee fund free to insure successive waves of student loans. In 1969, even though the statutory interest had earlier been increased to 7 percent, rising interest rates threatened to impede the program. In that year the "special allowance" was established. Under this concept the federal government paid to all eligible lenders an amount above and beyond the statutory interest rate for the purpose of more adequately compensating lenders for the cost of their money. During the next few years, the special allowance fluctuated between 1 percent and 2.5 percent in addition to the 7 percent rate established when the loan was made.

By 1972 the problem of lender liquidity was met through establishment of the Student Loan Marketing Association (known as Sallie Mae). This agency was authorized to create markets for student loans, either through direct purchase or through warehousing, wherein the student loans were pledged as collateral for loans to participating banks. This program went far to ease the problems that large-volume lenders had incurred by tying up large amounts of capital in long-term obligations. By 1976, partly as a result of the pressures of inflation, the family income level below which the interest subsidy would apply was raised from $15,000 to $25,000. In addition, the Education Amendments of 1976 provided cost overhead payments to state agencies functioning under reinsurance agreements created by the 1968 legislation.

With the 1978 Middle Income Student Assistance Act, the $25,000 ceiling on annual family income as a qualification for the interest subsidy during the in-school period was removed. This change made any applicant, no matter what the family's income level, eligible for the in-school interest subsidy and for the interest rate, which remained at 7 percent.

By 1979 interest and treasury bill rates had climbed to a rate that made the maximum cap of 5 percent on the special allowance clearly insufficient to provide lenders with a reasonable return on their loan portfolios. Congress responded by eliminating the cap entirely and tying the special allowance for 7 percent loans to the quarterly average of treasury bill rates minus 3 percent. This change would ultimately result in the payment of 12.5 percent special allowance rates in addition to 7 percent loans, for a maximum return to the lender in the fall of 1981 of 19.5 percent. Under the Education Amendments of 1980, the interest rate was increased to 9 percent on loans made after January 1, 1981. For these loans the special allowance rate became equal to the average treasury bill rate for the preceding quarter, minus 5 percent.

In addition, Congress enacted a program called Parental Loans for Undergraduate Students (PLUS), which was modeled on the existing student loan program. However, in the case of loans to parents, there was no interest subsidy whatsoever, and loan repayment was to begin within sixty days after the loan was disbursed by the lender to the student. The interest rate to be paid by the parents under the PLUS program was at 14 percent, unless treasury bill rates ultimately fell below 14 percent for an entire year, at which time the parent loan rate would be reduced to 12 percent. Furthermore, in its original version, the parent loan program was limited to dependent undergraduate students. In 1982 the interest rate was dropped to 12 percent; and the name Auxiliary Loans to Assist Students (ALAS) came to be used as independent undergraduates and graduates became eligible.

Changes in 1978 and 1979 in the eligibility of students and the floating special allowance rate served to increase the total volume of new loans from approximately $2.9 billion in 1978-

79 to $4.6 billion the following year and finally to $7.8 billion in 1980-81. This expansion had the added effect of increasing the loan portfolios of eligible lenders by the end of the summer of 1981 to approximately $20 billion. A large part of this singular increase in loan volume in 1980 and 1981 may be attributed to the entry of state lending agencies into the loan market. The difference between the interest rate paid on revenue bonds sold for purposes of raising loan capital and the return during 1980-81 on these same loans amounted to as high as 10 percent. Ultimately, Congress reduced special allowances by 50 percent for payments made to tax-exempt state lending agencies.

As long as treasury bills stay at relatively high levels, the on-budget costs of the Guaranteed Student Loan program will remain at $2.5 billion or more each year. Beginning with amendments providing for student-paid origination fees and other changes in 1981, both the Congress and the administration searched for ways of reducing costs, while at the same time maintaining the volume of loan activity. The issue of these cost reductions will be a major item in the education portion of the fiscal year 1983 federal budget.

General Program Administration

Student Eligibility. By 1982 regulations governing student eligibility were generally made uniform for all the federal programs. As a general proposition, students enrolled for at least a half-time program of study who are in good standing and making satisfactory academic progress, and, according to program criteria, demonstrate need for assistance, are eligible for federal student aid programs. Currently, the need test affects a guaranteed loan applicant only if the adjusted gross income of the family exceeds $30,000 per year.

With the exception of the Pell and SEOG programs, in which support is limited to undergraduate students, all the programs are available to students at the undergraduate, graduate, and professional levels.

Foreign students who are in the United States for other than a temporary purpose, such as permanent resident aliens and those holding other types of resident status that do not require return to the country of origin, qualify as students for federal assistance. Further, American students who are United States citizens may under certain circumstances use federal assistance to attend foreign colleges and universities if they are enrolled at a United States college or university and the credits they earn abroad can be transferred to that institution. GSL is the only program that, under specific legislation, provides support for students attending colleges and universities outside the United States; however, eligibility is somewhat complicated in that a financial need test must be performed by the foreign institution on applicants whose family income exceeds $30,000. Amendments are being sought from Congress to provide for the need test to be made either by the federal government or by some other educational agency located in the United States on behalf of the foreign institution.

Recent issues addressed by the Department of Education and the higher education community are (1) the establishment of reasonable and equitable refund policies for students holding grants and loans who withdraw from school during an academic period and (2) the basis for institutional establishment of criteria defining "satisfactory academic progress." Both issues have long vexed the student aid community, and their resolution will be most welcome in all quarters.

Establishment of Financial Need Criteria. Beginning with the National Defense Education Act of 1958, measurement of financial need in one way or another has been a consistent characteristic of each federal student aid program as it came into existence. (Need analysis is discussed in detail in Chapter Six.) At the outset the original NDEA legislation required only that eligible students be "in need" of loan assistance. It did not explain how or by whom such need would be measured. In the early years of the NDEA program, both the responsibility for assessing need for loan applicants and the establishment of a system for doing so were left entirely to the college or university administering the program. In the main, institutions elected to use the new College Scholarship Service (CSS) method, which was at that time in its early years of development.

In the mid-1960s, the statutes became somewhat more precise in at least defining the characteristics of financial need. For example, in the original EOG, institutions were required to confer grants only on students with "exceptional financial need," which clearly implied direction of these awards to students from very low-income families. Conversely, students were made eligible for loans under the Guaranteed Student Loan program without regard to financial need. However, Congress did establish $15,000 of annual family income as the point beyond which borrowers could not qualify for the interest subsidy.

With the establishment of the Basic Educational Opportunity Grant program in 1972, the federal government became deeply involved in establishing a system of measuring need in order to determine student eligibility. Observers of the need analysis systems now in use will point out many differences between the criteria and calculations employed in the BEOG (Pell Grant) program and those used in what is now known as the uniform methodology—the need analysis model used by the College Scholarship Service and the American College Testing Program. This latter approach generally governs the systems used not only for the federal campus-based programs but also for state and institutional programs.

Maintenance of the uniform methodology is in the hands of the National Student Aid Coalition, an organization of thirty educational associations. As explained in Chapter Six, the methodology is a collection of criteria, indexes, and related items used in assessing a student's financial need for aid. There has been considerable debate over whether need analysis should or should not be in the hands of the federal government. The position generally adopted by administrations since 1972 is that the commissioner of education (now the secretary of education) would approve the parameters of need analysis through a series of benchmark or test cases, leaving its operational design and further development with the coalition.

In 1981 and in 1982, the administration recommended to Congress that the entire GSL program include a test of demonstrated financial need as a condition of student eligibility. Congress moved toward this objective in the summer of 1981 by requiring that all applicants whose adjusted family incomes exceeded $30,000 per year must undergo a financial need test for loan eligibility.

Further, if support for the Pell Grant program is reduced in fiscal years 1983 and beyond, the assessment of a family's financial strength will, for purposes of the program, not be need analysis but, rather, a means of rationing grant funds among eligible students from low-income families. This is a marked departure from the earlier entitlement system for Pell Grants, wherein the criteria were established first and appropriations subsequently adjusted to meet the demand generated by these criteria.

Allocation of Campus-Based Aid to Institutions. The allocation of campus-based federal aid to colleges and universities has progressed from the early days of NDSL, when institutions simply told the government what they needed to have, to a process known generally by the acronym FISAPP, which stands for Fiscal Operations Report and Application. It is a combined annual report of expenditures under the three campus-based programs (NDSL, CWS, and SEOG) and an application for funds under these same programs for the year following that in which the report has been filed. The reporting portions are rather simple and straightforward and have generally remained unchanged over the past years. Actually, the accounts structure for the NDSL program is in the same format as that originally laid down in 1958. The application portion seeks data from the institution concerning cost of education, number of eligible students, other types and sources of financial aid, and estimated amounts to be contributed by families of eligible students. This information is analyzed in order to compute what is known as a fair share index. This index is then applied to that portion of the annual allocation of funds which is governed by discretionary criteria established by the secretary of education. At this writing, Congress, in light of stable or declining appropriations, is moving to tie the state allocation to a percentage of the funds received in the prior year, in order that all institutions be treated equitably.

Administrative Expense Allowance. Colleges and universities that participate in the three campus-based programs are entitled to draw from the Department of Education an administrative cost allowance to offset the expense of administering these programs. The amount of the allowance provided equals 5 percent of the first $2.75 million of the institution's expenditures in an award year for the NDSL, CWS, and SEOG programs; plus 4 percent of its expenditures that are greater than $2.75 million but less than $5.5 million; plus 3 percent of its expenditures in excess of $5.5 million. For purposes of calculating the allowance, College Work-Study expenditures made under the Community Service Learning Program or NDSL loans assigned for collection to the secretary of education may not be included.

Institutional Audits and Program Reviews. Each institution participating in the federal student aid programs is required to conduct an audit of these programs at least every two years. These audits may be conducted either by state or local auditors if the institutions are in the public sector or by certified public accountants for those in the private sector. Each audit is reviewed by units of the Department of Education and subsequently closed when all exceptions are resolved. Monetary liabilities that arise as a result of the audit are settled as part of the closure process. In many instances the institutions are required to make restitution to the federal government for any funds improperly spent.

A parallel activity conducted by regional offices of the department's Office of Student Financial Assistance is known as a program review. In practice these reviews are quasi audits of the actual management of the federal aid programs within the institution. The purpose of the review is twofold: first, to make certain that the institution is following appropriate rules, regulations, and statutes in the awarding of student assistance; and second, where necessary, to provide help to the institution in managing its student aid programs. As is the case with audits, these program reviews will in some instances identify dollar liabilities, which then must be satisfied in much the same way that audit exceptions are ultimately closed.

Sources of Funds. Beginning in 1982 the Department of Education established its own payment system for actual transmission of student aid funds to participating institutions. This was substituted for the former Financial Assistance Financing System developed in the Department of Health, Education and Welfare during the late 1960s. In brief, institutions that have been issued letters of credit are able to transfer funds from the Federal Reserve System into the institution as needed, with a stipulation that not more than a thirty-day cash supply may be requested at any one time. All other institutions are on a cash demand system; that is, in order to secure funds for a particular quarter, they must submit a quarterly report to the agency. With the expansion of the dollar flow in the federal student aid programs in recent years, fiduciary control has become a matter of concern to the fiscal managers in the federal establishment. Conversely, institutions themselves have continued to seek means to speed the flow of funds into institutional accounts, in order to maintain as favorable a cash position as possible. By the end of this decade, all the student aid programs will probably be driven by electronic fund transfer systems, in order to minimize paperwork and make the process of transferring funds from the federal government to institutions more efficient.

Conclusion

In the first year of the NDEA loan program (the 1958-59 academic year), 27,600 students borrowed a total of $9,501,000, primarily in the spring semester. During the 1980-81 academic year, the federal student aid programs generated nearly $12 billion in student assistance. This amount was comprised of $7.7 billion in Guaranteed Student Loans, $2.4 billion in Pell Grant awards, and the remainder from the campus-based programs (National Direct Student Loans, College Work-Study, and Supplemental Educational Opportunity Grants) as well as the State Student Incentive Grant program. That year may turn out to be the high-water mark in the flow of federal student aid dollars into the hands of students and ultimately into institutional bursar's offices, since the current administration is restructuring some of the programs and seeking marked reductions in appropriation levels recommended to Congress; at this writing, how-ever, the significance of these changes during the remainder of the 1980s is uncertain.

In the main, all types of institutions at the postsecondary level have done a creditable job in managing the federal student aid programs over the years. The most frequent criticism and notorious problem is that of the default experience in the vari-ous loan programs. In fact, the default experience is a product of the basic dilemma faced first by the colleges in the original NDSL program and ultimately by financial institutions in the Guaranteed Student Loan program. As each of these loan pro-grams was set in place by statute, a basic assumption was made that somehow these institutions would make collectible loans to students of unknown credit worthiness who were still at vari-ous stages in their educational preparation. Most of these stu-dents had not yet entered the labor market and seldom had con-ventional loan collateral or security.

Institutions can markedly reduce their default rates if, at the time the loan is authorized, student borrowers are made fully aware of the terms of the obligations they are assuming—especially the penalties related to default and the projected amount to be paid periodically over a long period of time. Insti-tutions also must maintain contact with borrowers after they are no longer enrolled and must send billing notices in a timely and consistent manner. These are examples of responsible mak-ing and forceful and diligent collecting of loans, which the De-partment of Education expects of institutions. Increased em-phasis on "due diligence" has helped to reduce default.

As a general proposition, there are four basic avenues open for collection of delinquent or defaulted NDSL loans. Accord-ing to the statute, a note is considered defaulted if no payment has been received for 120 days (when scheduled payments are made on a monthly basis) or 180 days (for those on less frequent billing dates). First, an institution may exert its own effort in attempting to secure payment from a defaulted borrower. One of the most common sanctions employed here—except where prohibited by state law or court decisions—is the withholding of academic transcripts or other institutionally produced documents that the former student may require in pursuit of a career. The second avenue is, of course, litigation. Some institutions operate a regular planned program leading toward a lawsuit under provisions of the note and have experienced promising results. A third and very effective approach is referral of the delinquent note to a collection agency that specializes in delinquent student loan accounts. A final and permanent cure for a defaulted note that is absolutely uncollectible under any of the methods noted above is assignment of the note itself to the Department of Education. In this instance the note must have been in default for two years, and the institution must present evidence of its own efforts to secure payment. Approximately 350,000 NDSL notes have thus far been assigned to the department. The department is in turn actively pursuing collection of these accounts through commercial agencies that have contracts with the department.

Further, as the baby-boom children entered college in the 1960s and as intensive recruitment activities among educationally and economically disadvantaged youth were carried out, the borrower population assumed characteristics hitherto unknown by major credit institutions in the United States. Massive collection efforts on the part of not only the federal government but state agencies and institutions alike have been mounted in the past ten years.

With the advent of a period in which loan demand may well far outstrip available resources, and given the general move in the country to a somewhat more conservative approach, in all probability the high-risk nature of these programs will be controlled during the 1980s, with a continued lessening of the default rate.

In the next several years, the federal government can be expected to persist in its efforts to improve all aspects of the administration of its student aid programs. Priority will be given to effective and efficient delivery of the assistance to needy students. Furthermore, attempts will be made to meet the intent of the legislation, even though resources may be shrinking, and to maintain a high level of institutional flexibility in the management of these funds.

Bibliographical Note

The major federal student assistance programs described in this chapter are authorized by Title IV of the Higher Education Act of 1965 and by subsequent amendments. The references identified here include the Title IV laws, regulations, handbooks, audit guides, and other publications. Except where otherwise indicated, these publications are issued by the U.S. Department of Education, Office of Postsecondary Education, Office of Student Financial Assistance (OSFA), and are available on request.

Laws. Primary authority for the federal student aid programs is in the enabling statutes. These may be found in the chapter on "Title IV—Student Assistance," in *A Compilation of the Federal Education Laws,* Vol. 3: *Higher Education* (Committee on Education and Labor, House of Representatives, 1980). (This chapter was updated by Public Law 97-92, sec. 124, Dec. 15, 1981.)

Current Title IV Regulations. The required administration of the federal aid program is accomplished through the application of regulations issued periodically by the Department of Education. These regulations—cited by volume and part number to the *Code of Federal Regulations* (C.F.R.)—as they apply to specific programs and to subjects are as follows:

	Date Published in *Federal Register*
Student Assistance General Provisions (34 C.F.R. Part 668)	Dec. 31, 1980
Amendments to Student Assistance General Provisions	May 4, 1982
Campus-Based Programs: National Direct Student Loan Program (34 C.F.R. Part 674), College Work-Study Program (34 C.F.R. Part 675), Supplemental Educational Opportunity Grant Program (34 C.F.R. Part 676)	
Campus-Based Programs Regulations	Jan. 19, 1981

	Date Published in *Federal Register*
Cost of Attendance and Treatment of Bankruptcy	Jan. 21, 1981
Revised Definition of Independent Student	Jan. 6, 1982
Campus-Based Funding Procedures	Aug. 1, 1982
Technical Corrections	Aug. 2, 1982
Guaranteed Student Loan Program (34 C.F.R. Part 682)	
GSL Program Final Regulation	Sept. 17, 1979
Amendments to GSL Program Final Regulation	June 24, 1980
Nomenclature and Technical Amendments	Dec. 30, 1980
GSL Deferment	Jan. 16, 1981
GSL Refund of Tuition Charges and Other Fees	Jan. 16, 1981
GSL Amended Family Contribution Schedule	May 3, 1982
PLUS Program (34 C.F.R. Part 683) (These PLUS regulations are effective, with the exception of certain record-keeping requirements.)	April 21, 1982
Pell Grant Program (34 C.F.R. Part 690)	
Pell Grant Program Final Regulation	Dec. 30, 1980
1981–82 Family Contribution Schedules	Jan. 19, 1981
Cost of Attendance and Treatment of Bankruptcy	Jan. 21, 1981
Revision to the 1981–82 Family Contribution Schedules	March 13, 1981
Cost of Attendance	July 22, 1981
National Direct Student Loan, College Work-Study, and Supplemental Educational Opportunity Grant Programs: Definition of Independent Student; Pell Grant Program: Expected Family Con-	Jan. 6, 1982

	Date Published in *Federal Register*
tribution (Document describes relationship of campus-based programs to Pell Grant program.) Amended Cost of Attendance	May 13, 1982
State Student Incentive Grant Program (34 C.F.R. Part 692)	July 14, 1981

Pell Grant Program Publications. As a result of the complexities of the Pell Grant and its significant variation from the other Title IV programs, a host of publications applicable only to it have emerged. These are as follows:

- *Pell Grant Payment Schedule, 1982–83.* Contains the charts used by financial aid administrators to look up Pell Grant awards.
- *The Pell Grant Formula, 1982–83.* Explains each step of the Pell Grant eligibility formula.
- *ADS* [Alternate Disbursement System] *Handbook, 1982–83 (Pell Grant Program).* For officials at schools that participate in the Pell Grant program but are not disbursing agents.
- *Pell Grant Validation Handbook, 1982–83.* Gives procedures for financial aid administrators to follow in validating information on student aid applications.
- *Audit Guide: Pell Grants* (June 1981). Sets forth the audit requirements of the Pell Grant program.
- *Pell (Basic) Grant Calculations Workbook* (March 1981). Explains the Pell Grant calculations process for financial aid administrators in a variety of unusual circumstances.

Other Publications. Several other important publications seek to provide interpretation of the law and regulations. The following should prove useful to the financial aid office in its day-to-day administration of the programs:

- *Federal Student Financial Aid Handbook, 1982–83.* A financial aid administrator's guide to administering Title IV student aid programs.

- *The Bulletin* (published several times a year). Contains articles on student aid issues of interest to the financial aid community.
- *Counselor's Handbook, 1982–83.* Gives general information about Title IV programs and the application and award process—for high school guidance counselors and financial aid administrators.
- *The Blue Book: Accounting, Record Keeping, and Reporting by Postsecondary Educational Institutions for Federally Funded Student Financial Aid Programs* (October 1981). Gives guidelines on federal requirements for bookkeeping practices for schools participating in Title IV student aid programs.
- *OSFA* [Office of Student Financial Aid] *Program Book* (July 1981). A statistical summary of the major federal financial aid programs.
- *Audit Guide: Campus-Based Student Financial Aid Programs* (June 1980). Issued by U.S. Department of Education, Office of Audit, Office of Inspector General. (Updated by the August-September issues of *The Bulletin.*) Sets forth the audit requirements of the campus-based programs.
- *Collections Manual: National Direct Student Loan Program* (November 1979). Guidelines for collecting National Direct Student Loans—for financial aid administrators and collectors.

3

State Student Aid Programs

Arthur S. Marmaduke

Higher education in the United States has historically been a state enterprise. It could hardly have been otherwise, since this country originated as highly individualistic colonies that established colleges for the preservation of their own culture and religion. There was no national government or national church to impose uniformity or create an intercolonial system of higher education. By 1776 the existing colleges had established firm patterns of support and control, which were taken up by the newly created states. Despite the urgings of the founding fathers for a national university, an aversion to nationalizing education at any level persisted through the succeeding two centuries. The first federal Department of Education was established in 1978, and the succeeding administration attempted to dismantle it by 1983. The language of the administration-supported bill to dismantle the department (S. 1821, introduced November 6, 1981) is relevant here: "The primary public responsibility for education belongs to the states, the local school systems, and other instrumentalities of the states; and a cabinet-level Department of Education threatens to preempt the role of parents, localities, and the states in determining policy for education."

Financial support for institutions of higher education for all purposes is divided as follows: 43 percent from state (and, to a minor extent, local) governments, 25 percent from the federal government, and 32 percent from private sources. "State support for institutions is heavily concentrated on public colleges and universities, although most states now provide some form of subsidy for the private sector as well" (Carnegie Foundation for the Advancement of Teaching, 1976, p. 55).

As noted in Chapter One, the historical emphasis on institutional support by the state can be viewed as a very basic form of student financial assistance. When California and other states pursued a policy of providing tuition-free colleges within easy commuting distance of all but a small percentage of the state's population, it was for the purpose of helping students enroll in college. Similarly, tuition and other costs at California's senior colleges and universities were held at a low level easily affordable by the vast majority of students and their families.

Despite the historic emphasis of the states on institutional support rather than support directly provided to students, a number of states created programs of student financial aid, including scholarships, grants, and loans. The motivation varied among the states, but often the goals were not only to reward the academically gifted and enable them to attend college, whatever their economic circumstances, but also to maintain the viability of the private sector by reducing the growing gap in costs between public and private colleges. Later many states established grant programs to widen access for economically disadvantaged youth, even those whose academic achievement was relatively modest.

This chapter will review (1) the growth and development of state involvement in student aid; (2) loan programs; (3) scholarship and grant programs, including state student aid policy and private higher education; and (4) the impact of state student aid on colleges and universities.

Growth of State Student Aid

The participation of states in student financial aid programs is not a recent development, although it may appear to be so because the level of participation became significant only during the past one and a half decades. The earliest state aid programs—three state scholarship programs established to meet three different goals—preceded World War I. In 1909 Connecticut began a program to recruit trained manpower. Four years later New York initiated its Regents Scholarship Program to honor its ablest high school graduates. Pennsylvania soon followed with a program designed to provide awards to students in each political district. Then, after a hiatus of twenty-two years, Oregon established its program in 1935. A considerable period of time again passed before a cluster of programs were established in the late 1950s in response to an awareness of the impending enrollment increases and a concern for preservation of the private sector. Programs in California (1956), Illinois (1958), Massachusetts (1958), and New Jersey (1959) were all established before the 1960s. By 1969-70 nineteen states had programs to which state-appropriated funds were allocated for financial aid, in the form of direct gifts (nonrepayable) or loans to students. Thus, as the 1970s opened, aggregate state expenditures for student aid exceeded the expenditure of the federal government; the states spent about $200 million in gift aid, compared to about $144 million for the Educational Opportunity Grant (EOG) program, the lone federal comprehensive gift aid program in 1969-70. From that year the number of states involved in student aid increased from nineteen to ultimately include all fifty states plus the District of Columbia and all eligible trust territories. The number of annual awards made to students during this period grew from about 470,000 to over 1.3 million, and the total funds awarded grew from just under $200 million in 1969-70 to over $975 million in 1981-82.

The College Entrance Examination Board recently sponsored a detailed analysis of the growth of state programs (Fenske and Boyd, 1981). The resulting report indicated that, during the period of major growth of state programs (since 1965), three stages of growth were evident. In the first stage (concluded by 1969-70), only nineteen states established programs for a variety of purposes—for instance, to recruit academic and other special talents, to provide access for economically disadvantaged youth, and to maintain freedom of choice by providing financial support for students who attended private colleges. In the second stage of growth, nine additional states established programs. Many of these also attempted to deal directly with issues of access and choice; however, during this period, which lasted from 1969-70 through 1973-74, there was a distinct shift in student aid from scholarship (ability-based) aid to grant (need-based only) aid. The third and final stage of growth occurred principally in response to the initiatives to the State Student Incentive Grant (SSIG) program, enacted under the Education Amendments of 1972. During this last stage of growth, all the remaining states and territories established programs providing state funds to students to attend postsecondary institutions. As will be shown, many of the states in the last stage of growth simply matched the relatively small amounts of SSIG federal funds with equally small amounts of state funds.

In their study of state funding levels over a recent eleven-year period, Fenske and Boyd (1981, p. 29) found that

[since 1969-70] a very marked imbalance or variability has been demonstrated in the level of funding and the number of awards provided among the states. Specifically, in all but one of the eleven years in this study, the five largest states in terms of dollars awarded were, in order, New York, Pennsylvania, Illinois, California, and New Jersey. During this period, these five largest states typically constituted nearly two thirds of the number of awards and of the total dollar amount of funds awarded. By 1979-80, about fifteen additional states had established programs of significant size even though the five largest states still provided well over half of the dollars awarded. The largest twenty states in 1979-80 provided 89.5 percent of total awards and 92.4 percent of all the dollars awarded. All of the remaining thirty-seven states and trust territories have relatively small programs, and nearly all of these have been only recently established.

The remarkably high variability among the states in student aid makes it difficult to find a common basis between New York, for example, which established its first program in 1913 and in 1979-80 provided over a quarter of a billion dollars to nearly half a million students, and such states as Alaska, Idaho, and Nevada, which among them awarded less than one and a half million dollars to fewer than two thousand students in the same academic year.

Table 1 shows the pattern of the establishment of state

Table 1. Year in Which States and Territories Established Student Aid Programs.

Year	Cumulative Total	State/Territory
Before or during 1969-70	19	California, Connecticut, Illinois, Indiana, Iowa, Kansas, Maine, Maryland, Massachusetts, Michigan, Minnesota, New Jersey, New York, Oregon, Pennsylvania, Rhode Island, Vermont, West Virginia, Wisconsin
1970-71	21	Florida, Ohio
1971-72	24	Oklahoma, Tennessee, Washington[a]
1972-73	28	Kentucky, Missouri, Nebraska, South Carolina
1973-74	28	None
1974-75	39	Colorado, Delaware,[a] Georgia, Idaho, North Dakota, Puerto Rico, South Dakota, Texas, Trust Territory, Virgin Islands, Virginia
1975-76	46	Arkansas, Hawaii, Louisiana, Montana, North Carolina, Utah, Guam
1976-77	53	Alabama, American Samoa, District of Columbia, Mississippi, New Hampshire, New Mexico, Wyoming
1977-78	56	Alaska, Arizona, Nevada
1978-79	57	Northern Marianas
1979-80	57	None

[a]Washington and Delaware did not respond to the annual surveys made by the National Association of State Scholarship and Grant Programs (NASSGP) until the years indicated. Both evidently had programs of undetermined type and size for some years before responding.
Source: Fenske and Boyd, 1981, p. 5.

student aid programs; Table 2 shows the growth in number of monetary awards and dollars expended from 1969–70 to 1982–83.

Table 2. Growth Since 1969–70 of State-Funded Need-Based
Undergraduate Scholarship/Grant Programs.

Year	Number of Monetary Awards	Dollar Awards[a] (Millions)
1969–70	470,000	$199.9
1970–71	535,200 (up 13.9%)	$236.3 (up 18.2%)
1971–72	604,000 (up 12.9%)	$268.6 (up 13.6%)
1972–73	661,700 (up 9.6%)	$315.5 (up 17.5%)
1973–74	733,300 (up 10.8%)	$364.2 (up 15.4%)
1974–75	913,100 (up 10.9%)	$440.8 (up 21.0%)
1975–76	901,900 (up 10.9%)	$510.2 (up 15.7%)
1976–77	1,104,400 (up 22.5%)	$651.4 (up 27.7%)
1977–78	1,161,400 (up 5.2%)	$737.0 (up 13.1%)
1978–79	1,217,750 (up 4.9%)	$789.2 (up 7.1%)
1979–80	1,278,429 (up 5.0%)	$864.5 (up 9.5%)
1980–81	1,241,851 (down 2.9%)	$873.3 (up 1.0%)
1981–82	1,210,126 (down 2.6%)	$890.6 (up 2.0%)
1982–83	1,253,262 (up 3.6%)	$975.8 (up 9.6%)

[a]All figures except 1982–83 are known enrolled recipients with award dollars; 1982–83 are best estimates. All figures are rounded and include both state and federal (SSIG) dollars.
Source: National Association of State Scholarship and Grant Programs, annual surveys.

State Governance Structures for Student Aid. In its annual surveys, the National Association of State Scholarship and Grant Programs (NASSGP) includes data on the constituency of the governing agencies for state student aid and the method of appointment selection of the members. These data show that the average size of the governing agency is about thirteen and that most of the members are laypersons rather than student aid professionals or public officials. The size of the governing body ranges from seven in four of the states to a maximum of twenty-one members in New Hampshire. All the states listed in the survey utilize a single agency for administering the state programs —except for New Jersey, which uses three different agencies. In most of the states, the governor selects and appoints the members of the agency governing body; in a small number of states, the governor shares that responsibility with the legislative bodies; and in Nevada the board of regents, which is responsible for state student aid, is elected by the public.

As might be expected from the fact that higher education developed independently in each of the fifty states, the structure and responsibilities of the state student aid agencies also vary widely. In many of the states, advisory committees are used in addition to the governing bodies (usually called commissions). Many of the commissions and advisory bodies include institutional governing board regents and/or institutional administrators. Many include students, either in a voting or an advisory capacity. Finally, many of the commissions and agencies include some legislators. However, the vast majority of members on the commissions and advisory committees are laypersons.

Role of Nonprofit Organizations. The College Scholarship Service (CSS) of the College Entrance Examination Board was started in 1954 to bring order out of a chaotic situation at a time when colleges were experiencing excess capacity and the competition for students was intense. CSS established a set of principles and standards and created a framework that assisted the enactment of state legislation. Its concepts of financial need analysis and packaging were adopted explicitly in government programs.

Early in the 1960s, the American College Testing Program developed a set of student aid services that accepted the assumptions and principles of the CSS system but included a separate means test. Consequently, students and parents had to cope with two nationally distributed need analysis documents, which, when processed into the separate means test, resulted in two different determinations of financial need. The differences between the systems became increasingly difficult for students to understand and increasingly unsatisfactory to government administrators and policy makers. The existence of the two organizations, however, did create a favorable political atmosphere for the development and administration of state programs. Both organizations first provided guidance to the state organizations and agencies; and both organizations, through testing and financial need and research services, provided significant administrative support.

National Task Force on Student Aid Problems. Against
the background of different need tests and multiple application
forms, the National Task Force on Student Aid Problems (better known as the Keppel Committee after its chairman, Francis
Keppel) was organized in May 1974, to explore ways in which
the existing financial aid system could be made more coherent,
equitable, and effective. The task force represented another effort to bring about voluntary governance and management. Implicit in its existence was the recognition that no governance
group, voluntary or public, was sufficiently comprehensive to
develop and maintain an orderly student financial aid process.
The principal, and highly significant, result of the work of the
task force was the development of the uniform methodology of
need analysis (see Chapter Six).

As the task force approached its goals of trying to bring
order out of the disarray of student financial aid, it developed
the concept of a federal-state-institutional-student partnership.
It considered a coordinated program, with all parties participating and working together, and discussed the importance of a
close working arrangement, so that aid to students could be distributed efficiently and equitably. It assumed, for purposes of
the study, that access, choice, and persistence are all achievable
student aid goals of equal importance. (See National Task Force
on Student Aid Problems, 1975.) Basic to the recommendations
of the task force is the concept of partners working together to
improve the delivery of student financial aid. Most of the partners showed positive attitudes and were most cooperative. The
Office of Education was initially reluctant to implement the
recommendations of the task force and showed few signs of accepting the partnership concept. Recently the stance of the
Office (now Department) of Education has changed considerably, and it has shown an increased willingness to work within a
partnership concept.

Loan Programs

The State Loan Programs section of the 1965 Higher
Education Act, Title IV, authorized the Guaranteed Student
Loan (GSL) program. The act encouraged state administration

of the guaranteed loan program and provided federal advances as reserves against defaults. It also provided for direct federal administration and loan guarantees through the Federally Insured Student Loan (FISL) program in situations where students could not obtain loans through state agencies or nonprofit corporations.

Substantial amendments to the Guaranteed Student Loan program were made in the Education Amendments of 1976, which provided incentives for states to establish Guaranteed Student Loan agencies if they had not previously done so. Currently, all but two states have some provision for student loan funding. Over half of the state loan agencies have been established since 1976. By 1980 the GSL program had grown to constitute 90 percent of loan volume, compared to 46 percent in 1974. Thus, by 1980 the states had become the dominant guarantee source, and direct federal guarantees assumed a minor role. The federal government—by virtue of paying in-school interest subsidies, giving special allowances to lenders, and providing reinsurance of defaults to state agencies—is the principal source of governmental expenditures for these loans. As such, it maintains through law and regulation the primary decision-making authority for Guaranteed Student Loans. While programs vary somewhat from state to state, the state agencies operate within specific federal laws and regulations and are really management agents of the federal government with some operational discretion but no major policy authority.

Interestingly enough, states first served as models for the massive federal programs as we now know them. The first Guaranteed Student Loan program actually was started in 1956 in Massachusetts. Other states commenced similar activities, as noted in Table 3. Massachusetts and New York in particular provided the models for the enabling federal legislation. The New York experience was probably most influential, and many specific features as well as the broad design were federal reflections of the New York structure (Hansen and Feeney, 1977). The early development was quite regional, occurring for the most part in New England, the mid-Atlantic area, and the South. No western states and only two midwestern states guaranteed loans before the federal program.

Table 3. States That Guaranteed Loans Before GSL Began in 1966-67.

State	Year
Connecticut	1966
Georgia	1965
Louisiana	1964
Massachusetts	1956
Michigan	1962
New Hampshire	1962
New Jersey	1960
New York	1958
North Carolina	1963
Ohio	1962
Pennsylvania	1964
Rhode Island	1960
Tennessee	1963
Vermont	1964
Virginia	1961

As noted in Table 3, fifteen states preceded the federal government as a guarantor of loans to students by commercial lenders. In 1965-66 state program appropriations totaled only a few million dollars. By fiscal year 1983 dollar volume had grown to 6.5 billion dollars in loans (including GSL and state-appropriated loans) to approximately 2.8 million students.

Guaranteed Student Loan Agency Structure. Johnson (1981), in her survey of state-level administration of Guaranteed Student Loan programs, found three structural configurations predominating among the participating states. In the first one, the state is the guarantor, and a state agency, board, public corporation, commission, or department directly administers the program. In the second, the state has delegated all responsibilities for the guarantee function and the administration to a nonprofit corporation. In the third, the state is the guarantor but has contracted all or part of the program administration to a nonprofit corporation. In addition, several of the states have separate boards, corporations, commissions, or authorities with specific authorization to issue tax-exempt revenue bonds and to establish a secondary market for lenders in Guaranteed Student Loan programs. Readers will wish to investigate how the program is administered in their state, so that they can determine how they can best observe and perhaps facilitate the process.

Approximately half of the states fall into the first category and act as the guarantor and administrator of student loans. An existing state agency usually performs this function, although in some states specifically established public authorities or state-chartered corporations take full responsibility for the guarantee and its accompanying administrative function.

Nonprofit corporations, such as the Higher Education Assistance Foundation or the United Student Aid Funds, have responsibility for the guarantee function or administration in about one quarter of the states. The Higher Education Assistance Foundation tends to perform both the guarantee and the loan-servicing function, doing so in five states and the District of Columbia. The United Student Aid Funds acts in the same manner for Hawaii but provides only loan servicing in about thirteen states. In one quarter of the states, a guarantee agency established by statute maintains responsibility for both the guarantee function and administration. These agencies have contractual relationships with a nonprofit corporation, such as United Student Aid Funds, or a locally chartered organization.

Financing the State Agency Enterprise. The major costs of the Guaranteed Student Loan program are (1) the interest subsidy paid for students in school and (2) the special allowance paid above the statutory interest rate while the student is in school and also when the loan is in the repayment period. Federal expenditures for interest payments in 1982 were $2,914,097,000. As a large number of loans are converted into payout status when students have completed their academic programs, the absolute number of defaults increases and provides the second largest demand for funds. In 1982 the total amount of GSL defaulted loans was over 1.5 billion dollars.

The federal legislation provides an attractive financial structure to induce state participation. After the state pays the insurance claims filed by lenders, the Department of Education activates the reinsurance provision, and the state is reimbursed for the major share of the defaults on student loans. The rate of federal reinsurance is as follows:

Agency Loss Rate	*Federal Reimbursements*
0–5%	100%
5–9%	90%
Over 90%	80%

In addition, state agencies are authorized under federal law to keep one third of any monies they have collected from student defaulters. With the total loan volume through state agencies in 1982 in excess of six billion dollars, the administrative costs, while quite small as a percentage of volume, still represent a sizable outlay of funds. In most states the Guaranteed Student Loan program is administered without requiring state support. There are several sources of funding for operational costs. The federal government provides an administrative cost allowance, which in 1982 totaled $55,781,000.

Many states rely primarily on the student insurance premium, which may, under federal law, be up to 1 percent of the amount of the loan and which may be front loaded to cover the period of the student's attendance and the grace period. This can amount to five years for an entering undergraduate student at a four-year college. Most states charge the maximum 1 percent, but six states charge .5 percent, and five charge no premium at all. In addition, a few states levy the premium over the life of the loan.

Approximately one fourth of the states receive state appropriations that cover various phases of their operational expenses. Generally, states also receive funds from their investment of reserve funds. The size of revenues ranges from as little as 1 percent of the outstanding loans to as high as 10 percent, although the preponderance of states are at the lower ranges.

Secondary Markets and Direct Lending. In order to ensure an adequate supply of capital to commercial lenders, several large and important secondary markets have developed. The best known, the Student Loan Marketing Association (Sallie Mae), functions as a secondary market, dealing directly with lenders and purchasing their notes under negotiated terms. Recently, to ensure a steady flow of capital to lenders, a number of states have established organizations that provide secondary markets. Seventeen states have directly or indirectly established or authorized such agencies. Frequently these are private non-profit corporations, and occasionally the secondary market organizations provide both secondary market and direct-lending services. Only infrequently are the secondary market sources organized under the aegis of the guarantee agency.

Some states, in addition to providing the guarantee function or assuring a secondary market, also provide direct loans to students. Twenty-one states have exercised this option.

For both direct-lending operations and secondary market programs, state agencies usually resort to tax-exempt revenue bonds, which are sold either publicly or privately, with the proceeds used to make either direct loans or to purchase outstanding loans from commercial lenders. Even at today's high interest rates, there is a sufficient spread in the cost of funds and the combination of the interest charged to students and the special allowance to make a secondary market operation or a direct-lending operation economically feasible.

Scholarships and Grants

Monetary awards—such as scholarships and grants—made with no expectation of repayment (sometimes called gift aid) represent the predominant type of student aid program. There is no consensus on the precise definition of scholarships or grants. However, common usage indicates that scholarships are generally awarded competitively on a basis of higher academic or other achievement and potential. Financial need may or may not be part of the process of selecting recipients. Grants are generally awarded solely on the basis of need to students who are admissible to designated postsecondary institutions.

Scholarships were originally the preferred type of award made by state programs. In 1969-70, 68.5 percent of all state awards required a measure of academic potential or achievement. By 1979-80 this percentage had dropped to 20.6, and grants comprised the other 79.4 percent. Clearly, this shift represents a major revision in the goals of the state programs.

Applications and Awards. The fourteenth annual survey

of the National Association of State Scholarship and Grant Programs (1982) estimated that there were over 2.6 million applications for the 1.3 million awards made in 1982-83, for a 50 percent award rate. It also estimated that approximately half of the students who were denied aid did not have financial need under the standards of the program. While only a portion of the states were able to estimate the number of unsuccessful applicants, about 468,000 applicants in slightly over half of the programs were denied aid because of lack of funds. The percentage of applicants who received awards varied considerably among the states. The middle two thirds of the state programs awarded aid to between 2.5 and 8.3 percent of their applicants.

In keeping with the differing needs of the states and the patterns of application for admission to postsecondary institutions, the patterns of application for aid also vary among the states. Nineteen programs have no deadline dates; nine allow the institutions to define the deadlines; sixty-one programs publish deadline dates, which range from early February of the preceding academic year through October of the academic year. The majority of programs require March, April, or May deadlines. Most state agencies notify students of their awards directly by letter, although 29 percent use notification systems in which the institutions announce their decision to students. The patterns again vary as to the time of the announcement, ranging from March to as late as August.

Twenty-four percent of state programs had award maximums greater than $2,000. Another 24 percent reported that their awards were between $1,500 and $1,999; 21 percent awarded between $500 and $999; and 7 percent awarded less than $500.

Selection Procedures. Most states use some formal system of financial need analysis. The CSS processing is used by thirty-three states, seven use the ACT processing, thirteen use either CSS or ACT, and seven use either ACT or the Basic Grant methodology. Six states use special methodology designed by the state; others use a variety of combinations. CSS and ACT processing of need analysis differs, but both determine the amount of need according to the uniform methodology. Each organization gathers somewhat different supplementary information.

Seventy-eight percent of the programs determine financial need by comparing all college costs, including tuition, with the applicant's resources. Seventeen percent of the programs use an absolute, rather than a relative, need concept; that is, they consider only the applicant's resources.

Forty-three percent of the programs require students to apply for a Pell Grant in order to qualify for an award in their program, and in all but two cases the amount of the Pell Grant is anticipated and subtracted from the applicant's need before an award is made.

Only slightly over a third of the states use merit criteria in determination of awards; high school or college grades are the most frequently used criteria. Test scores are used by twenty-six programs, and almost half of the states with the merit criteria use a combination of test scores and grades.

Only 20 percent of the programs use their own criteria for determining whether a student is independent of his parents for financial aid purposes, and 62 percent use the federal criteria (discussed in Chapter Six of this volume). Most programs have a minimum state residency requirement that varies greatly. About 52 percent of programs are open to students who are either citizens, admitted to permanent residency, or on refugee status. Forty-three percent are open to students who are citizens or permanent residents. Virtually all programs have some eligibility and institutional requirement.

The shift from scholarships to grants cited above may be somewhat misleading. Several large state programs—notably, in New York, Pennsylvania, and Illinois—have sufficient awards and dollars so that any qualified student receives an award. In this they are very similar to the Pell Grant program, having acquired the status of entitlement programs.

State Student Incentive Grants. Under the leadership of Senator Jacob Javits of New York, Congress added the State Student Incentive Grant (SSIG) program to the Higher Education Act of 1965 through amendments signed into law in 1972. The SSIG program became part of the Title IV Student Assistance Program, which established the Basic Educational Opportunity Grants (BEOG), Supplemental Educational Opportunity Grants (SEOG), College Work-Study (CWS), and National Direct

Student Loans (NDSL). (For a description and discussion of SSIG, see Hansen, 1979.)

Senator Javits envisioned a federal-state partnership, with the federal government providing dollar-for-dollar matching to states for expenditures in grants to undergraduate students. States apply to the Department of Education for their allotment, up to the amount they can match with qualified state funds. Federal funds not matched are reallocated to states with excess matching funds in proportion to total enrollment. State Student Incentive Grant funds must be administered by a single state agency. They provide grants not to exceed $2,000 per academic year to undergraduate students. The Education Amendments of 1980 allowed graduate students also to participate. States must appropriate funds that represent an increased state expenditure over the level of expenditures in a designated base year.

The goals for SSIG, as determined by the Department of Education's regulations interpreting the law, were (1) to encourage the creation of state student grant programs and (2) to encourage increased state expenditures on such programs. SSIG seems to have been very successful in meeting the first goal but only moderately successful with the second. In 1974-75, when SSIG funds first became available, twenty-eight states (California, Colorado, Connecticut, Delaware, Florida, Illinois, Indiana, Iowa, Kansas, Maine, Maryland, Massachusetts, Michigan, Minnesota, Missouri, New Jersey, New York, Ohio, Oregon, Pennsylvania, Rhode Island, South Carolina, Tennessee, Texas, Vermont, Washington, West Virginia, and Wisconsin) allocated funds for need-based undergraduate programs. By academic year 1977-78, all fifty states and the District of Columbia were participating. The immediate burst of growth of new programs after the enactment of the SSIG program suggests very strongly that the program provided considerable leverage and that it encouraged expenditure of state funds that otherwise would not have occurred. Both the law and the Department of Education took the position that the states should have considerable freedom in designing the grant programs and that federal legislative and regulatory requirements would be minimal. In operation it has been analogous to a revenue-sharing program.

The favorable state response and the absence of state complaints about legislative and administrative interference indicate that participating states strongly support the administrative mechanism of the program.

Index of Effort. The great differences in the size and complexity of various state student aid programs make a meaningful analysis most difficult. In 1980 New York had about 9 percent of all United States college enrollments but provided nearly one third of all state student assistance (Hauptman and Rice, 1980, p. 1). As a contrasting example, Arizona did not make an appropriation for student aid until 1980. The efforts in Arizona and a number of other states are late, small, and still somewhat uncertain. There is very little commonality between New York and Arizona in purposes, scope, impact, or administrative style.

States may be measured by the duration of their commitment to state aid and by their total annual appropriations. Their index of effort can be measured by total student aid dollars awarded per total state population. Table 4 shows a range from $15.31 in New York to 22 cents in Louisiana.

State student grant programs may be evaluated as they relate to total state expenditure for higher education operating expenditures. Fenske and Boyd (1981) interrelated the data from the annual surveys made by the National Association of State Scholarship and Grant Programs and the data from M. M. Chambers in his annual compilation entitled *Appropriations of State Tax Funds for Operating Expenses of Higher Education* (published by the National Association of State Universities and Land-Grant Colleges in Washington, D.C.). They found a substantial decline in state grant funds as a percentage of total state operating expenses from 1969-70 to 1979-80. In 1969-70 the total state grant appropriations were $199.9 million, compared to $3,794,831 for operating funds; that is, total grant appropriations were equal to 5.27 percent of the appropriations for operating funds. By 1979-80 this ratio had declined to 4.08 percent.

State grants have also decreased as a percentage of total state and federal grant funds, largely because of the enactment and the enormous expansion of the Pell Grant program. In

Table 4. Rank Order of Indexes of Effort: State Student Aid Dollars
Awarded per Total State Population, 1979-80.

State	Ratio	State	Ratio
1. New York	$15.31	26. Maryland	1.34
2. Vermont	8.82	27. Washington	1.30
3. Pennsylvania	6.88	28. Maine	1.25
4. Illinois	6.63	29. Florida	1.23
5. Minnesota	5.94	30. Utah	1.18
6. Iowa	5.30	31. Delaware	.95
7. New Jersey	5.18	32. Oklahoma	.80
8. Wisconsin	4.51	33. Arizona	.78
9. Rhode Island	4.50	34. Nevada	.77
10. Indiana	4.01	35. Virginia	.74
All States	3.94	36. Alabama	.67
11. California	3.82	37. Georgia	.67
12. South Carolina	3.69	38. North Dakota	.64
13. Michigan	3.30	39. Wyoming	.62
14. Colorado	3.07	40. New Hampshire	.61
15. Ohio	2.89	41. South Dakota	.61
16. Massachusetts	2.81	42. New Mexico	.60
17. Connecticut	2.77	43. North Carolina	.60
18. Oregon	2.39	44. Alaska	.58
19. Kansas	2.00	45. Idaho	.58
20. Missouri	1.87	46. Nebraska	.55
21. West Virginia	1.63	47. Montana	.54
22. District of Columbia	1.57	48. Arkansas	.51
23. Kentucky	1.53	49. Hawaii	.51
24. Tennessee	1.44	50. Mississippi	.46
25. Texas	1.44	51. Louisiana	.22

Source: Fenske and Boyd, 1981, p. 16.

1969-70 state programs represented 61.6 percent of the state and federal grant expenditures. In 1974-75 state expenditures had declined to 41.9 percent, although SSIG funds added 1.9 percent, while the Pell Grant program represented 35.4 percent and Supplemental Educational Opportunity Grants (SEOG) 20.9 percent. In 1979-80 state expenditures had fallen to 23.2 percent, with SSIG an additional 2.3 percent, but Pell Grant represented 66.4 percent and SEOG 8.1 percent (see Table 5).

State Student Aid and the Private Sector. An element of commonality among the earlier and larger state student grant programs was their goal of helping students attend private col-

Table 5. Total State and Federal Grant Expenditures, 1979-80.

Program	Dollars (millions)	Percentage
State Student Incentive Grant	$ 76.8	2.3
Pell Grant	2,220.0	66.4
Supplemental Educational Opportunity Grant	270.0	8.1
State Grants	775.5	23.2
	$3,342.3	100.0

leges. Fife (1975), in his study of college student grants, observed that equalization of public and private college tuition levels through state grants would favor many private colleges. He further estimated that perhaps 10 percent of national private college enrollment would not be there without state student aid. His studies and others demonstrate a definite attendance gain at private colleges. In the states that provide funds for students in private colleges (a majority of states), the state student aid can be a principal source of continued viability for many private colleges. For example, in a study of state student aid trends in Illinois over a recent ten-year period, the findings "underscore the special role that state grants and scholarships have in maintaining the continued vitality of the private sector in states where such monetary awards are applicable to costs at either public or private colleges. This impact derives from the higher costs and per capita grants accruing to students at private colleges. As tuition plays an increasingly important function in the finances of private colleges, and as state monetary awards increase as a proportion of that tuition, the state agencies administering those awards assume a growing de facto influence, passive though it may be, concerning private colleges and universities" (Fenske, Boyd, and Maxey, 1979, p. 154). Table 6 shows the distribution of state grant funds at public and private colleges.

Decisions regarding state student aid programs are made in relationship to federal programs and to institutional programs. Originally a program came into being because of a short-

Table 6. Distribution to Public and Private Colleges of State Grant
Awards and Dollars (Selected Years from 1969-70 Through 1982-83).

Year	Percentage of Awards		Percentage of Award Dollars		Mean Awards	
	Public	Private	Public	Private	Public	Private
1969-70	46.0	54.0	37.2	62.8	$317	$457
1975-76	59.6	40.4	44.6	55.4	431	789
1976-77	62.0	38.0	46.2	53.8	440	833
1977-78	61.8	38.2	45.3	54.7	460	896
1978-79	63.0	37.0	45.2	54.8	479	986
1979-80	61.5	38.5	41.1	58.9	451	1,034
1981-82	59.4	38.0	41.5	56.3	—	—
1982-83	59.4	38.6	42.3	56.0	—	—

Sources: 1969-70 through 1979-80 data from Fenske and Boyd, 1981, p. 27; 1981-82 and 1982-83 data from 13th and 14th annual surveys of the National Association of State Scholarship and Grant Programs; data not available for 1980-81 and for mean awards in 1981-82 and 1982-83. Percentages shown do not add to 100 because they exclude awards to students at out-of-state institutions.

age of institutional funds as colleges, particularly private colleges, documented their inability to provide adequate financial aid for their students through private funding. Because of the shortage of institutional funds, particularly at private colleges, most state programs are tuition sensitive.

Relationships Between Institutions and State Programs

The relationship between the campus and state student aid differs among the states. Campus administrators in states like New York, Pennsylvania, Illinois, New Jersey, and California are aware that the states' efforts in student aid have been and are a significant influence on higher education. These five states have collectively invested several billions of dollars in aid for students. At the other end of the spectrum, states like Nevada, South Dakota, Arizona, and Idaho have not established significant student aid programs. In the majority of states that do have significant programs, campus administrators are cognizant of the state programs and have an opportunity to become involved with and influence them. In such states both college student aid and academic administrators maintain a close working relationship with their state agency. Fortunately, the state agencies are typically structured for effective interaction with the states' campuses, public and private, through a network of advisory and planning committees and other devices.

An overview of state, as compared to federal, efforts reveals that the states have been much more consistent and reliable in student aid. As we enter an era of attempts to decrease student aid sharply at the federal level, will the states step in to fill the breach? And will they do so quickly enough to offset sharp federal decreases, so that the campuses will not experience a "roller coaster" effect of peaks and valleys in funding? These are questions that will be answered only within each state depending on the political efforts of state campus administrators as well as the long-term traditions of the state in student aid and the economic climate.

A retrospective look at the involvement of the fifty states in student aid leads one to expect that those states with a long-term tradition of maintaining access and choice through their own efforts will respond positively to the challenges immediately ahead. The SSIG program did bring many new states into the circle of states with student aid programs, and college administrators now have a record of sorts on which to base attempts at convincing legislators of the merits of continued student aid. Success in such attempts would probably be well worth the time and effort involved.

Bibliographical Note

The literature on state student aid is not extensive, but some of it is of good quality and highly useful, particularly the data-oriented research reports and the historical essays.

Basic to a thorough understanding of state involvement in student aid is a perception of the primacy of the states in control over public institutions and benevolent protection of private institutions in the United States. This perception is aided by review of a general historical work like *Higher Education in*

Transition by Brubacher and Rudy (1976) and further reading into authoritative publications like *The Capitol and the Campus: State Responsibility for Postsecondary Education* by the Carnegie Commission on Higher Education (1971), *The States and Higher Education* by the Carnegie Foundation for the Advancement of Teaching (1976), and *The States and Private Higher Education: Problems and Policies in a New Era* by the Carnegie Council on Policy Studies in Higher Education (1977).

Studies of state student aid are blessed with consistent, fairly comprehensive data compiled annually by the National Association of State Scholarship and Grant Programs. The surveys were initiated in 1969 by Joseph D. Boyd, then director of the Illinois State Commission, on behalf of the association and conducted by him for the first eleven years of the series. Subsequent surveys have been conducted and reported for the association by the staff of the Pennsylvania Higher Education Assistance Agency.

Drawing on this extensive data bank, Fenske and Boyd (1981), in a study commissioned by the College Scholarship Service, produced the first comprehensive analysis of state student aid. This chapter refers extensively to their findings, and the author wishes to acknowledge the kind permission of the report's publisher, the College Entrance Examination Board, to use tabular data and other direct findings. Readers should note that the Fenske and Boyd work includes only scholarship and grant programs. Loan programs are covered in the brief but insightful article by Johnson (1981) cited earlier in the chapter.

4

Expanding and Utilizing Private and Institutional Sources of Aid

Robert P. Huff

For purposes of this chapter, institutional aid is defined as assistance where the college or university decides on the recipient and makes the award from funds (other than federal or state funds) under its direct control. Private financial aid refers to awards controlled by a noncollegiate organization, which determines the aid recipient and makes the award from its own resources. Data on the extent of institutional and private financial aid resources are at best sketchy, but it is estimated that in the academic year 1980–81 institutional aid amounted to approximately $2.1 billion and private financial aid was just under $1 billion. This chapter describes both institutional and other private financial aid resources, recommends ways in which they can be generated, and suggests how they can best serve the particular interests of the institution.

As noted in Chapter One, institutional and private support for students actually predates federal and state aid programs by many years. History records that the first scholarship fund was established in 1643, when Lady Anne Mowlson presented Harvard College with an endowment of 100 English pounds, the income to be used to help a needy student. In the early years of American higher education, then entirely private, scholarships were used mainly to ensure the access and preparation of students aspiring to careers in education, public service, and religion. Scholarships were also used by the colleges as a means of generating income for their operation. For a fee a donor could purchase a "perpetual scholarship," which would forever cover the tuition of someone, often a family member.

Certainly not all institutional aid in the eighteenth and nineteenth centuries was limited to scholarships. Brown, Princeton, and Yale established separate dining halls to feed students of very limited means at a lower cost. Institutions provided students with opportunities to work as tutors, dining hall attendants, and field hands engaged in raising food crops for dining halls. Some students actually earned their expenses by assisting in the construction of their institutions. At the turn of this century, Yale University established a self-help bureau, which helped students locate term-time employment. Book loans were even available at some institutions to help students purchase their texts and other academic materials.

Prior to the 1950s and burgeoning enrollments in the nation's colleges and universities, scholarships were used mostly to attract students into certain disciplines and were frequently awarded to those with specific qualities, above all academic promise and achievement. For the most part, these awards provided all or a part of the recipient's tuition.

Concerned that a very limited number of mainly private institutions had significant scholarship resources and could virtually monopolize the most gifted students if they chose, a group of colleges and universities in 1954 established the College Scholarship Service. The members of this association, which was sponsored by the College Entrance Examination Board, agreed that student aid generally should be awarded in response to demonstrated financial need and that a standard means of assessing that need should be employed. Added impetus to the movement of basing financial aid on demonstrated need was provided by the American College Testing Program when it established a second national need analysis service in 1967.

While the College Scholarship Service and the American College Testing Program—in consort, whether intentional or not, with the federal and state governments—succeeded in moving most student aid to a need basis, the amount of scholarships and grants awarded without regard to the student's need has remained significant and even appears to be growing. In a 1974 survey of 1,875 four-year public and private colleges and universities (Huff, 1975), 54.5 percent of the 859 respondents reported that they awarded merit scholarships. The percentage rate was virtually identical for public and private institutions. About 77 percent of the institutions found the awards at least moderately effective in their efforts to recruit very talented and gifted students. Evidence of an increase in the use of scholarships awarded without regard to need was discovered in a 1977 survey of College Scholarship Service members (Potter and Sidar, 1978). Of the approximately 400 responding institutions, 71 percent reported that they were awarding merit scholarships or other scholarships not related to demonstrated financial need. Many colleges and universities, then, have chosen to make awards on a basis other than, or in addition to, need. The principal factors influencing whether an institution follows such a course appear to be competition for very talented students and the availability of the resources with which to award these scholarships.

A number of ways do exist for colleges and universities to recognize exceptional academic promise and achievement without necessarily resorting to a monetary payment to the student. Some institutions award "honors at entrance" to the top 10 or 15 percent of the incoming freshman class. Designating students who have earned an outstanding grade point average as the president's or the dean's scholars, which may or may not carry any financial reward, is yet another form of recognition. It seems virtually without issue that some means should exist for extending public acknowledgment to notable academic achievement beyond the honors normally conferred only at the time of graduation. These scholars, however they may be designated, instead of receiving monetary rewards, can be honored by a special ceremony, the presentation of a certificate, lunch with the president or dean of the institution, or in a variety of other ways.

As described in Chapter Seven, some colleges and universities recognize both accomplishments and need by combining scholarships and grants with loans and jobs. The presumption is that the higher the proportion of gift aid in the student's package, the more appealing the offer of support and the greater the probability of the student's acceptance of admission and subsequent enrollment.

The ability of a college or university to award its own resources provides for more flexibility, and hence independence, in the administration of its student aid program. Some institutions use a less demanding means test in allocating their own loan and employment resources to students, in order to help upper-middle-income parents with the sometimes excessive contributions that are expected according to national need determination formulas. Independence is important because the goals of the college or university may not be totally congruent with those of public programs. More specifically, most public funds are awarded in response to the strict demonstration of financial need, whereas an institution, as has been suggested, may wish with its own resources to recognize and promote the enrollment of students with exceptional academic accomplishment and promise or with other qualifications held in high regard by the academic community. Also, since public funding may vary from year to year in its availability, and even in its nature, an institution that has its own resources can respond in a more stable way to student demand for support. The positive effect of such stability for recruitment is obvious.

Sources and Uses of Institutional Funds

Institutional student aid funds, like public resources, may take three basic forms. They may be scholarships or grants, usually referred to as gift aid; student loans, either long term (that is, payable after graduation) or short term (normally payable before the next academic year begins); and student employment, both during the academic year and during vacation periods. The funds themselves may be restricted—that is, limited to expenditure by the college or university for student aid purposes; or they may be unrestricted and consequently usable for any purpose the institution chooses.

Restricted Funds. Restricted funds take the form of endowments or current gifts. Only the annual interest earned on an endowment's principal is ordinarily spent for student aid purposes. Occasionally, either as specified by the donor of the endowment or at the institution's option, a portion of the interest is returned to principal, with the purpose of increasing the size of the endowment and providing eventually for larger annual payouts. Funds that the institution is expected to utilize in their entirety during a specified period, normally an academic year, are referred to as "current gifts." On occasion a donor may specify that the current gift is to be spent over a period longer than an academic year; the institution then may have the option of investing the funds that will be used in subsequent years, and adding to the fund and increasing the amount of aid awarded.

Endowments and current gifts that carry the fewest restrictions are the most useful. Donors very frequently have definite ideas about how their gifts are to be spent, and they may not coincide with the institution's objectives. Where institutional representatives have the opportunity to confer with the donor over the terms of a prospective gift, every effort should be made to keep the terms as broad as possible, to ensure that the resource can be used in the best interests of the institution.

Federal and state laws generally preclude institutions from accepting gifts restricted by race or creed; if the conditions are stated as a matter of preference rather than an absolute restriction, however, these gifts sometimes may be accepted. Similarly, institutions have been prevented from accepting student aid gifts restricted to one gender; now, however, such a gift sometimes may be accepted if the college or university can establish that it has adequate support for both men and women. In all such instances, college and university administrators should consult legal counsel to determine whether the gift can be accepted (see also Chapter Sixteen).

Although at one time gifts for student aid purposes may have come with a minimum of solicitation, such is scarcely the case now. If student aid gifts are to be made a major target for private giving, institutional administrators must make a conscious decision to solicit this kind of support. Of course, these same officers will need to consider whether seeking gifts for student aid may conflict with other fund-raising objectives of the college or university. They will have to determine exactly what priority they wish to assign to student aid. If they decide that they want to meet the demonstrated financial need of all students, or possibly those students in a particular category, they should initially determine the amount of aid that can reasonably be obtained from public sources and then consciously seek to raise the remainder from private sources. One compelling argument that can be used in securing student aid from the private sector is that cutbacks in public funding dramatically reduce the opportunity of the institution to attract and retain able and talented students.

Colleges and universities seeking financial aid gifts should do so by selling their strengths. For example, if the institution boasts a particularly strong school or academic department, it should approach those corporations which, because of their products or services, may have an interest in promoting a related discipline or field of study by ensuring the enrollment and graduation of able students. Some corporations will view the recipients of the scholarships they support as potential employees. They may, for example, offer their scholars the opportunity for summer employment, allowing for an evaluation of the students as permanent employees after graduation. By the same token, the aid recipients will be afforded the chance to judge whether they would like to work for the sponsor.

Sometimes a corporate donor will seek to establish as a condition of awarding the scholarship the requirement that the recipient will, after the completion of his or her course of study, agree to become an employee of the company for a specified period. Undoubtedly, problems can be created if an institution accepts a gift that carries such obligations. If the college or university has very limited aid funds to offer, will the student be forced into accepting such a scholarship as the only means of earning a degree? Then, too, students frequently change their academic majors and career goals as they progress through higher education. There seems to be less disposition on the part of corporations to insist on a permanent employment requirement as a condition to receive one of their awards, but college and university officials would be well served to consider carefully the consequences, both for the institution and its students, of accepting such a gift.

An institution actively soliciting restricted gifts for student aid purposes should have available a brochure that describes the student aid program and its goals, explains how donors may assist with the program's advancement, and identifies specific staff members of the institution who will be glad to provide more detailed information. This publication is not to be confused with the one that the college or university is obliged to distribute to its students under the consumer information requirements of the federal government. The required brochure for students, as described in Chapter Five, deals with how applications for aid are submitted, what resources are available, the basis on which aid is awarded, the conditions that must be met to have the aid renewed, and other information related to the awarding process. The scholarship brochure suggested here should be written to promote the interest and hence the support of contributors. Naturally, it should be as attractive and appealing as practical. Development personnel, whether they be institutional staff members or volunteer fund raisers, should be thoroughly briefed on all aspects of the institution's student aid program and its particular needs. The development officer and the student aid administrator should, of course, consult constantly and coordinate their efforts to attract support.

Potential donors of student aid—businesses, foundations, community organizations, churches, and private individuals—can be identified in various ways. The heyday of corporate and foundation support of student aid occurred in the 1950s. Corporations like General Motors, Union Carbide, Procter and

Gamble, Texaco, and Owens-Illinois and foundations like Alfred
P. Sloan sponsored impressive national scholarship programs,
often with accompanying cost-of-education grants, at many colleges and universities. The emergence and significant growth of
federal and state student aid programs in the 1960s prompted a
significant reduction in this private support for students, although many corporations and foundations have continued to
contribute toward the other needs of higher education. (When I
asked the program officer at a foundation that was allocating
$2 million a year for scholarships at a number of public and pri-
vate institutions why the aid program was being phased out, he
responded that the federal government had preempted the area of
support for students, and he saw no reason why his foundation
should compete. Other corporate and foundation representatives offered similar explanations for the termination of their
programs.) Despite the substantial diminution of this private
support for scholarships, grants, and loans in the last two decades, foundation and corporate support for student aid is well
worth pursuing vigorously, particularly in the light of cutbacks
in federal and state funding.

The *Chronicle of Higher Education* in its weekly issues
carries a column listing private gifts and grants to institutions of
higher education. This regular column is an excellent source of
summary information about corporations and foundations interested in particular areas of giving. Annual reports of corporations also often indicate the nature and extent of their support
of student aid programs. The *Foundation Directory,* published
by the Foundation Center in New York City, lists, by state,
over 5,000 foundations that make grants of $25,000 or more a
year and have assets of at least a half a million dollars. Besides
identifying the officers of these foundations and their financial
circumstances, the directory describes the objectives and activities of the foundations. Colleges and universities can also learn
about the philanthropic efforts of businesses and foundations
through commercial services that provide this information for a
fee.

Community agencies and individual donors are usually
more difficult to identify as potential sources of student aid

gifts because of the lack of systematized listings. Wide and continuous publicity through the media about the institution's financial aid program and what it desires to accomplish can generate contacts. The aid administrator should actively seek invitations to make presentations before professional and service organizations, alumni clubs, and parent groups and can use such opportunities to solicit gifts for student aid purposes.

Personalizing relations with a donor from the point of initial contact is absolutely essential to promoting gifts for student aid purposes. Personalizing relations involves designating one staff member to be the principal contact with a donor. The staff member should concentrate on becoming as familiar as possible with the donor's interests and circumstances and be readily available to respond to the donor's questions and concerns. The donor must be made aware of the institution's goals and expectations with respect to its student aid program. If the donor specifies exactly how the gift must be used, the staff member may, in some instances, have to explain why it cannot be used that way. As mentioned, the broader the terms of any gift, the greater benefit it is likely to have for the institution.

Effective donor relations do not cease once a gift is made. A donor who is particularly pleased with the way in which his or her gift has been used by the college or university will be disposed to repeat the contribution and often will encourage support from others. At least once in an academic year, a donor should receive a report that, without divulging confidential information about the recipient of the aid, gives some descriptive information about the student and indicates how much the aid has meant. A typical paragraph describing an aid recipient in a letter to the donor of the award might read as follows:

> Mary C. has been selected to receive your scholarship this year. She is one of our most outstanding students, with close to an "A minus" average for the year she has completed at the college. Although she has yet to declare her major, she has indicated a strong preference for the premedical program. Despite averaging seventeen units a semester, she finds time to perform with our award-

winning college orchestra as first violinist and to do
volunteer work at the local mental hospital. Since
Mary's father suffered a severe stroke last year and
is disabled, the family of five is supported by her
mother, who is a secretary. Without your scholarship, which provides her tuition and required fees,
Mary would be unable to continue her studies. To
meet a portion of her educational costs, she works
twelve hours a week in the college library and also
is borrowing under a federal loan program.

An institution administering restricted student aid funds
might want to include in its application form a consent agreement by which the recipient authorizes the institution to report
academic and personal information to the donor.

Everything possible should be done to ensure that the
recipient writes a personal expression of gratitude to the donor.
Several steps can be taken to help accomplish this important objective. The award notice itself, where possible, should identify
the donor, provide the donor's address, and encourage the sending of a communication of gratitude to the donor. The institutional aid office may also want to request the student to furnish
a copy of the letter of gratitude to the office and thus be able
to maintain a checklist on which students do, in fact, write. Students who fail to do so can be sent a second request. The aid
office may also make available sample "thank-you" letters and
notify aid recipients, through policy and procedures statements
that typically accompany award notices, where the samples can
be reviewed. When an aid fund is large and supports a number
of awards, the institution may wish to consider developing a
pamphlet that describes why the fund was established and how
important it is to the institution. Copies of the pamphlet can be
shared with aid recipients as well as with the donor.

Personal contact between the donor and the recipient
can also be very effective and can be accomplished by inviting
the donor to the campus to meet with the aid recipient over a
cup of coffee or lunch. In the event that the donor lives some
distance from the campus, recipients can be selected who reside
close to the donor and therefore, when they return to their

home communities during vacations, can offer to stop by for a personal visit. It cannot be overemphasized that personal contact between the donor and the student aid recipient generates continuing and increased support. Promoting this relationship is an important responsibility of the student aid department of the institution, in close cooperation with the development office.

Unrestricted Funds. In the best of all possible worlds, a college or university would have sufficient restricted financial aid funds, beyond public aid programs, to meet its needs. Unfortunately, it is rarely possible to ensure that gifts for scholarship and loan purposes will be sufficient to meet whatever institutional goals are established for student aid. Even the few institutions that are relatively well endowed with restricted student aid funds find it necessary to use some of their unrestricted funds. Unrestricted income—sometimes referred to as general funds—is derived mainly from unrestricted endowment income, unrestricted gifts, and appropriations from state legislatures, as well as indirect cost recovery from government research contracts and tuition and fee income. These funds can be used to respond to a variety of important institutional needs—among them, student aid.

The use of unrestricted funds can help an institution maintain stability in the student aid program, and this in turn can have a positive effect on the institution's applicant pool. Certainly, an important factor in recruiting is providing assurance to potential student candidates that a specific number of financial aid awards will be available annually for those who enter and that the support will be renewed, if certain conditions are fulfilled, during the period of time required to complete degree objectives.

The use of general funds is perhaps most critical when the college or university finds it necessary to raise its tuition and fees significantly. Unless a part of the increased income is allocated to the student aid program, there is a risk that enrollment will adversely be affected. Unfortunately, there is no accepted formula for determining how much of a tuition and fee increase should be returned through the aid program to students who are unable to afford the higher costs. In practice, however, student aid allocations have frequently worked out to about three to one. That is, for every three dollars realized from the increase in the institution's tuition or required fees, one dollar is placed in the student aid budget. Undoubtedly, the ratio appropriate to a campus must be determined on the basis of such quantifiable factors as the institutional priorities for use of the incremental income resulting from higher fees, the existing unmet need of students, the availability of external and institutional restricted funds to meet the higher costs, and the growth in parental and student ability to make larger contributions toward the higher costs.

One very important area in which colleges and universities can make general funds available for student support is campus employment. Virtually all financial aid packages include a work component, and institutions that are not already doing so may wish to consider utilizing some of their regular employment funds to support student jobs. For entering undergraduate students, appropriate jobs typically include those in services, such as the dining halls, typing pools, libraries, and buildings and grounds maintenance. More advanced undergraduate and graduate students might be employed as course assistants, research aids, and residence proctors. The literature on student aid contains a number of studies showing no adverse educational consequences and even some social value from student employment. Gaston (1973) found no significant differences in academic performance between students at Western Washington State College (now Western Washington University) who were required by the terms of their financial aid packages to engage in term-time employment and those who were not. Barnes and Keene (1974) reported similar findings among a selected group of freshmen at Southern Illinois University at Carbondale. Earlier, Adams and Stephens (1970) concluded, on the basis of their investigation, that a student's social maturation benefits from part-time work of reasonable dimensions. They contended, further, that there could even be positive educational benefit if the student's employment experience were academically relevant. From a practical standpoint, the employment of students in campus jobs, with the salaries paid out of general funds, can benefit the college or university, as well as help students pay their bills. Such a program can also supplement employment opportunities under federal College Work-Study.

Harnessing Outside Private Awards

Of the estimated $1.2 billion available in private student aid resources, the amount available for individual students varies from a one-time payment of one or two hundred dollars to, in some instances, the full educational costs for four years of study. This support—in the form of scholarships, grants, or loans—may come from national or local foundations, civic or service clubs, churches, or corporations. Sometimes the funds are highly restrictive—for instance, limited to the offspring of an employee of a certain business or to students with a particular religious affiliation—or they require the preparation of a paper or the undertaking of some project that demonstrates the academic interest and potential of the aid candidate.

One of the greatest challenges to harnessing the thousands of outside awards is first to identify them. Fortunately, a few publications—such as *Scholarships, Fellowships and Loans* (Feingold and Feingold, 1982), *How to Get Money for Education* (Human Resources Network, 1975), and *Barron's Handbook of American College Financial Aid* (Proia and Di Gaspari, 1978)—list the various aid funds available; these publications are updated periodically. Especially useful is the "Vocational Goals Index" in the Feingolds' volume. This index lists the award criteria established by 1,415 private and state student aid programs in the United States—criteria such as course and level-of-study conditions, geographical requirements, and affiliations that the students or parents are expected to have. The description of each program, presented in alphabetical order, contains detailed information on the number of awards, the amount of stipends, and the application procedures. Information of this kind can be of great value if it is constantly revised to maintain its currency.

Institutional financial aid brochures should encourage

prospective students to consult with their high school and community college counseling staffs about the various outside awards available. In their information brochures for aid applicants as well as in their catalogues, colleges and universities will also wish to identify a significant number of outside awards that are typically available to their students, and to include the authors and titles of publications containing comprehensive listings of outside awards.

Public institutions in particular often will award their limited scholarship resources principally to their continuing students who have successfully completed a specified term of study. This policy comes from the fact that most scholarships awarded by or through high schools and community colleges are one-time gifts. The student in these circumstances uses the outside award to finance the initial year of study and then seeks institutional support for subsequent years.

In a few instances, a scholarship search organization may prove helpful. A student seeking financial aid can submit certain specified biographical and academic information to the organization and, for a fee, will receive a list of support programs for which he or she is likely eligible. Undoubtedly, the search can result in the identification of some obscure scholarship or grant about which the user of the service might not otherwise have been aware. In many instances, however, the user receives mostly information that can be found without cost in an institutional aid brochure; therefore, college and university aid administrators will want to investigate the benefits of these search organizations before endorsing their use and bringing their services to the attention of students and parents. As an alternative to referring their prospective and current students to commercial scholarship search organizations, a few institutions with automated data processing facilities available to them have created data files of information on external financial aid resources; this information can then be matched with individual student characteristics. The main problem is keeping the data base current on the many and constantly changing sources of external funds that do exist, and this difficulty is prompting at least one group of institutions with similar characteristics and numerous common candidates for admission to examine the creation and maintenance of the data base as an associational activity.

Almost equal to the challenge of identifying outside awards is ensuring that students who may be eligible for them do in fact apply. Obviously, there is no incentive to do so if the student feels that an outside award will replace whatever aid the student might ordinarily expect to receive from the institution. However, the availability of outside awards will usually enable the college or university to increase the number of students who receive support and, in some instances, will enhance the attractiveness of the support package to students. As an incentive to promote student applications for outside awards, institutional policy might provide that a portion of any external scholarship and grant support obtained can be used to replace a part of the student's self-help expectation. (The matter of combining gift aid and loans and jobs is treated in Chapter Seven.)

Outside awards—especially such prestigious scholarships and grants as those awarded by the National Merit Scholarship Corporation—can benefit an institution whose students receive these awards, since other students, who may look to the winners of these outside awards as role models, may thereby be attracted to the institution. Just as in the development of restricted gifts to the university for scholarship and loan purposes, campus aid administrators and other officials should make it a point to contact off-campus associations, organizations, churches, and corporations that administer their own financial aid awards. Meetings with these groups to describe the financial aid needs at the institution and to request support can, as suggested earlier, pay dividends. On occasion the aid officer may even offer to take over the administration of an outside aid program, or at least to help with it.

Conclusion

An aggressive financial aid director and development officer can promote gifts for financial aid purposes, and this support should be viewed as an essential adjunct to public funds. To carry out such a campaign, there must be a clear determination of the role that student financial aid plays in achieving the institution's mission, as well as a plan stipulating how much is needed over what time span and how and where the funds will be raised. These fund-raising efforts, in addition to being carefully planned, must be sustained and will likely be most effective if they personalize the relationship between the donor and the student. Despite some of the disenchantment over student rebellion in the late 1960s and early 1970s, there is within society a strong commitment toward supporting students of all ages in their educational pursuits.

Bibliographical Note

Of the general works on student aid administration and the historical development of student aid programs, the most significant are *Perspectives on Financial Aid* (College Entrance Examination Board, 1975a), *Guide to the Literature of Student Financial Aid* (Davis and Van Dusen, 1978), and *A Design for a Model College Financial Aid Office* (Van Dusen and O'Hearne, 1980).

For readers who wish to pursue the topic of awarding scholarships without regard to financial need, the following two sources are suggested: "No Need Scholarships: What 859 Colleges Said About Granting Money to Students Without Regard to Financial Need" (Huff, 1975) and *No Need/Merit Awards* (Potter and Sidar, 1978).

Two sources that should prove useful to institutional administrators in their search for financial aid resources are the *Chronicle of Higher Education,* published forty-eight times a year, and the *Foundation Directory,* published annually by the Foundation Center in New York.

Among the studies on the effects of term-time employment on students' academic achievement and social adjustment, the following three sources are recommended for readers who may wish to explore in detail some of the findings: *College and University Student Work Program: Implications and Implementations* (Adams and Stephens, 1970); "A Comparison of the Initial Academic Achievement of Freshman Award Winners

Who Work and Those Who Do Not Work" (Barnes and Keene, 1974); "A Study of the Effects of College-Imposed Work-Study Programs on Grade-Point Averages of Selected Students at Western Washington State College" (Gaston, 1973).

Finally, on the subject of where to find listings of external financial awards, three sources in particular should be considered for inclusion in the library of the student aid office and called to the attention of students who are being encouraged to identify and apply for outside aid. These publications are *Scholarships, Fellowships and Loans* (Feingold and Feingold, 1982); *How to Get Money for Education* (Human Resources Network, 1975); and *Barron's Handbook of American College Financial Aid* (Proia and Di Gaspari, 1978).

Part Two

Delivering Aid to
Students on Campus

The operational link between the sources of financial aid and the student recipient is referred to as the delivery system. Its importance to the whole process can hardly be overstated; the delivery of assistance to the student is the very heart of student aid. A successful delivery system manifests the intent of the donor, whether a philanthropic person or foundation, or of state and federal legislators expressing the will of the electorate in laws and regulations. In contrast, an unsuccessful delivery system may well create more problems than the student aid programs were intended to solve. Part Two is the most technical of the four parts of the book, but the importance of the techniques of the delivery system warrants thoughtful attention, not only by the aid officers directly involved but also by the academic and business affairs officers of the institution.

Complexity and lack of coordination have characterized

the delivery system over the last two decades. What was historically within the college or university a simple process of uniting a locally available loan or grant with a deserving student has become one of the most complicated, continually changing, and demanding tasks required of any professional in higher education. In fact, one would be hard put to identify any other that requires so much detail of process yet is so vital to the very life of the institution. At the same time, the process is ringed with pitfalls of legal requirements, constantly changing regulations, and fiduciary duties toward programs whose schedules often are disruptive of rather than synchronous with academic calendars. Over all this, one must overlay the traditional and persisting view that student aid is at its heart an individualized counseling process between aid officer and student.

The four chapters in Part Two (Chapters Five through Eight) cover the four main stages of the delivery system: information dissemination and the application process, financial need determination, packaging the financial aid award, and disbursement and control. The coherence of the delivery system's structure suggests an orderly process; but that impression belies the annual struggle on campuses across the nation to deal with the rising tide of applications, uncertain funding levels, and the continual change of regulations and schedules inherent in politically based programs. The fact that there actually is systematic annual delivery of billions of dollars from many sources to millions of students in thousands of institutions is a tribute to the efforts of financial aid professionals everywhere.

In Chapter Five Norman Beck discusses research findings on the importance of effective information dissemination to potential applicants. He also describes the legislation enacted in 1976 and 1980 to protect the rights of student-consumers to timely and accurate information on financial assistance. In his section on "Providing Information to Students," Beck emphasizes the role of the aid officer as "an integral part of the institution's marketing team"; describes the communication resources that can be used by the aid officer; and reviews various successful methods of reaching out to high school students. He points out that students must become aware of the application procedures and the awarding policies that govern federal, state, institutional, and private aid programs. Beck also treats in detail the kinds of information that must be obtained from aid applicants so that the financial aid officer can make an award decision.

Once a financial aid application is complete, the next step in the awarding cycle is to determine the amount of the financial need demonstrated by the student. In Chapter Six Joe Paul Case introduces the reader to the theoretical and practical foundations of need analysis. His analysis of the theory and philosophy underlying need analysis is both stimulating and perhaps provocative to the aid officer accustomed to viewing need determination solely as a computational procedure guided by precise formulas. However, the bulk of Case's discussion is on the principles and practices of need analysis. His cogent review will be very informative to institutional aid administrators other than aid personnel and will provide a handy reference text for the aid officer. In addition to considering the elements that go into estimating the expected parental and student contribution, Case offers advice on how a student expense budget can properly be developed. Financial need, as is explained in the chapter, equals that budget minus the expected parental and student contribution.

The actual determination of the amount of support awarded to the student and of the aid forms in which it is provided has come to be referred to as "packaging." In her chapter on this subject, Shirley Binder describes certain generally accepted principles which she believes should influence the determination of an institutional packaging policy. She discusses various packaging approaches that are currently in use and suggests several techniques by which the aid administrator can implement the award policy of an institution. Binder emphasizes the importance of an institution's first establishing a philosophy that stipulates the goal it wishes to accomplish with its financial aid program. Such a philosophy must be sensitive to the applicant's self-help capacity (work, loans, savings), academic ability, demands of the academic program, availability of aid funds, and so forth. Binder concludes the chapter by listing the principles that an institution should carefully consider in developing its own packaging policies and strategies.

In Chapter Eight Donald Ryan provides detailed information on the procedures to be followed to ensure that the financial aid funds awarded end up in the hands of the student or are credited to the student's institutional bills. The proper use—or, more specifically, the control—of these funds becomes particularly acute at this stage of the awarding cycle. Ryan also deals with such important issues requiring institutional attention as refunds and repayments, audits and program reviews, procedures for ensuring student eligibility, and fiscal record keeping. His chapter emphasizes the fiduciary role of the aid officer. It is in this role that the aid officer maintains the institution's eligibility to continue receiving aid funds. Ryan points out that each institution must have an effective system for auditing and reviewing funds handled by the office.

5

Disseminating Information on Aid and Processing Aid Applications

Norman E. Beck

Although this chapter deals primarily with the dissemination of information about student financial aid and the application activities performed within the financial aid office, information dissemination is really an ongoing process. That is, students need detailed information not only when they are applying for aid but also at the time of award notification, during the periods when they must reapply for assistance for subsequent academic periods, and upon graduation if loans are to be converted to payout status.

The message, the medium of communication, and the environment within which the message is communicated must vary with the audience to be addressed and the purposes to be achieved. Because of the multiple facets of the aid administrator's role, proper planning of the communication activity is essential to ensure that all the publics with whom the administrator interacts are kept informed at a cost that can be borne by the institution with its own funds and with the administrative allowances provided by the government programs.

As an institutional officer, the aid administrator is an integral part of the school's marketing effort. As a counselor, he is concerned about the students' welfare. He helps achieve the societal goals of government aid programs as he encourages students to finish high school and to attend a postsecondary institution. Thus, the aid administrator assumes a multiple role when contacting students, parents, feeder school personnel, community agencies, and directors of programs for disadvantaged youth.

Research Findings

During the early 1970s, a number of state and federal studies had shown clearly that the lack of information about postsecondary institutions and about the means to finance education after high school formed a major barrier to prospective students. Evidence was also uncovered that students had been victimized by the marketing practices of some unscrupulous educational institutions. The congressional response to this situation was twofold: (1) Several major consumer protection provisions were included in the Education Amendments of 1976; (2) in 1975 the Fund for the Improvement of Postsecondary Education (FIPSE), United States Office of Education, was awarded over one million dollars to fund grants for studies of the quality of information available to prospective students and to make recommendations for improvement of the information delivery system. In addition, several federal and state agencies sponsored conferences on consumer protection in postsecondary education.

Some consensus emerged among the groups that have studied the problem of providing information to students: (1) Students want and need information about the cost of education and about financial aid to help them meet that cost. (2) The information that students are receiving is generally inadequate. (3) If prospective students are to understand fully the process and the options available to them, the various institutions, organizations, and agencies involved in the financial aid delivery system must make a coordinated effort to inform students about financial aid.

While there is almost total agreement on the need for better information for students, opinion is divided on how to coordinate the efforts of the various participants in the financial aid delivery system: federal, state, institutional, and private programs. Each of these programs has its own eligibility requirements, and many of the programs have unique application processes. Furthermore, programs are constantly being added, deleted, and changed. It is this multiplicity of available programs, each one of which has unique characteristics, that makes information dissemination regarding financial assistance to students so difficult. The Federal Interagency Committee on Education (1975, p. 116), concluding that "there is no coherent plan or responsibility for the dissemination of information to students and their families," recommended that the secretary of health, education and welfare (now the secretary of education) establish a clearinghouse to coordinate the dissemination of financial information to students regarding federal, state, institutional, or community-based programs.

The most thorough study of providing information to students regarding financial aid was performed by the College Scholarship Service (CSS) of the College Entrance Examination Board under a grant from FIPSE and the United States Office of Education. This study (College Scholarship Service, 1977) was undertaken in conjunction with the National Task Force on Better Information for Student Choice, which sought to examine all aspects of the communication flow between institutions and students. The CSS researchers recognized the need for a cooperative, comprehensive program of information dissemination to students and identified the following participants required to undertake such an activity: (1) the United States Office (now Department) of Education, (2) state scholarship and loan agencies, (3) the national need analysis services, (4) postsecondary institutions individually and as groups, (5) secondary schools, (6) information and counseling services and community agencies, (7) the Veterans Administration and the Social Security

Administration, (8) public and private media, (9) students and parents. They recommended a "Student Aid Awareness Campaign" to be carried out in September and October of each year at a cost of $300,000.

The CSS researchers found ample evidence to support the contention that prospective students are not well informed about educational costs or financial aid resources. The researchers analyzed questionnaires distributed to prospective postsecondary students in California, Massachusetts, Virginia, Illinois, Oregon, Michigan, and Ohio to discover what they wanted to know about educational costs and student aid. A very high proportion of all of the students surveyed wanted more information about both costs and financial aid, and the need for more information was virtually universal among students from low- and middle-income families and for students from racial or ethnic minorities. Specifically, the students wanted to know how need is determined. They also wanted a detailed description of aid programs, sample aid packages for students with varying characteristics, a statement about application dates and procedures, information on available student jobs, and information about the repayment of loans.

The student respondents were more interested in the total cost of their entire program than they were in the costs for a single year or term. Further, they sought information about the probability of changes in cost from year to year. While a detailed breakdown of costs was deemed important, of greater interest was an explanation of how and when the educational costs would be paid. The request for cost information for the entire program may reflect an emphasis being placed by students on the economic return from an investment in postsecondary education and the "opportunity costs" such an investment involves. The concern of how and when costs must be paid may reflect an awareness of cash-flow problems within the family unit.

In 1975 the states of Pennsylvania and Iowa surveyed high school seniors who intended to enroll in postsecondary education (Pennsylvania Higher Education Assistance Agency, 1976b; College Entrance Examination Board, 1975b) and found that students consistently underestimated the total cost of education at the institutions they planned to attend. Some of their estimates were understated by as much as 55 percent, and the percent by which the students underestimated the costs of attendance was greater among those who were considering higher-cost institutions.

Because of errors in estimating educational costs, a student may decide not to pursue postsecondary education, or he may choose an institution just because he assumes that it will be relatively inexpensive. The Iowa and Pennsylvania studies found that nearly 40 percent of high school seniors who failed to enroll in postsecondary schools stated that the reason was lack of money.

Additional studies completed in New Jersey, Pennsylvania, California, Oregon, and Washington (New Jersey Commission on Financing Postsecondary Education, 1976; Pennsylvania Higher Education Assistance Agency, 1976a; California State Scholarship and Loan Commission, 1973; Dent and others, 1973; College Entrance Examination Board, 1972) revealed that eligible aid recipients fail to apply for assistance from state-supported grant programs; and two thirds of that group indicated that they lacked adequate information about the program and application process. Failure on the part of students to apply for aid because of the lack of adequate information becomes increasingly significant in light of Astin's (1975b) finding that "financial difficulties" was the second most frequently cited reason for student withdrawal from postsecondary institutions.

The CSS study cited earlier concluded that "the data make two things clear: finances are a major factor in determining a student's access to, choice among, and retention in postsecondary education; and there is a major lack of correct information about costs and aid on the part of both prospective and present college students" (p. 12). Further, the study found that many institutions were purposely withholding information about costs and financial aid. Among the reasons cited by these institutions were the following: "The truth will scare them away." "It's too complicated to be truthfully communicated." "We couldn't handle any more students than we have now."

"Our policies are so unclear that we cannot communicate them" (pp. 13-14). Apparently, the advocates of the student consumerism movement had ample reason for concern. The Federal Interagency Committee on Education (1975, p. 1) arrived at the same general conclusions: "The general picture shows that federal efforts in protecting the student consumer are under way, but have yet to achieve a fully developed thrust. Policies are largely reactive. Information provided to students is inadequate. Safeguards against outright fraud and abuse are weak. Few agencies have systematic procedures for handling complaints from students and parents, or redressing valid claims. Coordination between federal agencies is at an embryonic stage, and the educational community itself has not activated consumer protection concepts or mechanisms where consumer problems exist. Among the federal departments and agencies, the response to educational consumer problems varies considerably."

Legislative Amendments

It was within this environment that Congress included in the Education Amendments of 1976 several major provisions aimed at protecting the educational consumer. Section 493A of the amendments required institutions receiving administrative allowances under one or more of the programs authorized under Title IV of those amendments to provide students with basic information about student assistance, student retention, and, when available, student completion rates at that institution. The institution had to designate an individual responsible for providing such information when requested by students. Section 493B instructed the commissioner of education to survey current institutional practices and to study the possibility of using students within the institutions as peer counselors who are trained by the Office of Education. The amendments also provided for grants to states to establish Educational Information Centers to supplement the counseling efforts of the high schools and postsecondary institutions. Finally, Section 335 instructed the Office of Education to provide career guidance information to students and schools.

The most recent changes to the federal legislation governing information dissemination to students occurred in the Education Amendments of 1980. Section 485 sets forth the federal requirements for "Institutional and Financial Assistance Information for Students," as indicated in the following excerpts:

(a) (1) Each eligible institution participating in any program under this title shall carry out information dissemination activities for prospective and enrolled students regarding the institution and financial assistance under this title. The information required by this section shall be produced and be made readily available, through appropriate publications and mailings, to all current students, and to any prospective student upon request. The information required by this section shall accurately describe—

(A) the student financial assistance programs available to students who enroll at such institution;

(B) the methods by which such assistance is distributed among student recipients who enroll at such institution;

(C) any means, including forms, by which application for student financial assistance is made and requirements for accurately preparing such application;

(D) the rights and responsibilities of students receiving financial assistance under this title;

(E) the cost of attending the institution, including (i) tuition and fees, (ii) books and supplies, (iii) estimates of typical student room and board costs or typical commuting costs, and (iv) any additional cost of the program in which the student is enrolled or expresses a specific interest;

(F) a statement of the refund policy of the institution for the return of unearned tuition and fees or other refundable portion of cost, as described in clause (E) of this paragraph;

(G) the academic program of the institution, including (i) the current degree programs and other educational and training programs, (ii) the instructional, laboratory, and other physical plant facilities which relate to the academic program, and (iii) the faculty and other instructional personnel;

(H) each person designated under subsection (b) of this section, and the methods by which and locations in which any person so designated may be contacted by students and prospective students who are seeking information required by this subsection;

(I) special facilities and services available to handicapped students;

(J) the names of associations, agencies, or governmental bodies which accredit, approve, or license the institution and its programs, and the procedures under which any current or prospective student may obtain or review upon request a copy of the documents describing the institution's accreditation, approval, or licensing; and

(K) the standards which the student must maintain in order to be considered to be making satisfactory progress, pursuant to section 484(a)(3).

(a) (2) For purposes of this section, the term "prospective student" means any individual who has contacted an eligible institution requesting information concerning admission to that institution.

Subsection (b) requires each eligible institution to designate one employee or a group of employees to assist students in obtaining the information listed above. Institutions must comply with the provisions outlined in Section 485 if they participate in any of the Title IV programs. Under the 1976 amendments, the requirement for compliance was contingent on the institution's withdrawing funds under the administrative allowance provisions of the act.

The necessity for an institution to comply with the requirements of Section 485 is reinforced in Section 487, which sets forth the provisions to be included in an agreement that must be signed by any institution participating in a Title IV program and by the secretary of education.

Providing Information to Students

Several private, mostly nonprofit companies have tried to institute a service whereby students, after submitting certain descriptive data, would be provided with lists of sources of financial assistance for which they would be eligible. This service normally is provided to the student for a fee. Because of the high cost of establishing and maintaining an adequate data base to provide a current list of resources at a price that students are able and willing to pay, such endeavors generally have not proved satisfactory.

While efforts by the Department of Education, state agencies, and others to provide financial information to students have improved, the fact remains that the major burden for financial aid information dissemination lies with the financial aid administrator at the postsecondary institution. It is doubtful that this situation will change in the near future. The federal and state governments are experiencing severe budgeting shortages. The aid administrator is in the best position to be aware of financial assistance from all the potential sources—federal, state, institutional, and private. Finally, the institutional aid administrator has established communication links with student, parents, and secondary school personnel. It is imperative, therefore, that the institutional financial aid administrator perform this function in the best manner possible.

In performing this function, the financial aid administrator becomes an integral part of the institution's marketing team. The offer of financial assistance, in and of itself, will not usually attract students to a particular campus; however, the failure to offer adequate assistance in a timely fashion will often discourage students from enrolling. Furthermore, the method of combining gift aid, loans, and employment in the financial aid package will attract various segments of the prospective student population differently; and the method of combining the various types of aid in the financial aid package will have an effect on the retention of students.

Chapter Fourteen deals extensively with the impact of student aid on marketing. However, some mention of marketing is appropriate in a discussion of dissemination because, as part of the institution's marketing and enrollment management effort, the financial aid administrator must inform the student about assistance at the institution and also from appropriate external sources. By helping the student secure resources from external donors, the aid administrator expands the total amount of financial assistance available to the aid applicants, enables a greater number of students to be awarded aid, and frees institutional funds to be used in a discretionary manner so as to complement the overall enrollment strategy of the institution. Examples of such external assistance would be benefits for veterans and their families; Social Security benefits; vocational rehabilitation benefits; tuition or fee waivers funded through the state; and programs sponsored by private donors at the local, state, or national level. Information regarding these programs can be included in the institution's financial aid publications, and specific questions added to the school's financial aid application can reveal the student's probable eligibility for such assistance. For example, questions such as the following might appear on the institution's financial aid application:

1. Was your father killed or disabled in either World War I, World War II, or the Korean or Vietnam conflict?
2. Do you suffer from any disability that might limit your ability to secure a job?
3. Do you or your family currently receive Social Security benefits?
4. Was your father an Indiana law enforcement officer or fireman killed in the line of duty?
5. Does your father or mother work for the Magnavox Company?

The application procedures for these programs are separate from the process for applying for institutional, state, or federal assistance. Student aid applicants are often unaware of such benefits and need guidance in how, when, and where to apply for this assistance. A form letter providing the student with instructions on how to apply for such aid will often assist the student in securing externally funded gift assistance and thus release institutional funds for other students.

Because publications are expensive and because the students' need for information will vary according to where they are in the decision-making process regarding institutional choice, the content, comprehensiveness, purpose, and quality of the publications will vary. For example, information given to students in their sophomore and junior years in high school, and to their parents, might include such basic topics as (1) college costs, (2) need determination, (3) sample aid packages at various types of institutions, (4) a general description of aid programs, (5) unique aspects of an institutional aid program, and (6) application dates and procedures. For such purposes as simply introducing prospective students and their parents to the basic concepts of financial aid, brochures published by the service agencies and the federal or state government might be utilized. They are normally free or very inexpensive. Institution-specific information can be provided in mimeographed form.

As students move closer to the point of the admissions decision, the quality of the publication is normally upgraded, and the content becomes more institutionally specific. For example, an attractive flier describing a particular scholarship program might be sent to a particular category of students in the admissions office's contact file. Financial aid inquiries to the admissions or financial aid office will require a publication that complies with Section 485 of the Education Amendments of 1980 as it applies to prospective students. It should be easily mailed and relatively inexpensive.

Many postsecondary institutions have prepared a single publication containing admissions, financial aid, and housing applications, designed for high school seniors who have indicated an intent to apply. Specific instructions for completing the three applications are also included, along with more general promotional material. Such a publication has the advantage of ensuring that every student who applies for admission receives an application for financial aid as well as information regarding institutional costs, financial aid application procedures, eligibility requirements, and deadline dates. Because this publication is sent only to students who have indicated an interest in enrolling, it is generally of high quality and very institutionally specific in content. In addition, such a publication ensures that the strategy utilized to distribute admission and financial aid materials will always be parallel.

Upper-class initial or renewal applicants present a different problem in the dissemination of information. The goal of the aid administrator in regard to enrolled students is primarily to inform them how to reapply for assistance during their sophomore and subsequent years. It can be assumed that the availability of financial aid has a positive effect on the student's decision to remain in college. (See Chapter Fifteen for an extended discussion on the impact of student aid on retention.)

Many financial aid offices publish a periodic newspaper to advise currently enrolled students about programs, reapplication procedures and schedules, new legislation, increases in costs, and other current information. This publication can be printed as a supplement to the campus newspaper and distributed to newspapers in other localities if a campus news bureau is available.

If the campus also has a radio and television station, they can be used effectively to communicate with currently enrolled students. Campus stations will normally accept spot announcements regarding school activities without charge, and they are often looking for material for "talk shows."

Also, presentations can be made directly to student groups if the financial aid administrator offers to attend evening meetings. Such groups might include fraternities and sororities, student associations, and residence hall councils. Small-group sessions (one hundred students or fewer) enable the financial aid representative to address individual questions or problems.

During the month of December, some institutions hold financial aid sessions where renewal application materials are distributed and information is disseminated. Students can then take the materials and information home over the Christmas vacation to share with their families. Distributing the reapplication forms at these meetings encourages attendance where the major goal is to relay information regarding application procedures, projected cost increases, and program changes. Other means of communicating information to enrolled students include the use of taped telephone messages, microfilm and computer terminal displays with or without printout capability, and tape cassettes. Although these methods require the availability of specialized equipment, the reproduction of data under such systems is relatively cheap if the equipment has been purchased for other purposes. Furthermore, the students can initiate an inquiry at their own convenience.

Material distributed at the time the financial aid is awarded is unique in two respects. It becomes part of the contractual offer of assistance, and it includes the information mandated by federal or state consumer information legislation. To protect the institution from future legal liability, it is a good idea to enclose a statement on the financial aid award acceptance form, which all aid recipients must sign, to the effect that the student has received, read, and understood the information enclosed.

The information provided to students with the award offer should be clear and complete and should fulfill the institution's legal responsibilities. The following topics might be included in such a publication:

1. General Information
   a. Purposes of financial aid
   b. Institutional costs
   c. Institutional method for need determination
   d. Institutional eligibility requirements
   e. Institutional policy on satisfactory academic progress and good standing
   f. Institutional policy on confidentiality of student records
   g. Institutional policy on packaging
2. The Financial Aid Award
   a. How to accept or decline a financial aid award
   b. How financial aid payments are made to students
   c. How refunds are calculated and paid to students
3. Program Regulations and Student Eligibility Requirements
4. Grievance Procedures for Students
5. Aid Recipient Rights and Responsibilities

While the advice of marketing and communication experts should be sought in the preparation of financial aid publications, the contractual nature of the award offer and the award acceptance is such that legal counsel is also recommended.

Several innovative methods have been adopted by practicing financial aid administrators to communicate with the various publics who have an interest in student assistance. General information that is not institutionally specific can be disseminated more effectively and efficiently through cooperative efforts between representatives from institutions, state agencies, federal agencies, service agencies, and professional associations.

Some state financial aid associations, like the one in Kentucky, have organized a "Student Financial Aid Week" to be held between November and March. They have sought and received cooperation from the state and local governments, radio and television stations, newspapers, and local businesses. A virtual communication blitz is achieved during that week. At the local level, this includes the distribution of information by aid administrators in supermarkets and other areas with high-density traffic patterns. Newspaper copy and radio scripts, as well as film footage for television stations, are prepared by faculty members with expertise in mass communication on the various campuses within the state. This information is released by the media as a public service. Adequate lead time of up to two months is required by the radio and television stations to program such spot announcements. The National Association of Student Financial Aid Administrators (NASFAA) has recently undertaken a project to assist states in the planning and execution of such a program. (Additional information can be obtained from the Executive Director, NASFAA, 1776 Massachusetts Avenue N.W., Washington, D.C., 20036.)

Other states have organized a speakers' bureau within their state associations. Secondary schools can call the association and request a financial aid presentation at school convocations, parent night programs, or college night programs. While college night programs are generally directed toward college admission presentations, a general financial aid session held before or concurrently with these presentations is normally very well attended. If aid administrators are assigned by the state association on a geographical basis, no individual aid administrator has to travel long distances or commit himself to an excessive number of speaking engagements. All postsecondary education institutions profit from such a cooperative endeavor because the overall college-bound population is enlarged, financial aid forms are submitted in a more timely fashion, and the information that is submitted tends to be more complete and accurate.

The use of overhead transparencies, slides, or motion pictures tends to enhance an oral presentation. Overhead transparencies and slides tend to be less expensive initially and are more adaptable to the frequent changes in federal and state aid programs and application procedures. It is also a good idea to have printed material available, so that parents and students can reinforce what they have learned by subsequent reading at home.

Reaching students from low-income families can be very difficult. Many students from the inner-city and rural poverty areas receive little encouragement to pursue postsecondary education from their families or their peers. These students and their families may not attend functions held in the high schools or on a college campus, and written material made available through high school guidance offices may not reach home or be read. For this type of student, an oral or visual presentation delivered in a familiar environment is often the only means of effective communication. Local community centers or churches can usually be secured at no expense for such a program. Finding a local leader in whom the community has confidence to coordinate such a venture is an important key to its ultimate success or failure. Frequently, students from these areas who are already in postsecondary institutions, or the parents of those students, can help in locating such a person.

For the more sophisticated parent and student, who will travel longer distances to meetings held on the campus of a postsecondary institution, financial aid workshops for parents and students have been employed successfully. The workshop can be offered as part of a series designed to assist prospective students and their parents by covering such topics as choosing a career, choosing an academic major, choosing a postsecondary institution, or taking entrance examinations. While the information presented during the financial aid session should not be institutionally specific, the host institution does benefit by getting prospective students to their campus.

Informing High School Counselors

The transition of students from grade 12 to grade 13 requires a team effort between the representatives of the high schools and the postsecondary institutions. It is important, therefore, that the financial aid community keep high school administrators informed of changes in financial aid programs and application procedures. This is not an easy task because the high school guidance personnel typically have little or no formal training in financial aid, are not exposed to financial aid on a daily basis, and have limited travel funds for attending meetings. Nevertheless, high school personnel are key figures in the financial aid delivery system, and every effort must be made to give them adequate information and guidance to perform their tasks effectively and on a timely basis.

Some state associations hold conferences on an annual basis for directors of high school guidance departments and for personnel from private and government-supported agencies. During these sessions information should be disseminated about changes in programs or procedures that have occurred during the year. Because of the nature and size of these meetings, the instructional cadre normally can be supplemented with representatives from the state and federal governments as well as the service agencies.

Because of limited travel budgets and restricted travel time away from the high schools, many guidance counselors cannot travel away from their local community and cannot be gone for more than one day. The financial aid community must, therefore, take the information to the counselors in the form of "mini-workshops." These workshops can be a combined effort between the state financial aid association and the state agency responsible for administering comprehensive, state-administered scholarship, grant, and loan programs.

While the effort to keep high school personnel updated on financial aid is time consuming and costly, the effort is well worth the expense. The guidance counselor has frequent face-to-face contact with the student, knows the student's abilities and needs better than the financial aid administrator does, and is readily available to counsel the parents. Furthermore, a guidance counselor is in a position to monitor the student's progress through the initial stages of the application process and to contact the appropriate financial aid administrator if problems arise.

Obtaining Information from Aid Applicants

To this point we have concentrated on the flow of information from the financial aid administrator to the prospective students. In the remainder of this chapter, we will analyze the process by which the applicant supplies sufficient data to the institution so that the financial aid officer can make an award decision. This flow of information from the student to the institution is called the financial aid application process.

A financial aid application process should not be viewed in isolation. Much of the information required to process a financial aid award is also required by other offices within the institution to perform their separate functions or to complete the delivery of aid to students. For purposes of control, completeness, and accuracy, student data shared by several offices should, whenever possible, be integrated into a single record or depository of student information. The use of computer technology and the development of the master student data base have broadened the concept of the financial aid processing system to include the admissions, registration, accounts receivable, student loan collection, payroll, and accounting systems and, in many cases, the alumni and development system as well.

An Integrated Data-Base Approach. The maintenance of a student master record and the resulting integration of several previously independent systems within institutions have had two major positive effects. Much of the redundancy in student data collection has been eliminated. As former students many of us are familiar with the multiplicity of forms that were required by numerous offices within the institution. Many of the

questions on these forms were repetitious: name, student identification number, home address, local address, parents' names,
sex, marital status, and college major. Not only is this repetition
aggravating to the student, but the chances for error in data collection and maintenance are increased proportionately. A data-
base approach can result, therefore, in better service to the student as well as more timely and accurate information to the
various offices within the institution.

Another result of systems integration has been heightened awareness of the interdependence of offices within the institution. Direct lines of communication have been opened
between offices that cross the formal lines of communication
suggested by the administrative structure. For example, a
change in the information gathered or stored by the admissions
office regarding a student suddenly has ramifications for offices
within student affairs, academic affairs, business affairs, and
public affairs. Because the administration of financial aid is virtually an institution-wide process, this holistic approach to information gathering, storage, and utilization is helpful. The
availability of information to the financial aid administrator
through a comprehensive, on-line data-base system has also led
to better counseling of students and has reduced the amount of
student traffic between offices.

The ready accessibility of complete information provided
by such a system has many advantages to the financial aid administrator in developing and maintaining the application process. However, even institutions with manual or nonintegrated
computer-assisted systems can benefit from a thorough review
of how student data are gathered, stored, and utilized. Such a
review often will reveal opportunities for cost efficiencies and
better service to students through an integrated and coordinated
student information system.

In the design of any financial aid information system, the
need to ensure the confidentiality of student data must be considered. Much of the student information gathered and maintained by the financial aid administrator cannot be shared with
institutional colleagues, or with parties external to the institution. The Family Educational Rights and Privacy Act, which is

included in a section of Public Law 93-380, the Education Amendments of 1974, speaks specifically to the institution's rights and responsibilities in relation to this sensitive issue.

What Data Should Be Collected? The purpose of the institutional financial aid application is to identify those students seeking campus-based assistance and to gather the information necessary to determine their eligibility and need for that assistance. The amount and type of information to be collected will depend on the requirements of the program administered by the institution and the degree to which the application is used as a counseling or research tool. To properly identify the aid applicant, the student's full name and Social Security number are required. While there is some debate about the legality of requiring students to reveal their Social Security number, it can be justified as the only basis on which federal reporting and financial aid transcript requirements can be met. The frequency of name changes during and after enrollment renders all other student identification procedures inadequate.

A question regarding the specific period for which assistance is requested is necessary in order to establish an appropriate budget, family contribution, need assessment, and fund distribution schedule. An inquiry about the anticipated hours of enrollment is helpful in projecting the eligibility for, and amount of, funds to be awarded from programs that are enrollment sensitive. For example, the level of an award made under the Pell Grant program will be reduced proportionately as a student moves from a full-time to a three-quarter-time or half-time status. Institutional or private scholarship programs may require that a student maintain a full-time status.

A student's permanent and campus address will be needed, since an institutional reply to the application for assistance is required whether or not funds are awarded. The amount of the Pell Grant award varies according to the student's housing arrangements during the period of enrollment. Many institutions use housing as a variable in budget construction. If students are frequently contacted by telephone to request additional information or to follow up on missing documents, home and campus telephone numbers will also be required.

There are three potential sources of information to establish a student budget. They are the financial aid application, records from other institutional offices, and the need assessment form. The financial aid director will have to decide which of these information sources will provide the appropriate data on a timely basis for the particular needs of his or her institution.

The type of family financial information required to assess financial need and program eligibility is determined by the donor of the financial aid funds. Because of the predominant position of the federal government in providing financial aid, most institutions and states adopt a federally approved system of need assessment. The two federally approved systems, the uniform methodology (described in Chapter Six) and the Pell Grant eligibility system (discussed in Chapter Two), are updated on an annual basis by the Department of Education with congressional approval. Because of these annual changes, most institutions require student applicants to file financial statements with one of the financial aid service organizations or directly with the federal government under the Pell Grant program. The Pennsylvania Higher Education Assistance Agency, like the service organizations, is approved by the federal government to perform the need analysis function. The College Scholarship Service (CSS) and the American College Testing Program (ACT) are the two largest nonprofit corporations providing a financial aid service. Their analysis is based on the uniform methodology, but they also provide an estimated eligibility index for the Pell Grant. To apply for the Pell Grant, the student must either complete the Pell Grant application or request CSS or ACT to forward the required financial data to the federal government. The federal government informs both the student and the institution or institutions he delegates of his eligibility for a Pell Grant.

The student is charged a user fee by the service organizations to process his or her need assessment form. However, the Pell Grant form is processed without charge to the student. For the following reasons, most institutions and states still require the student to file a family financial form with one of the service organizations:

1. The processing of the forms by the service agencies is normally accomplished much earlier in the year than that performed for Pell Grant eligibility.
2. Historically, the service agencies have provided a more reliable service than the federal government.
3. The Pell Grant eligibility form is also a voucher that the student can present to any accredited postsecondary institution for payment. The form is sent to the student rather than to the institution. Therefore, the institution is dependent on the student for the timely delivery of that form.
4. The student can apply to several postsecondary institutions simultaneously.
5. The Pell Grant application and need assessment process is primarily designed to determine an effective contribution for families with incomes below $25,000. In the opinion of many aid administrators, additional data elements are required before the financial strength of families with higher incomes can be adequately evaluated.
6. The service agencies offer management and other auxiliary services to institutions; such services are not provided by the federal processor.
7. The service agencies will make the need analysis forms "state specific," to meet the needs of various state agencies that offer comprehensive assistance.

All institutions awarding federal funds must use a federally approved need analysis system. The particular system adopted by the institution will depend on (1) the system adopted by the agency awarding funds within the institution's home state, if the school has a large in-state enrollment; (2) the institution's admissions and registration cycle; (3) the need for supplementary services; and (4) the compatibility of the processor's reporting mode with the institution's data collection system.

If academic scholarships are awarded by the school, entrance examination scores and class rank may be needed for entering freshmen. For upper-class students, the student's current grade point ratio will normally be required; and, in some cases, the academic performance of students in particular classes may be required. Awards based on other talents—for instance, in journalism, music, leadership, athletics, or debate—will necessitate the collection of appropriate information.

Certification Procedures. A Declaration of Educational Purpose must be filed by a student with an institution before Title IV funds (those funds awarded by the Department of Education) may be distributed to that student. The student completing this form certifies that all funds received through Title IV programs will be used solely for educational or educationally related purposes.

In addition, before receiving any Title IV assistance, students who have been previously enrolled must be certified by the institution as having maintained satisfactory academic progress. The institution may establish its own standards of academic progress within rather specific federal guidelines. Once the policy has been established, however, the financial aid administrator must have access to the data required to make a determination that the student has progressed adequately.

The financial aid administrator must be aware of any financial resources made available to the student—resources such as veterans' benefits, vocational rehabilitation allowances, CETA grants, corporate reimbursement programs, state agency awards, departmental scholarships, grants-in-aid, on-campus student employment, graduate assistantships, graduate fellowships, and traineeships. If the institution awards or administers funds, or certifies the student's enrollment for award eligibility from these donor programs, the financial aid administrator must have access to all this information. Failure to take these resources into consideration when awarding federal and, in some cases, state funds can result in overawards. The institution assumes a liability when such an overaward occurs.

Any action taken by the student financial aid office in regard to the student's application for funds must be communicated to the student and made a part of the student's permanent file. Such an action may include an award offer or adjustment or a denial of assistance because the student did not demonstrate financial need or did not meet other programmatic requirements for eligibility. In some instances the student may be refused financial aid because of a lack of donor funds.

As indicated earlier, the award offer and award acceptance or declination is a contractual process. In addition to setting forth the amounts and sources of assistance to be awarded to a student, the award notification form can be used as an effective communication instrument for providing information to the student that will assist him or her in the decision-making process. For example, the inclusion of specific dollar amounts calculated for the budget, parental contribution, student contribution, and remaining financial need will help the aid recipient and his or her parents evaluate the total cost of education, their responsibility for meeting that cost, and the basis on which the aid offer was rendered. Historical data regarding cumulative financial aid awarded to the student will help the student evaluate his or her current level of indebtedness and remaining eligibility for assistance under the various programs.

It is a good policy to inform the students on the award notification form of their obligations to advise the institution if any changes occur in their family financial status or their marital status or if they receive other awards. In addition, a caveat should be included on the award notification that the award is subject to federal and state appropriations and changes in federal and state legislation and regulations.

Conclusion

The application process provides the financial aid administrator with the information required for the award determination, for student counseling, and for preparation of reports. While many of the data elements collected on the application and supporting documents will be common to all institutions, some of the information collected from students will be determined by the unique configuration of the financial aid programs administered at a particular institution. The degree to which information is gathered and shared by offices within a school to eliminate the redundancy in the collection of student data will depend on the available computer technology and adherence to the concept of a master student data base.

The dissemination of information and the application process are two very important responsibilities of the financial aid administrator. They form the foundation on which the entire financial aid delivery system is based. The importance of these two financial aid functions is further evidenced by the amount of research and legislative effort directed toward them. Much of the financial aid administrator's time must be spent in designing and maintaining this communication process; but a successful completion of this task will benefit the student, the institution, and the society of which both are a part.

Bibliographical Note

One of the projects funded by the Fund for the Improvement of Postsecondary Education (FIPSE) was the National Task Force on Better Information for Student Choice. The report of that task force, *Better Information for Student Choice* (El-Khawas, 1977), is probably the most comprehensive analysis of why better information is needed and describes the meaning and characteristics of better information. Specific guidelines and examples for the development of institutional informational materials are included in that report. *Improving College Information for Prospective Students* (Chapman, 1980), published by the Council for Advancement and Support of Education, is similar in scope.

A companion work to the report of the task force is a handbook entitled *Inside Information: A Handbook on Better Information for Student Choice* (Stark, 1978). This publication contains extensive examples from several institutions that voluntarily undertook projects to improve the quality of information given to students. The National Center for Higher Education Management Systems has prepared a similar handbook, *Guidebook for Colleges and Universities* (Lenning and Cooper, 1978), with the support of a grant from FIPSE.

The Center for Helping Organizations Improve Choice in Education (CHOICE) is an organization that also received funding from FIPSE. The center was established to assist educational institutions in the development of better information to college applicants. *A Guide to Choice* (Center for Helping Organizations Improve Choice in Education, 1978) describes both the purpose and the services of that organization.

The most extensive study regarding the need of applicants to postsecondary education for information regarding costs and financial aid was undertaken by the College Scholarship Service of the College Entrance Examination Board. This report, *Making It Count* (College Scholarship Service, 1977), was also prepared under a grant from FIPSE and would be very helpful to anyone involved in the development of financial aid policy or operations.

Because of the complexities of applying for financial assistance to attend postsecondary education, many students and families need individual counseling. Institutional budget restrictions, however, limit the number of professional financial aid administrators available for this purpose. The Coalition of Independent College and University Students, a nonprofit corporation administered by students, prepared the *Financial Aid Peer Counseling Manual* (Rudley, 1980) to be used as an instructional tool and handbook by students and paraprofessionals working in a financial aid office. This is also an excellent resource book for senior clerical staff.

Many of the recommendations included in the Student Financial Assistance Study Group's (1977) *Report to the Secretary* have been enacted into legislation. The findings of this study group further illustrate the reasons for concern by the federal government in the areas of student consumerism. Additional information regarding the federal thrust in student consumerism and financial aid can be found in a report entitled *Reaching Students: Student Views on Communication About Financial Aid* (United States Department of Education, 1980b).

6

Determining Financial Need

Joe Paul Case

Need analysis is the process of determining the amount that a student and his or her family may reasonably be expected to contribute toward the expenses of attending a postsecondary educational institution. The amount of the expected contribution, when subtracted from the cost of attending a particular institution, determines the student's financial need. This remainder—the amount by which the family's "ability to pay" falls short of covering the bill—is the student's eligibility for financial aid.

This chapter will examine the theoretical concerns in development of need analysis rationale and need analysis in practice. Construction of student expense budgets will also be discussed.

Theoretical Basis of Need Analysis

Financial aid is the practical manifestation of a commitment to equal educational opportunity. That commitment is historically grounded in the society at large and especially in the higher education community. Inherent in it is sufficient financial support to permit access to higher education, as well as additional funding to provide choice among available alternatives. For over three centuries, scholarships provided through private philanthropy were the means of broadening educational opportunity. More recently the public commitment to equal educational opportunity has been evidenced in the appropriation of state and federal tax revenues for student financial aid. Because education is held to be a public good, egalitarian principles require that it should be equitably available to all who can benefit from it. Therefore, if the cost of education presents a barrier to a student's academic pursuits, financial assistance should be available to ensure, if not to create, equal educational opportunity.

Because the distribution of most financial aid is based on need, let us briefly explore why need, rather than some other criterion, is the basis for distribution. Distribution of a good or the means of achieving a good is a question for philosophical or ethical reflection: How can a good (or the means to it) be justly distributed? In this case the good is higher education, and the means to it is financial aid. The question restated, then, is: How can financial aid be justly distributed? The answer is not a clear one.

Justice—in this case, distributive justice—is itself relative. The question can be turned around: What is the end to which just distribution is a means? If, for example, the objective is to recognize commitment to an institutional goal, then distribution on the basis of work or productivity or sacrifice would be "just." Similarly, if the objective is to recognize achievement, then merit or worth (or perhaps even birth or station in life) might be the means of "just" distribution. Sometimes institutions distribute financial aid on the basis of commitment or achievement. Scholarships based on academic promise, athletic prowess, or other special talents or attributes are examples of such aid. In these cases it must be acknowledged that equal educational opportunity is, at best, only tangentially served. If the objective is the equalizing of opportunity, however, need is the only "just" means for achieving the greatest equity in distributing aid resources.

Once need is established as the criterion for distribution, the next question is: How is need to be measured? Aid administrators answer this question by approaching it from the other side. They determine a family's ability to pay for education, and in so doing measure its *in*ability to pay—that is, its need for financial assistance. To measure ability to pay, need analysis procedures have been developed over the past three decades to assist aid administrators in coming to an objective, realistic evaluation of families' resources and, thus, their ability to pay for their children's educations.

A need analysis method is basically a taxation structure. Available resources are measured, allowances are made for various reasons, and the remainder is subject to taxation. Like tax theory, need analysis methods employ certain principles, the foremost of which are horizontal and vertical equity.

The principle of horizontal equity, put simply, is that persons in like circumstances should be treated the same. If they are not, horizontal equity is violated, and a just distribution does not result. The problem, however, is in deciding which persons are in like circumstances. Because of the distinctive character of each family's situation, need analysis methods attempt to take into account as many factors as possible. Even so, the final result can be only an approximation of horizontal equity because of the limited information examined and the scope of the situations typically accommodated in the need analysis method.

As applied to tax theory, the principle of vertical equity requires that persons with greater resources should be expected to pay more than those with smaller resources. Because the intent of need analysis is to measure ability to pay, vertical equity is, therefore, best served if the distribution of aid favors those less able to pay. There are two primary taxation models that require greater contributions from those with greater resources and smaller contributions from those with smaller resources: flat rates and progressive rates. Flat taxation rates—such as sales taxes—tend to be regressive because they ignore the need to provide for fundamental costs of living before taxation is imposed. For example, the relative tax burden of a general sales tax is many times heavier for a low-income person than it is for a wealthy person. Even if the situation is ameliorated somewhat by exempting certain resources from taxation, the rates are still regressive, since persons with greater resources retain a greater capacity for discretionary spending than do their counterparts with smaller resources. On the other hand, progressive tax rates —such as income taxes—tend toward equity through redistribution of resources. This progressivity is familiar to us in the federal income tax schedules, where a greater percentage of income is taxed in each successive "bracket" of taxable income. Persons with greater resources have not simply a proportionately larger tax burden but, rather, a burden that grows at an increasing rate as resources increase. Therefore, in order to achieve vertical equity through a distribution of aid that favors those less able to pay, need analysis methods also employ progressive taxation schedules.

Need Analysis in Practice

A need analysis system is necessarily a compromise. The data collected by the aid administrator must be sufficiently broad and detailed that a reasonable evaluation of the family's resources can be made. However, assembling the data should not be so onerous as to deter a family from completing an aid application, nor should the data be so plentiful that the aid administrator is kept from efficiently performing his or her responsibilities. At best, it is hoped that a need analysis method will place families in a fair rank order of need, with an indication of the magnitude of that need, so that the intended just distribution of financial aid is achieved.

It is important to distinguish between need analysis and eligibility determination. Ideally, they are identical; however, if financial aid resources are limited, an institution or aid program may find it necessary to resort to restricting eligibility for assistance. This may be done in a number of ways. For example:

- Need may be determined according to standard procedures, but the resulting aid award may be limited in some way, such as fulfilling only a portion of a student's need, or restricting aid to a set percentage of a student's expense budget, or assisting only those students who have the greatest needs.

- A method that resembles need analysis may be devised in a way that produces the desired results in distributing aid—that is, the same general framework may be used, but the "need analysis" method might not have so reasonable an economic basis as the standard procedures (for example, allowances might be defined much more austerely).

- Certain aspects of the need analysis formula may be adjusted to achieve the desired end—for example, the assessment schedules used to "tax" a student's family resources may be made harsher or more lenient.

- Particular elements of need analysis may be omitted or additional elements included—for example, assets may be excluded altogether, or private elementary and secondary schooling costs may be included.

At this writing there are three major "need analysis" schemes: the Pell Grant method, the Guaranteed Student Loan need test, and the uniform methodology. As the labels of the first two methods indicate, each focuses on a single federal aid program. Determination of eligibility for the particular programs is the objective of the two methods. They do not necessarily produce realistic measures of family ability to pay. The uniform methodology, on the other hand, is used by most postsecondary institutions in the country to determine the financial needs of their students.

The uniform methodology was a product of the National Task Force on Student Aid Problems, which in 1974-75 brought together representatives of the principal national groups having an interest in financial aid programs. The methodology has been maintained since that time through ongoing cooperation of those groups. The cooperative effort was formalized in 1981 by creation of a National Student Aid Coalition. Among the coalition's activities are maintenance of the methodology and fostering of research in the financing of postsecondary education.

Fundamental to the uniform methodology of need analysis is the assumption that the student and his or her family recognize an obligation to contribute as much as they are able toward the student's educational expenses. A family's ability to pay is influenced by a variety of factors, including income, asset holdings, indebtedness, family size, and the number of family members in postsecondary education. Special accommodation is made in need analysis for circumstances beyond the family's control, such as unusual medical and dental expenses, that affect its financial capacity. On the other hand, expenses that are a matter of family discretion are not accommodated in need analysis. With these general rules in mind, then, let us examine the steps of need analysis according to the uniform methodology.

Parents' Contribution. The uniform methodology produces a "family contribution" figure (see Table 1) that comprises the parents' contribution and the student's contribution. The parents' contribution is a combined measure of the parents' ability to contribute from their income and their assets. For the majority of families, parents' income is the most important factor in determining the contribution, but assets may also play a significant role. The parents' contribution is derived by using a progressive assessment schedule that is applied to the parents' "adjusted available income." There are two components to adjusted available income: the parents' "available income" and their "income supplement" from assets.

Available income is the amount of income left after allowances for family maintenance, taxes, and extraordinary expenses are subtracted from the parents' total income. Total income, for need analysis purposes, includes earnings, interest and dividend income, income from a business or farm, rental income, alimony, taxable pensions, and other forms of taxable income. Also included are nontaxable resources, such as Social Security, veterans', and welfare benefits; nontaxable pensions; and child support. In general, the Internal Revenue Service's definition of taxable income is used, though many aid administrators reject the use of federal tax rules to exempt certain kinds of income from consideration in need analysis. For example, Individual Retirement Account payments, excluded from

Table 1. Uniform Methodology:
Total Family Contribution for Dependent Students.

	Parents' total income
−	U.S. income tax
−	F.I.C.A. taxes
−	State and local taxes
−	Standard maintenance allowance
−	Employment allowance
−	Medical and dental expenses
−	Other extraordinary expenses
=	Available income
	Home equity
+	Other real estate equity
+	Cash, savings, and bank accounts
+	Investments
+	Adjusted net worth of business and farm
=	Net worth
−	Asset protection allowance
=	Discretionary net worth
×	Conversion percentage
=	Income supplement
	Available income
+	Income supplement
=	Adjusted available income
×	Progressive assessment rate schedule
=	Total parents' contribution
÷	Number in college
=	Parents' contribution for student
	Parents' contribution for student
+	Student's contribution from past savings
+	Student's summertime employment
+	Student's benefits
=	Total family contribution

income for tax purposes, may be regarded as income by aid administrators. Likewise, losses from a business or farm are usually disallowed, especially if the business or farm is a secondary source of income for the family. The same is usually true of losses from rental property, particularly if the losses are attributable to depreciation. On the other hand, many aid administrators contend that capital gains should be treated as assets for need analysis purposes, rather than treated as income in accordance with tax rules. This is especially true if the gain is long term and thus probably not reflective of the ability of the family to contribute toward educational costs on a year-to-year basis. The calendar year preceding the year for which aid is sought is the "base year" for need analysis of parents' resources.

Allowances are made in the uniform methodology for expenses that reduce the family's available income and that are not matters of discretion. Federal income taxes and Social Security (F.I.C.A.) taxes are subtracted from the family's income, as is an allowance for state and local taxes. Normally, a standard table of allowances, derived from data reported to the Internal Revenue Service, is used for state and local taxes; in some cases, however, actual state and local tax data are available from the student's family and are used in place of the standard allowance.

Another standard allowance is granted according to the size of the family. This allowance, called the "standard maintenance allowance," is derived from data published by the Bureau of Labor Statistics and is updated annually for economic changes. The standard used is that for a family of four living at the BLS lower budget standard. BLS equivalency scales are used to calculate the allowance figures for other family sizes. The student's expenses for the anticipated nine-month academic year are subtracted from the allowance because it is expected that the student's maintenance costs will be considered in developing his or her expense budget. If other family members are also in postsecondary education, their maintenance costs are subtracted from the standard maintenance allowance as well.

The standard maintenance allowance is based on the Bureau of Labor Statistics' lower budget standard on the assumption that a student from a family at or below this level cannot realistically expect any income to be "available" for educational expenses. Thus, below this level no parents' contribution is expected for the student's educational expenses. If the family's after-tax income is above the lower standard, it is assumed that the family can make at least some contribution toward the student's maintenance (living) expenses, and perhaps toward other educational costs as well.

The costs of employment for one parent are included in the standard maintenance allowance. If the other parent in a two-parent family is also employed, an additional allowance is made for employment expenses. The allowance is based on the smaller income of the two parents and is calculated as a percentage of income up to a maximum allowance. The percentage and allowance maximum may be adjusted annually because of economic changes. For single-parent families, there has been continuing debate over whether the standard maintenance allowance adequately provides for extra employment costs, especially if child care is involved. At present the allowance is granted for single-parent families, and aid administrators generally accommodate child care expenses as an additional allowance if such costs are incurred.

To address further the concern for horizontal equity in need analysis, allowances may also be made for extraordinary expenses that are beyond the family's control. The only standard allowance granted in this category is for unreimbursed medical and dental expenses (excluding insurance premiums) that may be claimed as a deduction for federal income tax purposes. The aid administrator may make other adjustments to total income for additional unusual expenses, such as funeral costs, legal fees, child support and alimony payments, or sewer, water, and street assessments. Some institutions also have the policy of allowing at least a portion of unreimbursed elementary and secondary school tuition expenses to reduce available income. Such a policy parallels federal procedures for determining eligibility for the Pell Grant program.

Once the standard maintenance allowance, taxes, the employment allowance, and any allowances for unusual expenses are subtracted from the family's total income, the remainder is called "available income"—income that the family can use to supplement its standard of living beyond the standard maintenance allowance. This income, then, is available for discretionary expenditures and for contributions toward the children's postsecondary education expenses. Before a parents' contribution is calculated, however, the available income sometimes is adjusted by the addition or subtraction of an "income supplement."

The concept of an income supplement has been borrowed from welfare economics. There it is used to evaluate, in income terms, the strength added to the family by its possession of assets. By combining the income supplement with available income, the aid administrator may obtain a comprehensive measure of family wherewithal to undertake postsecondary education costs. The label "income supplement" does not mean that the family is expected to convert its assets into cash, although some students' parents do take this step. Rather, it is an indicator of the flexibility that assets add to the family's use of its income. In addition, from the standpoint of horizontal equity, the concept of an income supplement is useful as a tool for equating the financial strength of families at disparate income and asset levels.

The income supplement is the end product of a process that begins with the family's net assets. Not all assets are evaluated in need analysis. The assets included are those most frequently encountered and whose valuation is most readily determined: the home, other real estate, cash, savings, bank accounts, investments, businesses, and farms. Other assets, such as life insurance and pension holdings, have been suggested for inclusion, but the debate on these is presently unresolved. In some program eligibility determinations, such as for Guaranteed Student Loans, assets are not considered at all for most families; in other programs, such as Pell Grants, consideration has been given to excluding home equity. In the uniform methodology of need analysis, however, assets are not distinguished by their form, except for businesses and farms. In these cases, only a discounted value of the business or farm is included, so that the income-producing capacity of such assets is not affected. The total of a family's equities in the home and other real estate; cash, savings, bank accounts, and investments; and the adjusted net worth of any businesses and farms is designated "net worth" for need analysis purposes.

Against a family's net worth, an "asset protection allowance" is granted. This allowance is based on the composition of the family and the age of the older (or only) parent. An annuity formula is used to derive the allowance, which is equal to the amount needed to buy an annuity policy that would produce sufficient income in retirement to make up the difference between the cost of living and prospective Social Security benefits. The retirement basis of the allowance has been criticized for its complexity, its dependence on annuity and longevity tables, and the uncertainty of future Social Security benefits. Nevertheless, the allowance in practice permits a greater offset against assets for older parents than for younger ones and has some theoretical substance as well. For these reasons, and because an agreeable alternative has not been found, the allowance continues to be used.

Subtraction of the asset protection allowance from a family's net worth leaves "discretionary net worth." The family's discretionary net worth is converted to an income supplement by multiplication by a percentage factor. The percentage varies according to whether the discretionary net worth is positive or negative and, if negative, according to the family's available income level. On the positive side, the conversion percentage is related to the expected return on and/or appreciation of the family's asset holdings; on the negative side, the income supplement becomes an allowance against the family's available income to permit—theoretically, at least—the accumulation of retirement assets.

Available income and income supplement together constitute "adjusted available income." In respect to horizontal equity, families with equal adjusted available incomes are deemed to be equal in financial strength and in their ability to pay for postsecondary education. This is so even though overtly the families' income and asset holdings may appear to be quite different. In respect to vertical equity, a progressive taxation schedule is used to assess the portion of adjusted available income that is considered a reasonable contribution from the parents toward educational costs. The marginal taxation rates presently range from 22 to 47 percent for undergraduate students and from 18 to 47 percent for graduate and professional students. The brackets of adjusted available income against which the marginal rates are applied are adjusted annually for changes in the economy. Thus, because of this and other annual adjustments in the methodology, the parents' contribution is indexed to inflation. It will remain approximately constant from year to year, in constant dollar terms, if the parents' income keeps pace with inflation and if there are no other fundamental changes in the methodology or in taxes. Table 2 gives examples of parents' contributions for the 1983–84 academic year.

The parents' contribution figure obtained from the adjusted available income assessment schedule is a total contribution figure. That is, because the standard maintenance allowance does not include nine months' worth of maintenance costs for all family members in college, the contribution derived at this point is for all college students in the family. The contribution is divided among the students, so that each has an equal share. Some institutions, however, practice variations on this procedure. Many institutions do not include parents in the count of number of family members in postsecondary education. Instead, an allowance is made against available income for the parents' direct educational costs. In such a case, the standard maintenance allowance is not adjusted for the parents, nor does the division of the total parents' contribution include the parents. In addition, some institutions evaluate the costs of education of the student's siblings in order to decide whether an equal division of the parents' contribution is appropriate. If it is found that a sibling is attending a much lower-cost institution or that the sibling is the recipient of substantial financial aid, the parents' contribution may be adjusted accordingly.

In cases where the family's income is quite low, a negative parents' contribution may result from need analysis. When this occurs, some aid administrators adjust the amount of self-help required of the student in the financial aid package, or they determine whether the student's summer earnings are consumed in providing support for the family. Federal regulations prohibit the outright funding of a negative parents' contribution, but aid administrators who are alert to the particular financial difficulties of students from such families may appropri-

Table 2. Parents' Contributions for the 1983–84 Academic Year.

Net assets:	$30,000				$40,000				$50,000				$60,000			
Family size:	3	4	5	6	3	4	5	6	3	4	5	6	3	4	5	6
Total income																
$12,000	$ 110	$ 0	$ 0	0	$ 380	$ 0	$ 0	0	$ 640	$ 200	$ 0	0	$ 910	$ 470	$ 50	$ 0
16,000	720	280	0	0	980	550	140	0	1,240	810	400	0	1,520	1,080	660	200
20,000	1,290	870	460	0	1,570	1,130	720	270	1,870	1,400	990	530	2,220	1,690	1,250	800
24,000	1,900	1,420	1,020	570	2,250	1,720	1,290	840	2,640	2,050	1,570	1,100	3,080	2,400	1,870	1,370
28,000	2,640	2,050	1,580	1,120	3,080	2,410	1,880	1,380	3,560	2,820	2,230	1,670	4,120	3,280	2,620	1,990
32,000	3,500	2,780	2,220	1,660	4,050	3,230	2,590	1,980	4,610	3,740	3,010	2,330	5,180	4,300	3,490	2,730

Note: The following assumptions have been made in deriving these figures: two parents, one with earnings from employment, the other with no gainful employment; the age of the older parent is forty-five; no unusual expenses; no business or farm assets; standard deductions for income tax purposes; one child in undergraduate postsecondary education.

Source: Federal Register, 48:17 (Jan. 25, 1983), p. 3, 402.

ately adjust financial aid awards for justifiable, documented reasons.

Divorced and Separated Parents. Divorce and separation have significantly increased in the United States in recent years. Such cases can pose particular problems for aid administrators. The federal government's view is that the student's custodial parent and current spouse, if any, are to report their financial situation for financial aid purposes and are responsible for the student's education insofar as they are able. The noncustodial parent is officially excused from any contribution by the federal government's definition. If the custodial parent is not gainfully employed, and if continuing financial obligations to a previous family draw heavily on the stepparent's resources—or if premarital agreements assert that the stepparent has no legal obligation for the education of the children from the custodial parent's prior marriage—the official income for federal need analysis purposes may even be zero.

Some institutions have the policy that both parents of the student continue to be obligated to contribute toward the student's education costs regardless of the parents' current relationship to each other. If the parents are divorced, these institutions prepare separate need analyses for each parent, taking into consideration whatever present family responsibilities the parents may have. For purposes of the Pell Grant and Guaranteed Student Loan programs, however, federal rules are employed in determining aid amounts.

Dealing with cases in which the parents are divorced or separated is time consuming and requires special sensitivity to what is often already a strained relationship, not only between the parents but maybe also between the student and the parents. Professional judgment in evaluating the situation and skill in counseling are essential in all need analysis cases, but particularly in these.

Student's Contribution. The student is expected to contribute toward his or her education costs through past savings and through summer employment. Usually about one third of a student's current savings and other assets is expected to be available during each year of college. An exception might be made if the student's parents have placed investments in the student's name under certain tax provisions, such as the Uniform Gift to Minors Act. In these cases some aid administrators consider assets above a certain level to be the parents', rather than the student's. Student assets in the form of trusts and estates are not included in this adjustment procedure. Such assets, even those that are "inaccessible," are regarded as available—if nothing else, they can at least act as collateral for borrowing.

Summer employment is most often the principal contribution of a student toward his or her education costs. Most institutions expect a student to earn at least a modest amount during the summer (generally $700 to $900), although the amount is determined by the institution. In the event a student does not realize the expected summer savings amount, many institutions will expand term-time employment or loan amounts in the financial aid award to cover the shortfall.

Benefits received from the Social Security Administration, the Veterans Administration, and other governmental and social welfare agencies are also included in the student's resources, usually at 100 percent of their value.

The "total family contribution," then, is the total of the parents' contribution for the student and the student's contributions from past savings, summer employment, and benefits. The total family contribution has sometimes been called the "net price" of a college education. That is, regardless of whether a student attends a lower-cost community college or a higher-cost private institution, the same amount is expected from the family. Of course, if the cost of attending a particular college is less than the total family contribution, no need-based financial aid will be available to the student. In such cases the comparative savings to the family that a lower-cost institution can represent may be an important factor in a student's deciding which college to attend. Nevertheless, for students whose families are not able to pay the entire college bill, the total family contribution becomes the common denominator of financial aid eligibility. Ideally, the contribution figure is the same at all institutions that a freshman or transfer student might be considering. If this is so, then one of the purposes of need analysis is achieved: The student can make a decision about his or her education for educational reasons, rather than for financial ones.

Independent Students. Not all students are dependent on their parents for financial support. The circumstances in which students may be regarded as independent are defined by the federal government. In addition to orphans and wards of the state, independent students are those students who, for the year in which aid is received and in the preceding year, are not claimed on their parents' federal income tax returns, do not live at home for more than six weeks, and do not receive substantial financial help from their parents. Many aid administrators use this federal definition. Determination of which students are independent rests finally with the aid administrator. In many instances the situation is quite clear; in others it is quite obscure. Frequently documentation, such as rent receipts and paycheck stubs, is required of students when their dependency status is uncertain. The aid administrator's judgment is the key element in such cases. Ultimately, the question to be decided is whether there is sufficient evidence in the particular case to justify excusing the parents from their obligation to contribute to the student's education costs.

For independent students the present uniform methodology procedures are very straightforward (see Table 3). The "base year" of analysis is the academic year for which aid is sought and the preceding summer, although some aid administrators consider only the nine-month academic year. The student's income for the period, less any federal income taxes, Social Security (F.I.C.A.) taxes, and state income taxes (together with the spouse's after-tax income, if the student is married), constitutes the student's "available income." If there are nontaxable income sources, such as governmental benefits, these are included as well. There are no allowances made for family support or unusual expenses because it is assumed that these will be built into the student's expense budget.

The independent student's assets are evaluated in a fashion similar to the way that the assets of a dependent student's parents are treated. An asset protection allowance—basically an emergency reserve—is granted according to the student's age and

Table 3. Uniform Methodology:
Total Family Contribution for Independent Students.

	Student's (and spouse's) total income
−	U.S. income taxes
−	F.I.C.A. taxes
−	State income taxes
=	Available income
	Home equity
+	Other real estate equity
+	Cash, savings, and bank accounts
+	Investments
+	Adjusted net worth of business and farm
=	Net worth
−	Asset protection allowance
=	Discretionary net worth
×	Conversion percentage
=	Contribution from assets
	Available income
+	Contribution from assets
=	Total family contribution

family responsibilities. If there are assets remaining after subtraction of the asset protection allowance, they are assessed at approximately one third.

The total family contribution for the independent student, therefore, is the sum of the student's (and spouse's) available income and contribution from assets.

In the method used to determine Pell Grant eligibility, the independent student with children is treated much the same as a dependent student's parents are treated. Allowances are made for family size and unusual expenses, and a marginal assessment rate is used to determine the contribution. It should be noted, however, that the budget used for Pell Grant purposes is not a comprehensive one; thus, the effect of the more generous procedures is diminished considerably. For independent students who do not have children, the Pell Grant method is roughly parallel to the uniform methodology.

Need Analysis Documents

Standard forms for collecting the information required in need analysis are published by a number of organizations, including the College Scholarship Service of the College Board, the American College Testing Program, the Graduate and Professional School Financial Aid Service, and the United States Department of Education. The form that a given institution uses depends largely on its particular needs and the services provided by the organization that publishes the form.

Each of the organizations noted above (or its contractor) can process its forms by computer at a central location. The product of the central processing is a need analysis report that reproduces the information reported by the student and his or her family on the form and that outlines the steps of need analysis (or at least gives the end result of need analysis), including the total family contribution computed according to the uniform methodology.

The need analysis report is reviewed by the aid administrator, who must rely on his or her professional judgment and experience to decide the appropriateness of the analysis. In the course of review, various adjustments may be made according to established institutional policies or because of the particular circumstances of a given case. In addition, further information or clarification of reported information may be sought from the student or his or her family. Documentation, such as a copy of the parents' or student's federal income tax return, may be required; and verification may be sought for important factors in the need analysis, such as the size of the parents' household and the college attendance of the student's siblings. Close scrutiny of need analysis reports yields the dual benefits of conserving the institution's aid resources and ensuring that financial aid is distributed as equitably as possible.

Student Expense Budgets

Realistic student expense budgets are just as important to the equitable distribution of financial aid as is the determination of the ability of a student and his or her family to contribute toward those expenses. Without the student expense budget, the work of need analysis is not complete, for need cannot be decided unless there is something with which the family contribution can be compared.

The principal components of student expense budgets are readily apparent to institutional administrators: tuition and fees, books and supplies, and room and board. To this list the aid administrator routinely adds allowances for personal expenses and transportation. (See Table 4.) Each of these, however, bears closer examination.

Table 4. Student Expense Budgets.

	Tuition and fees
+	Books and supplies
+	Room (or rent and utilities)
+	Board (or food)
+	Transportation
+	Special expenses
=	Student expense budget

Tuition and fees may vary in a number of ways. Tuition may be charged by the credit hour; additional amounts may be charged for out-of-district or out-of-state students; different rates may apply to students in different divisions of the institution or even in different programs within a school or college of a university. Fees may be assessed for student activities, parking privileges, health services, and laboratory breakage, and they may be added for special academic programs, such as music, art, dance, or engineering. All possible combinations of tuition and fees ideally are accommodated in a student's expense budget for financial aid purposes. Sometimes, however, it is necessary to use averages in determining awards. Nevertheless, the more closely tailored the student's budget is to his or her actual costs, the better the student is served—and the more equitable is the distribution of financial assistance.

The cost of books and supplies has increased sharply in recent years, mainly because of higher paper prices. Most institutions include at least $250 a year for books and supplies, although the allowance may need to be higher for students in certain disciplines, such as law, medicine, art, architecture, and literature.

Room and board charges are set by the institution for resident students, but room costs may vary because of differences in accommodations and location, and board costs may vary because of the meal plan selected. Again, some aid administrators must use average expenses to determine aid awards. If it is possible to do so, however, the actual charges to individual students should be used. If some meals are omitted from the meal plan, an allowance for additional food costs should be included in the budget. Extra allowances are also necessary for resident independent students and others who are unable to return to their family homes during vacation and break periods.

For the dependent student who lives with his or her parents, room costs are omitted from the budget, but food costs, both at home and away from home, should be included. The standard maintenance allowance used in need analysis, it should be recalled, excludes the student's living expenses for the nine-month academic year. Because of this, even the commuter student's expense budget should provide reasonable allowances for food and other expenses. The federal government presently specifies that, for federal student aid purposes, the commuter's allowance be set at $1,100.

For dependent students who do not live with their parents and who do not live in institutionally owned or operated residences, the aid administrator should determine an appropriate allowance for rent, utilities, and food. Many institutions, as a policy, do not grant off-campus students an allowance greater than the room and board allowance provided to students living in college housing. Such a policy typically has been adopted to conserve aid resources and to encourage maximal occupancy of campus housing.

Rent, utilities, and food costs for independent students are often quite difficult to determine with any precision. Surveys of rental prices for various-sized apartments in the community are usually necessary to set standard allowances. Even so, in a community with limited housing, some students will not be able to find anything other than higher-priced housing. Food costs can also be determined through surveys and through researching published data from the Department of Agriculture or the Bureau of Labor Statistics.

Personal expenses include such costs as clothing, laundry, cleaning, and recreation. For dependent students these expenses are usually the same regardless of whether the student lives at home, off campus, or on campus. Most institutions allow $550 to $700 for such miscellaneous costs. For independent students, especially those with families, personal expenses may be sizable. Periodic surveys of currently enrolled students (not just aid recipients) are probably the best tool for collecting data on which to base allowances. Special family circumstances, however, may necessitate further adjustments to the standard allowances in individual cases.

Transportation costs obviously differ according to whether a student is a resident or a commuter. For dependent resident students, most institutions allow the cost of two round-trip economy fares on a public carrier for travel between the campus and the student's home. Because of great fluctuations in air fares since deregulation of the airline industry, some institutions now assume that students traveling by air will be able to take advantage of "super-saver" rates for at least one of the two round trips. Commuting students, whether dependent or independent, should be allowed expenses for public transit, if available, or for fuel, maintenance, parking, tolls, and insurance costs. In general, the cost of purchasing a motor vehicle is beyond the scope of any financial aid program and thus is excluded from student expense budgets.

Additional special costs should also be included in a student's expense budget when appropriate. For example, additional costs associated with a handicap, child care expenses for younger dependent children, and a spouse's expenses of employment should be accommodated. Likewise, if a student is involved in a program that is a regular part of the institution's curriculum, such as study abroad, fieldwork, or internships, any additional expenses should also be included.

In summary, the student's expense budget includes tuition and fees, books and supplies, room and board (or rent, utilities, and food), personal expenses, transportation, and additional special costs. When the student's total family contribution is subtracted from the student expense budget appropriate to the student's circumstances, the difference is financial need, which presumably will be met with a package of assistance, including work, loans, and scholarships or grants. (Table 5 gives the average expenses for the 1982–83 academic year, as reported by postsecondary institutions to the College Scholarship Service of the College Board.)

Table 5. Average Student Expense Budgets, 1982-83 Academic Year.

	Public 4-Year Institutions	Private 4-Year Institutions
Resident students:		
Tuition and fees	$ 979	$4,201
Books and supplies	279	298
Room and board	2,087	2,226
Personal expenses	714	604
Transportation	329	326
Total	$4,388	$7,475
Commuter students:		
Tuition and fees	$ 979	$4,201
Books and supplies	279	298
Room and board	1,038	1,118
Personal expenses	673	625
Transportation	570	519
Total	$3,539	$6,581

Source: Reprinted with permission from *College Cost Book, 1982-83*, pp. 56-57. Copyright © by College Entrance Examination Board, New York.

Conclusion

In this chapter we have seen that financial need determination, or need analysis, revolves about a simple formula:

Budget
— Resources
———————
= Need

The problem for the financial aid administrator is, in each student's case, to define these elements in such a way that the individual is treated fairly and that equity within the overall group of aid recipients is achieved and maintained. To these ends standard procedures have been developed over the past thirty years.

The student expense budget is seemingly straightforward —it includes tuition, fees, books, supplies, room, board, personal expenses, and transportation. However, when the aid administrator attempts to tailor the budget to a given student's circumstances, the complexities may be manifold. The procedure that many aid administrators follow is to develop standard budgets that accommodate typical situations. Often these standards are based on surveys of students' actual expenses or on information available from secondary sources regarding student expenditure patterns. The use of standard budgets allows aid administrators to focus on atypical cases and, through comparison with the benchmark figures, to make reasonable judgments about modifications to the standard allowances.

Central to need analysis is determination of a student's resources—the amount that the student and his or her family can reasonably be expected to pay toward college costs. The present need analysis procedures are part of an evolutionary process that began in the Ivy League colleges in the early 1950s and continues on a national scale today. The process was sometimes more revolutionary (or even reactionary) than evolutionary, and there have been occasional threats of federal intervention. Common agreement on the framework of need analysis, however, was achieved in 1975, when the uniform methodology emerged. Since then the uniform methodology has been sanctioned by federal regulation, although its future use is somewhat precarious because the Education Amendments of 1980 call for a single "need analysis" system for four federal programs, including the Pell Grant program. From its inception, the Pell Grant program (formerly the Basic Educational Opportunity Grant program) has used a separate system for determining eligibility. Temporary legislation continues that separation of need analysis methods at least for the 1983–84 academic year.

Whether a single system will ever be stipulated in practice is problematical. For most aid administrators, such a move would not be welcome because of the prospect of government intervention. The present uniform methodology, although not completely free from government restrictions, is largely the product of voluntary cooperation and is regarded as a reasonable, objective, and economically informed procedure for calculating a family's ability to pay for college.

The key elements of the uniform methodology are a family's income and assets, the size of the family, and the number of family members attending college. Various adjustments are made to income and assets to help achieve greater horizontal equity from case to case; and, in recognition of vertical equity, a progressive taxation schedule is used to derive the parents' contribution from income that remains after subtracting allowances and making adjustments. Additional contribution figures are calculated on the basis of the student's own resources. These are combined with the parents' contribution to produce the total family contribution, which amounts to the "net price" to the family for the student's college education. For students who are independent of their parents' support, special need analysis procedures are followed which compare the student's total resources—minus a few allowances—with a comprehensive student expense budget.

For both dependent and independent students, "financial need" is the amount by which the total family contribution falls short of covering the student expense budget. This need figure usually represents a student's maximum eligibility for financial aid. The kind and amount of aid that a student receives depend on the aid resources available to the institution and its policies regarding the packaging of that aid. These topics are discussed in Chapter Seven.

Bibliographical Note

The major need analysis service organizations annually publish manuals that describe in detail the rationale and computation procedures of need analysis. See, for example, *CSS Need*

Analysis: Theory and Computation Procedures (College Scholarship Service, 1982b) and *Handbook for Financial Aid Administrators* (American College Testing Program, 1981). Details of the original rendition of the uniform methodology are included in the *Draft Final Report* of the National Task Force on Student Aid Problems (1975). A summary of the modifications made in the uniform methodology during its first five years is provided in *The Uniform Methodology: Past, Present, and Future* (Case and Finello, 1980).

   Philosophical discussions of ways in which the means (such as financial aid) to a social good (such as higher education) may be distributed are contained in *Distributive Justice: A Constructive Critique of the Utilitarian Theory of Distribution* (Rescher, 1966) and in *Toward a New Theory of Distributive Justice* (Bowie, 1971). More general treatises on justice and distribution include *Aristotle's Nicomachean Ethics,* especially book V, section 304 (translated by Rackham, 1968); Marx's ([1891] 1971) *Critique of the Gotha Programme*; and Rawls' (1971) *A Theory of Justice.* Particularly supportive of equal educational opportunity is *Education, Equality, and Income Distribution: A Study of Public Higher Education* (Windham, 1970).

   Taxation theory is the focus of *Public Finance in Theory and Practice* (Musgrave and Musgrave, 1980). Especially relevant to need analysis theory are chapter 5, "Theory of Optimal Distribution," and chapter 11, "Approaches to Tax Equity." Further consideration of tax theory is contained in "The Anatomy of Justice in Taxation" (Blum and Klaven, 1973).

   Construction of student expense budgets is the focus of *A Handbook for Use in the Preparation of Student Expense Budgets* (Clark, 1983). The College Scholarship Service conducts annual surveys of student expense budgets used by postsecondary institutions. The most recent findings are published in *The College Cost Book, 1982-83* (College Scholarship Service, 1982a).

7

Meeting Student Needs with Different Types of Financial Aid Awards

Shirley F. Binder

Developments of the past several years—such as changing economic conditions, the projected decrease of traditional college-bound students, and threatening memoranda from the Department of Education concerning the responsibility of each postsecondary institution for proper administration of federal student assistance dollars—have made chief executive officers aware of the importance of the funds expended for financial aid. As a result, there has been a general upgrading of the administration of the financial assistance programs at most colleges and universities. There has been, further, the realization that student enrollment and persistence in postsecondary education are highly dependent on the supply of financial resources, on the provision of information to prospective and continuing students about those resources, and on the delivery of those resources to students in a timely manner. In most cases, and certainly at state-supported institutions, fiscal officers are unwilling or unable to carry students on an accounts receivable system.

Nor are the owners of privately owned residence halls, apartments, and bookstores eager to extend credit to financially needy students. Therefore, financial resources equal to the need of financially needy students and proper administration of those resources, resulting in delivery of funds to students when needed, are of vital importance both to student and institutional health.

Of equal, if not greater, importance both to students and to institutions than the *amount* of resources awarded each student is the *kind* of resources awarded. Basically, there are two kinds of financial assistance: self-help and everything else. For the purposes of this chapter, we will refer to the "everything else" category as non-self-help. Self-help resources may be further described as current earnings, savings from past earnings, or loans against future earnings. Non-self-help includes scholarships, grants-in-aid, fellowships, gifts from relatives, parental contributions, and the like; in other words, those resources that do not carry with them a commitment either to past, present, or future employment or to repayment.

Most students would argue that the "best" funds are those that do not require either work or repayment. However, the supply of non-self-help funds—from all sources, including parental contribution, private, state, federal, and institutional— is not equal by any means to the total estimated financial need of students enrolled in postsecondary education today. In fact, the total of non-self-help *and* self-help funds is not equal to that need. The problem, therefore, is to stretch those funds as far as possible to meet the need of academically qualified, financially needy students and to award them in a combination or "package" that is in the best interest of both the student and the institution. How funds are combined in the financial aid award or "package" is the focus of this chapter.

On the surface the topic appears to be simple and straightforward: to distribute long-term student loans and part-time employment in such a way that students are not forced to subordinate their studies to their jobs or to face a burden of loan payments that are unrealistic in light of the students' expected income and/or family obligations.

Various need-related factors complicate the problem:

- *Variations in the cost of education by type and location of institution and by the course of study pursued.* Generally included in the cost of education are tuition and fees, room and board, books and supplies, transportation, and personal expenses. The cost of education is also affected by the student's marital status and number of dependents (if any).
- *Differences in student aptitude and in the capacity of the student to meld work and study.* Certain students—for instance, those with preschool dependents for whom they are the sole support, those who must take a number of time-consuming laboratory courses, and those with severe physical handicaps—may find the combination of school and part-time employment an overwhelming burden.
- *Length of study associated with different career and degree options.* Undergraduates who plan to continue their education through graduate or professional school face much greater overall costs than those for whom the baccalaureate is the terminal degree. The financial returns to the student resulting from that added study do not necessarily correspond to the added expense. Students forced by circumstance to assume large loans as undergraduates may be influenced by this factor to abort their plans to pursue graduate education. Those who persist and who add to their loan burden face a long-term obligation that can result in modification of career as well as personal plans or even in maladaptive behavior such as avoidance and default of their loan obligation.
- *Effect of cultural differences on student acceptance of loans.* As a result of unpleasant experiences with unscrupulous lending institutions, poverty-level families (among whom are a high proportion of minority students) are sometimes reluctant to allow their children to accept loans of any kind.
- *Differences in expected family contribution.* There are two variables on which financial need is determined: cost of education and expected family contribution. The financial need of students is determined by subtracting the expected family

contribution from the cost of education, which in turn reflects differences in tuition and fees and the marital status and number of dependents of the student. Therefore, identification of disadvantaged or "truly needy" students is a function of the expected family contribution, which, in turn, is based on an assessment of the relative financial strength of the family.

• *Family and other obligations.* In poverty or low-income families, the welfare of the family is often dependent on the contributions of all family members. Transfer of one or more of those family members from wage earner to college student translates to income forgone for the family. The pursuit of a college degree represents a long-range goal, a concept that is in conflict with the immediacy of the needs of a poverty-level family.

A financial aid award package also depends on the resources available at the institution selected by the student. The availability of student aid resources at the institutional level is affected by internal and external forces. The largest programs of student aid, in terms of dollars and students assisted, are funded by the federal government under Title IV of the Higher Education Act of 1965 and subsequent amendments. Changes in the executive and legislative branches of the federal government can result in abrupt changes in appropriations as well as in the regulations governing the various programs. Institutional contributions to student aid can be affected by the institution's response to changes in enrollment, student mix, and retention and by competing institutional needs. As a result of these internal and external factors, the resources available for packaging the financial aid award at the institutional level can range from Basic (Pell) Grant only to the full gamut of federal financial assistance program funds, a heavy commitment of institutional dollars, and privately donated scholarship resources.

Effective administration of a financial aid program at any institution is based on an in-depth knowledge of the student population and of the resources available to students at that institution. Those resources will not necessarily be under the control of the financial aid administrator. Nonetheless, that individual is responsible by federal regulation (where any Title IV federal financial assistance funds are involved) for coordination of all student assistance funds available on campus and for prevention of awards in excess of need to students.

Effective administration of a financial aid program at any institution is, further, dependent on a packaging philosophy that is consistent with the mission and goals of the institution. A packaging policy, whether developed by the financial aid administrator, by the committee on financial aid to students, or by others, should be communicated for approval to the chief executive officer or the chief administrative officer responsible for financial aid to students. The packaging policy of the institution can emphasize and further the mission and goals of the institution and can contribute to the health of the institution and the students it serves.

Several ethical issues should be considered in the development of a packaging policy. The use of institutional resources for scholarships/grants-in-aid rather than for increased faculty salaries or facility repair may be a short-range solution to enrollment management and thus may result in an even greater long-range problem. An offer of an extremely attractive financial aid package that is heavily weighted toward scholarships and grants may assist in the recruitment of desirable students; however, if students are not told at the time of the initial award that gift aid may be reduced in subsequent years, the institution may be confronted with an attrition problem and/or a resentful student body. One of the greatest dilemmas for institutional aid administrators today is the reemergence of merit no-need scholarships at the very time that federal financial assistance funds for needy students are being reduced. Certainly, the argument can be presented that scholars should be rewarded for their prowess in the same way that athletes are rewarded. On the other hand, it is difficult to condone the use of institutional and private funds for merit scholarships to students without documented financial need if needy students are thereby denied access to postsecondary education. Separation of the recruitment function from the financial aid award function, and separation of the financial aid award function from the disbursement function, can avoid the misuse of scholarship funds.

In authorizing the federal student assistance programs and appropriating funds for them, Congress intended to enable access, choice, and retention of postsecondary education for qualified students with financial need. Federal regulations define the eligibility of students for each federal student assistance program, as well as eligibility for student assistance in general. If an institution's financial aid package includes federal dollars, it must recognize these regulations.

Another packaging goal should be the optimal utilization of available resources. Unmet student need or underutilized funds can result from restrictions placed on scholarships by donors, an inflexible packaging philosophy or policy, the unwillingness of institutional administrators to hold back assistance funds for late applicants, or a general inadequacy of funding.

Certainly, any packaging policy should provide an equitable distribution of funds. This statement does *not* imply that each student aid recipient will receive an equal amount of the available scholarship and grant dollars or an equal amount of self-help. It does, however, imply that students with like characteristics can expect to be treated in like manner. It also implies that financial aid, regardless of the source, when offered by the financial aid administrator, will be offered justly and not arbitrarily and capriciously. In other words, the amount and kind of award should not be influenced by personal feelings toward any student or class of students. The financial aid administrator must often weigh the "special" needs of one individual against the aggregate needs of the total population of aid applicants. Adherence to a packaging policy and an appeal or review process can provide equity for the whole as well as response to the special needs of individuals.

Review of the Literature

The development of various financial aid packaging theories has been chronicled in the literature and is summarized here.

Among the earliest groups to attach importance to the "kinds" of assistance as well as the "amount" made available to an individual student was the College Scholarship Service Panel on Student Financial Need Analysis. This group was convened in 1968 under the chairmanship of Allen M. Cartter, chancellor of New York University, to conduct a critical review of the aid delivery process. The Cartter panel paid little attention to packaging but did report on how the ratio of grant aid to total aid varied with financial need, ability, and race. The panel members suggested that students with the greatest need should receive the greatest proportion of grant funds in their financial aid award. They found, however, that grants were more frequently awarded on the basis of ability than high need and were therefore used more as a reward than as an attempt to *undo* inequity (Cartter, 1971, pp. 77-86).

The Education Amendments of 1972 introduced the Basic Educational Opportunity Grant (BEOG) program, which was designed to provide a "floor" of grant assistance to needy undergraduate students. Unlike the earlier campus-based Educational Opportunity Grant (EOG) program, replaced in 1972 by the Supplemental Educational Opportunity Grant (SEOG) program, BEOG was a "direct" federal grant to students and followed students to the eligible institution of their choice. The State Student Incentive Grant (SSIG) program, also introduced by the Education Amendments of 1972 to encourage state support for grants to needy students, involved many states for the first time in the delivery process. As a result of BEOG and SSIG, the packaging of financial aid became not only more complex but cumbersome. Students were confused and, through lack of understanding, did not in many cases receive the full advantage of the wide range of programs suddenly available.

In 1974 a task force consisting of representatives of twenty-five different organizations was assembled by the College Entrance Examination Board, under the leadership of Francis Keppel, former Commissioner of the U.S. Office of Education. As stated in its report, "The primary thrust of the task force's activities was at the beginning of the student aid process, whereby students or potential students receive information about available aid, make application, are notified of the aid which can be made available specifically to them, and use that aid to begin or continue their education" (National Task Force on Student Aid Problems, 1975, p. 5).

The task force members further limited their deliberations on the delivery system of student aid to undergraduates, leaving graduate and professional issues to be taken up by others. The task force identified the elements of the student aid system as follows:

Types	Processes	Sources	Purposes
A. Grant	A. Direct	A. Federal	A. Access
B. Loan	B. Institutional	B. State	B. Choice
C. Employment	C. Third Party	C. Institutional	C. Retention
		D. Private	

In its chapter on packaging, the task force (p. 171) reiterated three packaging concepts identified earlier by Phillips (1973): (1) "the 'ladder concept,' in which the Basic (Pell) Grant program, in combination with such student and parental resources as are available, provides a guaranteed 'first step' for all needy undergraduate students, a floor from which students could advance up the ladder of successive steps until unmet need is fully satisfied"; (2) "the 'packaging or combination concept,' which implies no particular order in which resources normally should be explored, except [that] everything else should be built upon the 'floor' supplied by the parental/student Basic [Pell] Grant combination of resources"; (3) "the 'self-help concept,' [which] routinely builds in a self-help component composed of student savings, work, and/or loan assistance immediately on top of the floor provided by parental contribution and Basic [Pell] Grant." A fourth approach identified by the task force has become known as "equity packaging." The objective of this approach is "to distribute institutional aid funds in such a manner as to come as nearly as possible to equalizing the non-self-help components" (p. 72). To accomplish this, the aid administrator must first know the resources available to each student—family contribution, entitlements, and so forth. A reasonable expectation from student self-help is added next.

Institutional grants and scholarships are then applied to bring each applicant to a nearly equal start. Loans and/or work are added last to bridge the remaining need factor.

The task force recommended that each institution develop its own packaging policy, that such policy be designed to maximize equity and ensure that priority for grants not be on the basis of academic achievement or special talent, and that the National Association of Student Financial Aid Administrators provide training workshops to assist aid administrators in developing improved packaging policies and techniques.

In 1979 the Carnegie Council on Policy Studies in Higher Education recommended that "the basic building block of student financial support for postsecondary education be a substantial self-help component" (p. 5). A specific dollar amount of self-help was proposed for upper- and lower-division students, and the emphasis was on part-time student employment to provide this self-help component. The council did concede the possibility of borrowing by those students for whom term-time work would be difficult if not impossible, such as handicapped students, students in areas of high unemployment, students experiencing academic difficulty, and students with minor dependents. Expected cuts in federal programs and the inability of institutions to replace those funds with institutional or private funds suggest a much greater self-help expectation from students and their families in the immediate future.

The National Association of College and University Business Officers (NACUBO) (1981), in a monograph funded by the Department of Education, Office of Student Financial Assistance/Student Financial Assistance Training Program, promotes the use of self-help in the form of student employment because self-help supplements gift aid, which probably is insufficient to meet the demand, and part-time employment gives students an opportunity to socialize and to build a work record. Long-term student loans are presented positively as "deferred earnings" and are related to the increased salaries available to the student after graduation, thereby allowing the student to pay for his education with "cheap" money.

According to the monograph, most institutions use a ladder approach to packaging; that is, they apply institutional funds only after taking into account available federal and state funds. Some of these institutions use gift aid above a certain level of loans and work (the "self-help threshold" approach); others use loans and/or work to fill unmet need after an equal sharing of available gift aid (the "equal sharing of gift aid" approach). A summary presentation of equity packaging principles is also included.

Two other points are made: (1) The self-help component of a student's package may be increased as he or she advances academically. This principle, of course, relates to the investment of the student in his or her education. (2) In the self-help component, the student should, if possible, have a choice between loan and work.

Although traditionally student aid policy has in most institutions been made at the operational level—that is, by the financial aid administrator—recent developments have focused the attention of chief executive officers and governing boards on this subject. William Clohan, former undersecretary of the Department of Education, in a recent interview in the *Higher Education Management Letter,* was asked the following question: "If you were named university president or provost, and recognizing the constraints on federal funds, what steps would you take?" In response, Clohan said: "I would then familiarize myself with federal student aid programs, regardless of the institution's endowment size. I would select a first-class student aid officer and enhance the office. In the past, many student aid officers have been given short shrift. I believe the president and the student aid officer should be a team in the marketing of the institution. Student aid packaging is one of the best marketing tools available. The president can use this package to reach out to potential students. Too many students never look at the higher-cost private institutions, as they are unaware of the financing available" (Coopers and Lybrand, 1981, pp. 2-3).

The NACUBO monograph also encourages fiscal officers to increase their awareness of the relationship between governmental and institutional student aid dollars and tuition revenue and of trends in that relationship that will affect institutional health: "Student aid, through changes in enrollment patterns, can have a positive or negative effect on an institution's goals and mission. . . . Aid programs may be need based, as in most federal, state, and institutional programs, or awarded on the basis of merit in specified fields of study. Careful planning is needed to design a student aid program using federal, state, private, and institutional funds that will support, or at least not subvert, the institution's goals and mission" (National Association of College and University Business Officers, 1981, pp. 3-4).

The interest of admissions officers in financial aid packaging as a recruitment and retention device is obvious. The College Entrance Examination Board and the American Association of Collegiate Registrars and Admissions Officers (AACRAO) (1980), in a document entitled *Undergraduate Admissions: The Realities of Institutional Policies, Practices, and Procedures,* describe merit scholarships as an inducement for highly desirable students. "Another form of aid is the modified package which offers the sought-after student an unusually attractive combination of kinds of aid. The package is most likely disproportionately high in grant aid and low-interest loan and low in employment and conventional loan, although generally totaling no more than the estimated amount the student needs" (p. 42).

Sanford (1981) offers a contrasting viewpoint to the use of a modified package that provides a disproportionate amount of scholarship funds to highly sought-after students. He concedes that financial aid has generally facilitated access to postsecondary education for many who could not otherwise have afforded it; however, because of the loans that form part of the financial aid package, he questions whether the neediest of those recipients have been able to escape the cycle of poverty. He further suggests that employment offered to the neediest students *denies* opportunities for socialization and participation in extracurricular activities and, in effect, serves to ensure continuation of the domination of the middle and upper classes.

A contradictory view to Sanford's is presented by Astin (1975b, p. 63), who found a positive correlation between student success and persistence and part-time employment on campus of less than twenty-five hours a week. Astin attributes the positive effect of on-campus employment to the greater degree of student involvement resulting from that employment. In his analysis of various "packages" of financial aid, Astin found a negative correlation between student persistence and most combinations of loan, grant, and work. The only positive effect was between a package containing work-study and major (rather than minor) loan support. He suggests, in his summary (p. 71), the need for more in-depth study of the effects on student persistence of various combinations of aid, especially as they relate to race, sex, and parental income.

The Title IV Committee of the National Association of Student Financial Aid Administrators developed suggested packaging guidelines, which were published in the November 20, 1980, *NASFAA Newsletter* (p. 15). They are as follows:

1. All need-based federal financial aid awards shall be based on the results of a need analysis approved by the U.S. Congress.
2. The institution should award Title IV funds [first] to the students with the greatest need [whose applications are received by or before the institution's deadline date].
3. Each institution should develop student expense budgets reflecting direct educational and realistic living costs.
4. Each institution should develop a reasonable, expected contribution from summer or other employment earnings (including spouse) for all financial aid recipients before packaging aid.
5. Each institution should develop packaging policies that incorporate both "gift" and "self-help" aid on an equitable and consistent basis.
6. Each institution should make students aware of any specific packaging policies.
7. The Pell Grant should be used as the foundation program for all undergraduate awards.
8. The institution should ensure that the financial aid administrator is responsible for coordinating all resources received by each student as: vocational rehabilitation, CETA, BIA, veterans' benefits, Social Security benefits,

private, state, and institutional scholarships, and earnings from summer employment.

9. Financial aid award packages should be based on documentation considered necessary to validate the data provided in order to assure integrity and equity in all student aid programs.

10. Financial aid administrators have an obligation to provide students with the terms and conditions of their financial aid awards.

Although these guidelines met with the general approval of the aid administrators' community, questions were raised on some specific issues. Item 2 suggests that needy, late applicants may be eligible only for funds remaining after awards are made to those whose applications are received by the deadline date. It is a well-documented fact that disadvantaged students, among whom are a high percentage of ethnic minority students, are more likely to be late in applying for admission and financial aid than are middle-income students. Since increased access to postsecondary education for disadvantaged students is dependent on funds being available for those students, many institutions choose to hold back a certain percentage of grant and low-interest loan funds for late, needy applicants.

Criticism also has been levied against the words "the greatest need" in Item 2. Obviously, there is a vast difference between the net need of a single freshman dependent student and a married dependent graduate or professional student with dependents. The "greatest need" does not necessarily correlate with the "most disadvantaged." However, the emphasis should be determined by the institution and be in line with institutional policy.

In response to questions raised by aid administrators, Item 6 of the packaging guidelines, which states that each institution should make students aware of any specific packaging policies, refers in fact only to the specific packaging policy of *that* institution.

Item 8, which makes the financial aid administrator responsible for coordinating *all* aid resources available to students, is perhaps unrealistic. Certainly, the aid administrator is responsible for all funds that flow through institutional accounts and for all resources for which the institution provides certification of enrollment, such as Social Security and veterans' benefits. However, for some resources, such as off-campus employment, the aid administrator must rely on the student's own report.

Finally, guideline 10, concerning the obligation of the financial aid officer to provide students with the terms and conditions of their financial aid awards, might be improved by expanding the wording to include "or denial of aid awards."

Jay Snow, of Snow College, Utah, a member of the committee that produced the packaging guidelines, expressed the feeling of many aid administrators when he wrote in a letter to his fellow committee members in June of 1980: "Budgeting, need analysis, and packaging to me cannot be totally separated. Your budgets have an effect on how you have to package, the results of the need analysis affect the need, the individual situation may affect all three areas. However, I firmly believe in the financial aid officer having the discretion to package the award to best meet the student's particular situation, keeping in mind the overall goal of being as equitable to all recipients of aid as possible."

In summary, the literature reviewed presents some contrasting views on the packaging of financial aid, depending generally on the resources available when the views were expressed and on whether the author is relating a "student" or an "institutional" viewpoint. There are, however, several themes to be found. One is that the financial aid package should *not* exceed the amount of need of the student recipient. Obviously, when federal funds are used, this is imperative. The exception to this axiom is the non-need or merit scholarship made with private or institutional funds. Second, a financial aid packaging policy that is consistent with the mission of the institution and that is communicated to students is essential. Third, if retention is to be one of the goals of student financial aid, not only entering students but continuing students need to know what they can expect in the way of financial assistance. Finally, chief executive officers and members of governing boards of postsecondary institutions should become aware, if they are not already, of the effect of student aid on the health of their institutions and should include student aid in their fiscal planning.

Principles of Packaging

The first step in the development of a packaging philosophy is to know and understand the mission of the institution. Most colleges and universities have statements of mission that are long on rhetoric but short on concrete statements of goals and objectives. However, by asking certain questions, the financial aid administrator may be able to find other indicators of the institution's mission:

- What is the length of the student's program?
- Is the emphasis on teaching, research, or public service?
- What is the type, size, and control of the institution?
- Is admission to the institution open, selective, or competitive? If the institution is competitive, with whom does it compete and what are the pricing policies of those competitors?
- Is emphasis placed on undergraduate, graduate, or professional education?
- Does the institution serve primarily students from within the state or the district, or is the student body representative of the region and/or the entire country?
- Does the institution have a special commitment to serve disadvantaged students?
- Is this a four-year college or university with a large transfer population and a strong emphasis on research? Or is it a two-year junior/community college with both clock-hour and semester-hour programs, a four-year liberal arts college, or a professional school?
- What is the average age of the students? Are they traditional, college-age students, living in college-owned housing, or is this an urban institution with a heavy commuter population?
- Is the student population composed mainly of full-time students or of part-time students with full-time jobs and family commitments?

- What, in general, is the socioeconomic status of the families of the student body?
- Are most students first-generation college students, or are they the sons and daughters of college-educated professional/technical parents?
- What is the educational/career aspiration level of the student population?
- Do most of the students complete a baccalaureate degree and then enter graduate or professional school, or are they more likely to pursue a career immediately after graduation with a bachelor's degree?
- Are they vocational/technical students with a two-year program?
- In summary, what is the nature of the institution and of the students it serves?

An institutional policy might begin with a general statement such as:

- We believe that no qualified student should be denied the right to pursue the postsecondary education of his or her choice because of a lack of financial resources.
- We believe that student expense budgets should include the cost of tuition, fees, books, and a modest but adequate allowance for room, board, transportation, and personal items.
- We believe that the estimated family contribution provided by the uniform methodology is reasonably accurate, and we will not make across-the-board revisions in these estimates for the purpose of lowering the aggregate need figure.
- We will expect every undergraduate applicant to apply for the Pell Grant and will use the Pell Grant as the base of financial aid packages for all eligible recipients.
- We will make every effort to validate personal data supplied by applicants for financial assistance.
- We will award federal financial assistance in accordance with federal regulations and make every effort to protect against awards that exceed documented financial need.
- We will seek to identify and obtain maximum funding from

all available sources to meet the needs of students at this institution.

From this point on, the policy statement must become specific to the goals and characteristics of the institution. As an example: Big State U is a four-year, public, state-supported institution with a large endowment fund. It has a commitment to provide excellence in teaching, research, and public service to residents of the state in which it is located. Although, as a state-supported institution, its admissions standards are not rigorous, Big State has a commitment to recruit and retain the brightest and the best. Several of its colleges and departments offer scholarships to high-achieving, prospective freshmen, and Big State U is an institutional sponsor of National Merit Scholars. The aid policy of Big State U might also include the following statements:

> Subject to the availability of funds, we will attempt to meet the documented financial need of every aid applicant.
> Although priority consideration for federal assistance funds will be given to qualified undergraduates, financially needy graduate and professional students will be considered for College Work-Study awards and National Direct Student Loans as well as departmental and university-wide grants and fellowships, subject to the availability of funds.
> We believe that all students should make an investment in their education through self-help awards. We further believe that the further along they are toward their educational goal, the greater that investment should be. Therefore, financial aid packages for upper-division, graduate, and professional students should contain substantially more self-help resources than should those of freshmen.
> We believe that special attention should be given to students identified as disadvantaged rather than to those with cash-flow problems and that the financial aid awards of truly disadvantaged students should reflect that fact with substantially higher non-self-help resources.
> We believe that priority treatment, including modified aid packages with substantially higher gift

aid percentage, should be given to minority students and to academically superior students through the use of institutional scholarship funds.

In the event that funding is not sufficient to meet the needs of all financially needy students, the amount of unmet need should be assigned proportionately, with the neediest students being protected.

We believe that, whenever possible, students should be allowed a choice of working or borrowing to meet the self-help component of their financial aid award.

We believe that students who borrow should be limited to an amount that is congruent with their ability to repay, based on their career goals. We further believe that borrowers should be counseled and given regularly updated information with regard to their level of indebtedness and their repayment obligations.

We believe that institutional and state scholarship funds should be targeted to students who are residents of the state. We further believe that, in the spirit of the federal policy on choice as a goal, federal financial assistance should be awarded without regard to residency except as it affects student expense budgets and, therefore, financial need.

We believe that this policy statement should be reviewed by the Committee on Scholarships and Financial Aid on an annual basis. We further believe that it should be summarized and disseminated to students in the informational brochure prepared and disbursed by the Office of Student Financial Aid.

The principles of packaging might be summed up by the question "How much is too much?" In other words, for each individual student, is the total amount of aid offered enough to provide the student with his or her documented financial need? Further, is the form in which that aid is offered in the best interest of that student and of the institution? Will the student be able to accept the award, pay back any loans offered, work the number of hours assigned, and still attend to classwork and have some leisure to think and grow and learn from fellow students? Or is there too much of an unmet need, too many hours of work required, and too much of a loan for the student to accept and the institution to offer and still know that the student can take full advantage of the educational offerings of the institution?

Techniques of Packaging

The techniques of packaging are, simply stated, the tools by which the financial aid administrator carries out the packaging policy of the institution. As stated in the "Review of the Literature" section, there are several packaging concepts which are helpful in carrying out policy. The financial aid administrator's decision to select one or the other will probably be based on the resources available and the level of sophistication of computer and programming support. In other words, at a junior/community college with only federal assistance and manual processing, the aid administrator may resort to the ladder concept—adding work-study and loan awards to the Basic (Pell) Grant eligibility of the students, in order to meet need. Private high-cost institutions with available scholarship resources are more likely to require a self-help commitment from students in the form of institutional or Guaranteed Student Loans, and any remaining need will be filled by institutionally controlled scholarships, grants, and work-study funds. Equity packaging, probably the most sophisticated concept of packaging, is usually found in an environment with heavy dependence on computer support and with sophisticated programming assistance available. Such packaging might be compared to the art of filling to the top a group of test tubes that are already partly filled to different levels. The equity level, as determined by the financial aid administrator, can be a dollar amount or a percentage of the budget and can be adjusted for year in school, academic excellence, ethnic background, or other reasons as dictated by the packaging policy.

Bibliographical Note

The problems associated with the delivery of student aid are thoroughly discussed in the report of the National Task Force on Student Aid Problems (1975). The principle of equity packaging was first proposed in this work, and emphasis was placed on the development of a coherent packaging policy.

One of the major purposes of student financial aid has been to provide *access* to higher education for qualified, needy students—preferably, access to the institution of their *choice.* From the institutional point of view, financial aid offered in a timely fashion and in a combination or package that is attractive to selected needy students becomes part of an institution's *marketing* or *recruitment* strategies. The joint College Board–AACRAO (1980) publication *Undergraduate Admissions: The Realities of Institutional Policies, Practices, and Procedures* presents this point of view.

Preventing Students from Dropping Out (Astin, 1975b) is a classic that describes the relationship between student attrition and institutional policies on financial aid, employment, and residential arrangements. The chapters on financial aid and employment describe the impact not only of single forms of financial support but also of combinations (or packages) of aid.

An excellent description of the various forms of institutional aid and the purposes for which institutional funds may be used in support of students can be found in *Institutionally Funded Student Financial Aid* (Dickmeyer, Wessels, and Coldren, 1981). According to this work, institutional funds are used for several purposes—for example, to fund students with financial needs; to recruit scholars, athletes, and other talented students; and to provide work programs. The flexibility of institutional aid is stressed and formulation of policies with regard to student assistance is encouraged. The work also contains a number of references regarding pricing and college choice determinants. The national training project involving the United States Department of Education and the National Association of Student Financial Aid Administrators provides excellent technical training in the management of student aid, including the techniques of packaging.

8

Disbursing and Controlling Aid Funds

Donald R. Ryan

The final product of the financial aid delivery system is the receipt of the financial aid funds by the student consumer. From the student's perspective, actually receiving the funds is the most important part of the financial aid delivery system. The payment of funds to students involves different procedures for each type of aid allocated to the student. While the frequency and method of payment may vary from institution to institution, certain basic conditions must be met: (1) The donors of the financial aid funds—including federal, state, and private donors—are assured that the conditions under which their funds were granted to the institution are being followed. (2) The students who receive the funds are entitled to those funds. (3) Controls have been established in the disbursement process to ensure that conditions 1 and 2 have been met.

Internal Control

According to basic accounting principles, the most important control is an internal system that "consists of all measures employed by an organization to (1) safeguard assets from waste, fraud, and inefficient use; (2) promote accuracy and reliability in the accounting records; (3) encourage and measure compliance with company (donor) policies; and (4) evaluate the efficiency of operations" (Meigs, Larsen, and Meigs, 1977, p. 139). A carefully established system of internal controls in the financial aid process assures the donor that the funds are being administered as they were intended. It involves all steps of the entire financial aid process—including application, need determination, and packaging of the aid, as well as disbursement of the aid. Auditors of financial aid programs are usually concerned only with "internal controls of an accounting nature—those controls that bear directly on the dependability of the accounting records and the financial statements" (Meigs, Larsen, and Meigs, 1977, p. 140). Any discussion of internal controls in relation to financial aid must include not only accounting but also administration, organization, and operation of the aid office, as well as the training of its staff. Since the organization of the aid office and the training of staff are discussed in other chapters of this book, this chapter will discuss only those controls of an accounting nature as they relate to the internal operation of the office.

Federal funds have become the primary source of student financial aid. The Department of Education, which administers these funds, mandates that "an institution must establish and maintain an internal control system of checks and balances that insures that no office can both authorize payments and disburse funds to students" (United States Department of Education, 1981b, pp. 16-17). Small as well as large institutions must ensure that the functions of *authorizing* payment and *disbursing* funds are separated, so that no one person or office exercises both functions for any student receiving financial assistance—although the regulation does not require an institution to have two full-time individuals to award and disburse funds. For example, in a small institution the individual responsible for admissions, veterans' affairs, and services for disabled students could also *authorize* financial aid payments; the individual who *disburses* the aid could also have responsibilities for the institution's accounting functions, payroll, and purchasing functions.

In all postsecondary institutions, the student financial aid office will interrelate with many other offices in the institution, including the admissions office, the registrar's office, the alumni office, the placement office, the data processing center, the student counseling office, and the fiscal or business office. The interrelation with the fiscal office is the most critical, since that relationship is mandated both by federal requirements and normally accepted internal control procedures. As financial aid programs have increased in size and complexity, the interrelationship between the two offices and the sharing of like responsibilities have increased in importance. For example, because of the mandated requirement to conduct entrance and exit interviews for loans, the business office, on the one hand, is assuming more counseling responsibilities; the financial aid office, on the other hand, is increasingly being asked to reinforce fiscal responsibility and accountability by counseling with students regarding loan obligations. These two offices must work cooperatively to ensure that students receive their funds in a timely and efficient manner. The "team effort" between the two offices is most critical in the disbursement phase.

The Disbursement Process

As mentioned earlier, the disbursement process usually involves a different process for each type of aid awarded to a student. Normally, scholarships and grants are provided after the instructional term begins, with a check dispensed directly to the student; alternatively, if the institution has established an account for the student's educational and housing expenses, it can be credited by the amount of the award. Loan aid is provided in a similar manner after instruction begins, after the loan note and truth-in-lending statement are signed, and after the preloan entrance interviews are held. Campus employment, including the College Work-Study (CWS) program, is provided in the form of wages applied against the amount the student is eligible to earn. Paychecks are issued at least monthly or are credited to the student's account as wages are earned. Further information about the timing of disbursements and how they are made will be given later in this chapter.

The disbursement process involves several distinct but interrelated phases. The initial phase involves the securing or "drawing down" of funds from the donor—including the formal acceptance and acknowledgment of the funds by the institution. Normally, the fiscal office has the responsibility for "drawing down" the funds. Once those funds have been secured, the business office must be informed by the financial aid office of the amount of the funds approved for the student from each financial aid account. After the aid package has been formally approved and authorized, all costs to be made against a student financial aid package must be determined, including applicable tuition and fees; in-state, county, city, or district charges; residence hall fees; or other special charges. Outstanding bills to the institution—such as emergency loans, library fines, housing bills, overawards, bad checks, and other debts—might also be charged against the student's approved financial aid package. In such cases the financial aid office must ensure that aid funds approved for the current academic year are not being used to cover costs from a previous academic year. The final phase of the disbursement process is the payment of the funds to the student.

The Systems Approach. The actual method of disbursement of financial aid funds will vary with the size of the institution, the accounting system used by the institution, and the availability of computer or data processing support. As financial aid programs have increased in size and complexity, many institutions have developed sophisticated data processing support to assist with the disbursement process. Many institutions lacking the necessary institutional resources to convert their total financial aid operation to data processing have at least been successful in securing assistance from the computer in the preparation of checks for the disbursement process. At my own institution, even though we are not scheduled to convert our total financial aid operation to data processing for two or three more years, we found it necessary to acquire computer support for our disbursement process at an earlier date. With over 12,400 individual student checks to prepare at the start of each semester, we found it impossible to accomplish this task without data processing support.

Ideally, financial aid delivery would be accomplished through an integrated computer-assisted system in which each phase of the entire operation flows smoothly to the following phase. The application phase should flow to the award determination and packaging phase, which, in turn, results in the disbursement phase. Within the disbursement phase itself, the procedure should be (1) the "drawing down" of funds, (2) approval for expenditures from each aid account by the authorization of the individual aid package, (3) the determination of the obligation of charges against that package, and (4) the final crediting of the funds to the student's account or payment of the funds to the student by check. Converting manual financial aid operations to electronic computer-assisted operations is a time-consuming and costly task. However, if institutions, especially larger ones, wish to maintain the required internal controls and service students in a timely manner, such conversion is an absolute necessity.

Many commercial computer packages for the financial aid operation are now available. As institutions consider a particular program, they should determine whether it has proved adequate in service at other institutions and whether it is adaptable to the institution's special environment and needs. Institutions considering conversion to an electronic data processing system for financial aid are encouraged to review a recent article in the *Journal of Student Financial Aid,* which describes in detail the matters to consider (Pennell, 1981). Miller (1975) explains how Washington State University developed its initial computerized system. This system has since been expanded to include the total financial aid process. In addition to assisting with the disbursement process and the preparation of checks, it provides timely management reports, which include total financial aid offered, total aid accepted, and exact amount of disbursements. As financial aid funds become more difficult to secure, it is increasingly important that the institution know at all times the amount of uncommitted funds, especially since future federal allocation of funds is dependent on utilization of current funds. Timely status reports of disbursements will assist the institution in servicing more students. A monograph entitled

A Guide to Evaluating and Acquiring Financial Aid Software
(National Association of Student Financial Aid Administrators,
1983) provides an excellent review for institutions that are considering establishing data processing in their financial aid areas
and lists in detail all the factors to be considered by an institution before purchasing data processing software.

 The Voucher Approach. Many institutions have developed voucher systems to assist with the disbursement process. A
voucher normally eliminates the necessity for the preparation of
checks immediately following the beginning of each instructional term and serves as an excellent internal control to ensure
that students are actually registered before they receive their
funds. A system established at a community college in Georgia
helped to ensure that students were able to meet the immediate
costs of fees and book charges, yet provided the financial aid
office with the assurance that the students were actually attending classes before any checks were disbursed (Edwards, 1978).
The disadvantage of such a system is that students often must
wait several weeks before they receive funds to meet their other
living costs. Many institutions, particularly high-cost institutions, have established student accounts for individual students
and record there the total charges assessed students, including
tuition fees, room and board charges, and all other charges
billed by the institution. The total financial aid awarded the student is applied against those charges, and any balance of aid is
then disbursed directly to the student. Such a system must
clearly provide the student with a detailed record showing how
the aid was awarded and credited to the student account against
institutional charges. The system also should provide "a clear
audit trail of expenditures from source documentation to recording in accounting control records" (National Association of
College and University Business Officers, 1979, p. 48).

 The voucher approach, like any other disbursement system for student aid that an institution might adopt, must ensure
that the student receives the aid in a timely manner and is given
a detailed record of the expenditures and that there is a clear
audit trail of the expenditures. Since federal aid cannot be disbursed until after verification of the student's registration, and

since some institutions, particularly public institutions, require payment of fees at the time of registration, some financial aid offices have developed a system that guarantees payment of fees to the registrar or cashier's office at the time actual financial aid disbursements are made. Since disbursement often occurs after the registration process, such a system allows the financial aid student to complete the registration process yet still guarantees the payment of fees at a later date. At my institution the financial aid office guarantees the payment not only of registration fees but also of room and board fees for financial aid recipients who live in the residence halls. This system requires careful monitoring of a student's financial aid package to ensure that there are sufficient funds in the package to cover the costs guaranteed. Every effort should be made by an institution to develop some type of procedure to provide payment or guarantee of payment of institutional charges for financial aid recipients.

Pell Grant Disbursements. Under the federal Pell Grant (Basic Grant) program, there are two systems through which a student can be paid a Pell Grant award: the regular disbursement system and the alternate disbursement system. The regular disbursement system provides the institution with extensive control of the student's funds, ensures that the student will receive the funds in a timely manner, and enables the institution to coordinate the Pell Grant award with other institutional aid. The institution enters into an agreement with the Department of Education to act as an agent in disbursing Pell Grant funds to eligible students. The institution agrees (1) to determine the eligibility of students to receive awards; (2) to compute the amount of the Pell Grant according to the program regulations and the payment schedule provided by the secretary; (3) to validate, verify, and document the information on the Student Aid Report for students selected for validation by the Department of Education; (4) to pay the funds to the student; (5) to recover award overpayments; and (6) to maintain records and accounting of funds.

The Department of Education provides the participating institution with a payment schedule that allows the institution to determine the amount of Pell Grant for which the student is eligible, depending on the approved costs for the institution and the student's eligibility index. To determine this eligibility index, the Department of Education uses a system of need analysis approved by Congress. The payment schedule is based on expected family contribution schedules, attendance costs at the institution, and the amount of federal funds available in a given fiscal year for making Pell Grants. In addition, the institution receives disbursement schedules showing the grant amounts that full-time, three-quarter-time, and half-time students would receive for an academic year. Funds for Pell Grants are sent by the Department of Education directly to the participating institution in advance of the start of each academic term. The amount is based on an estimate of the institutional needs for that period. The institution makes payment directly to the student or credits the student's account. The payment may not be made to a student until a student is registered for that term. The earliest an institution can directly pay a registered student is ten days before the first day of classes of a payment period. The earliest date an institution can credit a registered student's account is three weeks before the first day of classes in a payment period. The participation agreement also specifies that unused or repaid funds must be returned to the federal government and provides procedures for notifying students of their scheduled award.

If an institution does not wish to participate in the regular disbursement system, it may select the alternate disbursement system as a method to calculate and pay Pell Grant awards. This system involves an extra step for the student and, as a result, takes longer than payment through the regular disbursement system. As with the regular disbursement system, institutions participating in the alternate disbursement system must enter into an agreement with the Department of Education. The student submits the Student Aid Report to the institution; the institution, in turn, requires the student to complete the Request for Payment of a Pell Grant award form, which includes the Affidavit of Educational Purpose, and return it to the institution. The institution certifies the form, signifying that the student meets the eligibility criteria, is maintaining satisfactory academic progress, does not owe a refund on any federal aid programs, and is not in default on any National Direct Student Loan or Guaranteed Student Loan at that institution. The student then returns the completed and certified form to the Department of Education, which makes payment directly to the student. The institution also agrees to maintain records on Pell Grant recipients, including enrollment costs and the period of enrollment. These records must be made available to the Department of Education on request by the department. The alternate disbursement system provides a much easier process for the institution than the regular disbursement system, although students must wait much longer to receive their funds and the institution cannot as easily coordinate the Pell Grant with other institutional aid funds.

Disbursement of Campus-Based Funds. The Supplemental Educational Opportunity Grant (SEOG) and the National Direct Student Loan (NDSL) programs also have a number of specific requirements that must be met before funds can be disbursed. Before making a payment for either program, the institution must get written acceptance of the grant and/or loan from the student and provide a statement to the student explaining the nature and source of other aid made available through the institution, as well as the continuing eligibility requirements for SEOG or NDSL—namely, that the student must maintain satisfactory academic progress according to the institution's published standards and must continue to be able to demonstrate financial need for the funds. The student must also have on file at the institution a signed statement of educational purpose, in which the student declares that the funds will be used solely for educational expenses in connection with attendance at the institution.

Both the SEOG and NDSL programs require any institution that uses a semester, trimester, or quarter system to allocate an equal portion of the funds to the student each academic term (each academic term comprises a payment period). Within each payment period, an institution may pay the student at such times and in such amounts as it determines best meets the student's needs. Before an institution makes its first advance to a student receiving an NDSL, it must provide the borrower with a "truth-in-lending" statement that informs the borrower of his or her obligation to repay the loan and clearly explains all the conditions of the loan, including the repayment terms, the interest rate, the minimum monthly payment, the maximum number of years in which the loan must be repaid, a definition of default, and the consequences to the borrower if he or she should default.

Disbursement under the College Work-Study (CWS) program should normally be made in the same manner as the payments to students working in other positions on campus. An institution must pay students at least once a month by check or by other similar instruments that students can cash by their own endorsement. If an institution pays CWS students in some form other than individual checks, there must be a method established for the student to endorse the document. The institution must have documentation in its files to show that the students actually received payment in the amount charged to the program. There must be a clear audit trail of all transactions. An additional consideration with the CWS program is a monitoring function to ensure that students' earnings under the program do not exceed the amount allowed in the financial aid package. If such earnings do exceed the amount allowed, an adjustment must be made in the financial aid package: either an increase in the student's original budget (if unanticipated costs have been incurred by the student since the establishment of the initial budget) or a decrease in other aid. If earnings have exceeded eligibility and an adjustment cannot be made in the financial aid package, the excess earnings can be used as a resource in the next academic year. Since the employment-monitoring function affects the total financial aid package, responsibility for the function should be maintained in the financial aid office.

Another program that provides a major source of funds to students and requires disbursement of those funds by the institution is the Federally Insured Student Loan (FISL) or Guaranteed Student Loan (GSL) program. Even though the funds are provided directly from the lending institution, they are usually routed through the educational institution for disbursement to the student. Internal procedures within the financial aid office need to be established to ensure that the date of receipt of all such checks is recorded and that the checks are logged into a master control record. To be consistent with proper internal control procedures, the checks received by the financial aid office should be relayed to the fiscal office for disbursement. A record of the date of disbursement should be maintained. Some lending institutions make the check payable to both the student and the educational institution. In such cases procedures need to be established for endorsement of the check by the student; the check is then deposited to the institution's account, and another check is issued to the student from that account. An alternate approach would be for the institution to endorse the check and then release it directly to the student to endorse and cash. The institution must inform the lender if a student withdraws, fails to maintain satisfactory academic progress, or drops below the required number of academic credits. Procedures must also be established to ensure that unclaimed checks are returned to the lending institution in a timely manner, normally thirty days.

Disbursement of Nonfederal Funds. Disbursement procedures also must be established for nonfederal scholarships, grants, and stipends from sources within and outside the institution. As with the GSL program, a system of logging and monitoring the receipt of all checks must be established. Controls must be instituted to ensure that the donor's instructions for disbursement are followed and that the donor's gifts are properly acknowledged. State-sponsored financial aid programs sometimes require the establishment of additional procedures for disbursement of funds. For example, if tuition and fees are to be paid directly by the state agency, a system for the billing of that payment by the institution to the state agency must be established. Coordination of these sources of aid with all other institutional aid must be handled by the financial aid office, to ensure that students are not overawarded. Disbursement again should be made by the fiscal office.

Amounts and Timing of Disbursements. The method of disbursement developed by an institution will vary according to the type of data processing support available, the accounting system used, and available staff. Depending on the type and the source of funds, certain controls are required. Once the institution decides on the type of disbursement system it will use, it must then decide how often disbursement will be made, what amount students will receive at each disbursement, what priority will be given to different types of funds, and how students with special needs or emergencies will be handled.

Also, financial aid offices have the responsibility of counseling students on how to budget their available resources to meet their total costs during an academic period. The counseling function in the financial aid process is of equal importance to providing the funds required to meet the students' costs. The majority of financial aid recipients have never had the responsibility or experience of budgeting and paying monthly bills. In establishing its policy on the number of disbursements, the institution must keep in mind the financial circumstances of its financial aid recipients. If students receive their total financial aid funds at the start of each semester, will they be able to budget those total funds to meet the costs of the entire semester? Most persons would have difficulty in budgeting total funds and meeting total expenses if they were to receive their paycheck for the semester at the beginning of the semester. The frequency of disbursements during a term is a major consideration in the disbursement process.

The amount of funds students receive at each disbursement should be determined by the costs at the institution and the amount of the financial aid package. High-cost institutions might very well have only one disbursement, since tuition, fees, and room and board charges might be equal to or greater than the total amount of the financial aid award and all be due at the beginning of the term. The balance of aid may be sufficient to cover only books and supplies. In such situations the balance should be paid to the student directly at the beginning of the term. "For institutions that have no tuition and fees and no housing charges, more than one payment within the academic term may be desirable to avoid loss of funds to students who enroll, receive their aid, and then immediately terminate their enrollment" (National Association of College and University

Business Officers, 1979, p. 51). Some institutions grant a larger percentage of the funds at the start of a semester (such as 60 percent) and the balance at mid-semester, since the costs at the start of the semester are normally greater. Within the nineteen campuses in the California State University and Colleges System,* the following system-wide policy on the maximum amount of funds in any single disbursement was developed and agreed on: "Whenever the total of grant and loan aid from any term is to be $600 or more, disbursements shall be made at least two times per term. An exception is authorized when deductions from the total amount, such as fees, nonresident tuition, and campus residence hall charges, would result in a second installment of less than $100" (California State University and Colleges System, 1975, p. 54).

Another essential factor in the disbursement process is the order in which different types of funds will be disbursed. Should students first receive grant funds or loan funds or a combination of each? If there are funds, such as those from many state scholarship programs, designated for payment of fees only, those funds should be disbursed first. Otherwise, students should first receive entitlement awards, such as the Pell Grants. The National Association of College and University Business Officers (1979, p. 46) suggests four general aid categories for assigning funds: (1) grant aid awarded to the student for tuition and fees, (2) grant aid awarded for housing, (3) loan aid for tuition and fees or housing, (4) advance payments and advance deposits. Once the priority of types of funds has been established, the priority for assignment should be (1) tuition and fees, (2) housing, (3) the balance paid directly to the student for out-of-pocket costs.

Before any assignment to tuition and fees can be made

---

*In this and the following chapter, reference is made by various names to one of the systems of higher education in California. The official name of the system through the 1950s and 1960s, California State Universities and Colleges System, was changed in 1972 to California State University and Colleges System. In 1982 the current name, California State University, was adopted. To maintain accuracy of reference to the publications of the system, the official name of the system *at the time of publication* is the one that is used in reference citations.

for Pell Grant recipients, it is necessary to determine whether the student will be full time, three-quarter time, or half time, since the amount of fees is normally affected by that status. Once the priorities for the order of funds and the assignment of those funds against charges is established, it is a simple step for institutions that have a computer-assisted disbursing system to build those parameters into the process.

Notification of Disbursement. After the institution has decided how it will handle all phases of its disbursement process, it must notify the students of that process, so that they will know exactly how they will receive their funds. Normally, students are notified by a disbursement schedule that includes all the required information: how and when students will receive their funds; where the funds came from; whether any of the funds will be applied against tuition, residence hall fees, or other assessed charges; and whether the balance of financial aid funds, if any, will be released directly to the student. The disbursement schedule also informs the student of any deadline dates for claiming financial aid funds. This deadline date is especially important, since the financial aid office must know at an early date if for any reason students cancel their registration or fail to register. If these funds remain committed for the academic year, the institution often is unable to award them to other qualified students. The disbursement schedule must be as clear and concise as possible, and students must be given an opportunity to obtain clarification on any item that they do not understand.

Refunds and Repayments

If financial aid funds have been disbursed to a student, and the student then withdraws from the institution, a procedure must be established to return the funds to the accounts from which they were paid. If a student is entitled to a refund, the funds should be credited to the aid accounts that were used in assigning aid funds to the institutional charges. The amount of the refund should be prorated among the various aid funds as they were applied to institutional charges. Federal regulations specify a formula that must be used by institutions in prorating funds returned to Title IV student aid accounts. The regulations also state that the portion of a refund allocated to a specific program may not exceed the amount a student received from that program. The institution must also return any portion of the GSL funds a student received to the lender.

In 1978 the Department of Education suggested the establishment of a federal regulation requiring a refund policy for any institution participating in federal student assistance programs. The department was concerned about the potential for misappropriation of federal funds, since some institutions did not have a refund policy. The National Association of College and University Business Officers (1979, pp. 52-53) responded by preparing a detailed set of policy guidelines to assist institutions in establishing a refund policy. Those guidelines were reviewed and approved by most of the other appropriate educational associations and recommended for use by their members. Because the postsecondary education community developed its own procedures for refunds, the Department of Education withdrew its proposal for a statutory regulation.

Whatever refund policy is established by an institution, that policy should be well publicized and uniformly applied to all students. The amount or percentage of the refund may decrease according to the number of weeks elapsed in the academic term. For example, if a student withdraws during the first week of classes, the refund might be 100 percent; if during the second week, 90 percent; if during the third week, 80 percent—and so on until a refund is no longer granted.

In addition to having a refund policy for students who withdraw, an institution must also have a procedure for repayments by students to the institution. Repayment may be required because a student has received financial aid funds and then withdraws from school or because a student's resources have increased and demonstrated need has been exceeded. The financial aid office is required to coordinate all resources of financial aid recipients. Frequently, after financial aid funds have been disbursed, financial aid recipients are approved for aid from sources outside the institution. This additional aid may result in the student's being awarded a higher total of aid than is needed according to the formulas that determine need. This condition is termed an overaward. If so, the original aid must be reduced to the determined need level. If the overaward occurs early in the term, and if the student has not received his total financial aid funds, an adjustment downward is possible. If a student has already received his total aid, a repayment may be required. For a student withdrawing from classes, the amount of the repayment due is normally calculated from the last recorded day of class attendance. The distribution of the repayment funds to the Title IV student aid accounts is handled in the same manner as refunds. If a repayment is required, the student should be told why the aid must be repaid and when it must be repaid. Repayments must be recorded in the accounting office. The financial aid office cannot approve the student for aid in subsequent academic terms until the repayment has been made.

Audits and Program Reviews

Federal regulations require institutions that participate in Title IV programs to be audited at least once every two years. One of the primary objectives of the audit is to determine whether "the institution has implemented and utilized financial and other administrative procedures and internal controls to effectively discharge management responsibilities and to protect the federal interest" (United States Department of Education, 1980a, p. 4). The importance of separation of functions between the financial aid office and the fiscal office was emphasized earlier. Every aspect of the operation of the financial aid office and the fiscal office should be reviewed to determine whether controls have been implemented to ensure compliance with donor requirements and to safeguard against waste, fraud, and inefficient use. Experienced financial aid administrators and fiscal officers welcome the biennial audit because it provides an opportunity to assess and evaluate their operation. Whenever possible, financial aid offices should secure institutional internal audits of the total financial aid operation. These internal audit reviews are to be differentiated from the biennial audits required by the Department of Education. "Some institutions have highly skilled internal audit staffs which can provide management services well beyond an evaluation of internal controls" (National Association of College and University Business Officers, 1979, p. 101). Whereas the normal audit concerns itself primarily with the internal controls of an accounting nature, the internal audit can review the total "administrative" controls within the financial aid office. The internal auditor is not involved in the daily operational activities of the financial aid office and, as a result, is able to review the total administrative controls in an objective manner. "As a specialist in management control, the auditor evaluates systems to identify current or potential weaknesses, and recommends improvements to avoid, as well as to correct, problems" (National Association of College and University Business Officers, 1979, p. 102).

In addition to regular and internal audits, the Department of Education periodically conducts program reviews concerned with the total operation of the aid office in institutions that participate in federal programs. The Western Association of Student Financial Aid Administrators has established a financial aid consulting service, which provides experienced financial aid administrators who conduct comprehensive program reviews of an institution's financial aid program. The National Association of Student Financial Aid Administrators (NASFAA) can also recommend qualified, experienced aid administrators throughout the country to conduct program reviews. (NASFAA can be contacted at 1776 Massachusetts Avenue N.W., Washington, D.C. 20036.) Institutions generally find the review by independent financial aid administrators less threatening than a review by the Department of Education. However, institutions that prefer a program review by the Department of Education can request one by contacting their regional Department of Education office.

Procedures for Ensuring Student Eligibility

While some of the internal controls established in an institution's financial aid office are mandated by federal regulations or donor policies, others are simply good management procedures to ensure the efficiency of the operation. Before awarding any funds to students, the financial aid office must make sure that the student has met every eligibility requirement and is fully qualified to receive the aid. If the financial aid process is separate from the admissions process, as it is at most public institutions, the financial aid office must at some point make sure that the student who has been authorized aid has been officially accepted for enrollment at the institution. This verification of acceptance is especially important at community colleges, which have an open enrollment period and a continuous admissions policy. At all institutions, but especially those that have a separate admissions and financial aid process, the student should be informed that the offer of financial aid is dependent on acceptance to the institution by the admissions office. If the institution has an integrated data processing system, verification of acceptance before disbursement can be done through the student master record file. In any case, the financial aid office must have proof that the student is registered and must know the exact number of units for which the student is enrolled, since the number of units affects the extent of the student's eligibility for certain aid programs and the actual amount of the student's aid. If the institution has multiple disbursements, the verification of the number of units for which a student is enrolled must be completed prior to each disbursement, to ensure that the student continues to carry the required number of units and has not withdrawn or dropped classes.

Further procedures require that the student's aid be properly authorized and that the aid be accepted in writing by the student. An Affidavit of Educational Support signed by the student, certifying that the aid will be used only for educationally related expenses at that institution, must be on file. The student must also file Financial Aid Transcript forms from all other postsecondary institutions attended. Those transcripts must be screened to determine whether the student is in default on any previous loans or whether any repayments are owed. The fiscal office within the institution also must be asked to verify that the student is not in default on any loan at that institution and does not owe any repayment. The transcript also serves as a method to determine the amount of eligibility the student has utilized for certain funds. Finally, to ensure that the correct student is actually receiving the aid, the disbursing agent must obtain positive identification from the student.

One of the conditions for students to continue receiving aid from any of the Title IV programs is that the student "is maintaining satisfactory progress in the course of study he or she is pursuing according to the standards and practices of that institution." The financial aid office must be able to monitor the academic progress of all financial aid recipients, to make sure that the students receiving funds are making progress toward their educational objective and are not merely attending classes with no specific goal in mind. The basic purpose of financial aid is to enable students to attain their educational goals.

Normally, students are regarded as "maintaining satisfactory progress" if they are in good standing as either full-time or half-time students; have completed a required number of units, as defined by the institution; and are enrolled at the time of subsequent disbursements. NASFAA and the American Association of Collegiate Registrars and Admissions Officers (AACRAO) have developed guidelines for institutions to use in establishing satisfactory academic progress standards for students receiving federal financial aid assistance. These guidelines were accepted by the American Council on Education (ACE) and recommended by that organization to all its member associations and institutions. The Department of Education stated in 1980 that it will propose a federal regulation identical to the standards adopted by ACE. A copy of the "satisfactory progress" guidelines can be obtained from ACE, One Dupont Circle, Washington, D.C. 20036, or from NASFAA or AACRAO.

Student and Institutional Records

The focal point of all the internal controls for students on aid is the student master record, whether manually filed in a folder or stored on magnetic tape. Student master records serve several purposes. First, they contain the documentation needed to determine eligibility for aid. Second, they furnish the information for reports to donors of the student aid funds. Third, they establish a clear audit trail. The records must show that the funds were awarded to qualified applicants, that the recipients received all of the funds to which they were entitled, and that all student aid funds can be accounted for. The final purpose of maintaining student records is to provide data for the research necessary to help the financial aid administrator evaluate the effectiveness of aid programs and to make policy decisions. The length of time student records must be retained as active or storage files at the institution may vary from one institution to another. Institutions receiving federal student aid funds are required to retain student and institutional records for a period of five years following the submission of the annual fiscal report for a program unless a longer retention period is necessitated because of audit questions. National Direct Student Loan files must be retained until the loan has been repaid.

In addition to student master records, complete and accurate institutional records or source records are essential to ensure that all the basic principles of internal control are being met. No office within the institution has more need for thorough source records than the student financial aid office. Let us consider the different types of records that must be maintained. Since the majority of student aid funds come from the federal government, copies of enacted legislation should be readily available for those federal programs in which the institution participates. In addition, legislation for state-sponsored aid programs should be retained. A list of all federal legislative acts can be obtained from the regional office of the Department of Education or from the NASFAA office in Washington, D.C. In addition to the legislation, the administering agency of a program issues administrative regulations, which must be readily available. Copies of all institutional agreements between the institution and administering agency must be retained. Copies of all documents submitted to a federal or state agency must be maintained for at least five years following the submission of an annual operating report on a program, or, in the case of an audit exception, until relevant questions are resolved. All applications for funds, including all the required documentation that was used to support the funds requested, should be on file. Federal student aid programs require the submission of the following periodic operating reports: Pell Grant progress reports, annual student validation roster for Pell Grants, GSL confirmation reports, NDSL reports on defaulted loans, Law Enforcement Education Loan Program certification sheets, Nursing Student Scholarship Program annual reports, and Health Professions Student Loan Program annual operating reports. Copies of all reports should be maintained, as well as official letters of authorization containing the amount of funds awarded to the institution. All these materials are required as a part of the review for the audit. Copies of all audit reports, official correspondence, and responses must be retained. It is also important to maintain a complete record of all originating documents that describe the conditions of donor scholarships (National Association of Student Financial Aid Administrators, 1978b, *Record Maintenance Phase*, pp. 27-39). Finally, to assist with the institution's initial application for federal funds as well as to ensure proper utilization of all funds received, a historical data base should be maintained on the demographic characteristics of the student population.

The financial aid office must organize its records in an orderly manner. The management guide developed by NASFAA suggests that a record-keeping system must fulfill three specific needs: (1) The system must provide for the internal informational needs of the institution. Information on what has happened in the past is helpful in projecting the future. (2) The system must provide institutional administrators with a means of measuring and controlling the financial aid operation. It must assist the aid administrator with daily management of the aid office. (3) The system must provide for the external information needs of the institution—that is, all the information required for reports to the federal government and to private donors (National Association of Student Financial Aid Administrators, 1978b, *Record Maintenance Phase*, pp. 23-26).

Bibliographical Note

The *Institutional Guide for Financial Aid Self-Evaluation* (National Association of Student Financial Aid Administrators,

1982b) should be in the library of all offices of financial aid. This essential work, first published in 1977, has been updated and revised in 1978, 1979, 1981, and 1982; the edition cited here is the fifth.

Principles of Auditing (Meigs, Larsen, and Meigs, 1977) is, in my view, the most generally useful and accessible book on auditing now available to student aid administrators. It approaches the subject of auditing from a fundamental perspective; yet it is more than sophisticated enough for the depth of knowledge required by the aid administrator. Other helpful books on audits are the audit guides of the United States Department of Education (1980a, 1981a).

Part Three

Ensuring Effectiveness
in Administering
Aid Programs

In a function as complex and important as student financial aid, the effectiveness of an institutional program is dependent on adequate numbers of properly trained staff, the logical organization of the aid office, the place of the office in the institutional structure, and the measures adopted to evaluate program effectiveness and efficiency. Chapters Nine through Twelve deal with these subjects.

In Chapter Nine Donald Ryan describes the various staffing formulas currently being used in financial aid offices, distinguishing among counseling, technical, and clerical positions. He also discusses such methods of supplementing staff as the use of peer counselors. Finally, he furnishes very detailed information on how the personnel of the financial aid office may

191

secure in-service and other training to equip these staff members to carry out their functions more efficiently and sensitively. Ryan, long in the forefront of those creating opportunities for the professional development of the aid administrator, offers numerous recommendations on materials and programs that can be of benefit in these training efforts. He notes that the profession has largely developed its own training function rather than using formal certification procedures such as examinations or the attainment of graduate degrees.

In Chapter Ten Merle Lange, a veteran community college student aid officer, briefly describes how student financial aid evolved into a centralized function on campus and identifies the various factors that influence the organization of the typical student aid office. These factors include the influence of the traditional counseling approach to student aid, the nature of the student population to be served, the management style of the office's chief aid officer, and the expectations of the administrator to whom the chief aid officer reports. Lange also discusses the impact of recent technology on office operations. He describes two of the most common types of office organization, the programmatic and the functional, and suggests that under current conditions the office might serve students best as a "networking" or coordinating function which interrelates closely with other student services, such as counseling, placement, veterans' advisement, and the business office. Finally, he explains how the office's location and appearance can affect service to the student clientele.

Almost inseparable from the determination of how the financial aid office itself is organized is the matter of where it should be situated in the institutional structure. The authors of Chapter Eleven, D. Bruce Johnstone, a university president who has also researched and written extensively on student aid, and Robert Huff, student aid administrator at a leading private university, treat the long-debated issue of whether student aid is logically a part of the business function or the student service function of an institution. They then stress the importance of communication and move on to identify critical institutional matters with which the aid administrator will need to be involved. Johnstone and Huff also provide a description of what the senior management of an institution should expect of the individual who is selected to administer the aid program, and they emphasize the need for senior officers and other policy makers to remain involved with the program. Their discussion of the role of the aid office in key functions and policies of the institution provides a unique basis for further systematic study of organizational placement of student aid. They present a valuable matrix that interrelates functions such as budgeting, enrollment planning, and governmental relations with institutional policy issues and the role of the aid officer and senior administrators and others. Finally, they remind the reader that the aid officer is, after all, an educator who should not lose sight of his or her vital role in providing students with an opportunity for postsecondary education.

Stressing that evaluation is fundamental to proper management, Dallas Martin, executive director of the National Association of Student Financial Aid Administrators, gives in Chapter Twelve a detailed description of the four usual ways in which an institution's program can, and in certain instances must, be evaluated. These include self-evaluations, peer reviews, mandated program reviews, and audits. Stressing the need for these reviews to take place on a continuing and systematic basis, Martin deals with the differences among the four types. He also suggests several other measures, beyond the more formal types of evaluation, that can help the institution gain the maximum contribution from its student aid program. One such measure is the evaluation of technology—specifically, computerization—as a tool for increasing efficiency. Another is goal-oriented evaluation—that is, evaluation of the extent to which the aid office advances the mission and goals of the institution.

9

Staffing the Aid Office and Improving Professional Expertise

Donald R. Ryan

Prior to 1958 very few separate offices of financial aid existed at postsecondary institutions. Separate financial aid offices at public institutions and at many independent institutions were not needed, since the limited funds were administered by other offices within the institutions. The incredible growth of financial aid programs and funds between 1958 and 1965 resulted in increased responsibilities and work loads within college and university financial aid offices. The impetus of the federal government programs initiated during this period accelerated the establishment of separate financial aid offices.

With the establishment of the National Defense Student Loan (NDSL) program in 1958, the College Work-Study (CWS) program in 1964, and the Educational Opportunity Grant (EOG) program in 1965, the need for an office in each institution to administer those programs became readily apparent. Regulations for the EOG required that colleges and universities applying for funds under the EOG program must provide the necessary administrative support: "In undertaking to support students with Educational Opportunity Grants, the institution also explicitly agrees to provide the administrative support necessary to operate the program. Failure to provide administrative support through trained, competent professional and clerical staff may result in depriving students of EOG funds urgently needed to finance an education or result in unauthorized expenditures which must be repaid by the institution. Institutions are therefore advised to consider carefully the additional responsibilities, as well as the additional opportunities which they may afford students, before entering the Educational Opportunity Grant program" (United States Office of Education, 1966, p. 6).

Consequently, separate offices of financial aid were established on many campuses and became the norm rather than the exception. Public institutions, which had relatively few financial aid programs and dollars prior to 1959, began to realize the significance of the development of federal programs and the potential impact on their student populations. For example, in 1965 the California State Universities and Colleges System (CSUCS), in order to coordinate the developing financial aid programs, established separate offices of financial aid on each of its campuses. As these programs expanded, almost all postsecondary institutions began to provide a small number of professional and support positions to administer the programs; however, it soon became apparent that additional staff was required.

Staffing Formulas

In developing staffing formulas for other areas, most institutions measured the work load against the number of full-time students enrolled. Since this basis for authorizing staffing positions was already established for other areas within the institution, it was also used to authorize new positions in the financial aid area. The initial staffing formula for financial aid developed in 1964 by CSUCS, for instance, relied entirely on total enrollment at an institution. The staffing formula originally proposed for financial aid for the system had been based on the number of applications and transactions, but that approach was abandoned and the enrollment variable was adopted, since it was the measure that had been used for other established staffing formulas within the system. But financial aid administrators soon began to realize that the enrollment variable alone (as it was then being applied) was not sufficient to determine the work load within the financial aid office. The enrollment variable did not produce adequate staff because it was being applied in the financial aid area exactly as it was in other areas. A ratio of one staff member per 500 or 1,000 students might produce adequate staff for the counseling or health service areas, but it did not produce sufficient staff for the financial aid area. College budget officers had difficulty understanding why there should be any difference in the staffing ratio for the financial aid area. However, auditors of financial aid programs soon began to recognize that financial aid offices were not sufficiently staffed to handle the work load required for the functions within the office. They also felt that additional staff was needed to ensure proper internal financial controls. In 1972 the chief auditor of the CSUCS Trustees Audit Team stated: "Many of the problems that have resulted in the financial aid area could be resolved if there were additional staffing" (California State University and Colleges System, 1972, p. 4). The *Governor's Task Force Study on Higher Education: Student Financial Aid,* issued in May of 1971, recommended that staffing standards reflect the aid office's actual work load (State of California, Office of Governor, 1971).

As mentioned, federal regulations mandate that institutions participating in federal student aid programs must demonstrate that they have the capability to administer the programs. One section of the "Standards of Administrative Capability," which is included as a part of the General Provisions of the Education Amendments of 1980, lists adequacy of staff as one of the criteria that the secretary of education must use to assess the administrative capability of an institution—specifically, whether the institution "uses an adequate number of qualified persons to administer those programs. In determining whether an institution uses an adequate number of qualified persons to administer these programs, the secretary considers the number of students aided, the number and types of programs in which the institution participates, the number of applications evaluated, the amount of funds administered, and the financial aid delivery system used by the institution" (45 Fed. Reg. 668.16(c), 1980). The basic question then becomes how the adequacy of staffing is determined. What may be viewed as an adequate staff at one institution may be insufficient at another institution. For example, the amount of data processing support available at an institution may influence the number of individuals required to perform all of the necessary functions.

Van Dusen and O'Hearne (1968, p. 26) originally suggested a staffing formula for financial aid based on the total enrollment variable; in the 1973 and 1980 revisions of their publication, however, they acknowledged the need for additional variables: "Most early staffing formulas were based on the number of students enrolled at the institution. Subsequently, formulas were developed on the basis of the number of financial aid recipients. It now appears that a more appropriate basis is the number of students who apply for financial assistance. It requires at least as much staff time (if not more) to process an application that must be denied, communicate that decision to the applicant, and assist in the identification of alternative sources of financing for him as it does to process an application that is ultimately approved" (Van Dusen and O'Hearne, 1980, p. 35).

Budget officers who have the responsibility of approving staffing positions for financial aid offices, and of including the required funds in the institutions' total budget to pay for the cost of those positions, prefer to use traditional staffing formulas. This approach has the advantage of being simple and straightforward. It addresses the total financial aid staffing needs at one time. There is no need to justify an extra position or prepare extensive budget presentations. The budget officials can merely look at the total full-time enrollment figures, make a decision, and move on to other matters. But realistic staffing formulas should provide a clear and concise method to measure the work load of an office and to establish new positions. They must, therefore, include variables that can be audited, justified, and verified. The work load in the financial aid area is quite different from that in other offices in the institution; therefore, the variables included in a formula for financial aid will differ from the variables for other offices. Those variables can change and must be reassessed periodically. The changing nature of those variables is illustrated in the following chronicle of the evolution of the staffing formulas for financial aid within CSUCS.

In 1973 I served as chairman of a task force committee comprised of directors of financial aid from within CSUCS. The committee had the responsibility of recommending changes in the staffing formula, which had been based solely on the enrollment variable. Additional work-load variables considered were the number of financial aid recipients, the number of applications processed, and the total dollar amount of financial aid expenditures. A detailed staffing work-load survey instrument was developed and completed by the financial aid offices at each of the nineteen campuses in the system. The results of the study clearly demonstrated that the staffing formula based on the enrollment variable needed to be expanded to include other variables. The set of revised formulas (which were not finally adopted until the 1976–77 academic year) included the following variables: (1) the dollar amount of financial aid expenditures for which nomination and/or selection of recipients was determined by the aid office; (2) the dollar amount of financial aid expenditures for all programs administered by the aid office, even if nomination or selection (such as for outside scholarships) was not a function of that office; (3) the number of financial aid applications received from new entering students; and (4) the total number of students enrolled for more than six units. The task force recommended that all input variables, with the exception of projected enrollment, reflect actual data for the most recently completed academic year. Since the budget process required aid offices to provide actual, rather than estimated, data prior to the beginning of the new budget year, the figures provided for the total dollar volume and the number of applications had to be taken from the previous year's totals. This resulted in a time lag of two years before staffing adjustments could be implemented to reflect changes in the work load as measured by the input variables. The formula was again adjusted in 1980 to include continuing as well as first-time applicants. In a paper describing the CSUCS staffing formula, Robinson (1981, p. 11) notes that the Middle Income Student Assistance Act of 1978 brought about increased work loads in financial aid offices: "It became apparent that the expansion of student eligibility under MISAA and the increase in loan funds being made available by private lenders were appreciably increasing work load in the financial aid offices. In January 1980, a proposal to augment the 1980–81 CSUCS budget for additional financial aid staffing was presented to and approved by the Board of Trustees. The augmentation request was based on a proposal to revise financial aid staffing formulas to reflect projected budget year input variable values as opposed to values that lagged two years behind actual work-load and staffing requirements. The staffing augmentation was incorporated in the final 1980–81 budget, and the formula budgeting procedures for financial aid were changed accordingly."

The financial aid staffing formula for CSUCS for 1980–81 was a three-variable formula: one component was related to enrollment; the second component, to total financial aid funds administered; and the third, to total applications received. The basic formula automatically established one director position and a secretary to the director for each campus. Additional positions were established according to three distinct formulas used to produce counselor positions, technical positions, and clerical support staff positions. Robinson (1981, p. 4) indicates that "the current 1980–81 financial aid staffing levels were generally regarded as adequate by the California State University and Colleges directors of financial aid." In my view, the formulas did provide adequate counselor and technical staff, but the clerical support staff formula did not provide sufficient staff to perform all the necessary functions in a timely manner, particularly in a manual system with little computer support. Tables 1–3 show the three-variable formula of CSUCS for counselor, technician, and clerical positions. These positions are in addition to the director position, which is automatically established on each campus.

The purpose of presenting the foregoing extended case

Table 1. Three-Variable Staffing Formula—Counselor Positions,
California State University and Colleges System, 1980-81.

A. *Component Based on Number of Regular Students*
0.5 counselor when 0–5,999
1.0 counselor when 6,000–12,999
1.5 counselor when 13,000–20,999
2.0 counselor when 21,000–29,999
2.5 counselor when 30,000–39,999
3.0 counselor when greater than 40,000

B. *Component Based on Financial Aid Funds Administered*
0.5 counselor when 0–$999,999
1.0 counselor when $1,000,000–$1,599,999
1.5 counselor when $1,600,000–$2,299,999
2.0 counselor when $2,300,000–$3,099,999
2.5 counselor when $3,100,000–$3,999,999
3.0 counselor when $4,000,000–$4,999,999
3.5 counselor when $5,000,000–$6,099,999
4.0 counselor when $6,100,000–$7,299,999
4.5 counselor when $7,300,000–$8,599,999
5.0 counselor when $8,600,000–$9,999,999
5.5 counselor when greater than $10,000,000

C. *Component Based on Number of Financial Aid Applications Received*
0.5 counselor when 2,500–5,999
1.0 counselor when 6,000–9,999
1.5 counselor when 10,000–14,499
2.0 counselor when greater than 14,500

Example: For a campus with 22,000 students that received 14,000 applications for aid and administered a program of $8,500,000, the formula would produce 8.0 counselor positions (students, 2.0; funds, 4.5; applications, 1.5 = 8.0 counselor positions).

Source: California State University and Colleges System, 1981, pp. 1-2.

study of formula development and the accompanying tables is threefold: First, except for Robinson's study, there is a nearly total lack of published material describing how an institution can effectively deal with the challenging dynamics of staffing in student aid. Second, the formulas presented here may well be directly usable by colleges and universities similar to those in the CSUC System; other types of institutions should be able to interpolate their needs, given the extensive narrative provided

Table 2. Three-Variable Staffing Formula—Technician Positions,
California State University and Colleges System, 1980-81.

A. *Component Based on Number of Regular Students*
    0.5 technician when 0-9,999
    1.0 technician when 10,000-15,999
    1.5 technician when 16,000-21,999
    2.0 technician when 22,000-27,999
    2.5 technician when 28,000-33,999
    3.0 technician when 34,000-39,999
    3.5 technician when greater than 40,000

B. *Component Based on Financial Aid Funds Administered*
    0.5 technician when $1,000,000-$2,499,999
    1.0 technician when $2,500,000-$5,999,999
    1.5 technician when $6,000,000-$10,000,000

C. *Component Based on Number of Financial Aid Applications Received*
    0.5 technician when 1,500-3,999
    1.0 technician when 4,000-6,999
    1.5 technician when 7,000-10,499
    2.0 technician when 10,500-14,999
    2.5 technician when greater than 15,000

Example: For a campus with 22,000 students that received 14,000 applications for aid and administered a program of $8,500,000, the formula would produce 5.5 technician positions (students, 2.0; funds, 1.5; applications, 2.0 = 5.5 technician positions).

Source: California State University and Colleges System, 1981, p. 3.

here. Finally, the wide dissemination of these formulas in this volume may provide a useful norm or basis that institutions can use to measure the adequacy of their staffing practices.

The work load in the financial aid office fluctuates and can change more quickly than the work load in any other office in an institution. Work-load increments can fluctuate as the result of a change in federal regulations or state regulations. In 1972, for example, the federal government mandated that institutions perform a need analysis for all applicants applying for Guaranteed Student Loans. This resulted in an immediate increase in the work load of the financial aid office. These changes in work load have taken place almost every year since that time, and indications are that they will continue in the future. Over

Table 3. Three-Variable Staffing Formula—Clerical Positions,
California State University and Colleges System, 1980-81.

A. *Component Based on Number of Regular Students*
    0.5 clerical when 0-5,999
    1.0 clerical when 6,000-7,499
    1.5 clerical when 7,500-9,499
    2.0 clerical when 9,500-11,999
    2.5 clerical when 12,000-14,999
    3.0 clerical when 15,000-18,499
    3.5 clerical when 18,500-22,499
    4.0 clerical when 22,500-26,999
    4.5 clerical when 27,000-31,999
    5.0 clerical when 32,000-37,499
    5.5 clerical when greater than 37,500

B. *Component Based on Financial Aid Funds Administered*
    0.5 clerical when 0-$999,999
    1.0 clerical when $1,000,000-$1,699,999
    1.5 clerical when $1,700,000-$2,499,999
    2.0 clerical when $2,500,000-$3,399,999
    2.5 clerical when $3,400,000-$4,399,999
    3.0 clerical when $4,400,000-$5,499,999
    3.5 clerical when $5,500,000-$6,699,999
    4.0 clerical when $6,700,000-$7,999,999
    4.5 clerical when $8,000,000-$9,399,999
    5.0 clerical when $9,400,000-$10,899,999
    5.5 clerical when $10,900,000-$12,499,999
    6.0 clerical when greater than $12,500,000

C. *Component Based on Number of Financial Aid Applications Received*
    0.5 clerical when 0-799
    1.0 clerical when 800-1,699
    1.5 clerical when 1,700-2,699
    2.0 clerical when 2,700-3,799
    2.5 clerical when 3,800-4,999
    3.0 clerical when 5,000-6,299
    3.5 clerical when 6,300-7,699
    4.0 clerical when 7,700-9,199
    4.5 clerical when 9,200-10,799
    5.0 clerical when 10,800-12,499
    5.5 clerical when 12,500-14,299
    6.0 clerical when greater than 14,300

Example: For a campus with 22,000 students that received 14,000 applications for aid and administered a program of $8,500,000, the formula would produce 13.5 clerical positions (students, 3.5; funds, 4.5; applications, 5.5 = 13.5 clerical positions).

Source: California State University and Colleges System, 1981, pp. 4-5.

the past twenty-five years, each new round of federal student aid legislation has produced additional work-load increments for the financial aid office. Any staffing formula that is adopted must be reviewed periodically to allow the work-load increments to be reflected.

In a study of Michigan financial aid staffing patterns, Petersen, Tatum, and Winegar (1977, p. 12) concluded that the "number of applicants" variable, as suggested in the 1973 Van Dusen and O'Hearne formula, should be expanded to include the number of "applications": "This 1973 statement seems to be based on the assumption that most applicants file only one application. However, a variety of 'applications' may now need to be processed for each aid applicant as a result of recent developments. These developments include Basic Grants [and] increasing school involvement with Guaranteed Loans. . . . Perhaps the time has come to measure the staff needs by application rather than by individual applicant."

Another input variable of staffing formulas that can change rapidly is the total dollar volume administered by financial aid offices. The Budget Reconciliation Act of 1981 reduced the total federal dollars available for the Guaranteed Student Loan program and the Pell Grant program. However, the work load in financial aid offices did not decrease as a result of the reduction in total federal dollars; it actually increased as a result of the new federal requirement that need analysis be completed for all Guaranteed Student Loan applicants with adjusted gross incomes above $30,000. The federal government also requires validation and verification of income of a certain percentage of Guaranteed Student Loan applicants. Total dollar volume can also be misleading as a work-load factor, since it does not necessarily require more work to award a large amount of money to a student than it does to award a small amount. Clearly, any staffing formula should not rely too heavily on total dollar volume administered.

Enrollment can also fluctuate, but a drop in enrollment may not necessarily mean a decrease in the work load of the financial aid office. Many postsecondary institutions in the United States are experiencing declining enrollments; yet, as a result of increasing costs for postsecondary education and the general state of the economy, they find that more of their students apply for financial aid support. Two institutions with the same enrollment may, as a result of costs of education and the economic backgrounds of their students, have a substantially different number of financial aid applicants. As with total dollars administered, a staffing formula should not rely too heavily on the enrollment variable.

What, then, are the best variables to include in the development of a staffing formula? The original approach of basing staff on the enrollment variable alone has not proved adequate (Van Dusen and O'Hearne, 1973). Other variables—such as total dollar expenditures, total financial aid recipients, total financial aid applications, and total enrollment—also present problems because they are not directly and solely related to the criterion of determining financial aid staff needs. In discussing the CSUCS study, Robinson (1981, p. 27) indicated that "despite general agreement on the part of campus aid directors and other California State University and Colleges administrators that the 1980-81 level of staffing generated by these formulas is adequate, it cannot be assumed that the input variables continue to be valid and reliable work-load indicators."

An environmental or contextual variable (as opposed to an input variable) of particular importance is computerized data processing: "Computerization plays an important role in the staffing issue but is definitely not a panacea for limiting the number of staff. . . . Depending on the [extent] of automation, computerization may quickly reduce the need for clerical work and improve accuracy, as for routine functions like award letters" (Anton and others, 1981, p. 13). Total staffing needs are not necessarily reduced as a result of data processing; however, the efficiency of the operation is improved, since information is more accurate and the processing of applications and notifications of aid packages to students are handled more quickly. Financial aid offices must gain data processing support to assist with the enormous amount of application documentation and paperwork required, since a budget including sufficient support staff to perform all the required clerical functions for a medium to large office probably would not be approved.

Perhaps, as the Michigan study suggests, the best input

variable to measure staff needs might be the number of applications processed (Petersen, Tatum, and Winegar, 1977, p. 12). As a result of the recommendations of special study groups, the California State University system (the name of the California State University and Colleges System was changed to California State University on January 1, 1982) is revising its financial aid staffing formulas to rely solely on the total number of application documents received by a financial aid office. The resulting one-variable formula developed for the California State University system's student aid director and counselor, technician, and clerical-secretarial positions is shown in Tables 4, 5, and 6.

Table 4. One-Variable Staffing Formula—Director and Counselor
Positions, California State University, 1982-83.

Formula provides 1.0 financial aid director per campus and additional financial aid counselor positions as a function of the number of various aid applications received.

General Formula

$$Y = Y_1 + Y_2$$

Where Y_1 = Financial Aid Director/Associate Dean
Y_2 = Financial Aid Counselors

1. Financial Aid Director/Associate Dean (for all campuses)

$$Y_1 = 1.0$$

2. Financial Aid Counselors (for all campuses)

$$Y_2 = \frac{SAAC}{1,070} + \frac{SAR}{45,750} + \frac{ISA}{2,790} + \frac{GSLA}{15,130}$$

SAAC = total student aid applications for California received for budget year; SAR = total student aid reports received from students eligible for Pell Grants for budget year; ISA = total applications for institutionally administered scholarships for budget year (for campuses that do not use a separate application form, the number of aid applicants whose files are evaluated in a separate scholarship process is used as a proxy); GSLA = total applications for Guaranteed Student Loans and Federally Insured Student Loans received for budget year (applications for auxiliary loans filed by parents, independent undergraduates, and graduate students are included in this total).

Note: The denominator figures on all the formulas are based on the results of system-wide work-load surveys.

Source: California State University, 1982, sec. 5.4.0, p. 1.

Table 5. One-Variable Staffing Formula—Technician-Level Positions,
California State University, 1982-83.

Formula provides 0.5 positions per campus and additional positions as a
function of the number of various aid applications received.

General Formula

$$Y = Y_1 + Y_2$$

Where Y_1 = Basic complement
Y_2 = Marginal complement

1. Basic Complement (for all campuses)

$$Y_1 = 0.5$$

2. Marginal Complement (for all campuses)

$$Y_2 = \frac{\text{SAAC}}{5,120} + \frac{\text{SAR}}{4,730} + \frac{\text{GSLA}}{32,850}$$

For explanation of SAAC, SAR, and GSLA, see note to Table 4.
Source: California State University, 1982, sec. 5.4.0, p. 2.

The three-variable formulas that appear in Tables 1, 2,
and 3 produce approximately the same number of staff as produced by the one-variable formulas in Tables 4, 5, and 6. Institutions must decide whether a multivariable formula or a single-
variable formula would best meet the staffing demands of their
financial aid office. If enrollment, the number of financial aid
applications received annually, and total dollar expenditures remain constant, a multivariable formula may be appropriate.
However, if those variables fluctuate annually, a single variable
based on applications might be more appropriate.

The 1980 National Association of Student Financial Aid
Administrators (NASFAA) study on staffing (Anton and others,
1981) investigated staffing patterns by function in relation to
the number of financial aid applicants. The study examined
three measures of work load: number of financial aid applicants, number of need-based recipients, and total dollars administered. The results of the study indicated that the number of
applicants demonstrated a much more consistent relationship
with staffing than did the other two factors. The study also
identified economies of scale in financial aid offices and the
level of operation at which efficiency is maximized. Some econ-

Table 6. One-Variable Staffing Formula—Clerical-Secretarial Positions,
California State University, 1982-83.

Formula provides 1.0 position per campus and additional positions as a function of various aid applications received.

General Formula

$$Y = Y_1 + Y_2$$

Where Y_1 = Basic complement
Y_2 = Marginal complement

1. Basic Complement (for all campuses)

$$Y_1 = 1.0$$

2. Marginal Complement

When SAAC > 4,500:

$$Y_2 = \left[\frac{4,500}{540} + \frac{SAAC - 4,500}{1,640} \right] + \frac{SAR}{4,770} + \frac{ISA}{2,070} + \frac{GSLA}{1,670}$$

or

When SAAC < 4,500:

$$Y_2 = \frac{SAAC}{540} + \frac{SAR}{4,770} + \frac{ISA}{2,070} + \frac{GSLA}{1,670}$$

For explanation of SAAC, SAR, ISA, and GSLA, see note to Table 4.

Source: California State University, 1982, sec. 5.4.0, p. 3.

omies of scale were found, particularly in the support staff functions. The results "of staffing averages at institutions categorized by numbers of financial aid applicants provides a gauge by which institutions may evaluate their staffing levels" (p. 13).

Additional Methods to Supplement Staff

Overtime and Temporary Help. The financial aid office, like other offices within the institution, experiences certain peaks and valleys in work load. Most financial aid officers would agree that there are no valleys but that some peaks are higher than others. Consideration should be given to alternate methods of staff support to assist the office during peak demand periods. Overtime can provide temporary relief; however, it is not recommended for extended time periods. Staff morale and productivity will both show noticeable declines with extended use of overtime. The cost of the use of overtime must also be considered in relation to the total operating budget of the office. Overtime salaries can quickly add up to prohibitive amounts. The use of temporary help and College Work-Study students is another alternative. This requires special training and supervision. Many institutions have identified a cadre of temporary help who wish to work only periodically and are willing to come to work during peak processing periods. Another alternative is to share staff with other offices in the institution. This "staff loan" process takes advantage of slack periods in other offices and will save the institution additional personnel costs.

Use of Peer Counselors. The benefits of students counseling students in financial aid offices have been documented by Stegura and Olsen (1978). A 1977 survey conducted by the National Center for Education Statistics showed that 79 percent of the higher education institutions in the United States enrolling undergraduates employed part-time staff in their financial aid offices. Thirty-three percent of the institutions reported that they used part-time staff for counseling students. The report also showed that over 10,000 students were employed in financial aid offices, and institutions generally rated their counseling services "adequate" or "very good."

As a result of findings from projects undertaken by the National Student Education Fund and the College Scholarship Service's Student Committee on Student Financial Aid Problems, the early drafts of the Education Amendments of 1976 contained a "provision which would have required every institution participating in the College Work-Study program to employ a specified number of students, related to the [full-time-equivalent] enrollment of the institution, for the purpose of providing financial aid information and counseling to enrolled and prospective students" (Tombaugh and Heinrich, 1977, p. 2). The final legislation did not include such a requirement; however, it did have a "Student Aid Information Service" section, which stipulated:

In order to assist in the expansion and improvement of campus student aid information services, the commissioner shall (1) survey institutional practices of providing students with complete and accurate information about student financial aid (including the employment of part-time financial aid counselors under work-study programs, hiring other part-time persons from the community, using campus or community volunteers, and communicating through use of publications or technology), collect institutional evaluations of such practices, and disseminate the information described in this clause; (2) convene meetings of financial aid administrators, students, and other appropriate representatives to explore means of expanding campus financial information services and improving the training of part-time individuals involved in such services; (3) whenever possible, include student peer counselors and other part-time financial aid personnel in training programs sponsored by the Office of Education; and (4) make recommendations to Congress, not later than October 1, 1977, concerning his findings and legislative proposals for improving the use and quality of services of part-time campus financial aid personnel.

A recent study by a student advisory group in Michigan (Petersen and others, 1978) provides an excellent description of how an institution might systematically develop a program of peer counseling in financial aid. The study group lists eight steps that must be considered before a peer counseling program is implemented: (1) identify the specific role of the peer counselor, (2) define the activities to be undertaken by the peer counselor, (3) decide on the method to remunerate the peer counselor, (4) establish a method to identify and select the students, (5) decide on a method to be used to train the students, (6) establish a method to evaluate their performance, (7) identify a physical location for them, and (8) establish a system to ensure confidentiality of the information with which the students will be dealing. The experiences of two institutions in establishing peer counseling programs in California (Morris, 1972) and Connecticut (Cunningham, 1981) are described in articles in the *Journal of Student Financial Aid.* These and other writings all stress the important support that student peer counseling can provide financial aid offices and the necessity for careful planning and training prior to implementation. The Coalition of Independent College and University Students (1980) has published a manual that can be used in the training of financial aid peer counselors. Copies of the manual may be obtained from the COPUS Research Project, 1730 Rhode Island Avenue, N.W., Suite 500, Washington, D.C. 20036. A further discussion of the training of peer counselors appears later in this chapter.

Training of Financial Aid Administrators

With the growth of the financial aid offices, there has been a corresponding need for individuals to administer those offices. The combination of skills required to function as a professional financial aid administrator is unique. The individual must be skilled in working with people individually and collectively and must also have good administrative skills to manage the funds, paper flow, personnel, and administrative budgets. The aid administrator must also have a high level of technical competence in areas such as program regulations, need analysis, packaging, and legislative processes. Although separate financial aid offices were being established at institutions in the mid-1960s as a result of the emerging federal student aid programs, there were no formalized programs at postsecondary institutions to train the administrators needed to staff those offices. As a result, the financial aid administrators, in the early stages of the profession, were drawn from many different backgrounds. In an early article on the training of financial aid administrators, Smith (1964, p. 90) noted the "remarkable diversity of backgrounds. To mention a few, there are men and women drawn from law, business, engineering. . . . There is at least one philologist, one high school principal, one retired officer from the armed services, one political scientist with a special interest in the Orient."

In a study of the training needs of financial aid personnel in Arizona, Fenske (1979, p. 11) describes some national problems in training for the financial aid profession: "There are no consensual professional standards such as those which exist in some education fields like counseling or teaching. . . . Neither are there competency-based measures like those reflected in state board examinations in professions like nursing or law." As a result of the lack of any formalized training program for aid administrators, on-the-job training has been the primary method used to train financial aid administrators (Petersen and Holmes, 1980). The financial aid profession, unlike most other student service professions, has not established any preservice programs. Consequently, completion of such formal educational programs has not been required for admission to the profession. Instead, the financial aid profession has been responsible for establishing its own standards of professionalism and in-service training programs.

Within a few years after its founding in 1954, the College Scholarship Service (CSS) began to provide training in the need analysis system developed by its member institutions to assess parents' ability to contribute toward the costs of postsecondary education. Through regional and national meetings, the membership of CSS developed program agendas that expanded the need analysis training to other areas of interest in the developing financial aid profession. These included student budgets, packaging of aid, resource development, and coordination of resources. In 1967 the American College Testing Program (ACT) developed a separate system of need analysis and began to provide training for financial aid administrators at institutions that used its system. The training programs of CSS and ACT were geared primarily toward need analysis, rather than the total administrative training of aid administrators.

Preservice Training. Formalized degree-granting training programs are still very rare in financial aid administration. Many postsecondary institutions have, however, included as a part of their curriculum for master's or doctoral programs (such as in higher education administration) a special course in financial aid administration or an internship in a financial aid office. For several years a special master's degree program in financial aid administration was offered at Loyola University of Los Angeles, but that program has since been terminated. Many recent dissertations for doctoral degrees have pertained to the area of financial aid administration, but the doctoral programs themselves have not focused on financial aid. Consensus has not been reached on what courses should be included in a graduate program for financial aid administration. In 1974 a group of doctoral candidates from Boston College, as a part of their doctoral studies, developed a curriculum model for a master's degree in financial aid administration (Delaney and others, 1974). The study recommended that any graduate program for the training of financial aid administrators must establish proficiency in a wide variety of skills—particularly skills in counseling, general administration and organization, and basic research. Because the technical aspects of financial aid administration are so complex, they are best taught by an individual who has experienced them. Since the profession is still relatively young and since financial aid administrators with extensive experience are still actively involved in administering their own financial aid offices, there has not been a cadre of professionals with sufficient time available to teach the technical courses. A recent proposal to obtain funding to finance training of financial aid administrators in California included a request for funds to support the development of a master's degree program in financial aid administration at two institutions in the state: "The curriculum would be developed jointly by a committee of experienced aid administrators and by the faculty of the schools of education at the two participating institutions. The program would be taught by the regular faculty at the institution and two aid administrators who would collaborate in teaching a combination of typical education courses, along with courses in the theory and practice of student aid administration" (Huff, 1981, p. 4). Financial aid administrators must provide the leadership in establishing formalized degree-granting programs in financial aid administration.

In-Service Training and Development of Materials. Because of the lack of formalized training, financial aid administrators began to band together to develop informal types of training. The need to share ideas and explore new approaches for managing the expanding programs led to the establishment of state and regional financial aid professional associations. These groups had as one of their primary goals the training of their members. A week-long summer institute for training of new financial aid administrators was held in 1964 at Indiana University under the joint sponsorship of that university and the College Scholarship Service. The workshop has been held annually since that time, with the Midwest Association of Student Financial Aid Administrators assuming the sponsorship in 1970. Other regional and state associations developed similar summer institutes.

The need for a core of training materials soon became apparent. In 1970 a group of financial aid administrators, through the support of CSS and later with support from the Office of Education, developed the first set of comprehensive training materials for financial aid training. In 1972 those materials were compiled into a manual by NASFAA, with the intent that they would be used as the curriculum for a national series of workshops. Even though they were not used for that purpose, they did serve as the basis for the development of further materials.

As new federal financial aid programs were established by Congress, the United States Office of Education began to sponsor training workshops to train financial aid administrators on program regulations. National workshops were held in 1966 to explain the purposes of the Educational Opportunity Grant program and to provide suggestions to institutions on how to administer the program. The Office of Education recruited full-time practicing financial aid administrators to assist with the teaching of those workshops. In 1973 the Office of Education expanded its support of student aid training to include fiscal officers at postsecondary institutions and high school counselors as well as aid administrators. Because the Office of Education did not have sufficient staff or background to conduct the comprehensive training, it contracted with a consortium of three professional associations to carry out that training. The consortium included the National Association of College and University Business Officers, the American Personnel and Guidance Association, and NASFAA. The training project has been funded each year since that time, and the agendas have been expanded to include not only programmatic items for specific federal programs but also the total aspect of administering a financial aid office. The Office of Education and the Department of Education, which superseded it, also sponsored and provided training workshops to explain the procedures that institutions must follow in order to participate in the federal student programs.

In 1977 the training committee of NASFAA agreed that a series of training modules needed to be developed that would cover the total range of training for the financial aid administrator. The committee members prepared a detailed syllabus for each of the six individual modules to be completed. They then contracted with five experienced financial aid administrators, who had assisted in preparing the original core of materials in 1972, to assist with the project. They also contracted with a graphic arts firm to ensure that the final materials were printed in a highly professional and usable format. The six modules prepared by NASFAA were (1) *Professional Development Phase,* (2) *Management Planning Phase,* (3) *Need Analysis Phase,* (4) *Awarding Phase,* (5) *Record Maintenance Phase,* (6) *Student Relations Phase* (National Association of Student Financial Aid Administrators, 1978b). These training modules were then used by both NASFAA and its affiliated regional associations in presenting workshops for its members. They were also used as the curriculum for several week-long summer workshops sponsored by regional associations and in programs presented under the national consortium mentioned earlier.

The federal government became further involved in training as a result of the Education Amendments of 1976. Because of the large amount of federal funds being approved for financial aid programs, Congress was concerned whether these funds were being properly administered at postsecondary institutions. In addition to the participation of traditional postsecondary institutions in federal student aid programs, proprietary/vocational institutions began to participate in increasing numbers after 1976. Audits of federal student aid programs indicated that, in many cases, the programs were not being properly managed.

The reason often cited by the audit reviews was the lack of experience and training of the individuals administering the programs. As a result, Section 493C of the amendments stated: "It is the purpose of this section to make incentive grants available to the states, to be administered in consultation with statewide financial aid administrator organizations, for the purpose of designing and developing programs to increase the proficiency of institutional and state financial aid administrators in all aspects of student financial aid."

Most of the states applied for and received funding through the Section 493C funds to establish training workshops within their respective states. The state agencies and the financial aid professional association in each of the states were jointly assigned the responsibility to assess the training needs in that state and plan training activities to address the needs that were not being met. Federal funding for these projects continued through the 1980-81 academic year but was not continued through the Education Amendments of 1980. Many innovative approaches to the training of financial aid administrators and staff were carried out through these 493C projects.

The training committee of NASFAA summarized in booklet form all the state projects for the 1979-80 and the 1980-81 years (National Association of Student Financial Aid Administrators, 1980). The state training project in Michigan developed a comprehensive questionnaire to assess the training needs in that state. In their responses to the questionnaire, financial aid administrators indicated that training programs funded under Section 493C (1) should not be limited to novices in the field, (2) should not be focused only on the newest segment participating in student aid programs (proprietary/vocational schools) but should include personnel from all sectors, (3) should coordinate all training activities, (4) should further develop preservice training opportunities and consider certification standards, and (5) should increase opportunities for development of peer counseling as an avenue of career exploration and preparation (Petersen and Holmes, 1980, p. 22).

Coordination of Training Activities. By the late 1970s, then, training programs included the national training project under the management of the consortium, separate workshops sponsored by the Office of Education, workshops sponsored by the need analysis services to explain the methodologies of their systems, workshops sponsored by state agencies to explain the administrative requirements of their programs, and workshops at the state level through the funding of the 493C legislation. Many of these training programs were beginning to overlap and to cause a great deal of concern and confusion on the part of the aid administrators for whom they were intended. They were all held outside the aid office and required the individual to be away from the day-to-day management and operation of the office. A need for coordination of all training activities became apparent. The training committee of NASFAA attempted to provide some coordination by establishing a national coordinating calendar. Every state, regional, and national group that planned any training activities was supposed to coordinate those activities through the central office of NASFAA. This plan was only partially successful, since there were no enforcing mechanisms to ensure that groups would cooperate. The national training project offered by the consortium also attempted to coordinate its activities through state financial aid associations and high school counselor associations. Because the national training project operated by the consortium was usually late in receiving federal funding to begin its programs, the dates for state-sponsored workshops had often already been established.

According to a 1977 survey of the profession, conducted by NASFAA, 84 percent of the respondents regarded the training programs being held at that time as adequate (National Association of Student Financial Aid Administrators, 1978a, p. 67). However, the profession must continue its attempts to ensure that training efforts of individual groups are not being duplicated excessively and that the financial aid administrator not be required to be away from the office for training purposes any more than is absolutely necessary. Since the requirements of administering a financial aid office are in a constant state of change, due to federal and state regulations, financial aid administrators must keep abreast of all current changes. It is, however, equally important that they be allowed sufficient time to manage the office properly.

Training Programs for Support Staff

A great many training programs have now been developed for the training of the professional financial aid administrator. However, very few programs have been developed for the training of the support clerical staff, who are usually trained on the job. The support staff, work-study students, and peer counselors are essential to the effective operation of an aid office. They are the "front line" of contact in the aid office for parents and students, and their proper training is vital to ensure that the office is fulfilling its purpose. A few state financial aid associations have established workshops outside of the aid office for the training of support staff. The states of Arizona, California, and Michigan established such programs through their 493C projects. Because support staff find it difficult to leave the office setting to attend training programs and because few training programs have been available, it is essential that training opportunities within the institution be established. Procedures manuals and desk manuals need to be maintained for each support staff function within the office, so that individuals can understand what they are required to perform and why they are required to perform the function. They are an important part of the financial aid team and need to know what financial aid is all about, how it fits into the structure of the institution, and what the institution is trying to accomplish with financial aid funds.

To assist financial aid offices with the training of the support staff, work-study students, and peer counselors, the training committee of NASFAA has developed a comprehensive training manual and workbook (National Association of Student Financial Aid Administrators, 1979). This manual is designed to be used in the financial aid office as part of the on-the-job training and is intended to give the support staff member a total understanding of the entire financial aid process.

The financial aid office also must sponsor informative meetings and in-service training opportunities for other campus offices whose operations require an understanding of the internal operating procedures of the aid office—specifically, the business, accounting, payroll, admissions, registrar's, and placement offices, as well as the counseling bureau.

Additional Opportunities for Professional Development

In addition to the numerous training materials, seminars, and workshops available for the financial aid administrator, the meetings of state, regional, and national professional associations provide excellent opportunities to keep abreast of changes in the field. Especially valuable for the continued professional development of a financial aid administrator is membership in the National Association of Student Financial Aid Administrators and its regional and state associations. The national organization, regional associations, and state associations all have a close working relationship with one another. NASFAA, which currently has an institutional membership of close to 3,000, was formed in 1969 to coordinate the effort to improve student financial assistance resources on a nationwide basis. From its inception, the association has sought to improve access to post-secondary education for the many needy students of this nation through coordinating a variety of efforts. It is governed by a national council composed of twenty-five elected members who have the responsibility of planning, organizing, and directing the activities of the association. To ensure an interlocking and close working relationship with the regional associations, twelve of the council's members are elected by the members of each of the six affiliated regional associations, and ten of the members are elected by the membership at large. The remaining members of the council are the immediate past president, the president, and the president-elect, all of whom are also elected by the membership at large. Various committees carry out the work of the membership, under the direction of three commissions: the Commission on Associational Activities, the Commission on Governmental Affairs, and the Commission on Professional Development. NASFAA has as one of its preliminary objectives the continual professional development of the financial aid administrator. Included as a service for its membership is a direct-access telephone line that provides a weekly recording of current activities in legislative and regulatory areas and other important notices.

The continued professional development of a financial

aid administrator is essential to ensure that the goals of an institution's financial aid program are being achieved. The foremost ingredient to that development is the continued and active *involvement* of the aid administrator in all the appropriate activities, training, and resources described in this chapter.

Bibliographical Note

To the best of my knowledge, no single publication in any form or length has previously covered the topic of staffing and professional development in student financial aid. Earlier in this chapter, I cited various journal articles and other sources that dealt with certain limited aspects of the topic. Here I will review the most noteworthy publications, which, in aggregate, give a comprehensive overview to the reader who wishes to pursue the topic.

The publications of NASFAA are a continuing, invaluable resource for professional development. The principal ones are (1) a *Federal Monitor,* which contains copies of regulations, congressional testimony, analysis, and other materials important to the administration of financial aid programs; (2) a *Newsletter,* which provides news and analysis of legislative and administrative activity of NASFAA; (3) a *Membership Directory,* a ready reference and communication guide to all members and federal and state agencies; (4) the *Journal of Student Financial Aid,* published three times a year, which includes articles on current literature, as well as reports on current research activities in the field; and (5) copies of all publications prepared by NASFAA's committees and commissions. Two such publications closely related to the subject of this chapter are the *Institutional Guide for Financial Aid Self-Evaluation* (National Association of Student Financial Aid Administrators, 1982b), which enables financial aid administrators to conduct an internal review of their operations to ensure compliance with regulations and legislation; and the *Guide for the Development of a Policies and Procedures Manual* (National Association of Student Financial Aid Administrators, 1982a). Also invaluable are the *Financial Aid Support Staff Training Guide,* published in 1979, and the

1981 publication *Fundamental Financial Aid Self-Learning Guide.*

Several news publications on financial aid provide timely information and analysis on developing legislation, regulations, and other areas of interest to the financial aid administrator. Most noteworthy are the *Student Aid News,* a biweekly news publication published by Capitol Publications, and the *Chronicle of Higher Education,* a weekly newspaper. Periodic newsletters from the College Scholarship Service and the American College Testing Program, as well as memoranda and monthly bulletins issued by the United States Department of Education, are also essential reading material.

10

Factors in
Organizing an Effective
Student Aid Office

Merle L. Lange

A critical question in financial aid administration is how a college or university can best structure its financial aid office. This chapter describes how financial aid offices have evolved, considers the factors that influence how the aid office is organized, treats the more prevalent ways in which most aid offices are organized today and, finally, offers suggestions about the physical appearance and location of the office. Obviously, for a small office with one or two staff members, what this chapter presents about how to organize may have limited applicability. On the other hand, location and attractiveness of the facility are relevant to any size operation.

Evolution of the Financial Aid Office

Prior to the enactment of the National Defense Education Act of 1958, only a handful of colleges and universities had moved to centralize in one office the administration of all the various financial aid programs and functions. The major reason why this was true is that massive federal and state aid, as we know it today, had not emerged. Just a few, mostly private, institutions—such as Harvard, Yale, Massachusetts Institute of Technology, and Stanford—had concentrated in a single office most aspects of the delivery of aid, at least to their undergraduate students.

Prior to 1958 and the beginning of the first sizable federal student aid undertaking, some financial aid resources were, of course, available to students at many four-year institutions, but their administration typically was the responsibility of a variety of individuals and departments on the campus. Awarding of scholarships, for example, might be in the hands of a faculty committee served by a scholarship secretary. At institutions where these kinds of awards were seen as having a significant recruiting value, the director of admissions was probably a key figure in the selection process. Loans, for the most part, were likely to be of a short-term nature and authorized by such student personnel officers as the dean of students, the dean of men, or the dean of women. They might alternatively be within the province of fiscal officers such as the business manager, the bursar, or the controller. Work opportunities on the campus were not considered an integral part of a financial aid program; therefore, campus jobs might be listed with the institution's placement service or a bureau of student employment. Perhaps the most important consideration was that the various individuals who administered student aid did not have it as their sole, or even their primary, responsibility. They performed a variety of other duties and were involved in part with student aid as it existed then.

With the advent of federal student aid programs, commencing in 1958 and continuing through 1970, most student aid resources and functions became consolidated in a single institutional office. Indeed, the federal government stipulated that one individual on each campus must be charged with the responsibility of coordinating all student aid. There are other factors, too, besides the specific insistence of the federal government, that promoted centralization. The advent of financial need as a major determinant in the awarding of financial aid, as promoted by the College Scholarship Service commencing in 1954, created the need for staff members who had the particular expertise and technical training to perform need assessment. As the cost of college attendance began to rise, senior administrators at many institutions perceived the need to bring together in one office the various financial resources available to help students meet these growing expenses. Higher costs, too, prompted more requests for help and hence correspondingly larger processing requirements.

Factors Influencing Organization of the Aid Office

While virtually no college or university is today without a financial aid office, institutional management may, from time to time, wish to consider whether a restructuring of the office's organization might result in a more efficient, sensitive, and expeditious delivery of aid to its students. There are a number of factors which bear on what appropriate form this restructuring might take. The more obvious of these are, of course, the number of students to be served, the dollar volume and complexity of the programs to be administered, and the size of the staff. Donald Ryan, in his chapter on staffing and professional development, treats the ratio of staff to program size. This section focuses mainly on nonquantifiable factors that have to be considered in structuring an office properly.

Student aid might be viewed as primarily a counseling function—that is, an activity closely related to the student's development. The goal is primarily one of wishing to help the student to achieve his or her educational objectives by means of providing a variety of student aid resources. In most instances the counseling approach seems to predominate because of aid's historical roots and the fact that many of today's aid personnel come from a student personnel or academic background.

Contributing to the historical evolution was the emphasis placed on the contact between the student and the personnel involved in the financial aid process. Rather central to this contact experience is the counseling relationship, which is held to be a common denominator of all student personnel activities, since all personnel workers seem likely to need skills in counseling from time to time (Reilley and Cauthern, 1976). The student financial aid administrator assumes the role of a counselor when dealing with matters involving the student's values and ambitions; therefore, the officer must be sensitive to the student's needs in a cooperative decision-making process.

According to Frantz (1969, p. 195), student personnel administrators differ from other administrators in that they are more "sensitive to personal, humanistic, social, and emotional influences and the least sensitive to material, abstract, and analytical influences." To accommodate this difference, the preparation of student personnel professionals ideally should include attention to such areas as college student characteristics and needs; history, philosophy, setting, and objectives of colleges and universities and social institutions; counseling theories and procedures; principles of administration and decision making; theory and practice of organization and fiscal management; selection and in-service training of staff members; communications with college departments and constituents; group dynamics; human relations and skills; an overview of student personnel work; and practicum, field work, or internships.

Because of the influx to the campuses of students from other than traditional backgrounds, specifically minority and disadvantaged, the counseling approach seems to have continuing viability. The need to treat students as individuals with special problems in the face of computer-determined financial need and packaged awards offers additional justification to placing the emphasis on counseling as opposed to treating student aid as little more than a strictly fiscal transaction.

As the amount of financial aid has risen dramatically on college campuses, there has been a growing insistence, particularly by the government, both federal and state, that the delivery process be grounded in sound and responsible business practices. This approach can be termed fiscal or transactional. It places particular emphasis on effective accountability and controls. A view distinctly in the minority, however, is that student financial aid personnel merely disburse money to students. Even the federal government has emphasized the need to protect student rights, particularly by providing useful and accurate consumer information, in the delivery of aid. With cutbacks in financial aid resources, or at least an end to the increases that could be counted on almost annually from 1958 through 1981, there is bound to be even greater emphasis on such activities as verifying the accuracy of the financial information submitted as the basis for an award, the maintenance of satisfactory academic progress by the recipient, and the timely repayment of student loan obligations.

Yet another approach, not at odds with either the counseling or the fiscal emphasis, might be considered in determining how a financial aid office should be organized. It is viewing the office in a "networking" context—that is, in close relationship with the other student services of the institution, such as counseling, placement, educational opportunity programs, veterans' advising, and the business office. This approach—which might be viewed as a holistic approach to student personnel services—emphasizes informed referral, so that the student is assured of obtaining sensitive and expert help in all areas.

How an institution selects the approach which predominates in determining how to organize its financial aid office should be dictated primarily by institutional mission. Does the institution see itself as highly selective or seeking to maintain an "open door"? Is the emphasis on certification, "value added," or remedial education? In short, what does the institution hope to achieve with its student aid program? The organization of the financial aid office also will be influenced by the position of the person to whom the director reports. If the director is, for example, on the staff of the dean of students or the vice president of student affairs, the counseling or student personnel approach can be expected to predominate. If, on the other hand, the director reports to the business officer or the vice president for fiscal affairs, the office's organization is likely to be influenced significantly in ways that promote sound fiscal accountability and emphasize the business transaction itself. In actual practice financial aid personnel most frequently report to the dean of students (Van Dusen and O'Hearne, 1980; National Association of Student Financial Aid Administrators, 1978a).

Among other factors influencing the organizational structure of the financial aid office is the concept of function versus personnel. For example, when one examines the activity level of an off-campus College Work-Study program, he may discover that the institution has failed to expand the program, not because it is an unimportant function but because of the personnel factor—namely, insufficient staff (Russo, 1972). In this instance, personnel considerations are dictating the performance of an activity rather than the merits of the function and its value to students and the institution. Staffing policies and decisions can play a significant role with regard to the organizational structure of the financial aid office. Personnel policies are often tied to budgetary considerations; therefore, salary and hiring freezes will influence office organization.

The staff members currently employed in a financial aid office will exert an influence on its organizational structure according to their personality characteristics. Their training and background will bear on, or at least limit, the degree of flexibility of the organizational structure. For example, if the individual is task oriented, the structure may take on certain overtones of task relatedness; if the individual is person oriented, a different set of behavioral patterns and activities may prevail.

The management style of the aid administrator cannot be overlooked as influencing, at least to some extent, the way the office is structured. Rensis Likert (as described in Koontz and others, 1982) identified four management styles in his treatment of leadership behavior. These are exploitive-authoritative, benevolent-authoritative, consultative, and participative-group. The exploitive-authoritative system places little trust in subordinates, while the benevolent-authoritative approach is more patronizing toward subordinates. Applying these concepts to a financial aid office organization might result in a structure where the exploitive-authoritative director retained virtually all decision-making authority and turned to a staff of strictly clerical and technical personnel to carry out specific tasks with little discretion. The benevolent-authoritative director, on the other hand, might appoint some principal assistants with the illusion of sharing authority with them but, in the final analysis, reserve to himself or herself virtually all the decisions. The consultative system utilizes subordinates' ideas but exhibits some lack of confidence in them. Translating this concept into an actual financial aid organization might entail the delegation on paper of significant responsibility to assistants who had clearly defined responsibility but, when the truly critical decisions had to be made, were aware that they would emanate from the director. The participative-group approach has been demonstrated to be the most beneficial and achieves greater total group involvement. To gain an understanding of how this concept would apply to a financial aid office, imagine the prior example but with the important distinction that the counsel of subordinates would, more times than not, have a marked effect on the major decisions in the aid program, although they would likely be made in the name of the director. Yet another management approach—an approach that may be necessary in a particular set of circumstances—is known as the "continuum of leadership." This approach finds the supervisor moving from a boss-centered position to the other extreme, a subordinate-centered position (Trewatha and Newport, 1979).

Electronic Data Processing and Organizational Considerations

The application of electronic data processing (EDP) to financial aid administration is, relatively speaking, so new and so important that its effect on how a financial aid office is organized merits separate treatment. With the wide availability of micro or personal computers at low cost, even the smallest program can consider the use of EDP.

Frequently, the financial aid administrator will allow certain routine activities within his or her office to gain a dominant role—for example, the process of individually reviewing and packaging a student's award. This domination may result in the overshadowing of other important activities, such as determining an institutional philosophy for awarding funds; setting goals and objectives for the financial aid office and evaluating their implementation; preparing for and conducting institutional research which evaluates the student financial aid program; or simulating the effect of various disbursement patterns for aid dollars. Some of the advantages of using EDP are the savings in time, speed, accuracy, and consistency, especially for routine tasks. Adherence to federal and institutional management policies, simulation ability that permits assessment of various policy decisions, and relief from clerical and mathematical functions are additional advantages.

In this time of austere college and university budgets, it is just not feasible to meet all needs of the financial aid office by simply adding personnel (Hartshorn, 1981). EDP can perform virtually any function not requiring human judgment, such as record keeping, need analysis, packaging, award letter preparation, student check production, fiscal and research reports, tape exchange for Pell Grants, normal academic progress tracking, and loan billing.

There is not complete agreement regarding the ability of EDP to reduce the need for personnel, since the computer is not a panacea for constricting the number of staff members (Anton and others, 1981). EDP does, however, offer a high degree of accuracy and accountability, both of which are highly sought-after characteristics of the financial aid office. The rapid expansion of EDP has caused personnel problems in the financial aid office, particularly in the case of the employee who has been with the office for many years. Pennell (1981, p. 8) writes that "experienced employees may feel threatened by change because the existing system provides them the respect of their less experienced peers." To negate the problem as much as possible, it is well to keep all staff informed at each stage of the planning and implementation of EDP.

Hartshorn (1981) suggests that the successful implementation of an EDP program consists of (1) securing an up-front commitment from the institution that will provide computer service, programming time, and software; (2) developing a comprehensive plan; and (3) describing each module. Before making a final commitment to a particular EDP system, the aid administrator should determine whether the system can (1) effectively perform the data processing task; (2) provide reliable data processing; (3) permit EDP activity to integrate readily with the environment, organization, and professional standards; (4) be obtained within a proper business relationship between its seller and the institution; and (5) be secured at a justifiable cost.

If the decision is made to incorporate EDP into the financial aid office, there are numerous and different arrangements or combinations available. One such possibility is known as time sharing. In this case the institutional terminal equipment, either video or printer, is connected by telephone to a computer. The location of the computer may be within the institution or within another institution or in a private firm. This approach is usually more costly than is the microcomputer concept. The microcomputer is a more recent technology that can embrace different approaches. For example, one such arrangement would be utilizing a microcomputer that handles communications between terminals and a central computer; another arrangement would be where the microcomputer performs independent applications and requires no active link to the central computer but permits periodic interchange of data; still another approach would be where the microcomputer stands alone.

Microcomputers have now developed to the point where it is the financial aid administrator's responsibility to develop an understanding of the appropriate way to integrate microcomputers into the work of the organization. This increasingly sophisticated and versatile equipment is not fundamentally different from computer systems of the past several years, except that the equipment has been made more reliable, faster, of greater capacity or memory, and less expensive.

Still another option open to the financial aid office is what is referred to as semiautomation. These are electromechanical magnetic ledger card machines and programmable calculators. The ledger card machines were largely responsible for opening the market. The programmable calculators are the latter-day vehicle for semiautomation and have been improved in capability to include storing programs and data and printing output.

Whatever decision is made relative to EDP, several guidelines should be observed in order to achieve the desired end product. For example, the purchaser should investigate the vendor's history, stability, and financial position before making a commitment to buy either a computer or a software package. Also, the delivery schedule and the location of the vendor's headquarters and of the support and service personnel, parts, and backup should be checked. A check of the vendor's record with other customers should be made. The vendor should offer protection against complete loss of data, with adequate ability to recover after a failure. In addition, the purchaser should establish whether the vendor or the purchaser will assume responsibility for maintaining the system and determine whether there is a prime contractor or several separate contracts for the hardware and software. Additional items to investigate might include the Dunn and Bradstreet rating of the company, sales and profitability, references, technical support, and documentation. As inviting as computers are for the typical financial aid office, expectations are often set too high for the computer and do not reflect what can realistically be accomplished. On the other hand, the full potential of the system should be understood and utilized (Wedemeyer, 1978; Hartshorn, 1981). Before deciding to automate an aid program, one should by all means consult with personnel in institutions that have done so and arrange to visit a college or university that already has something similar to the type of equipment being considered.

Typical Financial Aid Office Organizations

The earliest financial aid offices were structured on programmatic lines. In that configuration, specific staff or units of the office dealt with distinct forms of financial assistance. For example, one section of the office would devote itself exclusively to processing scholarship awards. The others would deal with student loans and with jobs. In no small measure, this kind of arrangement reflected the fact that various forms of financial assistance, prior to the establishment of a centralized financial aid office, were likely on most campuses to be the responsibility of different offices. Also contributing to a programmatic structure was the consideration that the various forms of financial assistance could have vastly different eligibility criteria. For example, scholarships might be based on the recipient's academic record or promise. Loans, on the other hand, with the advent of the National Defense Student Loan program, were authorized in response to computed financial need. Prior to about 1965—when federal loan, work, and grant programs all were in existence—the typical student rarely received a predetermined combination of all three forms of assistance. The programmatic approach to organizing a student financial aid office, then, largely predated the notion of financial aid packaging, which is described in Chapter Seven of this book.

With the significant increase in governmentally provided student aid in the late 1960s and early 1970s, existing and new aid offices came to be organized along more functional lines. Because of the growth in aid recipients and more complicated application procedures, as well as increased funding, greater attention came to be directed toward the delivery process. Specifically involved were efforts to make the delivery of aid—from the filing of a single application to the disbursement of the award—a more efficient and timely process. In offices dealing with a large volume of students and dollars, distinct units of the office might be assigned such functions in the awarding cycle as application and supporting document collection, need analysis, packaging or awarding, and aid disbursement.

As the financial aid delivery process became more complex for students and conscious institutional commitments were forged to recruit ethnic minorities, disadvantaged students, and nontraditional students, counseling and advising sections became an essential part of many larger offices. Even offices which remained in the programmatic mode frequently added personnel who assumed the responsibility for personalizing the aid delivery process and ensuring that sight was not lost of the needs of the individual.

While concerns over function came to predominate in the second-generation financial aid office, within certain units staff might still be assigned responsibility for working with only certain programs. For example, within the awarding unit of an office, there might be a section dealing exclusively with the processing of Guaranteed Student Loans.

One interesting variation of the functional approach involves a team approach to the awarding process. The team is assigned to the total delivery of aid to specific groups of students. They might comprise a segment of the alphabet of all aid applicants or an academic level such as an undergraduate class or graduate status. Within a class or an undergraduate or graduate division, there might be a further alphabetical breakdown. The team is responsible for contact with the student at all phases of aid delivery, as well as for advising. It collects documents, performs need analysis, determines the award, and sees to its disbursement. The value of the approach is that it personalizes the process, particularly at larger institutions, and results in a better understanding of the circumstances of individual students.

In spite of the growth of federal funds and the government's requirement that one individual on a college campus be assigned responsibility to coordinate student assistance, some universities—mainly those with substantial resources of their own—still handle undergraduate and graduate financial aid administration as separate activities. In large measure, this situation has resulted from the fact that fellowships, teaching assistantships, and research assistantships are not awarded on the basis of computed financial need, as is much undergraduate aid and all federal campus-based aid. Differences in awarding philosophy between graduate deans and faculties and administrators charged with the responsibility for undergraduate and federal support have likely been a contributing factor in preventing the complete centralization of all financial aid activities at a university into a single office.

Similarly, within a university such professional schools as health sciences, law, and business administration often have their own financial aid office, distinct from the university's aid office. To some extent, this decentralization has been encouraged by agreements reached among the graduate schools to use their own separate financial aid application form, such as the Graduate and Professional School Financial Application, and their own awarding calendars. Whether the decentralization in student aid administration, which is to be found in many universities, is a positive or negative circumstance seems counter-productive to debate. The fact of the matter is that it is a reality and, because of the dynamics involved, is not likely to change. In light of these circumstances, it becomes imperative, in a university where more than one financial aid office is functioning, to provide for coordination and constant communication among the several offices. While these offices may have different perspectives on student aid and resources to administer in varying amounts and type, close contact among the various offices can at least promote an understanding of why there are differences and result in less rivalry.

Regardless of what kind of an organizational structure is chosen for a financial aid office, it will not likely be the most effective and efficient for all times. Institutions, aid programs, technology, and personnel can all change over time, with significant consequences for that structure. Formal evaluation techniques should be used periodically to determine whether the student financial aid office is achieving the objectives set for it by the institution's philosophy and by the functional requirements of the aid office itself. The National Association of Student Financial Aid Administrators Committee on Institutional Management Services is developing a staff evaluation instrument. In Chapter Twelve of this book, Dallas Martin describes the very useful *Institutional Guide for Financial Aid Self-Evaluation* (National Association of Student Financial Aid Administrators, 1982b).

Location and Appearance of the Financial Aid Office

An institutional aid office, even with the best possible organization as measured against institutional mission, will be ineffective if it is not accessible to the students that it serves. An office located on the fifteenth floor of a dormitory high rise where the elevators are not always operating, as occurred at one large university, can scarcely be viewed as readily accessible to students. While administrative space on most campuses is virtually as dear as operating funds, every effort should be made to locate the financial aid office in an established student traffic pattern. To the extent that choice is possible, such a location might, for example, be adjacent to the student activities center, the post office if the college has one, the library, or the bookstore. Ready access to the facility or alternate arrangements should be available to handicapped students.

It is highly desirable that the office be situated in close proximity to the other student services with which it must relate closely, such as admissions, the registrar, the counseling center, and the business office. While it is readily apparent that the convenience of both students and staff will be served by this proximity, the fiscal soundness of the program also can be helped when not too great a physical distance is placed between the financial aid office and the fiscal office. For example, the need for a student to carry an award check, or perhaps a loan authorization, from the aid office to a business office located clear across the campus can result in bills not being paid or other aspects of the financial aid transaction not being completed in a timely fashion.

As important as the location of the financial aid office are the physical conditions to be found there. Is it reasonably attractive? Is there space available for students to complete forms and study while they wait for appointments? Is a maximum amount of privacy provided for students to discuss their financial circumstances with staff?

Steps short of requiring the expenditure of substantial sums of money can often be taken to make the financial aid office more attractive. Signs pointing out where the various activities within the office occur and identifying the staff who are servicing them can help reduce confusion and congestion. Painting the office in pleasant colors and hanging posters or suitable art can be helpful steps. Potted plants and flowers can also contribute to the warmth and friendliness of the environment. Wherever possible, sturdy yet attractive furniture should be considered for purchase. Also, neat and well-organized student files will give the students coming to the office more confidence in the processes that take place there. On the other hand, a luxuriously appointed office, particularly on campuses where student aid resources are sparse, may cause students to feel that there is an imbalance between funds being spent on the administration of the program and the support which they need and may not be receiving.

Certainly the benefits of an attractive office, well lighted and ventilated, with the maximum work space assigned to each staff member, is bound to promote productivity and efficiency. A name plate at each staff member's work station can help identify that person to those who must deal with him or her and emphasize the fact that the process of student delivery is in the hands of individuals. Within the office, it is important to group together units or individuals performing the same or closely related functions. To the extent that space permits, arrangements should be made so that staff members assigned to tasks that require quiet and concentration—for instance, need analysis and document evaluation—can be separated from those who are involved in heavy student contact, such as reception service. Both space and operating funds are always at a premium, and the challenge is realizing the very most from what is available.

Conclusion

The most important issue in determining how an institution's financial aid office should be organized is how the aid program supports the institutional mission. If the emphasis is principally one of recruiting and serving student needs, a strong emphasis on counseling and advising is in order. If, on the other hand, student aid is viewed as mainly a fiscal transaction, the structure of the office is likely to reflect control and accountability. In most instances, an effective aid office is likely to combine the best of both approaches. The growing resort to electronic data processing has its effect on organization.

Whether the office is organized along networking, programmatic, or functional lines, it must be able to maintain an effective linkage with such other offices and departments of the institution as student personnel, the registrar, the director of admissions, and the fiscal office. A mutual and thorough understanding of the responsibilities and functions of these various offices is highly desirable. Periodically, too, evaluations should be made of how well the office's structure is serving institutional mission and the office's functional requirements.

In addition to the matter of how an aid office is organized, it must be accessible to students and preferably situated in the student traffic pattern. Furthermore, its physical arrangement and furnishings should be such that it is comfortable and as attractive as possible for both the students and the staff. Since space and funds for administrative purposes are always in short supply on college and university campuses, a major challenge is to make the very most of these resources in situating the office and making it as functional and as attractive as possible.

Bibliographical Note

There are no books dealing exclusively with the broad topic of the organizational structure of a financial aid office. Undoubtedly, the most useful work bearing on many of the factors related to it, however, is Van Dusen and O'Hearne's classic *A Design for a Model College Financial Aid Office* (1980). The report by the National Association of Student Financial Aid Administrators (1978a) on the *Characteristics and Attitudes of the Financial Aid Administrator* presents useful and interesting data on office patterns and reporting arrangements.

On the more specific subject of management practices and styles, the reader is referred to *Essentials of Management* (Koontz and others, 1982), *A Guide to Selected Financial Aid Management Practices* (Miller, Dellefield, and Musso, 1980), "Financial Aid Office Management" (O'Hearne, 1973), and *Management: Functions and Behavior* (Trewatha and Newport, 1979). The application of computers to financial aid functions is receiving increasing treatment in the literature, and articles by Pennell (1981) and Wedemeyer (1978) are worthy of review. Also suggested is Hartshorn's (1981) paper for the National Association of Student Financial Aid Administrators.

11

Relationship of Student Aid to Other College Programs and Services

D. Bruce Johnstone
Robert P. Huff

Once there was a brand-new university. It had stone buildings and dormitories and a field house and lots of brand-new traditions. It had students, faculty, and administrators. The budget was approved, the catalogues were all printed, and the computer was up and running and on line. The only task left was to position administratively the financial aid office, for which task the president solicited the counsel of his colleagues.

"With over seven million dollars at stake plus thousands of disbursements, collections, and journal entries, it absolutely has to be under the vice president for business affairs," said the controller, glowering under his green eyeshades.

"Financial aid is to help the kids," said the kindly dean of students, "and it can't be run by someone with a bursar mentality. It belongs in student affairs, where we put people ahead of dollars."

"Financial aid may be the most powerful recruiting tool we have," ventured the director of admissions, "and it ought to be tied directly to this office."

The vice president for public affairs and chief lobbyist then spoke. "Ninety percent of my attention in Washington and 50 percent of my attention in the state capitol is devoted to legislation, regulations, or appropriations for financial aid. I'm probably the only senior administrator who understands the stuff."

"I assume you mean undergraduate aid," said the chairman of the history department, who, it turned out, had come to the wrong meeting but had stayed on lest the administration be tempted actually to make a decision without proper consultation, "and I don't care where it goes; just keep your administrative hands off our graduate fellowships."

The aid officers seated in the back of the room spoke up:

"The only way we'll have any clout is to report directly to the president," said one.

"The only way we'll have any standing with the faculty is to report directly to the academic vice president," said another aid officer.

"Just don't move us far from the computer," said still another, "or we'll never get the job done."

The president of the new university pondered this wisdom for three days and nights, and then called together his advisers to announce his decision. "It's clear," he said, "that financial aid is critical to recruitment, retention, and the long-range financial health of our great new university. It cannot be separated from business affairs, from student affairs, from admissions, or from governmental relations. It needs knowing, day-to-day attention, but it also needs strong support from the very top.

"I have concluded that the only solution is for all of you to report to Director Jones, here, in financial aid. I'd rather teach anyway." And with that the president handed the financial aid director, Jones, the keys to the presidential office, the presidential parking sticker, and the gold medallion of the university, and he (the former president) went off to check some books out of the library.

Jones threw himself into the job of being both president and director of financial aid. He was soon spending so much of his time with the vice presidents and trustees on fund raising, legislative relations, long-range academic planning, budgeting, faculty senate relations, the energy crisis, and a dozen other critical tasks that he all but forgot about his former bailiwick, the office of financial aid, the administration of which he had delegated to Riley, his associate director of financial aid. Riley, it seems, was becoming frustrated at never being able to see her boss. She was not getting the cooperation she needed from the bursar or the director of administrative computing or the counseling center. In the meantime, the vice president for finance was having fits about overspending in financial aid, and the director of admissions was complaining to everyone that no one in financial aid really cared about recruiting a class anymore. In desperation, Riley wrote a memo to the president and director of financial aid, asking if she might possibly report to someone else—someone who might give her a bit more direction and support and who could, when necessary, convey her most serious needs and problems up to him.

The president and director of financial aid said he understood her problem, and he called together his vice presidents and other advisers and asked where administratively he might locate the associate director of financial aid.

This parable illustrates a common administrative problem: the proper location, within a traditional college or university organizational chart, of a key office (in this case financial aid) that requires extensive linkages to many other offices, not all of which can be assembled within the same reporting structure. The office of financial aid must have close ties to the bursar's office, as well as to the admissions office and to all the "helping offices" of the division of student affairs. It must also have close ties to budget, planning, and governmental affairs. It needs close management attention, yet it also needs ready access to the president and the chief academic officer.

The point of the parable, of course, is that there is no conceivable perfect solution to this set of needs within a hierarchical organizational chart. "Solutions," such as they are, must come from a set of essentially horizontal relationships that cut across vice presidential and other departmental boundaries and that recognize the difference between the policy and the operations of student financial aid. The remainder of this chapter explores these relationships. The chapter also presents certain expectations which the chief executive officer should appropriately have of the institutional financial aid administrator and concludes with some administrative principles for a more effective financial aid operation.

The Search for Structure

Offices of student financial aid can be found administratively situated in about every possible arrangement, and it is a rare college or university that has not tried more than one. In the early days—before the 1958 National Defense Student Loan program, before Title IV of the Higher Education Act of 1965, and certainly before today's enormous volume and complexity of governmentally sponsored loans and grants—there was practically no financial aid whatsoever in the public sector. Even the private colleges had little need for an "office," as such, of financial aid. The admissions office typically handed out and collected the scholarship applications and notified the bursar or business office which term bills were to be deferred or forgiven, up to the limit of available scholarship dollars, which usually emanated from an endowment fund. Combined admissions and financial aid offices were often located administratively either within student affairs or academic affairs, or perhaps in a very small college reported directly to the president.

As financial aid grew in dollars, in the number of transactions, and in the complexity resulting from the regulations of external donors (particularly state and federal programs) and the inclusion of work-study and loans, each with its own special demands for paperwork and personnel, student financial aid emerged as a major operation needing staff, space, an operating budget, and an organizational location. Even after emergence as a major operation, the student aid office was frequently kept in student affairs, an area that increasingly has been separated from, rather than subsumed within, the office of admissions.

Often, because of the enormous volume of dollars and transactions and the natural tie to the bursar and the payment window, student aid was moved under business affairs, sometimes along with admissions.

Because the kinds of students admitted are enormously important to the academic mission of the institution, the admissions function, with or without financial aid associated, has sometimes been moved under the vice president for academic affairs or the dean of the college. In one college consulted for the preparation of this chapter, financial aid had been moved under the chief academic officer, mainly to protect what was thought to be an otherwise vulnerable budget. In another college financial aid had been moved away from the chief academic officer because there it had seemed too competitive with other academic demands—and could be better protected under a less visible "administrative" budget line.

Probably the newest organizational scheme to affect financial aid is the elevation of the combined functions of admissions, financial aid, and marketing to a vice presidential level. While not yet a common form, such an office reflects the heightened concern in nearly all colleges over the future of enrollments. This concern has resulted, particularly in the private sector but increasingly as well in the public sector, in larger recruiting budgets, the use of financial aid as an avowed recruiting tool, and an improvement in the salary and status of those charged with maintaining both tuition revenue and the academic quality of the student body.

Figure 1 illustrates some of the alternative organizational locations for the office of student financial aid. Clearly, there is no "correct" organizational placement of the office. Informal inquiries for the preparation of this chapter revealed that changes in reporting from one vice president or dean to another had been made (or would be desired) often for *ad hominem* reasons—that is, more on the basis of the personality, competence, or interest of the respective vice presidents or other senior officer than on the basis of some detached theory of the ideal collegiate administrative organization.

The best short answer to the question of organizational placement, then, is that a financial aid office can probably func-

Figure 1. Alternative Organizational Locations for the Office of Student Financial Aid.

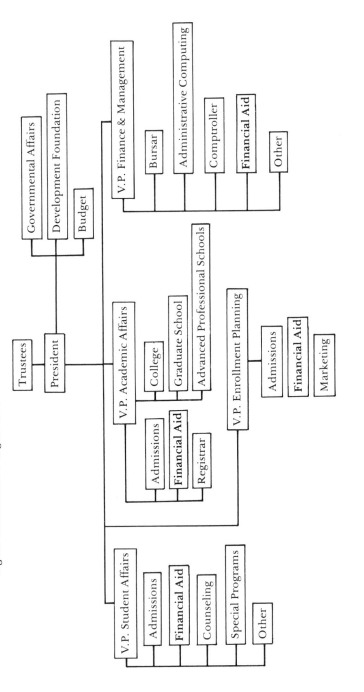

tion effectively under any senior administrator who has the respect, as well as the ear, of the president and other administrative colleagues *if* this individual brings interest, understanding, and leadership to the institution's financial aid program *and if* he can speak persuasively on behalf of financial aid when budgetary, admissions, and legislative lobbying strategies are being formulated.

Regardless of which administrative or academic officer the financial aid director must report to, the president or chief executive officer must be able to mediate conflicting views on financial aid policy and budget matters where irreconcilable differences appear to prevail. An example is an aid officer who insists to his superior in the student affairs division that the required fees of students awaiting Guaranteed Student Loans (GSL) should be deferred without charge. The chief business officer of the institution, on the other hand, might point out that had students applied for their loans in a timely manner, no deferment of fees would be necessary; therefore, standard deferment charges should be collected.

To prepare for differences growing quite legitimately out of the perspectives of particular administrative and academic units of the institution, the president or chief executive officer must be prepared to make the final decision on any issue or refer it for a solution to a council of the principal policy makers. The point to be emphasized is that—whether it is viewed as a student affairs function, an academic function, or a business function—the policies and procedures of the financial aid office will undoubtedly be influenced by the interests and objectives of the particular division of the institution in which it is located. Other functions in the institution may challenge the policies and procedures proposed by the financial aid director and his or her superior, and differences have to be settled by an individual or a group of individuals who can best view the overall objectives and mission of the institution.

Functional Ties

More fruitful than a search for the elusive ideal organizational location of the office is a strategy for enhancing communication and shared decision making with those programs or activities of the college related to student financial aid.

Undergraduate Enrollment Planning. The nature and amount of financial aid is critical to the numbers and kinds of students a college or university can enroll. Several questions should illustrate why this is true. Are highly desirable students being lost who could be induced to enroll if offered merit-based, as opposed to need-based, aid or because of a better (that is, more grant and less loan and work) package of need-based aid? At what cost can enrollment of the most highly desirable students be procured? Can these students, to be blunt, be "bought"? Should self-help be increased, at least for some students, in order to save gift aid and thus make it possible to target more narrowly the scarce grant dollars on the most desirable students, whether or not they have financial need? Can retention be improved by more favorable aid for the upper-division student—and, if so, at what cost or other consequence in diminished aid dollars for the entering freshman? How important to the mission of the institution is the enrollment of the financially disadvantaged or the nontraditional students, and what kinds of aid maximize their enrollment at the least cost? How and when are the aid awards being communicated to the admitted students, and would more timely and effectively communicated awards increase the yield?

These questions are posed to illustrate the increasingly critical role of financial aid policies to enrollment planning. It is not enough to respond by putting financial aid under the admissions director, as in the old days, or even by having financial aid and admissions report to the same dean or vice president. As is discussed at considerable length in Chapter Fourteen, comprehensive enrollment planning can be done only by a team that includes the directors of admissions and financial aid as well as the chief financial and academic officers who have studied the institution's retention patterns, market shares, and the like. The responsibility of the financial aid director in such a council is not to advocate one or another packaging policy, or even necessarily to advocate a higher aid budget, but to help shape the formation of policy by identifying the principal alternative financial aid policies and their consequences to the numbers and kinds of students likely to be enrolled and retained.

Advanced Professional Schools' Enrollment Planning. A university's advanced professional schools (such as medicine, dental medicine, pharmacy, veterinary medicine, law, business, and architecture) have typically operated in virtual isolation from the undergraduate offices of both admissions and financial aid. There are several reasons for this. Aid dollars for advanced professional schools have generally been limited—mainly to loans, jobs, and a rapidly diminishing number of federal training grants. The number of applicants for most advanced professional schools remains strong, and "marketing," as such, has not yet become the preoccupation that it is for the undergraduate schools. Advanced professional students are (or have been) expected to come up with the resources needed to stay in school—parents, spousal earnings, part-time work, or loans—with much less of the trappings of need analysis, scholarships, and institutional loans characteristic of undergraduate financial aid.

However—because of the increasing awareness, as well as acceptance, of the responsibility of advanced professional schools to provide access to low-income and minority students; the burgeoning paperwork burden of all forms of aid, including externally originated loans; and the growing competition for students and the emergence of a new "marketing awareness" in many advanced professional schools—this traditional isolation may change. The future seems destined to see more and more cooperation, both analytical and operational, between the large, well-established university offices of (undergraduate) financial aid and the grant, loan, and job aid programs of the advanced professional schools.

At the analytical level, such issues as the relationship between enrollment/retention and aid, or the availability of parental and spousal resources for the adult student, are common to both undergraduate and advanced professional schools. At the operational level, both undergraduate and advanced professional schools at many institutions will soon be implementing on-line student data systems carrying information on amounts due, financial aid, and loans. In short, while university schools of medicine, business, and law may retain substantial autonomy in determining financial aid policy and will probably have their "own" aid officers, the future will see increasing cooperation, and even occasional consolidation, between undergraduate and advanced professional school aid operations.

Graduate Programs in the Arts and Sciences. Financial assistance to graduate (Ph.D.) students in the arts and sciences has also been generally disassociated from the undergraduate financial aid office. Graduate admissions are typically handled by the graduate programs, not by the university's admissions office. The sources of graduate aid are mainly in the form of tuition rebates, competitive fellowships, teaching assistantships, research assistantships, and loans. Need analysis and expected parental contributions play a limited role, except where federal College Work-Study (CWS) and National Direct Student Loans (NDSL) are involved; and federal training grants and other external sources of outright gift aid are disappearing. Competition nationally for the most promising students continues to be keen, and the consequence to a department of attracting or failing to attract them is profound. The awarding of graduate fellowships is a zealously guarded academic prerogative, under no circumstances to be entrusted to either formulas or administrators.

At the same time, as with the advanced professional schools, graduate financial aid has been turning increasingly to the tools of the trade of undergraduate financial aid. Need analysis and expected parental contributions are beginning to be employed, as has been noted, for federally sponsored work-study and student loans, and because of the growing attention to the role of aid in matriculation and retention. While the formation of aid policy and the actual awarding of fellowships are likely to remain with the graduate office and the Ph.D.-granting departments, the undergraduate aid office will probably have an increasing role in securing federal and state funds, administering need analysis, disbursing awards, and advising on the role of financial aid in the marketing of the graduate programs.

Budgeting. At a public college, the per student dollar volume of undergraduate financial aid depends on (1) the total cost of attendance; (2) the number of "needy" students and the average need (which generates the Pell Grant); (3) the success of the financial aid director in securing allocations of the campus-based federal aid programs of National Direct Student Loans, Supplemental Educational Opportunity Grants (SEOG), and College Work-Study funds; and (4) the existence and availability of state student aid funds. While the dollar volume may be high, the aid funds at a public college may be entirely restricted to externally determined, need-based financial aid and not available for any other purpose. The dollars may be directly significant to the students and indirectly significant to the institution in supporting a given enrollment and thus a given budget allocation. But if the aid funds have no conceivable alternative use, then nothing is forgone by their allocation to aid, and the financial aid program, to the institution, is effectively without cost. Furthermore, if the awards are mainly generated by entitlement, as with Pell Grants, or student choice, as with Guaranteed Student Loans, there may be little institutional discretion in making awards and little significance to a financial aid "policy" beyond securing for its students as many state and federal dollars as possible. Thus, financial aid at a public college without aid funds of "its own" may involve large amounts of money, of enormous significance to its students and a paperwork burden to the aid office, but may not present the administration with any particularly difficult policy issues, as such.

The aid budget of an independent college, however, often contains reallocatable institutional funds in addition to restricted sources of aid. The reallocatable dollars originate from tuitions or unrestricted gifts, which can be used for salaries or new landscaping or library books—or financial aid. Because a large portion of such aid comes right back to the college coffers in the form of tuition, room, board, fees, and bookstore profits, and because at least some of this income would not be forthcoming were there to be no aid, it is difficult to say how much of, say, a one-million-dollar institutional aid budget would really be available for staff salaries or for some other use if all the institutional aid were eliminated. Nevertheless, for most private colleges (and a few public colleges), institutional financial aid represents a decision to allocate resources to the goals of student quality and diversity rather than to some other purpose. As such, financial aid represents a significant real cost, probably vital to the mission and quality of the college but nonetheless costly and vulnerable, particularly as other seemingly unavoidable costs increase and as income falls behind. In such cases it is imperative that the alarms concerning the probable costs of cutting financial aid—that is, lost enrollment, lost quality, and lost diversity—are also heard in the circles where budgets are made and resources divided among all the competing claims.

Student Services. Unlike the office of admissions, which probably means nothing to students after their matriculation, the office of financial aid will continue to be a source of frustration, salvation, annoyance, and help. It is an office to which a good many students may carry poignant stories of personal financial troubles that could alter the course of their academic careers—and perhaps their lives. It is an office that requires patience, understanding, and faith—along with financial prudence and sometimes a little suspicion. It is an office whose clients are frequently having personal difficulties and are simultaneously calling on the other helping services of the college, ranging from counseling to health services to the student ministries. The office of financial aid reports to the dean of students or the vice president for student affairs not merely because it is manifestly a "helping" service but because it must have extensive communication with all the offices that deal closely with the out-of-classroom problems of students; also, it must share the basic "helping" orientation traditionally associated with student affairs.

Financial Stewardship. The stewardship of financial aid funds is a responsibility distinct from either the establishment of the financial aid budget (how much shall be spent and from where shall it be obtained?) or the formation of the financial aid policy (what students shall be given what kinds of aid within the overall budget constraint?). Stewardship, or comptrollership, requires that all funds be disbursed in conformity to the budget, to all applicable laws and regulations, and to generally accepted practices of accounting and control. Some senior officer or officers, possibly including such posts as comptroller, treasurer, or financial vice president, are given the responsibility of safeguarding funds. As the numbers of financial aid transactions and dollars have increased at a virtually explosive rate, so has the need for sophisticated, rigorous stewardship. Regardless of where or to what senior officer the financial aid administrator directly reports, the college comptroller (or similar officer) must have the authority to prescribe how cash shall be handled and books kept and must have the responsibility to call to the attention of all senior officers any significant departure from the budget or from approved financial procedures. In short, the director of financial aid need not administratively report to a senior financial officer, but he or she must still be accountable to that officer.

Influencing Federal and State Legislation and Appropriations. The total financial aid dollars from federal and state sources, including all loans, can easily reach $2.5 million in a private college with an enrollment of 4,000; $4 million in a public college with an enrollment of 8,000; and $20 million in a private university with an enrollment (all schools) of 16,000. Obviously, what happens in the new legislation, appropriations, and outlays associated with the federal Title IV programs (GSL, NDSL, Pell Grants, SEOG, and CWS) has enormous impact on the financial status of students and institutions. From the opposite perspective, about $6.4 billion, or 43 percent of all current outlays of the federal Department of Education, goes to programs of student financial aid. The government, too, has a substantial stake in level and trajectory of these outlays.

As these figures indicate, most of what the federal government can do for a college, at least in the short run, is tied up in the federally sponsored financial aid programs. It follows, then, that much of the time of the person who keeps track of such issues for the college president will be spent trying—with the help of the financial aid director—to determine how much a particular proposal will cost the students in that college. The Washington, D.C., higher education establishment, based largely but not entirely at One Dupont Circle, probably spends more time on issues relating to financial aid than all other issues combined. Although this observation carries little or no message regarding the appropriate reporting relationships of the financial aid director and the principal "Washington, D.C., person," effective communication between these posts is critical—and financial aid policy is probably better served if the financial aid director establishes some direct contacts with key congressional offices and the staff of the Department of Education.

While the amount of student aid being appropriated by state governments pales in comparison with federal support, it does, after all, approximate a billion dollars a year and thus more than justifies the institution's efforts to influence decisions in the statehouse. The pricing of higher education does continue to be determined largely by the states. They decide, for instance, whether, as a matter of public policy, to charge relatively high tuition in the public institutions and then to offer generous financial aid programs to ensure the enrollment of needy students or to do just the opposite. Obviously, decisions about tuition and fee charges in public institutions can have a significant effect, too, on the private institutions of the state. If funds are limited in a state aid program that serves students in public and private institutions, and if a hefty rise in fees occurs for the former, awards may drop significantly for the latter.

Two other problems have surfaced on the state student aid front. First, because of the availability of federal support, many states have not increased or have even reduced their student aid appropriations; institutional representatives must be prepared to respond to these kinds of initiatives. Second, state higher education planning and coordinating bodies are becoming increasingly involved in the development of educational policy; that is, they are attempting to influence state legislation and appropriations. A senior administrator for a large midwestern public university system has gone so far as to suggest that these bodies could dominate the development of educational policy at the expense of colleges and universities. It is his view that institutional representatives need to be able to provide data about the impact of student aid and to project simulated results of proposed program changes in dealing with state boards and agencies.

Table 1 attempts to summarize the complex maze of functional relationships in which the student aid office operates within the institution. Special contributions of the student aid director are described therein, relating to the five functional areas (enrollment planning, budgeting, serving students, stewardship, and governmental relations) discussed in this section.

Functions of the Financial Aid Administrator

Certainly every bit as important as the determination of where the office of financial aid should be placed in the institutional structure are the expectations that the central administrators of the institution should have of the individual who is selected to administer the program. These expectations, although alluded to in part in the preceding section, are grouped into the following five broad categories and explored in some detail in this section: serving students, informing the institutional community, promoting the efficiency of the program, maintaining the integrity of the program, and, finally, functioning as an educator in the institutional community.

Serving Students. As stated earlier, the aid administrator must be committed to responding in a sensitive and humane way to the students who apply for assistance, whether or not they qualify for aid. Because of the intricacies of the financial aid delivery process, with its myriad forms and formulas, it is easy to lose sight of the goals of student financial aid: access, choice, and retention. The watchwords are patience, understanding, and faith, with a little prudence and even suspicion thrown in.

Informing the Institutional Community. As even a casual observer of the financial aid scene quickly learns, changes in the rules and regulations that apply to federal and state programs, as well as the often uncertain funding of these programs, seem to create a state of constant flux. It is therefore an important responsibility of the aid administrator to keep the appropriate elements of the college or university community informed of what is happening. Senior administrators, for example, will need to know how changes in terms and funding of external programs are likely to affect the institution. The faculty should be made aware—to the extent that they are interested (and of

Table 1. Role of Office of Financial Aid in Key Functions, Issues, and Problems of the College.

Function	Key Question or Issue for the Institution	Special Contribution of Aid Director to Resolution of Key Question or Issue	Senior Officer with Primary Responsibility	Others with Role in Policy Making
1. Enrollment Planning	What kind(s) of aid package (mix of grant, loan, job) do we need to preserve or to increase, and then to retain, our share of the potential student market? What is the risk to enrollment and/or retention from alternative financial aid packages?	What is the "need profile" of present and potential applicants? What are the alternative aid packages? What are students now getting at our college, and also at our top competitor colleges? What are present job and borrowing policies, and to what extent are there financial hardships among our students or parents? What does the financial aid literature say about enrollment response to changes in tuition and aid?	President Vice Presidents	Financial Aid Director Admissions Director Director of Institutional Research Students
2. Budgeting	What should we spend of our "own" (unrestricted, reallocatable) funds for financial assistance?	What are the total reallocatable costs (from unrestricted institutional funds) of the principal alternative aid packages? What are the probable enrollment and gross tuition revenue consequences from each?	President Vice Presidents Board	Financial Aid Director Chief Budget Officer Budget Committee
3. Serving Students	How do we convey to all staff that service to the student is what we are here for, that a problem with financial need can be traumatic, and that financial aid problems will frequently accompany other "problems," many of which will need the attention of the student affairs community?	What is the magnitude of, and what are the major patterns in, student financial aid difficulties? What are most frequent complaints directed at the office?	Vice President for Student Affairs	Financial Aid Director Director of Counseling Director of Special Programs Other Advisers Students

4. Stewardship	Are all aid funds being disbursed in accord with applicable laws, regulations, and generally acceptable accounting standards? How are we minimizing or eliminating "overawards" to our students?	What is called for by the applicable federal and state laws and regulations? What are the costs—in staff time, money, and award delays—of preaudit verification? How are staff protected against any appearance of impropriety?	Vice President for Finance President Board	Financial Aid Director Comptroller Bursar Registrar Legal Counsel
5. Governmental Relations	What position should the president, trustees, and others take to their elected representatives on legislation and regulations affecting student financial aid?	What positions are being urged by the financial aid profession? What is most directly beneficial to our students? What is most directly beneficial to our long-range financial position?	Director or Vice President for Public Affairs President	Financial Aid Director Admissions Director

course some faculty members are not)—of how well the aid program, as it evolves, supports the goals of the college or university. Students and their families must be informed in a timely way about the availability of funds and about application and awarding procedures. This need to inform interested parties about all aspects of student aid requires that the administrator maintain a high level of knowledge and understanding of what is an almost constantly changing function and be able to distill this knowledge in a way that is helpful to all concerned. There is no shortage of detail, and synthesis is essential.

Promoting the Program's Efficiency. The aid administrator must strive constantly to make the student aid delivery process more efficient. Student aid threatens to become, if it really is not already, a "paper jungle." Because of the task-related nature of the function, the administrator should step back occasionally and view the entire process in a linear fashion, to determine how it can be streamlined and expedited. Unfortunately, expediting the process is no easy feat because the heavy dependence on governmental programs reduces the institution's ability to control the awarding process.

In the effort to make the institutional program function more efficiently, the aid administrator should be alert to the new technology available and ascertain how this technology can, if affordable, improve the process. The director also should establish an ongoing training program for the staff of the aid office and others in the institution with whom the program interrelates, so that the personnel of the institution may carry out their responsibilities in a knowledgeable and effective manner.

Ensuring the Program's Integrity. The misuse of aid funds, even if unintentional, can create problems of eligibility, restitution, and reduction in the level of funding, to say nothing of embarrassment and loss of public funds for the college or university. If difficulties do arise, or even threaten to develop, the aid administrator must be certain that the senior administrators are informed and also told what actions are being taken or should be taken to resolve the difficulties. Moreover, when the aid administrator prepares institutional applications for federal campus-based aid, the data that he or she submits as justification for the request must be verifiable through institutional records. Because in some instances unsupportable data have been submitted and detected, senior officers of the college or university will want to satisfy themselves of the accuracy of the information being used to obtain federal funds.

But despite the myriad "do's and don'ts" that seem to punctuate student aid, there remain many opportunities for the exercise of institutional discretion and judgment. The aid administrator should be aware of just what latitude does, in fact, exist and should inform the senior officers of the college or university about ways in which the latitude can be used to serve institutional goals and what risks, if any, may result.

Educating Students and Others. The financial aid director —as an expert in an area of great importance to the institution— should be expected to bring expert advice and counsel to the shaping and reshaping of institutional policy, and also should play a role in determining policies and procedures for which he or she will assume responsibility. In some institutional settings, the aid administrator may be called on to teach courses in various aspects of student aid or the financing of higher education; but even in the absence of those circumstances, the individual does, in fact, have a didactic role. In the day-to-day contact with students in the financial aid arena, the administrator and others on the staff of the financial aid office are, in fact, educating students by helping them develop good fiscal practices: constructing and living within a reasonable expense budget; utilizing available resources properly; and meeting obligations, such as loan payments, in a timely fashion.

Conclusion: Reporting and Relating

Financial aid, especially at private colleges but increasingly at public ones as well, is too important to leave only to the director and his or her staff. From the perspective of the institution, enrollment targets, budgets, and even the shifting fortunes of individual departments and programs may depend considerably on what kinds of students are offered what forms of financial aid. From the perspective of the student, not just the policies but the actual practices of financial aid—for example, the willingness to extend deferment when the bank loan is denied, or the help provided to those contending with federal forms—may mean the difference between staying in and dropping out, or between a challenging career and a dead-end job, or between feeling wanted and important or rejected. The senior officers in academic, financial, public, and student affairs, as well as the president of the college, must play a direct role in answering key questions shown in Table 1 concerning enrollment planning, budgeting, and student affairs. The financial aid director must help to shape these questions and, most of all, outline possible answers, or trade-offs, as suggested in Table 1. While the office of financial aid may not, under such a matrix of relationships, have the unambiguous authority it once had, it should, by virtue of its participation in the most crucial and immediate matters of budget, enrollment, and program planning, have considerably more influence than it traditionally has had.

Bibliographical Note

A fairly general, brief statement concerning the placement of the student financial aid office in the institution, now somewhat dated, is offered by Dejarnett (1975). Essentially, he recommends that the student aid office be accorded equal status with other functional offices in the division of "special services" (student affairs) and that the head be designated a dean.

The manual published by the National Association of College and University Business Officers (1979) contains an authoritative and comprehensive discussion of the fiscal relationships of the aid office to the financial operation of the college or university. Predictably, NACUBO views the fiduciary function of student aid as central and accordingly recommends close linkages of the aid office to the business office.

The American Council on Education (ACE) has recently published some highly useful monographs alerting its presidential constituents to the importance of student aid. For those interested in the organizational placement of the office, the key publication in this series is *Management of Student Aid* (El-Khawas, 1979). While not dealing directly with the topic, the author stresses presidential responsibility and the vital significance of the aid function to the institution. We recommend this work for academic officers who wish to study the policy implications of student aid as well as the financial and administrative relationships.

In a thoughtful and insightful review of "What Academic Administrators Should Know About Financial Aid," Atwell (1981) emphasizes the fiscal importance of student aid; however, he also indicates that both the academic and the administrative infrastructures should become involved with this vital function.

Van Dusen, Higginbotham, and Jacobson (1980)—in a monograph developed primarily as a guide to implementing data processing systems for student aid—provide an excellent treatment of organizational relationships of the aid office. They include flow charts of the major federal programs (Pell Grants, SEOG, NDSL, and CWS) within the institution, as well as a fascinating chart that shows the aid office at the center of a veritable spider web of lines leading to internal and external offices and programs.

Finally, Van Dusen and O'Hearne (1980) summarize some of the available survey data on organizational relationships of the aid office within the institution. They found that in two thirds of the public institutions, but only one fourth of the private institutions, "the most common chain of command was from the director of student aid to the institution's chief student personnel officer" (p. 26). Private institutions were much more likely than public institutions to have student aid directors report to the chief business officer (19.3 percent versus 4.6 percent) or to admissions (11.1 percent versus 2.1 percent), indicating an overriding concern for financial and marketing implications. As public institutions compete more vigorously with the private sector and with each other, "it will be interesting to see if the percentage of institutions aligning financial aid with the admissions office changes as more emphasis is placed on the role of aid in attracting students from a more limited pool of prospects" (p. 27). We agree that it will be most interesting, especially if changes in purpose and function accompany the change in organizational structure.

12

Evaluating and Improving Administration of Aid Programs

A. Dallas Martin, Jr.

Evaluation is the foundation of proper management. Institutional procedures need continued evaluation to ensure that they are doing what they were set up to do. Institutional policies need to be reexamined in light of changes in the financial or social environment. Financial aid management policies and procedures are no exception. Statutes, regulations, and institutional personnel change; and what is a correct procedure under one set of circumstances may not be under a new set. Unfortunately, these critical aspects of program management—that is, systematic planning and evaluation—are all too often neglected in the ongoing operation of the student financial aid office. The recent growth in the number of student aid programs provided by federal, state, and private agencies has certainly made it more difficult for institutional administrators to develop systematic planning and evaluation of their financial aid operations. Likewise, financial aid administrators have been plagued by dramatic increases in number of student aid applicants, constantly changing statutory requirements, and an ever-growing set of complex program regulations and record-keeping requirements. Consequently, instead of taking the time to evaluate the efficiency of their operations and the extent to which institutional and program goals are effectively being met, these administrators have simply concentrated on getting the aid delivered to the students.

For the purpose of analysis and training, the financial aid award cycle is normally divided into discrete steps. However, for the purpose of evaluation, any attempt to divide the award cycle into such distinct elements must be seen as somewhat arbitrary and simplistic because the aid administrator will be performing several of the activities within an award cycle simultaneously and may be processing applications for two or more award cycles at any one time.

The first step in the award cycle is normally labeled *preadmission.* This activity includes all contacts with the student prior to the submission of a formal application for assistance. The next step is the *application process,* which includes the identification of the aid applicant and the accumulation of documentation necessary to determine the student's eligibility for the federal, state, institutional, and private financial aid programs administered by the institution. In addition, sufficient data must be collected to facilitate internal control as well as for the preparation of institutional and external reports.

After the necessary documentation has been collected and verified, the aid administrator must *assess the demonstrated financial need* of each applicant. The system by which the assessment is performed is subject to governmental review, and the data collection and initial review of those data are normally performed by one of several service organizations. The largest of these service organizations are the College Scholarship Service and the American College Testing Program.

The aid administrator must then *analyze the total resources* available to the financial aid office from federal, state, institutional, and private sources. Once an effective review of these sources and their regulations has been performed, the aid administrator can effectively consider the requests from the applicant pool. At the time of the *award decision,* the actual amount and type of funds (gift aid, loans, and employment) to be awarded to each student are determined. This determination of the mix of the funds and the dollar amounts awarded to students is called "financial aid packaging," and that process is governed by institutional policy and donor stipulations.

Once the financial aid package has been developed for a given student, an *award notification* must be sent to the student in writing. The award notice is part of a contractual process and, as such, must comply with the general requirements of contractual law and with specific legislation regarding the awarding of financial aid. The offer of financial assistance must be followed by a formal *award acceptance*. The student normally has the option of accepting or declining the entire award or each of the various elements within the financial aid package.

Disbursement of the funds to students by the institution to pay their educational costs can be accomplished by crediting the student's account or by making cash disbursements to the student. However, federal, and sometimes state, regulations govern this process when federal and state funds are included in the award.

Review and evaluation of the award cycle is a continual process. Several questions regarding this process must be addressed frequently. For example, is the award process being performed efficiently and effectively? Are institutional goals and donor stipulations being satisfied? Are students' financial needs being met? Are students receiving notification of their financial aid awards in time to make adequate plans for the following academic period? Are the financial aid funds available to students in time to pay their educational expenses?

This chapter devotes more attention to evaluation of efficiency than effectiveness, since this is the type of evaluation most often required of aid officers. While both are important, the distinction between effectiveness and efficiency is crucial and revealing of the "state of the art" of student aid management at the institutional level. Effectiveness pertains to the extent to which a program reaches its goals, whether formally stated or implicit and actual. It relates to *why* the program is in existence and what impact it has on target populations or constituencies. A program is effective when it has positive effects in its societal environment; that is, when it advances desired policies. Efficiency focuses on a program's processes—*how* it operates in relation to costs in time, money, and energy.

The types of evaluation involved with these two concepts are quite different. Efficiency is evaluated by review and audit after a cycle of operations—a type of evaluation called summative, to denote its typical purpose of review and judgment by policy makers external and/or superior to the operation itself. Effectiveness is best evaluated by formative measures, since the program is in a continual state of flux and development in striving to meet societal goals such as access and retention.

Obviously, efficiency and effectiveness are closely related in an aid program, and ideally they are complementary: the more efficient a program is, the better chance it has to be effective. Nonetheless, the two concepts are distinctly different in important ways. For example, an aid office can be quite efficient—that is, it can process a large volume of applications quickly and smoothly—if it restricts its processing to applicants who need little or no counseling and offers no assistance with completion of necessary forms; but if the program's avowed goal is to assist those who most need help, financial and otherwise, the program would be most ineffective. Conversely, an aid program could be quite effective in meeting certain institutional goals but be inefficient in the process. For example, an institutional aid program for a private liberal arts college may have as its goal the use of aid in competing successfully with other colleges for a highly select, academically elite student enrollment. It is perfectly possible for this goal to be reached with spectacular success but with gross inefficiencies in program costs and use of personnel.

The congruence of goals between the aid office and the total institution is crucial, particularly for colleges and universities that are heavily dependent on student aid as a recruiting and retention tool. A strategy for an overall evaluation of the aid office could well begin by assessing the extent to which stated and actual goals (they are not always identical) of the aid office support the institution's goals. If the aid office does not have a goal statement, one should be developed as a precondition for an evaluation study. That developmental process must begin by reference to the mission statement of the institution. The aid office's goals should not only be congruent with those of the institution; they probably should be properly subordinated to or "nested" within the overall goals of the institution (see Fenske, 1980b, pp. 178-180).

Systematic Planning and Management

Today the increasing financial stress facing postsecondary education, coupled with the impact that financial aid programs have on the institution's enrollment and retention patterns, makes it essential that all schools develop and implement effective management techniques for use with these vital programs. The success of federal aid programs as a whole depends on proper management at the institutional level, especially in this critical period of cutbacks in federal spending, and an individual institution's continual access to federal student aid monies depends on its proper use of current aid funds.

Many management systems are available for study and adoption by the aid officer. Some are formal, general systems developed for use in business or in bureaucracies such as government agencies. For example, Management by Objectives (MBO) has been adapted for use by some higher education institutions in certain student service areas and in academic support programs. MBO can be and has been used for personnel management in student aid offices; however, because of the press of increasing work loads and shrinking resources, little has been done to evaluate the effectiveness of this and other formal systems in such settings.

The National Association of College and University Business Officers (NACUBO) (1979) has developed a comprehensive management system for the fiscal side of student aid operations. As a "companion piece," the American Council on Education (ACE) added a management guide for presidents (El-Khawas, 1979), outlining (1) the effect of student aid on the institution, (2) major policies and control points in the aid process, and (3) sound management practices as an example of effective self-regulation. Taken together, the NACUBO and ACE publications provide effective guidelines from the perspectives of the institutional business and academic officers, respectively.

The two major need analysis organizations have also provided management guides that are useful in certain aspects of aid operations. The American College Testing Program (ACT) (1981) publishes a frequently updated *Handbook for Financial Aid Administrators,* which instructs student aid personnel in administering the uniform methodology and ACT's need analysis system. The handbook also offers a limited number of suggestions for an effective office operation. The College Scholarship Service (CSS) of the College Entrance Examination Board publishes similar handbooks; the board has also published a revised version of *A Design for a Model College Financial Aid Office* (Van Dusen and O'Hearne, 1980), which is a valuable guidebook, especially for institutions establishing new offices or revamping present offices. The guidebook reviews the relationship of the aid office with external agencies and with other institutional offices and provides a general introduction to the impact of student aid on the institution. Despite its title, the guidebook contains only a brief four-page section on administrative organization of the aid office (pp. 25-29) and neglects the topic of program and operations evaluation altogether.

The set of published materials likely to be most useful to aid officers in planning and management are those published by the National Association of Student Financial Aid Administrators (NASFAA). (These are discussed in Chapters Eight, Nine, and Ten.)

An interesting perspective on planning and management in student aid programs has been provided by Binder (1980a), who suggests that the "open system" approach could be a useful model for student aid offices. "Effective administration of financial aid programs for students is the result of a systematic and comprehensive plan for those services. The financial aid administrator must be a manager, develop a management style, and approach the administration of aid programs with some understanding of planning or management theory. . . . The open system theory provides a framework for the administration of financial aid programs on a college or university campus" (pp. 85, 92). Whether or not one subscribes to the open systems approach, the selection and use of a formal, comprehensive system will greatly facilitate evaluation.

Types of Evaluation

Basically, four types of evaluations are used in examining federal student aid programs: self-evaluation, peer review, program review, and audit. No method in and of itself is sufficient to guarantee sound management practices; instead, the methods complement one another and, when used in combination, should ensure a sound student financial aid system.

Self-Evaluations. The concept of institutional self-evaluation is not new. The early colonial colleges studied various aspects of their programs and goals. The basis of regional and professional accreditation is self-evaluation. However, only in the past few years has this technique been much used in the area of student financial aid. Generally, informal self-evaluation occurs in the operation of an aid office on an ongoing basis. That is, subordinates routinely report to their managers on various phases of the operation—indicating, for example, how well a new aid disbursement system is working or how student need is being analyzed for freshman applicants. Such informal self-evaluation is a normal activity in any organizational unit. However, institutions are far better served by an ongoing formal self-evaluation. In the area of student financial aid, one tool that has proved particularly helpful is the *Institutional Guide for Financial Aid Self-Evaluation,* published by the National Association of Student Financial Aid Administrators (1982b). This publication was designed to assist financial aid administrators in evaluating the efficiency and effectiveness of their administration of the financial aid programs, as well as determining compliance with federal laws and regulations. First developed in the fall of 1977 and updated and reprinted each year (except 1980) since, to reflect federal regulatory changes, the guide contains all current regulatory citations as well as an up-to-date listing of all applicable public laws. If fully utilized, it could help the financial aid administrator perform the following functions:

1. Convey to the administration (or other target group) the magnitude and complexity of the financial aid operation.
2. Document the need for an operating budget, staffing, and physical accommodations commensurate with the size and scope of the institution's financial aid program.
3. Develop a profile of the financial aid operation for affirmation/revision of policies, office procedures, and administrative controls.
4. Train new staff and enhance the skills and knowledge of current staff.
5. Prepare for audits and program reviews.
6. Prepare financial aid and fiscal reports.
7. Make periodic checks of the financial aid operation, to determine progress being made in plans for improvement.
8. Develop a financial aid staff manual or institutional policies and procedures.

Other institutional self-evaluation projects can be designed and conducted to focus on a special program (such as the integration of the school's management information system) or a limited aspect of the institution and its programs (such as the development of criteria to determine and update student expense budget standards). Self-evaluation can also be used by administrators to (1) reexamine an institution's student aid philosophy and objectives, (2) validate or improve existing operational policies or practices, and (3) institute new procedures that are needed to provide greater accountability or coordination of student aid programs.

Peer Reviews. Some institutions periodically find that, in addition to conducting their own internal self-evaluation of their aid programs, it is desirable to supplement such activity by inviting experienced and well-qualified student aid administrators from other institutions to visit the campus to review the programs. The advantage of using an outside person or team of evaluators is that they are often likely to take a more objective look at the management procedures and ask critical questions about the institution's aid policy. Outside observers are also likely to bring with them new ideas and techniques that may be helpful in resolving current problems.

A peer review is a formal evaluation and should conclude with an exit interview and a written report. A peer evaluation should be taken seriously, but with the understanding that local conditions vary and some procedures and policies that are necessary in one institution would be inappropriate for another institution.

Peer reviews are a second opinion to be considered in evaluating student aid programs. They do not necessarily ensure that an institution is complying with the procedures required by the Department of Education or that the procedures reflect current law and the associated regulations. Therefore, the Department of Education has developed formal program reviews to ensure that institutions are administering their federal student aid programs in compliance with current federal regulations and to assist institutions needing technical assistance.

Program Reviews. Program reviews generally focus on the operational aspects of the institution's student aid system rather than on fiscal or accounting procedures.

In lieu of the Department of Education's preferred practice of reviewing each institution every three years (which it has been unable to maintain because of a lack of personnel), it has developed certain edit factors to determine which institutions need to be reviewed. Eighty percent of the program reviews conducted are based on this triggering mechanism; the other 20 percent are chosen at random.

Most often conducted by personnel from the regional office of the Department of Education, the program review is scheduled with the institution two weeks in advance of the review date. The first step in this review process involves the completion of a checklist by the institution prior to the visit. The checklist then serves as the basis for the program review. During the visit a selected sample of student files is reviewed to determine whether the students who received aid met the eligibility criteria of the program and whether they actually received the funds awarded them. The following minimum documents should be in the files for each student:

1. Financial aid application.
2. Need analysis documentation.
3. A signed award letter containing education costs, expected family contribution, amount of need, how need is to be met, and an explanation of the terms and conditions of the aid being awarded.
4. A signed document signifying that the student accepts the aid offered.
5. A statement of educational purpose.

The reviewer will examine the institution's policy and procedures manual to make sure it contains acceptable policies on satisfactory progress, packaging criteria, the financial aid appeals process, refunds, and determining the cost of attendance. The manual also should include a description of the procedures used for implementing these policies.

Consumer information will also be examined to ensure that all necessary information is provided to students. It is more acceptable to have all consumer information together in one publication rather than distributed throughout the institution's publications.

All recent reports on the financial aid programs should be available for the reviewers. Such required reports include the Fiscal Operations Report, the Progress Report, and National Direct Student Loan (NDSL) default reports.

A second part of the review will involve an examination of:

1. Accounting records detailing receipt of cash from the appropriate federal agency, disbursement of funds to students, deposits of matching or institutional share of funds, and calculations of administrative cost allowances.
2. Letter of credit drawdowns, monthly cash requests, reports of expenditures.
3. College Work-Study (CWS) payroll records, to ensure that

time cards, satisfactory progress reports, reports of off-campus earnings, and the like, are present.

4. NDSL records, to ensure that the promissory note has been properly executed, loan advances signed for, exit interviews conducted, and other steps taken to indicate that the institution has exercised diligence in making and collecting loans.

This portion of the review is conducted to ensure that certain program requirements have been met. For example, the bank in which the funds are deposited must know which accounts contain federal funds. Program funds may not be used for institutional operations at any time. There should be no excess federal cash in the accounts. The Fiscal Operations Report and the ledgers must be in agreement.

The reviewer may also examine a sample of CWS job descriptions and the procedures used to place students in these jobs. If the institution is participating in the Job Location and Development Program, the procedures and records for this program will be examined. The same will be true for institutions participating in a Community Service Learning Program.

The last phase of the review involves areas that reflect the institution's overall administrative capability. The reviewer will ask such questions as:

1. Is there a staff development program?
2. Is the institutional staffing adequate for the size of the financial aid program?
3. Does the institution have a financial aid committee to guide use of aid funds?
4. Are the facilities adequate for storage of confidential aid documents? Are NDSL promissory notes and student loan ledgers stored in a locked, fireproof container?
5. Are all student financial aid programs, federal, state, and institutional, coordinated to guard against overawarding?
6. Do the financial aid office and fiscal office records agree, and are there procedures for regularly reconciling this set of records?

Program reviews, like peer reviews, end with an exit interview, in which the reviewers meet with the financial aid administrators, the business officer, and, if available, the president of the institution. The findings of the review are summarized, and recommendations are made on better operating procedures or on modifications of present procedures. A written report is then sent to the institution within thirty days. Although the reviewer may assess liability against the institution, the program review is generally designed to assist the institution in implementing better administrative procedures.

A response from the institution should be submitted within thirty days from the date the program review report is received. Adequate documentation must be included to support the institution's responses or rebuttals. There is no formal appeals process for liabilities assessed under a program review. The program review is considered closed when any liability assessed is satisfied.

Audits. Legislative changes enacted by the Education Amendments of 1976 require that institutions have their federal aid programs audited on a two-year cycle. The audit must be performed in accordance with the Department of Education's audit guides for financial aid programs.

Program regulations require that the audit be performed by the institution or at the institution's direction, through the employment of an independent, private accounting firm or by the internal audit staff of the institution. If the institution uses its own internal audit staff, it must ensure that the staff meet the standards of independence as defined by the United States General Accounting Office (GAO). The Department of Education's audit agency is responsible for acceptance of the audit report and any necessary follow-up.

An audit is an independent examination of financial transactions, accounts, reports, and compliance with applicable laws and regulations; it is conducted to determine whether the institution is maintaining effective control over revenues, expenditures, assets, and liabilities; properly accounting for resources, liabilities, and operations; complying with applicable laws, regulations, and the Department of Education's directives;

and, in its financial reports, presenting accurate, reliable, and useful financial information. The audit also studies and evaluates the institution's internal accounting and administrative controls, as well as the policies, procedures, and practices used in administering student financial assistance programs. It should be viewed by the institution as a management tool that can promote operational efficiency and effectiveness and facilitate achievement of organizational goals and objectives.

Problems may arise if no audits are conducted or if the institution fails to schedule audits on a timely basis. The potential result in either instance is that the institution may continue operating from year to year with procedures that are assumed to be in compliance with regulations but, in fact, are not.

In its audit guides for financial aid programs, the Department of Education has established general objectives for the conduct of audits. The objectives ensure that:

1. The institution has established procedures for coordinating assistance provided under all federal and nonfederal student aid programs in which it participates.
2. The institution has implemented and used financial and other administrative procedures and internal controls to effectively discharge management responsibilities and to protect the federal interest.
3. The institution has established and has followed policies and procedures to ensure that the funds provided are being used only for the purposes set forth in the institution's agreement with the secretary of education and that the policies and procedures conform with applicable Department of Education directives.
4. The financial information submitted on the annual program reports is reconcilable with the financial statement and submitted on a timely basis.
5. The institution has documentation to support the enrollment data reported in its application for funding.
6. The balance sheet and related statements of changes in fund balances present fairly the financial position and changes in fund balances, in accordance with generally accepted accounting principles and/or terms of agreement

applied on a basis consistent with that of the preceding year.
7. The institution has established a control and self-evaluation system intended to monitor and evaluate the programs to determine whether their objectives are met.

The institution's evaluation by an auditor will include a review of the following financial areas:

1. Internal controls—methods used by the institution to safeguard assets and to ensure accurate and reliable accounting data, operational efficiency, and adherence to policies.
2. Accounting system.
3. Student file maintenance—acceptability of the program and student records.
4. Program funding—the timing and means by which the program funds are requested by or advanced to the institution.
5. Reconciliation of account balances.
6. Student participation—confirmation that students participating in the programs were actually enrolled and received the report awards.
7. Administrative cost allowance funds.
8. Federal and institutional contribution—confirmation that the federal percent of NDSL and CWS funds did not exceed that allowed by regulation and that the institutional contribution was timely and in the proper amount.
9. Maintenance of level of effort—confirmation that the institution expended the proper amount of its own funds for scholarship and student aid.

The following compliance areas are also reviewed:

1. Eligibility—all requirements are met by the institution.
2. Validity of the institutional application process—all data used can be documented.
3. Coordination of federally assisted aid programs—how federal and nonfederal aid programs are coordinated and integrated.
4. Use of a self-evaluation system—the method used to pro-

vide a continuous system of evaluation of program activities.

5. Calculation of total cost of attendance—how the allowable student costs are calculated and what costs are used.

6. Eligibility of participating students—whether all students aided meet the program eligibility requirements.

7. Calculation of the amount of award—how the amount is determined and how the aid is packaged.

8. Student file maintenance—whether student files contain complete and necessary documentation of aid actions, satisfactory progress, statement of educational purpose, admission date, enrollment status, and so forth.

9. Institutional disbursements—how aid is disbursed to the students.

10. Refund procedures—the institution's procedures for identifying Title IV financial aid recipients who receive tuition or room and board refunds, how these funds are refunded to the programs, whether the institution has a written policy on student refunds.

In addition to these general areas, each program will have its own areas of audit. The Pell Grant program will be examined for validation procedures. The College Work-Study program will be examined to ensure that student employment opportunities meet the eligibility requirements and that the payment system and amount of wages are proper. Methods used to carry forward or carry back CWS funds to succeeding or prior years will be reviewed, as well as procedures used to transfer funds from CWS to Supplemental Educational Opportunity Grants (SEOG) and vice versa. The amount of funds transferred also will be examined. In the NDSL program, the promissory note will be reviewed for proper format and student's signature for each advancement. Files will be examined to ensure that students did not exceed the loan limits. The institution's system for recording payments from borrowers will be reviewed, as well as deferments and cancellations. Student records will be checked to make sure that the due diligence requirements are being followed.

The institution can do a great deal to ensure that the audit process is conducted smoothly and that meaningful information is obtained. Advance preparation should automatically be incorporated into the institution's procedures and operations. The institution should (1) maintain complete files on each student; (2) keep all records current and reconcile all accounts monthly; (3) monitor the entire aid process; (4) establish an audit trail, by dividing the audit trail responsibility between the financial aid and the fiscal offices; and (5) ensure that the institution complies with the program requirements.

At the conclusion of the fieldwork and prior to preparing the final audit report, the auditor will hold a closing or exit conference with financial aid and business office personnel. This provides an opportunity to discuss the draft report and review any discrepancies uncovered by the audit. Sometimes, because of the complexity and changing nature of the program, an auditor may misinterpret regulations or use standards that are no longer applicable. Similarly, institutional personnel need to be aware of the auditor's reporting requirements. The exit conference can do much to alleviate the misunderstanding that can occur during an audit and improve the climate in which future audits are conducted.

During the exit interview, minutes should be kept that record any major revisions and disclosures. At the conclusion of the exit interview, there should be a clear understanding about the facts supporting the audit report. Sometimes these facts will be interpreted differently by the auditor and the institution. In these cases the audit report will contain the auditor's view, and the institution will state its disagreement in its response.

After the exit interview, the auditor will complete the final draft of the audit report. The institution should prepare a written response, indicating any disagreement with the auditor's conclusions; any remedial action taken to correct deficiencies cited by the auditor, or any planned actions that would alleviate or eliminate such deficiencies; and any facts or circumstances bearing on the issues cited in the audit. This response should be reviewed by all parties affected by the audit and by the institution's administration. Many institutions have agreed to include their response as part of the audit report; others treat it as a separate document. In either case, the response should accompany the audit report when it is submitted to the regional Department of Education's Inspector General for Audit. When the audit report is submitted to the regional office, it is reviewed for format, completeness, and the use of standards for government auditing. This office does not evaluate the merits of exceptions.

There are essentially three categories of findings available to an auditor: (1) no exceptions (or corrective action already taken) and no expenditures challenged; (2) exceptions (perhaps procedural) but no expenditures challenged; and (3) exceptions and expenditures challenged.

The Department of Education's Office of Student Financial Assistance (OSFA) personnel will review the report and either concur with the auditor; modify the auditor's recommendations, based on the institutional response; or ask the institution for more information. Amounts questioned by the auditor do not necessarily mean that these costs will be disallowed. The final determination as to the allowability of costs will be made by the Department of Education.

Institutions have the opportunity to appeal OSFA audit determinations when they believe that errors of fact are involved. In cases where an institutional liability is upheld, the institution has the option of accepting the amount projected from the audit sample, selecting a second random sample, or reviewing the entire population in question for a determination of the exact amount due.

Once an audit has been closed to the satisfaction of OSFA officials, the institution is advised of that fact in writing. This authorizes the disposition of records once the regulatory time limits have passed.

Other Evaluation Measures

In addition to these formal types of evaluation, there are other measures for ensuring an effective financial aid program. *Evaluation of Technology.* Various technologies have been introduced into student aid offices to increase efficiency by assisting with the growing work load. Some of the early introductions included ledger and key-sort cards to cope with the flood of manual paperwork in the late 1950s. These, in turn, led to new filing systems in which shelf-type, side access files were seen as a notable advance. The acceptance of the IBM data card (actually originated by Herman Hollerith for regular use by the United States Census as early as 1890) comprised a real revolution in many aid offices, since each card contained 960 positions for storing data. Keypunching and card sorting became new technological skills. In another area the leap from typist skills to advanced word processor operation represents an unbridgeable gap for many secretarial and clerical staff.

In still other areas, new word storage, dictation/transcription, and intercom systems have increased administrative efficiency and staff communication while contributing their share of bafflement to those coping with the new gadgets that operate the systems. Over the years students, also, have been required to deal with technological advances in forms, the most notable being the mark-sense systems developed by E. F. Lindquist in the 1960s. The bar-coded labels, now used for pricing in some modern supermarkets, are being adapted for various student forms for encoding confidential information easily read by electronic wand at certain processing stages.

However, to most student aid administrators, computerization is the primary way to increase efficiency through technological advances. Computerization preoccupies most administrators because it is at present the most ubiquitous, expensive, and significant of the new technologies. In many respects it is also the most challenging because the complexity of process, machinery, and even language represents a quantum leap over previous technologies. Evaluation of its contributions to efficiency (savings of time, energy, and money) is equally challenging. In this discussion of evaluation, however, the reader should bear in mind that while computerization is used as the prime example, the challenge it poses to evaluation is one of magnitude, not kind. All technologies have raised the same types of problems (such as staff training and morale, cost, and administrative controls), as well as prospects for efficiency. Resistance to new technologies is both timeless and universal. Such resistance is usually passive, but sometimes it is active. (It is interesting to note that the word *saboteur* derives from the wooden shoes worn by eighteenth-century European peasants who destroyed factory machinery in a vain attempt to save the cottage system which had allowed them to work at home with their families.)

For the vast majority of aid officers in all but the smallest institutions, the question now is not whether to computerize but how. Which functions (need analysis, packaging, award notification) should be included in the system? Should the office purchase a commercial system, develop one in-house, or contract for services with an external agency? Should the system be batch or on-line? Should the office purchase a self-contained minicomputer of limited capacity or plug into the institution's large main-frame computer?

The literature of student financial aid has recently included a number of fine contributions dealing with the technical and managerial aspects of computerization. Foremost among these is *The CSS Guide to Implementing Financial Aid Data Processing Systems* (Van Dusen, Higginbotham, and Jacobson, 1980). This guide begins with an emphasis on planning for the system and includes a commendable focus on the purpose of student aid. The main discussion, however, is on the various aspects of installing and implementing the system. A number of excellent articles and other sources on planning and implementing computer systems for the aid office are reviewed in the Bibliographical Note that concludes this chapter. In aggregate, these materials deal comprehensively with the administrative aspects of this particular technology.

The present discussion, however, focuses on evaluation of technology rather than its implementation. The evaluation measure likely to be of most interest to administrators is the extent to which the new technology frees time for the administrator from routine, repetitive chores to devote to loftier goals and more professional pursuits. Pernal (1977, p. 48) contends that computer and other technology "should be utilized to improve the management of the financial aid officer and allow the aid professional more time to work with students, develop innovative ideas, explore research possibilities, and coordinate his or her efforts with other administrative offices in his institution." Similarly, Van Dusen, Higginbotham, and Jacobson (1980, p. 9) point out that many of the activities in the aid office, particularly the counseling of students, "can be enhanced by a financial aid data processing system. By providing the aid administrator with up-to-date, accurate, and complete information about students and by freeing time for talking with students, the system can facilitate all the administrative functions of the aid office." Surely, the prospect of more free time for truly professional activities (as compared to mere "paper pushing") is one of the most attractive reasons for implementing computerization. It is also one of the measures amenable to evaluation. The administrator should be able to determine, by a before-after comparison, whether the new technology did indeed free him from routine tasks.

Goal-Oriented Evaluation. Whatever consensus exists about the goal of student aid is summed up in the statement of the National Task Force on Student Aid Problems (1975, p. 6): "The primary purpose of student aid is to provide financial resources to students who would otherwise be unable to begin and complete the type of postsecondary education they wish to pursue." One measure of an effective institutional aid program, then, is the general satisfaction of the students who are being served. In essence, the student aid office is student centered. An aid administrator can generally collect data to evaluate this measure by periodically asking students to complete simple questionnaires. The questionnaires may be distributed to all financial aid recipients, in the case of smaller institutions, or to a random sampling if the institution serves a large number of aid recipients. The questions should be designed as simply as possible, to ensure valid responses. Such a procedure should be conducted annually and can be used by the aid office to measure students' perceptions about the quality of service that they are receiving and to solicit ideas for improving administrative operations. Student evaluations of consumer materials, financial aid brochures, application forms, and award letters can also be very helpful in rewriting these documents to improve clarity.

Many larger institutions also use student questionnaires

to evaluate their financial aid counselors. While such a technique should not in and of itself be the sole evaluation criterion, it can provide honest feedback about the counselors' approach, sensitivity, and honesty in communicating with students.

Student questionnaires can also be used by administrators to evaluate current aid policies and to determine whether the needs of all students are being met. Many institutions serve large numbers of part-time students, older students, and educationally disadvantaged students, and yet the policies and the services being administered fail to address the needs of these people. Office hours of the typical aid office may make it virtually impossible for evening students or weekend students to come by the aid office to obtain information or counseling; student expense budgets may ignore the true financial expenses of disadvantaged students or single-parent students who need additional financial help in paying for an alarm clock or a bedspread for their residence hall room or an allowance for child care expenses; or institutional policies in general may fail to provide the amount of assistance that will enable any aid recipient to enjoy a full collegiate experience without being a second-class citizen.

A second measure of an effective aid program that has long been endorsed by financial aid professionals is whether or not the aid program on a campus is centralized: "One organizational issue of major concern a decade ago—the need to implement a centralized office responsible for the administration of all kinds of financial assistance—no longer seems a problem. ... While some graduate and professional divisions of complex institutions continue to maintain separate financial aid offices to serve their particular student clientele, the centralization of undergraduate financial aid into a single office at each institution seems virtually complete" (Van Dusen and O'Hearne, 1980, p. 34). Recent evaluations conducted for the Department of Education have also indicated that there is more likelihood of error and overawarding at schools that have decentralized administrative structures for their aid programs. Still, in spite of these facts, many schools continue to utilize existing decentralized structures for administering aid; as a result, other financial benefits that may be going to an individual student—most notably, Veterans Administration and Social Security educational benefits, as well as graduate financial assistance and employment earnings—are often ignored, since they are most likely administered by some office other than the financial aid office. In today's climate of scarce resources, the need for closer coordination, control, and management of all aid dollars makes it even more important for schools to develop centralized operations. It is axiomatic that financial aid awarded to a student who does not need or deserve it denies the aid to one who does.

Another measure of an effective aid program is whether it is predicated on a strong philosophical base that complements the institution's goals and objectives. Every institution in our country has an overall educational mission; yet, regardless of how it is stated, the primary reason for each institution to exist is to help people to learn. Therefore, every experience within the institution should promote the learning process and ensure that the student is receiving the finest educational experience possible. Student aid programs and operations should be structured to reinforce the educational mission of the school and to encourage individuals to be free, independent, positive, and productive members of society. Aid administrators must, therefore, think of themselves as teachers and educators and should always approach students in a warm, accommodating, sensitive, and fair manner. At the same time, they should be firm and consistent with those who are attempting to beat the system or who fail to carry out their fair share of the process. Aid administration should be conducted in the best educational environment that is possible. Surroundings should be pleasant and comfortable and should encourage privacy and confidentiality of materials and discussions. Staff sizes should be adequate to carry out accurately and efficiently the legal and regulatory requirements of the programs within a time frame that is responsive and reasonable to meet the needs of the students, the donors, and the institution.

As John Koldus, vice president for student affairs at Texas A&M University once said, "The entire thrust of the financial aids program should have a success motivation and a success orientation. Every possible opportunity and every educational program should be provided to aid the student in successfully completing his academic program."

Bibliographical Note

The most directly useful resource for student aid program evaluation is the *Institutional Guide for Financial Aid Self-Evaluation* (National Association of Student Financial Aid Administrators, 1982b). It was developed specifically to assist administrators in evaluating their programs and as a guide to ensure compliance with federal program regulations. The guide is the basis for much of this chapter's discussion of audits and program review.

The "bible" for evaluation in general is the *Encyclopedia of Educational Evaluation: Concepts and Techniques for Evaluating Education and Training Programs* (Anderson and associates, 1975). This book is the most comprehensive treatment of evaluation and should be consulted at every stage of an evaluation study.

The highly useful *CSS Guide to Implementing Financial Aid Data Processing Systems* (Van Dusen, Higginbotham, and Jacobson, 1980) provides a complete treatment of evaluating the effectiveness and efficiency of newly installed computer systems.

Finally, the *Journal of Student Financial Aid* has published a number of articles pertaining to program evaluation. Two that deal with the problems and prospects of computerization are by Wedemeyer (1978), who offers a generalized discussion, and Pernal (1977), who focuses on the small college.

Part Four

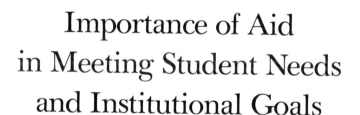

Importance of Aid
in Meeting Student Needs
and Institutional Goals

Administrators and policy makers at every college or university wish to ensure that their financial aid program supports the institution's objectives, however they may be defined. There have been numerous references in preceding parts of this book to the need to plan and revise policies and to consider using financial aid to meet enrollment goals and to achieve favorable retention rates. Chapters Thirteen through Fifteen are devoted to these critical topics. Chapter Sixteen discusses a relatively new area of concern—namely, legal implications of student aid. Chapter Seventeen identifies and evaluates the common themes and issues in the book, and Chapter Eighteen provides a look into the future by a leading scholar in the field.

In Chapter Thirteen James Nelson and Robert Fenske advocate conducting applied research into student aid matters in order to determine and enhance the impact of the aid office on institutional policy decisions. Nelson, former vice president of the College Scholarship Service and currently its project manager for new technology, has long advocated the involvement of aid officers in research, planning, and projections. Fenske has also advocated such involvement from his perspective as a university-based researcher. In this chapter they emphasize the need for institutional aid officers to project the amount and nature of the aid resources that will be needed in the future, and they detail the very specific issues that are part of developing a useful forecast. Nelson and Fenske then move on to treat the matter of policy analysis and pose the kinds of questions that must be answered in order to define a policy position. They also provide useful hints on how research results can be shared with others who should be informed.

In Chapter Fourteen Joseph Boyd and George Henning analyze the demographic factors and other critical considerations that bear on the college-going applicant pool and describe the options open to the college or university for achieving its desired enrollment goals. They treat the role of printed materials in communicating with applicants and explore how best to use the internal and external aid resources available. Their chapter is a primer on strategic use of financial aid in the highly competitive world of student recruiting. Boyd and Henning urge that student aid be used strictly in an ethical and responsible manner—specifically, that the college have available and actually deliver the proffered aid to the student and that only students be recruited who match the college's mission. The two authors have been active in marketing consultation with numerous colleges, and they describe a composite profile of colleges that have developed successful strategies and have met or exceeded enrollment goals with the planned, judicious use of student aid.

In Chapter Fifteen Leonard Wenc urges that, as a result of current demographic and fiscal circumstances, colleges and universities should evaluate their existing policies that bear on retention and attrition. He contends that much student attrition can be averted and that student aid can be a valuable tool in an overall strategy. Wenc emphasizes, however, that the entire institution must be mobilized to increase retention rates to satisfactory levels. His own experience, and a thorough review of the literature, are brought to bear on a series of recommendations for a retention plan. He observes that much of the attrition problem can be attributed to overzealous and indiscriminate recruiting, especially that done with student aid used as inducement without proper attention to student goals and capabilities.

Any thorough treatment of the various ways in which student financial aid can be used to further the objectives of colleges and universities must take note of the growing frequency of litigation in matters relating to student aid administration. In Chapter Sixteen Bruce Richardson, one of a handful of attorneys with recognized expertise on issues relating to student aid administration, identifies several areas of particular legal sensitivity. He treats such important issues as the conditions under which institutions of higher education can and should accept gifts for student aid purposes, the criteria for student aid eligibility, equal credit opportunity, contracting for off-campus employment, and the aid recipient's right of privacy. Richardson also provides a discussion of the legal problems related to collecting aid that is overawarded, secured by mistake or misrepresentation, or granted to a student who subsequently becomes ineligible, as well as aid that must be repaid as a student loan. One very useful section of the chapter describes the legal implications of terminating a student's aid. To the best of our knowledge, Richardson's chapter is the only current nationally published research focusing on the legal implications of student aid administration. The chapter is as useful to academic and business affairs administrators as it is to aid officers.

Chapter Seventeen provides an overview of all the preceding chapters. Robert Fenske and Robert Huff select salient points from each chapter and, using a narrative approach, synthesize and integrate key points made independently throughout this volume. Fenske and Huff then conclude the chapter with a discussion of two additional perspectives: the need for student financial aid to become a true professional field, which would include establishing preservice training and credentials, and the need for and potential of aid administrators to become much more influential in developing policy for their institutions.

Any treatise on the subject of student financial aid could well become an instant best seller among college and university administrators and policy makers if it were to include accurate predictions of what is certain to occur in the field in the next twenty, ten, or even five years. Being unable to identify an infallible prognosticator to author Chapter Eighteen, the editors turned to a knowledgeable and highly regarded observer—not only of the Washington scene but of state and private student aid programs—for his advice to administrators about what might happen to student aid and what trends to look for in the years ahead. Lawrence Gladieux, after taking stock of where student aid seems to be at present and noting some fundamental value judgments that are at stake, discusses current trends and suggests how these trends may affect student aid. He considers such topics as "student aid and the manpower issue," "a larger corporate role in student support," and "military needs and postsecondary financing." His discussion entitled "Filling the Gap: Who Will Pay" is one of the most insightful treatments of higher education policy issues now available.

13

Strategies for Improving Research, Projections, and Policy Development

James E. Nelson
Robert H. Fenske

This chapter is frankly evangelistic in tone and purpose. The intent is to convert dubious and even skeptical administrators to enthusiasm or at least acceptance about the value of research in student aid. We recognize that for most aid administrators there are both obstacles and seeming lack of incentives in doing research other than that mandated for reporting and evaluation purposes. To other administrators in the institution, student aid often is a "no man's land" where the institution's scholars and administrative staff analysts rarely if ever tread. However, we contend that research not only can help the aid office do its job better but can have further value and be satisfying and rewarding as well.

This chapter will emphasize applied research of the "operations analysis" type rather than the more abstract and theoretical type—research that deals more with the "what" and "how" of student aid than the "why" and "what if" questions. At the institutional level, few aid and academic administrators have the resources and opportunities to research the important but less urgent theoretical questions. Later in the chapter, however, we urge the wide dissemination of findings through presentation at professional conferences and publication as a professional responsibility.

Conditions in the student aid field are not usually conducive to research. One problem is that the field is process oriented, and the administrators who labor in it are immersed midstream in a sometimes overwhelming flood of paper and applicants. The work loads are heavy with the press of moving documents and money on tight schedules and coping with too many students who need help *now*. This continual press of things to do that have immediate results in one way frees aid officers from having to deal with the peculiar ambiguities and frustration that often accompany research. A day spent in processing so many applications, packaging aid for so many students, and awarding so many dollars may be exhausting, but it is somehow immediately satisfying; the results are there and can be tallied at the end of the day. In contrast, a day spent in futilely attempting to determine a relationship in a maze of stubborn data can result in pure, deep frustration. After a hectic day of processing, one can sink wearily into an easy chair and feel deserving when the family dog brings comfortable slippers. After a frustrating day of little progress after much cerebral wrestling with a research problem, the family dog may wisely stay well out of sight.

Because student aid is process rather than outcome oriented, it is not amenable to the "fun" kinds of research where one determines the results of manipulating variables—for example, deliberately withholding aid from an experimental sample of needy students to see how well they cope just isn't done. Furthermore, there is no single set of goals or philosophy or underlying theory of student aid; thus, there is no hypothesis testing.

Higher education middle managers in general and student aid officers in particular are not prime prospects for either the opportunity or the incentives in doing research. Scott (1979, p. 93) provides a rather bleak view of their role conflicts: "They enter the career field to work with students, but find that they work mostly with paper. They have high institutional loyalty, but must look off campus for training, guidance, recognition, collegueship, and rewards. They are highly oriented to service, but find increasing pressures to exert both administrative and financial controls. They have little substantial contact with faculty and senior officers, but want higher status on campus. . . . On campus, financial aid officers are thought of by both administrative peers and superiors to be paper shufflers in a basically clerical function. . . . The lack of a knowledgeable superior up the line seriously affects the condition of aid officers." To offset this pessimistic view, the National Association of Student Financial Aid Administrators (NASFAA) and the American Council on Education (ACE) have alerted many institutional chief executives to the importance of the student aid function on their campus. If aid officers can follow up on this sensitization with some valuable policy-analytic and operations research, the importance of their role will be solidified. One can, through dissemination of research findings, change "the lack of a knowledgeable superior up the line."

Improved communication, especially that which results in knowledgeable superiors, is one of the most important goals of research on student aid. The aid officer and/or the vice president for student services, for example, may need to convey to other administrators and the governing board the deep dependence of the institution on state and federal student aid. The degree of dependence may be so great that even relatively minor cutbacks at either the state or federal level would decimate enrollment. Simulation of some of the disastrous effects may not be a welcome message to the chief executive, but the information is vital for planning. And the president and board will certainly realize the importance of the aid office. Later we offer a number of specific suggestions and model formats for communicating with student aid's many constituencies, including central administration.

Projecting

Almost anyone responsible for administering a student aid program is confronted with the seemingly impossible task of projecting how much money will be needed for next year, or for the years ahead. The answer to that policy research question has enormous implications for an institution or agency and can lead to significant actions. Without an adequate and accurate knowledge of the aggregate financial need of the population to be served, it is impossible to assume that the optimum amount of financial aid can be made available. To develop such a forecast, a number of related issues must be addressed:

1. What is the aggregate financial need of the current student population?
2. How much financial aid will be required to offset increases in student charges and expenses for some or all of the students?
3. What will changes in the enrollment and composition of the student population do to the demand for aid funds?
4. What would be the impact of changing current methods of calculating student and parental contributions?
5. How would aid awards be affected if institutional policies or external economic circumstances resulted in modifications to standard or actual student self-help contributions?
6. What will be the impact of proposed changes in funding levels and eligibility requirements for existing federal or state student aid programs?
7. How would the implementation of a new or different student aid program or new dependency rules affect the need for total aid resources?
8. Will a particular packaging strategy result in overexpenditure or underexpenditure of available student aid funds?
9. What will be the unmet student need for aid, given the total resources available and certain packaging rules?

These are just a few of the questions that must be answered by financial aid policy analysis. The most accurate way to estimate the impact of these kinds of changes is to calculate individually what the changes would do to the financial need of each student in an actual or hypothetical population, and then to sum the cumulative effects. For all but the simplest situations, however, such a task is practically impossible. The populations are too large, the changes myriad, and the interactions too complex. Administrators seeking to determine the aggregate financial need of student groups must know the pertinent characteristics of those groups and the program requirements involved, must develop a reasonable set of assumptions about changes to take effect—and then must use a simulation model to estimate the overall impact.

Many aid administrators have developed their own modeling techniques and tools over the years. Some use only informal calculations and wild guesses on the backs of envelopes; others use the computer. Perhaps the most sophisticated approach is that used by institutions and agencies currently subscribing to PARS (Packaging Aid Resources System), a computer software system offered by the College Scholarship Service (CSS) of the College Board. By using a PARS coding form to analyze aggregate need, an administrator can invoke and control any number of changes to student records in a computer file to simulate the individual and cumulative impact of those changes. The PARS system can thus be used for a variety of projective purposes. It uses scientific sampling and weighting to determine packaging parameters. For example, both an inventory of funds available for awarding and student category groups are maintained separately from the data base and are called into the actual packaging program as desired. Since PARS assigns students to groups according to user-specified combinations of characteristics (ethnicity, high school academic achievement, and so forth), the system can simulate many different packaging and award configurations by varying the dollar amounts of various awards and the pattern of student group characteristics.

Many of the "home-grown" data systems also have considerable sophistication and potential for useful research. For example, the Office of Management and Financial Analysis at Arizona State University has developed a simulation model that enables the researcher to project the impact of enrollments of proposed federal Title IV cutbacks to college and even departmental levels within the university. The model develops a matrix based on historical data of student profiles according to percentage of need met by various federal programs. The loss of new enrollments and attrition of presently enrolled students are then estimated according to the increase in unmet need caused by program cutbacks. The model shows significant variation in potential enrollment losses among the university's colleges and departments.

Other modeling tools have been built and offered as services to aid administrators over the years (the Educational Testing Service's Financial Aid Planning Model in 1978 and CSS's Financial Aid Study Tool as early as 1972), but these models have not been updated for current use. A common feature with these approaches has been the use of a limited amount of readily available *summary* data, rather than individual student calculations, to simulate answers to a variety of "what if" questions. They commonly employ an estimate of number of student applicants, college expense budgets, inflation rates, distribution of family incomes, estimated growth rates of parents' income, student income and summer earnings, and eligibility and packaging rules for major student aid programs. A change in any one of these elements can be made on a coding form, resulting in a full recalculation of the estimated aggregate impact on financial need caused by that change.

The projective models described above generally imply the availability of a fairly substantial central computer system. But the capability to do useful research on student aid is by no means restricted to those at institutions with such hardware. For example, a pencil, a calculator, and a columnar pad can be used to accomplish the same research results as described above, with several hours of work involved if any variable is changed. Software on a "home" microcomputer has been successfully used to perform these tasks of resource forecasting in minutes rather than hours. Even small towns now have "computer stores" with many examples of management planning and research models available at low cost that can be used efficiently for anything from family budgeting to student aid resource planning. Computer or programming experience is not necessary to use such a tool, and, once a "worksheet" has been organized for the purpose, multiple "what if" calculations can be performed in seconds. Altering any number in the system results in instant recalculation of every other affected item, the "worksheets" can be saved on disk for future use, and simple graphs of the results can even be produced.

Policy Analysis

Responding to changing conditions in student aid requires extraordinary, and almost constant, change by most institutions—and by the administrators involved. The variety and number of skills needed for future success in the financial aid field will jump well beyond anything experienced in the past. Duties will be very different in most cases, and will require new skills and expertise.

Who on any given campus knows more about what is happening outside of the campus that is going to affect what happens inside campus, in terms of economics and resources, than the competent aid administrator? Almost always the answer is no one. Yet, how many deans or directors of aid are sitting on or have direct access to long-range planning committees? Fortunately, more and more each year, with a few even reporting directly to the president of the college. But others are being left out of such planning efforts altogether.

As institutions plan for the future, the realization becomes obvious that the student is indeed the lifeblood of the institution. Therefore, the long-range planning committee must have as much information as possible about the number and characteristics of past, present, and future students. It needs answers to such questions as: What are our students' needs, goals, and expectations? How can we meet these needs? At what rate of expansion should we plan to grow? Should we consider stabilizing our enrollment over the next ten years? Should we cut back enrollment? Should we consider special programs in order to capture some of the part-time and adult local population market? Should we increase our engineering offerings and decrease our education program? Should we begin to decrease the size of our faculty? Shall we increase our admissions standards and gradually decrease our enrollment? How much financial aid will be required to meet the needs of these student populations?

These and countless other critical questions face many institutions. Accurate and up-to-date data should be collected, tabulated, analyzed, displayed, and interpreted before decisions of such significant magnitude should be made. Financial aid offices can provide a great deal of the data. And this potentially places such an administrator in a position of real power—and responsibility.

Because of the recent importance of student financial aid to the financial health of most institutions, research on the topic can provide decision-influencing information at the highest levels of administration. The significance of the role of student aid is not yet fully understood by central administration in many colleges and universities. Changes in student aid levels can influence the institution's policies (such as admissions and tuition levels), operations (such as budgeting and physical facilities), and planning (such as enrollment projections). However, the student aid office is rarely involved in policy analysis (even though its role is vital) because it is usually at least one administrative layer removed from decision making and because the expertise and traditions of data analysis are lacking.

The unit on most campuses charged with developing information for policy analysis is the office of institutional studies. Typically, institutional studies officers have only limited and/or indirect access to student aid data, even though such data are fundamental to analysis of many policy questions. A liaison naturally suggests itself: By cooperating with the office of institutional studies in development and adaptation of data for policy analyses, the student aid office can create a symbiotic relationship. The office of institutional studies can get the data it needs more quickly and easily; the student aid office receives the necessary recognition of its importance.

Fenske and Parker (1981) suggest that the offices of institutional studies and student financial aid have great potential for a symbiotic relationship that can improve administrative decision making within the institution. They contend that student aid is probably the prime example of a newly emergent function on campus whose importance is undervalued because it is not recognized as related to most of the vital operations of the institution. Part of the reason is that data relating to student aid are not routinely incorporated into the administrative data system. Typically, student aid data systems relate only to fiduciary and application-processing functions. Yet models such as the one at Arizona State University mentioned earlier can easily show that even moderate changes in student aid parameters, such as funding levels or program eligibility requirements, can drastically affect enrollment, retention, public relations, affirmative action, and a host of other factors. Fenske and Parker propose a model by which the student aid office can become incorporated into the main "policy-building" administrative data and planning system of the institution.

Increasingly, recognition of student aid in maintaining the vitality of the institution is bringing collaboration with many other important functions. Sometimes the collaboration is in response to external pressures. An example of a state-sponsored study is the one undertaken by the University of Wisconsin System (Kauffman, 1982). Members of the system—representing Budget and Development, Academic Planning, Business Affairs, Financial Aid, Student Affairs, and Systems Administration—were brought together and charged with the task of defining a policy position with respect to the following questions:

1. What should be the role of financial aid in assuring access to the educational opportunities provided by system institutions?
2. What is the appropriate role of each of the three types of aid (grant, loan, and employment opportunities)? Is the existing mix among grant, loan, and work-study aid consistent with these roles?
3. How well do the existing aid programs serve the needs of the system's students?
4. What should be the responsibility of the state to provide

support for need-based grant, loan, and work-study programs?
5. What are specific recommendations for the future role,
administration, and funding for the Wisconsin Higher Education Grant program and the State Direct Loan program?
6. What policy recommendations on the future of federal financial aid efforts should be communicated to Wisconsin's
congressional delegation and to national associations of
higher education?

Who Are the Researchers?

Research can be conducted by anyone who identifies a
problem, understands its elements, and has some idea about
how to solve it. It is increasingly important that financial aid research be linked directly to the world of practice, and nobody
can do that better than practitioners. Perhaps it does take a
trained research specialist to conduct long-range, follow-up research, or studies dealing with highly theoretical behavior models. But much of what really needs to be done in financial aid is
more immediate, practical, short-term research. What is needed
is the skillful use of data that aid administrators are in the best
position to provide—not just collecting and analyzing data but
displaying and interpreting them, and then sharing them with
others on campus.

Many aid administrators have acquired some of the skills
that are and will be required to be central in planning for the future. And, in fact, some are very sophisticated users, managers,
and providers of information. Research can be conducted within a one-man shop with little or no computer support. The main
concern is to identify what research is needed by defining a
problem or an area for clarification. The results of these research studies need not be complex, but they can be enlighten-
ing to the office, other offices on campus, the faculty, and the
administration.

This is not a cookbook, and this chapter presents no simplistic recipes to follow in doing research. If the prospective researcher has had no formal academic training for the task, the

college library and bookstore will have an array of useful books, ranging from the most elementary to the most advanced. The bibliographical note that concludes this chapter suggests some sources. Beginner or brush-up courses are probably available in the institution, or through extension, evening, or correspondence courses of other institutions. Consultative help is available from a variety of sources, including state, regional, and national professional associations and from qualified faculty on the administrator's or a nearby campus. Many universities have graduate departments of higher education, educational psychology, and other fields, and can often provide graduate students on a paid or unpaid internship basis to conduct specific research projects. However, we believe the best source of help is the on-campus institutional studies unit, as described earlier, because of the quality of assistance there and the mutuality of interest in student aid.

While we provide no step-by-step recipe for doing research, following are ten rules for conducting easy policy research (slightly modified from the form first presented as an address by James E. Nelson at the annual meeting of the College Board, New York, October 1978):

1. *Know What Is Needed.* It is important to know what you want to do before you do it. It is of ultimate importance to identify the problems to be solved and the goals to be reached— whether for use on the job or for other decision makers who need the kinds of information that you can provide. Try to separate out the essentials from the "wouldn't it be nice to know" questions. Break down the complex questions to simple ones. In financial aid—rather than tackling the broad question of "How much aid is required to meet the needs of our students?"—the more focused question might be "How effectively are we matching the needs of our freshman applicants with attractive offers of aid?"

2. *Don't Wait to Be Asked.* If someone has to ask for information, you, as an administrator, have waited too long. The effective administrator has to anticipate the important issues that will be arising and try to be slightly ahead of them. Senior administrators on a campus are interested not only in facts about

the numbers of students applying for aid; they also need to know and understand the issues involved that influence student choice, such as the impact of a pending tuition increase on applications for admission and financial aid. Who is in a better position on campus to spell out likely effects than the persons responsible for aid? The presentation of such knowledge will be even more powerful if the aid office works together with the admissions office in combining information, experience, and clout. Partial information at the time it is needed is better than complete information after the fact. Even ambiguous or incomplete results will and should be used if they are the best available.

3. *Do It for More Than One Purpose.* In putting together information for a committee, for the state, for the U.S. Department of Education, or for any group, plan also to use selected results in memos to senior administrators or to others on campus who would be interested in the findings, and find ways to share what has been found with colleagues in letters, speeches, and published articles.

4. *Use What You've Got in the Desk Drawer First.* As a corollary of sharing work with others, make sure to first use the results of work that already has been done. "If you've got it, flaunt it." Others listen to someone who has something to say, particularly if facts and figures can be used to support opinion and supposition. This often is the way that "experts" are born. In financial aid there are a number of pieces of information of interest to others that can be pulled directly off the student's application form. Some might not think of this information as research, but others on campus would be amazed and impressed by the wealth of data that are annually compiled.

5. *Take Advantage of What Others Have Done.* Look for the experiences of others that can help to answer a question. (a) Take advantage of existing resources and of potential collaborators for policy research within your own institution. Seek out these people and gain their assistance. (b) Combining research efforts with other offices on campus will decrease the work load and increase the impact of the information provided by increasing the scope of your audience. Apart from financial aid office

data on hand, other valuable stockpiles of relevant information and assistance can be found in other offices on campus, such as the registrar's office, the placement office, and the admissions office. Try these places first before starting to collect new data. (c) As noted earlier, be sure to consult with personnel in the institutional research office. They are a source of invaluable data and can provide direction and assistance as you attempt your research studies. Collaboration with the institutional research office can be a vital link for the successful research project.

A number of outside agencies also regularly provide information that can be very useful in responding to policy issues. Available sourcebooks, such as the annual *ACE Norms for Freshmen,* can be used to compare freshmen at one institution with those at other institutions, or the research literature can be used to find out who else has studied a given issue, such as financial aid for minority students. The references in this chapter and in the Selective Guide to the Literature at the end of this book also note a number of resources.

In short, before mounting a large effort to collect new information, check to make sure that it does not already exist. And, in addition, use outside sources for comparison in checking results generated for your own institution.

6. *Keep It Simple.* What needs to be done with good data on hand is to abstract small bits of information that can be easily communicated to others who are involved in policy decisions and actions. One-page memos addressing a single issue, with an offer to provide more detailed information if requested, will gain a lot more attention than a thirty-page report. One approach to consider is the notion of a memo-a-month. Policy research that takes the form of a crisp, brief memo on a single page, once a month, can be a powerful way of gaining attention and action.

Don't expect the results of research work to be appreciated or used unless a question has been answered and findings properly communicated to the right people in an easy-to-understand form. Exhibits 1, 2, and 3 at the end of this chapter may serve to illustrate the point. They include (1) a report on packaging practices and policies, (2) a memo to the president's attention on the amount of new student aid money required with a tuition increase, and (3) a note to the faculty on academic quality of aid recipients.

7. *Don't Use Fancy Statistics.* Policy research does not have to be elegant and use fancy statistics. Administrators are sometimes reluctant to even begin a research study without having some training in research or statistics. Yet, for most audiences, the very same statistics are not understood and often tend to discourage potential users from reading reports. Again, if action is to result, someone must be able to read and understand your report. Head counts, means, ranges, and an occasional standard deviation can provide a wealth of useful information in policy research. If it is possible to illustrate the data with simple tables, bar graphs, or pie charts, so much the better.

8. *Do It.* The kind of policy research suggested here does not necessarily have to take a lot of time, but it does take discipline. "One pagers" can cover a variety of research issues, and most can be pulled together with available data in a few hours' time—or even less if there are good data access and report-writing capability through the computer center or a minicomputer in the aid office. The most critical step is then to disseminate a report. Too many administrators do all the work and then put the information away without sharing it. With appropriate copies to key administrators on campus, it is possible to establish the aid office as an important source of information critical to the process of policy planning.

9. *Do More—It Gets Easier.* As one looks over the professional publications in financial aid, the same names appear among the lists of authors again and again. Few of those listed are "professional researchers." They are other administrators who have shared what they have done. Having produced one article, they start working on a second, and a third, and a fourth. And finally they become recognized as "experts."

An attitude often encountered is best expressed by the statement "I don't have time to do policy research. I'm too busy putting out fires and handling crises." But the cry also can be heard "How do I get the president's attention? Why am I not involved in policy decisions that affect my program?"

Research—both routine analyses of existing data collected for another purpose and imaginative problem-solving investigations—is something every aid administrator should do, simply by picking an area where he or she has some experience and interest, where the results can be used, and where the necessary data can be obtained. And it should be a dynamic activity, one that is regularly used in the process of making policy and practice decisions. The problems—and the unanswered questions—are easy to list. What is needed are more practitioners interested in finding the solutions to the problems and the answers to the questions.

10. *Fight for Change with What You Know.* These ten rules end where they began. Policy research *can* and most often *should* present and support a position. Advocacy and action are legitimate goals. Efforts need *not* be neutral. At the same time, do not abandon intuition or experience simply on the basis of some limited information. The more research results challenge generally accepted assumptions or entrenched procedures, the stronger should be the data that support a recommendation for action.

And remember students in the process. When students are involved in policy research, they should not be treated as "subjects" but, rather, as participants in the process who stand to gain. Research outcomes should be communicated to students as important members of the decision-making chain, and student support can be a most effective mechanism for translating the results of policy research into action.

Bibliographical Note

This chapter attempted to proselytize student aid and academic administrators into initiating research activities if they have not already started and to urge more involvement of those already in the field. In keeping with the emphasis on why to do research rather than how to do it, the body of the chapter did not dwell on published resources. For those aid and academic administrators already doing sophisticated research on student aid (and there are many), advice is hardly needed from us on sources that will "get you started." However, for those who can use such advice, we offer the following suggestions.

A good, brief introduction to student aid research is "The Handyperson's Guide to Student Aid Research" (Van Dusen, 1980). We especially like the section on "Why Bother?"—probably because it presents a positive message similar to the thesis of this chapter.

Both the American College Testing Program and the College Scholarship Service of the College Board offer normative profiles of the student users of their financial aid services. These annual publications are models of data presentation and can be consulted for examining a variety of tables, graphs, and charts as done by experts.

For those who wish to consult very basic texts to refresh their memories from undergraduate or graduate courses on research design and statistics, or to find a beginning to learn about doing research, we recommend the following three books.

The first is very aptly titled *A Basic Course in Statistics* (Anderson and Zelditch, 1968). It has stood the test of time in innumerable sociological courses as the best introduction to a sometimes intimidating subject. "This is probably among the most elementary of all elementary texts on statistics. The book is designed with the specific and pleasant intention of attracting the student who is frightened of mathematics. There are no mathematical derivations whatsoever in the text. We presume only some knowledge of arithmetic. . . . [Nonetheless,] it is a book in which we are concerned, throughout, that the student should learn how to recognize just when to apply a given technique and when not to, and to understand what kinds of assumptions are implied in the application" (pp. vii, viii).

The second work, *Statistical Concepts for the Social Sciences* (Korn, 1975), focuses on descriptive statistics and provides a thorough, straightforward introduction to all of the basic techniques.

The third text, *The Research Process in Education* (Fox,

1969), is the most thorough and comprehensive elementary source we can recommend for learning how to think like a researcher. The chapters cover such topics as "A Case Study in Research Design," "The Nature of Data and Variables," "The Survey Approach," and "The Data-Analysis and Data-Gathering Plans."

We also recommend the encyclopedic book on educational evaluation edited by Anderson and associates (1975). It focuses on evaluation but is useful for all types of research.

The "computer stores" mentioned above that seem to be sprouting up everywhere will provide user-oriented classes and self-teaching modules on how to use the analysis and computer graphics programs of the equipment. The computer service units of colleges and universities typically offer such instruction also.

Finally, we urge those who do research for any purpose to present papers at professional meetings and to consider submitting their findings for publication in the *Journal of Student Financial Aid* or *College and University* or anywhere else the material can be brought to the attention of professionals in the field. This activity is a professional obligation, promotes the advancement of one's career and writing capabilities, and is immensely satisfying.

Exhibit 1. A Report on Packaging Practices and Policies.

TO: Financial Aid Committee   cc: President

FROM: Director of Financial Aid   Vice President

CONCERNING: Financial Aid Packaging Policies   Director of Admissions

It is important to review some of the results of our current packaging policies, as we look forward to possible changes for this coming year. The following graph illustrates the way in which aid (from all sources) was awarded to undergraduate students at the college last year.

% of Full-Time Undergrads	% of All Aid Recipients	Family Income Levels	Average Aid Package			Average Total Aid	Average Net Cost to Family
			Grant	Loan	Work		
11	26	Under $9,000	$3,043	$1,032	$387	$4,462	$1,138
17	40	$9,000–$15,000	2,300	986	387	3,673	1,927
16	20	$15,000–$21,000	1,650	1,035	387	3,073	2,527
18	9	$21,000–$27,000	1,120	1,026	387	2,531	3,069
35	3	$27,000 and above	791	1,015	387	2,193	3,407
3	2	Independent	2,190	916	387	3,493	2,107

Several observations about our current packaging policies are apparent:

1. All parents and students, including low-income families, make substantial contributions toward our typical educational expenses of $5,600. In aggregate, our 1,105 students on aid brought $2,323,000 of family resources to bear on their educational expenses, combined with $3,987,000 in student aid funds (all but $320,000 from federal, state, and private resources outside the college).

2. All students are expected to borrow and work like amounts before grant aid is awarded.

3. Middle- and upper-middle-income families do qualify for and receive student financial aid at the college.

With the assumption that costs and available resources will remain about the same for the next year, I will ask that you consider the following questions at our next meeting:

1. Are our current packaging policies fair and equitable, or do they need to be modified?

2. Should we include the above graphic illustration of our packaging policy in materials for our prospective students, giving them a reasonable indication of our typical aid awards?

Exhibit 2. A Report to the President on Potential Impact of an Increase in College Costs.

TO: The President   cc: Vice President
FROM: Director of Financial Aid   Director of Admissions
SUBJECT: Student Aid Requirements with Increased College Costs

I understand that serious consideration is being given by the trustees to an increase of $400 in student fees for next year. Such an increase in costs would have a considerable impact on the aid resources required to meet the resulting student financial need. The following table should help to illustrate my point:

Family Income Levels	Under Current Costs		With a $400 Increase in Costs	
	% of Undergrads with Need, and Average Aid Package		Additional % with Need, and Average Aid Increase Required	Total New Aid Required
Under $9,000	100%	$4,462	+ 0%	$400	$112,000
$9,000–$15,000	96	3,673	+ 3	400	182,000
$15,000–$21,000	56	3,073	+11	390	105,950
$21,000–$27,000	22	2,531	+ 6	365	52,045
$27,000 and above	4	2,193	+ 3	310	21,570
Independent	30	3,493	+15	380	13,360
Average	43	3,580	+ 5	367	486,925

In this table, it is assumed that:

1. Next year's student body will have similar characteristics of family income and ability to pay for college as is true for this year.
2. All continuing students who now have financial need and aid will require additional aid to offset a $400 increase in costs.
3. With a $400 cost increase, an increased number and percentage of students will demonstrate some need and require offsetting aid at all income levels.
4. We presently are expecting students and parents to contribute to the limits of their ability before awarding aid.
5. Unaided students with unmet need will not enroll with us next fall.

We have estimated our increased allocation of federal funds for this coming year to be $80,000. And we estimate additional state aid in the amount of $35,000. This $115,000 can be applied directly against the estimate of $487,000 in new aid required—leaving an aid deficit of $372,000.

Based on the above information and assumptions, I would suggest the following:

1. A portion of the tuition increase be set aside to provide an increased institutional source of aid for students.
2. Estimations of enrollment should be altered to project a possible decline in new as well as returning students.
3. The college should notify students at the earliest date that the increase is confirmed, so that alternative arrangements may be made if the college cannot meet their full need.

Exhibit 3. A Report to Faculty on Academic Quality of Aid Recipients.

TO: Dean of Faculty	cc: Department Chairpersons
FROM: Director of Financial Aid	President
SUBJECT: Quality Indicators of Students	Vice President
on Aid	Student Financial Aid
	Committee
	Director of Admissions

It is my understanding that some of the college's student financial aid policies and practices came under question at your last meeting with department chairpersons. Specifically, I have learned that there is concern about the need for additional scholarship and grant funds to be directed toward attracting and holding more top scholars.

There are several points about current policy and practice that should be made:

1. We are in the fortunate position of being able to meet, with a package of aid, the full documented financial need of all admitted and enrolled applicants. We did deny aid to twenty-two top students who applied for aid but who were unable to demonstrate financial need (although we do refer all such applicants to attractive loan programs external to the college). Sixteen of the twenty-two enrolled.
2. We do not offer aid in excess of need—and we do not have resources to do so unless we are to reallocate funds now committed to students with need—but we do take steps to be sure that aid offers to our best applicants are both attractive and competitive. Our experience is that the rate of acceptance on offers of admission and aid to top applicants is over 75%—compared to an average of 65% for all offers of admission and aid.
3. Over two thirds of our top students in the last entering class applied for and received aid sufficient to meet their need. The following chart illustrates the distribution of aid to freshmen who entered in 1982, with academic promise represented by indicator levels of high school grade point average (GPA) and SAT–Verbal (V) test scores. Clearly, the academic quality of our entering students would be markedly lower without our strong financial aid program.

Entering Freshmen, 1982

H.S. GPA	% on Aid	SAT–V	% on Aid
3.50–4.00 (28% of total)	68%	700–800 (12% of total)	76%
3.00-3.50 (36% of total)	52%	600-700 (38% of total)	62%
2.50-3.00 (22% of total)	46%	500-600 (26% of total)	40%
2.00-2.50 (11% of total)	58%	400-500 (16% of total)	36%
Below 2.00 (3% of total)	50%	Below 400 (8% of total)	52%

14

Using Student Aid in Recruiting and Admissions

Joseph D. Boyd
George E. Henning

Most managers of postsecondary institutions assume that stable or even declining enrollments will be the reality of the next two decades for most colleges. These same managers know that their colleges will need to sustain and even expand present tuition revenue levels in order to survive. To achieve enrollment goals in the years ahead, therefore, a postsecondary institution must understand marketing techniques and use them effectively. Kotler (1976, p. 5) has provided a widely accepted, process-oriented definition: "Marketing is human activity directed at satisfying needs and wants through exchange processes." Marketing requires hard work, sophisticated planning, tough evaluation, and well-selected personnel who can give clear, concise, and acceptable answers to a student's question "How can I afford to go to this college?"

Student financial aid is a vital ingredient in the marketing process. For many students, especially in high-cost colleges, it is a requirement for full-time attendance. In a longitudinal study conducted by the Illinois State Scholarship Commission (Boyd and others, 1981), about 60 percent of the students receiving state-funded grants or scholarships reported that they would not have been able to attend any college full time without the aid. How to market, manage, and use student financial aid is the supreme challenge and necessity for all colleges. The extensive and well-planned marketing efforts of a college and its personnel to interpret, offer, and use student financial aid can make the difference between success and failure in the competitive environment for students.

The Current Scene

A substantial majority of all students at private colleges and about half of the students in the public sector cannot meet total college costs with their own financial resources (savings, earnings, and parental contributions). If they are to be able to enroll, therefore, these students need financial assistance from outside sources—primarily from the state and federal governments (in the form of grants or loans) and from the institution itself (in the form of scholarships and grants paid to students and/or discounted costs by the use of waivers). The tuition revenues from outside sources and the student's own resources in turn provide the revenue to institutions to pay salaries and meet their other budgeted expenses.

Meeting college costs involves the agreement of many parties. Taxpayers and their elected representatives in the last decade have agreed that a growing part of the taxpayer revenue should be used for college grants and loans. This attitude is now changing. Parents, when financially able, now must invest a larger part of their resources in the postsecondary education of their dependent child. Similarly, the students must now invest more substantially in themselves by savings prior to college, earnings while in college, and by borrowing funds. The college now must raise more funds from friends or alumni to be used for scholarships, grants, and loans. Unless the parents, students, and colleges do their expected and required share at an ever-increasing level during inflationary times, enrollment and retention of students will be adversely affected.

In marketing terminology, the educational institution is a provider offering services to consumers (parents and students). Each provider has much competition. How to compete successfully is the vital question. Student financial aid is the required "means to an end," since it enables the consumer to consider the services (college attendance) to be purchased. When the college disseminates information about available student aid funds, it can also inform potential consumers about its educational services and their value.

Institutions must determine which potential student clienteles and geographical areas are their primary and secondary student markets. Dollars and efforts should be concentrated in the primary market because of the expected larger return in enrollment and retention of students. Dollars spent in other than primary or secondary markets are truly experimental.

All decisions in the marketing of student aid must conform to federal and state procedures and policies. No institution can afford the adverse publicity of audit irregularities. Books and files must be open to federal and state auditors for all institutions accepting federal or state student aid dollars. The institution must continually monitor the legality and conformance of student aid practices.

Student financial aid for postsecondary students is big business. Currently, about seven million students annually receive some type of state and/or federal grant and/or loan assistance to help meet college costs. Furthermore, for most colleges and universities, the dollars provided from government sources or programs represent a major portion of student aid revenues. During the last half of the 1970s and the early 1980s, the states and the federal government provided student grants and educational loans to a degree that almost any needy student found a loan and/or grant to meet educational costs at the college of his or her choice. Student aid thus helped stabilize enrollments at most colleges.

As the 1982-83 academic year approached, there was

much anxiety about enrollment and student aid. Other public priorities were successfully competing for limited government resources. Postsecondary education was no longer a growth industry. Federal and many state governments made plans to control expenditures, and student aid was under close scrutiny. Most educators and legislators assume that several dramatic changes of all types—reflected in levels of appropriations, definitions of financial need, maximum award amounts from government funding, need tests for guaranteed loans, and other policies and procedures—are ahead. State and institutional decisions about student aid are not made in a vacuum. Because many needy students use both state and federal programs to meet their needs, decisions made in Washington, D.C., and state capitols have dramatic impact on all states and institutions as they plan their student aid programs.

In November 1981 questionnaire responses were obtained by Joseph D. Boyd from twenty-one chief administrators of state student aid programs. (The study was commissioned by the Illinois Board of Higher Education; the results were not published.) The administrators had been asked to express their opinion of trends from 1981 to 1985, including known or estimated funding of respective state programs from 1978 to 1985, specific state reactions to reductions in Pell Grant funds, and potential responses to any other changes in federal student aid. States surveyed were California, Connecticut, Florida, Illinois, Indiana, Iowa, Kentucky, Massachusetts, Michigan, Minnesota, Missouri, North Carolina, New Jersey, New York, Ohio, Oregon, Pennsylvania, Tennessee, Texas, Vermont, and Wisconsin. The twenty-one states awarded $850 million in scholarships and grants in 1981-82.

The administrators expressed much anxiety about the planned reductions in federal and state student aid dollars, new definitions of the ability of a family to pay for college costs, new and higher expectations from the student in meeting costs, and the threat that certain colleges would not survive. More specifically, the state aid administrators believed the following trends were most likely to occur between 1981 and 1985:

- Parent(s) will be asked to conform to a standard formula requiring sacrifice of their resources to help meet college costs.
- A number of colleges, for financial reasons, will not survive.
- Tuition charges at public institutions will increase at a much faster rate than in the recent past.
- The role of student self-help (savings, earnings, and/or loans) will increase as a percentage of all resources to meet college costs.
- Tuition charges at private colleges will significantly increase.
- Changes at the federal level on student aid will be frequent and dramatic.
- New plans/procedures to make monthly payments of college costs will evolve.
- More detailed verification of income/asset information submitted by parents and student applicants will take place.
- More students will select colleges to which they can commute.
- Stricter academic progress requirements will be legislated or included in regulations for continued student aid.
- More states will establish enrollment ceilings at their public institutions.
- There will be a significant increase in half-time student enrollment.
- Federal decisions on how to calculate financial need will dominate student aid practices.
- Portability of state awards will decrease.
- The maximum Pell Grant award will decrease.
- Pell Grant dollars will decrease.
- Postsecondary education and its needs will become a less important priority in government decision making.
- State grant/scholarship award dollars for all states will significantly decrease.

State student aid administrators see difficult years ahead. Federal and state funding for scholarships and grants is assumed to increase only modestly, if at all. States appear to be willing to look at new and expanded loan programs and anticipate assisting the most needy where funds become limited. As dollars become more limited, there is a majority opinion that access (the opportunity to enroll at some college) will predominate over the goal of reasonable choice among many colleges.

State and federal decisions on student aid for postsecondary education in the early to mid-1980s are extremely important for both the thousands of students affected and the viability and continued existence of many colleges.

Institutional Options

The recent growth of state and federal student grant aid has made such funds the basic source of all student gift aid. A college's ability to reach desired enrollment goals is directly related to the availability and use of state and federal grants. Very few colleges can replace any decreases of federal and/or state appropriations for student grants with dollars from other resources. All colleges should follow the rule that other aid for students is secondary to the primary sources of federal and state aid.

Every student aid administrator must know both the federal and state aid programs and the people responsible for administering them, and must keep up with the annual changes in procedures and eligibility requirements. Letters, manuals, application forms, and procedures and legislation related to these programs must receive high-priority attention. Personal contacts with administrators of these programs can give an institution a competitive edge. Specifically, student aid directors should (1) read all correspondence, reports, and bulletins from federal and state program offices; (2) visit by telephone or in person the individuals who can provide further clarification of questions or concerns; and (3) issue frequent memos to presidents, financial aid personnel, admissions personnel, business officers, deans, and others, to make sure that all are currently informed and that each gives identical and accurate responses to students' questions dealing with federal and state student aid. Enrollments cannot be achieved at desired levels without the use of every federal and state grant, loan, or benefit for which the student is eligible. High school counselors, parents, and students need professional assistance to learn about, apply for, and receive these benefits. The college admissions and student aid personnel cannot evade the responsibility to provide such assistance. Every lost dollar from governmental sources places undue pressure on the institution to replace these funds from its own resources.

Even after a student receives every state or federal dollar that he or she is eligible for, a financial shortfall still may remain. That is when institutional creativity and action can make the difference. Funds from operational budgets, gifts from alumni and friends, and uncollected or waived tuition represent flexible ways to offer students funds to meet costs. The desired goal is to be able to ensure optimal or desired enrollment and achieve institutional objectives at the lowest possible investment of institutional dollars. To meet this goal, a careful and complete analysis of past aid decisions is required.

How well each college's aid package matches or exceeds that of competing colleges is another area for analysis. Packaging decisions—for example, when to offer loan and/or work funds instead of gift aid—require that an aid officer be sensitive to the individual needs of each student. The packaging process should be approached as a competitive marketing strategy. The colleges that will best survive the enrollment crises in the next decade will use more care and take more time to offer each student a package of aid that best fits individual circumstances. They will be cognizant of the continuing need of the student over the full period of college attendance.

Successful colleges will not only recruit new students but concentrate on the needs of continuing students. Introducing students to the campus and retaining them until graduation should be viewed as one integrated program. "Retaining live bodies already enrolled has much more potential and can be much cheaper than scouring the countryside amid increasing competition for a shrinking number for potential enrollees. For example, if the dropout rate is approximately 50 percent over a four-year program in a student body of 1,000 and if the rate could be reduced by one half, this has the same effect as locating, recruiting, and enrolling 250 new students over that period each year, assuming a consistent rate. Student services of many types can be effective in this process, including counseling, housing, financial aid, and others" (Fenske, 1980, p. 59). (Chapter Fifteen in this book contains a detailed discussion of the role of student financial aid in increasing retention.) An investment of funds in a student who is likely to remain and graduate will add to total enrollment and will keep enrolled a student who is likely to remain qualified for continuing state and federal student grant dollars. Pursuit of this objective requires an extensive analysis of the aid packages of students who withdraw and those who remain enrolled at the institution.

Institution options that make the payment of educational charges more flexible for a student may well be equivalent to offering other financial aid benefits to a student. Such institutional options include (1) the use of major credit cards as method of payment, (2) individualized monthly payment plans to meet tuition and other costs, (3) provision of a reserve account to the agency administering Guaranteed Student Loans, (4) awareness and use of innovative programs such as tax-exempt bond loans, (5) expansion of donations by alumni and friends of the institution and designation of these funds for scholarships or grants, and (6) a systematic search for off-campus jobs that will pay significantly higher salaries than on-campus jobs.

Since printed materials sent to prospective and enrolled students are the major tools for the marketing process, institutions also should analyze these materials. Simply updating the last material used may be the easy way to meet deadlines, but for many institutions major changes will frequently be required. Examples of ways in which recently enrolled students were able to finance their college education should be displayed. Parents and students need to learn how the college has typically responded to other families with similar incomes and assets. Publications and other contacts must make prospective students feel that someone cares and wants to give them good and honest answers.

Although major national services will provide mailing labels for prospective students of almost any category of students requested by the institution, many dollars can be wasted unless there are clear indications that large mailings make a difference. Therefore, every applicant for admission should be asked to state in his application the reason that he elected to apply to the college. Only after such data are analyzed can a college determine when it is best to mass-mail or narrowly target its publications and other communication efforts.

A happy and satisfied alumnus or currently enrolled student represents a powerful force for recruitment through word of mouth. Conversely, an unhappy one is a detriment to the institution and the marketing process. No marketing plan can ignore these types of influences. Time and money should be spent to keep alumni and enrolled students informed of existing student aid programs and policies. General information about the academic programs and student services is not enough, for a desire to enroll rests on a student's personal ability to afford the college under consideration. Any proposed publication and/or form letter should be shared with honest critics, and advice should be heeded. Enrolled and prospective students should be asked to review the drafts and to answer such questions as these: "What statements are confusing? What questions are not answered? Were you motivated to read with care? What suggestions do you have to improve the document? Does it meet your needs as a student?" Effective communication in marketing programs satisfies both institution and student needs.

Meeting the Challenge of Competition in Marketing

Each institution must know its major competition and select the most effective response to the efforts of its competitors. "The adoption of the concept of competitive financial aid packaging is an effective method of improving a college's market position. Such a process is really no different than the type of price discounting that takes place in other industries and has proven to be a successful marketing technique" (Ihlanfeldt, 1980b, p. 88). Each college must be aware that it cannot be financially competitive for all students that the institution encounters.

Most institutions, for the past several years, have publicly stated that no admissible student would be denied access because of financial need. The growth of federal and state programs of student aid, when combined with institutional aid, made this declaration attainable for most institutions. However, when appropriations for federal and state funds do not equal college costs, many institutions—especially those in the private sector—cannot easily achieve this goal. Every dollar diverted to student aid from institutional funds is a dollar not available for other institutional needs. When institutional funds are used for student aid in order to ensure enrollment at any cost, the quality of faculty and the strength of programs can be most adversely affected and many former marketing advantages can be lost.

Each institution should review the major decisions it annually faces in student aid. Management must strive to:

- Establish realistic estimates of earnings from endowment funds for student aid.
- Budget student aid out of funds provided from all operational funds of the college.
- Decide what costs can be waived for certain students as a form of student aid, and how such waivers affect the institutional operating budget.
- Determine what percentage of the funds given annually by alumni and friends can be designated for student aid and how such funds might be increased.
- Decide what type of student shall qualify for non-need-based aid (for example, athletes, debators, children of faculty and staff, academically gifted, and musicians).
- Determine how much of the operational funds shall be budgeted for college employment of students—beyond the available federal College Work-Study allocation.
- Determine the costs and benefits of publishing and distributing to each student the precise procedures for applying for federal, state, and institutional aid.

Each of the above items deals directly with how a college

shall market student aid. Until each item is addressed and all decisions are integrated, a sophisticated and well-developed student aid program cannot be a reality.

Institutions should avoid taking either a hard or a soft marketing approach. In a hard marketing approach, the institution states a precise dollar intention of aid without indicating what specific sources of aid are included in the offer. This is unfair and misleading. Every offer of student aid should specify the source of the funds being made available to the student. In a soft marketing approach, the institution states that it intends to help the student but provides no specifics. This approach is not only ineffective but as unfair as the hard approach. Parents and students should not be asked to put blind faith in good intentions. Proper marketing of student aid relieves student and parental anxieties without presenting further obstacles—for instance, by attempting to reduce the aid package—at a later time.

Parents and students develop considerable anxiety as they plan to meet the costs of college. College catalogues, separate financial aid pamphlets, letters, and telephone contacts, along with personal interviews and home visits, must be oriented toward reducing the anxiety and mystery of student financial aid. Every detailed student aid publication should carefully state estimated total college costs and specify, where possible, tuition, room and board, books and supplies, personal items, incidentals, and transportation costs. After costs are stated, proposed sources for the college cost package should be given as follows:

- Financial support, if any, from parent(s).
- Contribution expected from student earnings (prior savings, summer and/or term-time earnings).
- Specific gift aid offered, with identification of specific sources.
- Specific loan aid offered or suggested.
- Specific work-study and/or college employment offered.
- Renewal procedures and options.

Parents and prospective students should be told how each

of the above items will be applied each term to the college costs. Obviously, the closer the package of aid, including parental and applicant contributions, approaches the student's college budget, the more attractive it will be to the prospective student. Any institution should assume that its competitors will provide the student aid package in the detail outlined above. Therefore, as a provider of services to a client, a college must match or exceed in clarity, if not in exact dollars, the aid package proposed to a student by its competitors.

How a college communicates with a prospective student is often as important as the amount of aid offered. Needy students go through the same process up to four times in an undergraduate career, so they have a need for annual information on a timely basis. If they do not like the degree of cooperation or efficiency, they will turn to other colleges that better meet their needs. "The timing of the announcement of financial aid is critical in determining the choice of college. The earlier such information is available, the more likely a student with limited resources will consider private institutions and major state institutions. The longer such information is delayed, the more likely it is that not only college choice may be limited, but that access may be denied" (Ihlanfeldt, 1980b, p. 8).

We believe that the same attention as outlined above for financial assistance must be given to the delivery of preregistration and registration materials, prebilling or financing options, housing information, transportation and parking options for commuters, and other items of information for specific groups of students.

Reassessing Current Marketing Strategies

Flexibility and creativity are necessary to cope with continual change. Simply repeating what was done last year with standard incremental dollar or percentage increases may be the easiest strategy, but it often is not the best. A more meaningful measure may be to compute the dollar per enrolled student allocation of external and institutional financial aid each year. Consideration of funds in this way can do much to clarify the basic issues for all persons in the institution who have decision-making power. An annual reassessment of the following student aid policies is required:

- What respective role should institutional dollars for gift aid, loan(s), and work-study funds play in reaching desired enrollment goals and institutional objectives?
- Should different levels of expected contributions be established for parent(s) and applicants from their own income and assets?
- What new payment procedures can the institution suggest to assist parents and students to pay on specified future dates?
- What group(s) of students should be given priority for each component of the institutional aid package? (Among the groups to be considered are racial and ethnic minorities, foreign students, women, older students, and others grouped according to geographical origin, academic ability and achievement, athletic or artistic skills, religious affiliation, independent or dependent status, extracurricular interests, and other specialized interests, activities, and skills.)

Decisions about student aid strike at the very core of most institutional cash-flow problems. The highest-ranking administrative, academic, and fiscal officers must be involved in all decision making. The financial aid officer may be middle management in most institutional organization charts; however, the performance of this person and the office dramatically affects the financial health of the entire college. Acceptance of this reality by key management is an important part of institutional planning. (Chapter Eleven, on the organizational role of student financial aid in the institution, provides an extended treatment of this subject.) Additionally, trustees must be made aware of this reality. The very future of most institutions is directly related to the time and effort given the decisions relative to student financial aid. Meaningful discussion on improving academic programs, faculty and staff salaries, determination of tuition levels, and so on, is often not possible until a decision on funding and use of student financial aid is made.

In the buyer's (student's) market of today, how does the institution best market its financial aid services? The first priority is to carefully select the person who will serve as director of the financial aid office. Few institutional appointments are more important. It is essential to set high expectations and goals for the financial aid staff in efficiency, concern for detail, and dedication to their task. A college should expect a high level of performance and accountability and then compensate the individual accordingly.

In any marketing plan, it is necessary to set high, yet attainable goals. Failure to do this will encourage defeat and build continuing discouragement. Institutions should not expect the impossible. However, high goals that will stretch people to achieve what otherwise might not occur are desirable. "Objectives must be specified and performance in achieving them should be measurable. Marketing objectives are usually stated as standards of performance" (Tarpey and others, 1979, p. 11).

To achieve maximum success in reaching enrollment goals, all parties responsible for goal achievement must be involved in the decision making. The degree of motivation to achieve any goal is directly related to the extent of involvement of responsible persons in the goal-setting activity. Both long- and short-term objectives should be established. The objectives should be measurable. If original objectives turn out to be either too easy or too difficult to achieve, new objectives that are attainable only with strong team efforts should be formulated. Monthly reviews of admission, retention, and financial aid goals and their relationship to the budget are recommended due to the present unstable economy and the rapid changes in federal and state student aid programs.

Developing an Institutional Marketing Plan

The college must realize that an effort in so vital an area as recruitment of students is interrelated with the basic mission of the institution. Any significant change in the size or nature of the student body directly affects the way society will view the institution and will change the goals and operations of the college itself. The college must therefore determine its present goals and anticipate how these will be affected by the proposed enrollment changes. For example, if a small, moderately selective liberal arts college finds that it can no longer compete successfully for enough of the best and brightest students, it may have to choose between enrolling fewer students or recruiting less able students and offering vocational and professional programs to attract them. The latter option would require the most diligent soul searching and commitment to a new era in the college's history. These changes affect both the vertical structure (from the trustees and president down to the security and maintenance staffs) and the horizontal structure (for example, no member of the teaching faculty would escape the impact of installing new programs for a different student clientele).

Ideally, the college should precede marketing with a thorough study of its present goals and value system and an estimate of how these would change after the marketing project is completed. A systematic goals study can be aided by use of a standardized instrument such as the Institutional Goals Inventory published by the Educational Testing Service. In any such study, the college's institutional research office should work directly with the admissions and financial aid office.

In any marketing effort, the key working relationship is between the financial aid director and the admissions officer. Often-heard comments like the following are symptomatic of poor articulation between the efforts of student aid and admissions: "I could spend less money and yet do better for more students if only admissions would bring in a different type of student" or "I could recruit much more effectively if only financial aid were managed better." These types of comments reveal both a communication gap and a lack of cooperative planning. If the admissions officer is thoroughly familiar with the aid packaging process, he will know beforehand the competitive advantage or disadvantage he will have in recruiting the most desirable types of students. Conversely, if the aid officer can accurately anticipate the financial needs of incoming students, he can distribute the aid most effectively to the largest number of students. For example, if on-campus employment is found to be a cost-effective way to meet student financial needs and also increases retention, then the college's enrollment goals are best served if the admissions office recruits students willing to be employed while attending the college and if the aid office can provide sufficient employment opportunities for the students.

The financial aid office should reflect the overall goals of the institution and not only the orientation of the office director, who may focus solely on individual student needs. Financial aid administrators are typically student personnel oriented and are preoccupied with national financial aid policies rather than trying to preserve their institutions. The individuals engaged in a marketing program should have an institution-wide and long-term perspective. They should realize that the college has been in existence for generations and that the goal is to help the college continue as a viable institution capable of providing educational services to many future generations of students. Too often financial aid administrators manage budgets only and never catch even a glimpse of institutional perspective.

It is the responsibility of the president to see that there is a continuing review of all financial aid policies in light of the mission statement of the institution. Each policy should enhance the position of the institution and not work to its detriment. Unless there is clear statement of purpose and such purpose is protected with vigor, detrimental policies can creep in from individual campus-based interest groups or be imposed by groups external to the campus. One of the most valuable outcomes of the institutional goals study mentioned above is a heightened awareness of interdependence and common purpose of everyone involved in a marketing program.

The financial aid budget should not be thought of as resources to be expended but as an investment in individual students whom the institution would like to enroll for specific reasons. The student aid package is the primary inducement for enrollment of most students. Hence, there is nothing wrong in administrators asking what the return on the financial aid investment in students will be to the institution. Without a unified marketing plan, institutions may just dole out dollars without the thought or effort required for proper expenditures of such large and annually increasing sums of money.

Institutions need to research their students. They need to review and analyze their primary and secondary marketing areas and do this with relationship to the college's mission statement. Once the type of student desired is decided on and the marketing area from which they must come is defined, admission strategies must be devoted to attracting a large enough pool of qualified desirable students which will permit financial aid to be selective. The financial aid program that must assist every recruited student with as many dollars as each student seems to require, and needs all of those students to enroll to meet enrollment objectives, will spend larger than necessary amounts of financial aid dollars. There must be a surplus of students present in the admissions pool for truly effective utilization of student financial aid, and it is the responsibility of the admissions office to attract that pool.

Dollars will always be important to recruiting, but the student who desires to attend a specific institution—because of its academic quality, program, location, religious affiliation, athletic program, or for one of many other possible reasons—is more likely to accept loan or employment funds in addition to cash. And students attracted for reasons other than dollars are more likely to persist. One must recognize the need for a balance of strong personal reasons and dollars for strong continuing student interest and support. Too often administrators are not cognizant of the relationship between these two factors.

All institutions are on a continuum. On one end, program attractions are such that aid dollars per student can be sharply limited; on the other end, the attractiveness of the program is at such a low level that aid dollars must be excessive to overcome program deficiencies. Typically, the institution is somewhere between these extremes. Institutions must be aware of competitive forces in the market and know where they are on this continuum.

The foregoing comments suggest that it is quite difficult for an institution to have an objective view of its needs and problems and that the preexisting roles of key officials, such as admissions and financial aid, often will prevent the full development of a truly cooperative relationship in marketing. For these and other reasons, many colleges are considering the assistance of an outside consultant. If the decision is made to seek outside help, it is best to determine before negotiations whether the consultant is to lead the entire project or to provide assistance only in selected aspects. Such a consultant should be interviewed and selected with the same care one would take to employ a full-time person and should be able to supply numerous examples of successful consultation efforts and personal and professional references.

There are pros and cons to the use of a consultant and to a college "going on its own." Obviously, a college would seem to know its own problems and potentialities better than any outsider, at least at the outset of the program. Money would not have to be spent for honoraria and expenses if the college's own staff were used entirely in the project. There is usually no guarantee beforehand that outside help would yield better results. Finally, a college might have justifiable reservations about revealing the full extent of its problems to an outsider. On the other hand, an outside consultant can provide an asset that can never be developed within the college—namely, an unobstructed, objective view of the situation. He will not be concerned with who may have been to blame for whatever problem may exist, or with the nuances of the internal power structure. He is free to concentrate on the problem at hand and need not be deterred or distracted by protecting the egos of certain college officials.

It is particularly important that the consultant be knowledgeable about the particular type of college that is hiring him. For example, a consultant with experience only in large public universities may not be sufficiently knowledgeable about the special needs of the small, church-related private college. Few full-time financial aid/admissions consultants with broad management experience in a variety of higher education institutions over a number of years are available. Higher education will need to develop this resource in the same way that it developed the fund-raising counseling resource. Only then will all institutions have equal access to individuals who can help the institutions address the major issues fully and completely in a reasonable length of time.

A number of postsecondary professional organizations provide a clearinghouse or brokering function for consultation services at a modest charge to both member and nonmember institutions. While some of these efforts can be of assistance, they seldom can address the real problems effectively, since the consultants are typically full-time employees of other institutions and have not the energy or the time to devote to this challenging task, nor will they have the broad experience obtainable only through intimate association with a large number of institutions. Up to four full days a month over a period of a full academic cycle, and the active support of a president who wishes to solve an enrollment problem, are sometimes necessary to deal with the complexities of developing an institution-wide effort. Only this level of attention will result in meaningful, long-lasting, and financially constructive results.

To illustrate the development of an institutional financial aid/enrollment plan, the following composite profile (based on actual college cases) is offered. This case study involves a church-related private college in the Midwest. Before the enrollment project was developed and implemented, the college had about 950 full-time students, recruited from thirty-nine states and sixteen foreign countries. The overall quality of its academic programs existed more substantially in its promotional literature than in the reality of its classrooms. For many years this college had broadened its purposes as a general liberal arts college and in the process had, in a relative sense, deemphasized its role of service to the church; yet it continued to request and expect a high level of financial support from the church. The college had, over the previous ten years, annually increased its expenditures for student financial aid and for intercollegiate athletics, but these same years saw an erosion of church support, a decrease in the academic quality of students, and, despite strenuous efforts, no increase in enrollment. The college decided to engage the services of an external consultant to mobilize and coordinate its attack on these problems.

Today the institution has 2,341 full-time students, largely from the Midwest. The student body, because the students are selected with care, has greater diversity in characteristics important to the educational programs than when thirty-nine states were represented. Most of the students rank in the upper 40 percent of their high school class. All this was accomplished with reductions in financial aid for the first four years of the enrollment project, with maintenance of a relatively consistent level of financial aid expenditures for the next several years. At the same time, tuition revenues increased, allowing faculty salaries at all levels to be improved to the highest level on the American Association of University Professors scale and for academic programs to be improved. Finally, the retention rate increased as a result of the program improvements.

To reach this level of positive change, the following institutional decisions were made and vigorously implemented by key administrators supported by the president.

1. Enrollment must come from the primary marketing area, and precious recruiting dollars should not be used in the relatively unproductive competition for students in secondary areas.

2. Academic ability of students must be recognized, and such ability and promise for success must be made a crucial part of the decision to offer financial aid.

3. All students must be advised of, and then required to apply for, all external sources of financial aid.

4. The strong academic departments must be further strengthened and heavily promoted in recruiting efforts; then, as enrollment increases, weaker departments can be strengthened.

5. Facilities and equipment must be improved to be compatible with the ability level of students sought.

6. The reality must be accepted that people make programs and that the best people make the best programs. The highest-quality faculty must be recruited and compensated accordingly.

7. Students must be contacted initially at the sophomore/junior level in high school, and a program of admissions contact and publications must be implemented whereby the student desires to attend the institution because of its

attractions rather than the mere availability of financial aid.

8. Close contact must be established and maintained with all important private, state, and federal agency personnel, so that the institution can anticipate change in these sectors and react to it in advance intentionally rather than be dragged by national momentum. (This permitted the institution to anticipate and even run counter to trends at times.)

9. All matters related to financial aid/enrollment planning must be placed under the direction of one administrator.

10. All institutional financial aid used to enhance art, athletics, debate, drama, music, and other special interest groups must be coordinated by one administrator, so that institutional objectives can take precedence over department or activity interests.

11. Selection of potential graduates must be considered the most important aspect of enrollment of new students. This is judged to be the most positive means to improved retention.

These decisions comprised the essence of plans that have proved successful in many institutional settings, whether or not an external consultant was used to coordinate the effort. In the case study cited above, the use of a consultant was deemed necessary because of the broad range of the program. Support of the president was imperative because of the policy and personnel changes often required. The success of the financial aid/enrollment planning model helped the institution in its fundraising efforts—which succeeded well beyond initial expectations.

Such results require commitment, time, energy, and money. "Last-ditch" efforts are usually least successful because, by the time this stage is reached, the problems are often so severe, and the resources of the institution so eroded, that the college has little left to attract prospective students. Under these circumstances, a college in such desperate straits will lose out to far-sighted competitors with strong faculties, attractive academic offerings, and a well-organized student aid program.

Conclusion

Successful marketing in the increasingly competitive search for new students is vital to any college, and student financial aid is at the heart of such efforts. We have attempted to show the symbiotic relationship between recruiting/admissions and the availability, awarding, and packaging of financial aid. In our view, the entire institution must be involved at least tangentially in any significant marketing projects, even though the activities will be spearheaded by a relatively small percentage of the college staff. It is particularly important that the chief administrative officer be actively supportive, since coordination of efforts across the traditional organizational lines is necessary for success. Even more crucial, however, is that a unified effort be made across the entire administrative staff and faculty to offer the students enrolled through the marketing program a valuable, satisfying experience that will justify and validate the efforts by financial aid staff to bring adequate numbers of new students to campus each year.

Bibliographical Note

Marketing is a dynamic and exciting field of study. Much of the excitement and interest, however, is masked by the technical definitions and descriptions of marketing concepts that form the foundation of any marketing knowledge. For persons in higher education, additional interest is lost because most publications have reference only to corporate product marketing.

The marketing publication with closest direct application to higher education is *Marketing for Nonprofit Organizations* (Kotler, 1975), which contains some direct references to institutions of higher education. The basic marketing book by McCarthy (1981) is an excellent general reference work containing good sections on information gathering, behavioral dimensions, and promotion; however, the reader will need to interpolate the general information to higher education.

For those who wish to go beyond these two basic works and derive more technical marketing knowledge, the books by

Boyd (1981) and Cravens and others (1980) are both worth reading. The advertising theory text by Sandage (1979) is excellent and comprehensive. Whatever time one can devote to it will be well spent.

The writings of Doermann (1976) and Ihlanfeldt (1975, 1980b) illustrate how theory can be used in higher education to recruit and offer financial aid to students. In another work Ihlanfeldt (1980a) illustrates how marketing can result in financial stability for colleges and universities.

Finally, while all marketing programs include some measure of personal selling, much of higher education has not understood the relationship between personal selling and marketing. The book devoted to personal selling by Kurtz (1982) is extremely practical, interesting, and helpful.

15

Using Student Aid in Retention Efforts

Leonard M. Wenc

During the last two decades of growth in postsecondary education, the emphasis was on providing educational opportunities for what seemed to be unlimited numbers of students. With the initiation and growth of student financial aid programs by both the federal and state governments, newly enfranchised students sought postsecondary educational opportunities in increasing numbers. Selective institutions seemed to pride themselves on being known for whom they kept out rather than whom they admitted. Overwhelmed by applications, directors of admissions in such colleges seemed to function more like directors of rejections. Flagship state universities also felt the pressure of increasing enrollments. Building programs began that resulted in dramatic expansion of the physical plants of major state universities. Teachers' colleges and state colleges strove to change their image by incorporating the term "university" in their names. Expansion in name, physical plant, and enrollment was the rule. Enrollment growth expanded the horizon of most institutions from modest achievable objectives to complex and ambitious ones. As long as the increasing numbers of students generated income to finance such expansion, little effort was made to evaluate whether the institutions were achieving either their stated or their implied objectives.

In the heady days of mushrooming enrollments, the attitude seemed to be that education might not always do what it claimed but surely more education would not do anyone much harm. A piece of the "college experience" was certainly better than no piece. If only the system could whet the educational appetite of the new teeming population of recruited students, then certainly this was well worth the effort of family, governments, and the taxpayers. Postsecondary education now serves new kinds of students. Growth of remedial and developmental courses and grade inflation have diluted the traditional academic nature of many postsecondary educational institutions. In many instances a "college experience" has replaced a "college education."

Institutions now face a difficult dilemma: How can they sustain a national commitment to postsecondary educational access and choice in light of a smaller pool of traditional-aged applicants, reduced federal and state support in areas such as research and student financial aid, and a depressed economic condition? Sustaining academic standards under the above conditions will be difficult at best. Simply stated, institutions will be hard pressed to maintain enrollment-driven budgets while subscribing to traditional and increasingly unrealistic academic standards.

At the front end of this process, positioned precariously in the administrative hierarchy of each institution, is the financial aid officer. Logic seems to demand that appropriate institutional support and attention be given to this area if we are inclined to sustain our newly enfranchised constituencies through graduation. Unfortunately, student aid has been narrowly focused toward achieving access for new constituencies without attention to meeting other than the financial needs of a new clientele of students enticed onto the campuses. What has materialized is the development of financial aid as a means of meeting institutional needs for enrolling ever greater numbers of students, to the detriment of a responsibility for meeting the personal, financial, and academic needs of the students themselves.

Although by the mid-1970s the winds of demographic change were being felt and the future prospects of continued enrollment growth dimmed, little effort was made to help the newly enfranchised students complete degree programs once they were admitted. No attempt has been made to assess the cost to the taxpayer of the human resources lost to this turnstile approach that encouraged students to enroll but made feeble efforts to sustain them to the achievement of their degree objectives. Although fiscal accountability was emphasized in the administration of federal and state student aid dollars, little was done to ensure program accountability.

The influx of federal and state student aid dollars to institutions since the late 1960s was based not so much on institutional commitment as on federal and state inclinations. As a result of putting these programs into operation, a new administrator on campus was beginning to become visible—namely, the financial aid officer. He was often ill prepared for what was soon to become an awesome responsibility for both himself and the institution. Unfortunately, the administrative role of the financial aid officer was severely curtailed because the position's impact on the institution was not fully understood by the major policy makers. Major institutional decisions involving the recruitment, retention, and education of students seemed not to involve student financial aid personnel. In short, what should have developed as a broad influence on total campus planning ended up a more restricted role of applying for and administering federal student aid dollars within externally mandated parameters.

The symbiotic relationship between enrollment growth over the past two decades and the expansion of both federal and state student aid programs is unfortunately coming to an end. Recent federal and state budget restraints do not bode well for programs previously funded with little or no debate. In fact, the very role of the federal government in providing financing through previously funded programs is being called into question. More than ever before, opportunities for financial aid administrators to redefine their institutional roles are at hand.

Basic Dimensions of Attrition and Retention

In light of demographic and fiscal realities, all institutions must become ready to review their performance in a number of areas. A good place to start is with a review of retention and attrition.

Retention occurs when students complete, continue, or resume their studies; attrition occurs when students are no longer enrolled in a college or university. These two definitions, along with the following terms, are used by Lenning, Beal, and Sauer (1980, pp. 9-10).

> *Persister:* One who continues enrollment at the same institution without interruption, for a defined period of study. Graduation for a full-time persister is usually timely; that is, two or three years after matriculation in community colleges and four or five years after matriculation as a freshman in a four-year institution. Persisters are said to achieve on-time graduation.
> *Attainer:* A student who drops out prior to graduation but only after attaining a personal goal, such as a limited course of study.
> *Stopout:* One who leaves the institution for a period of time but returns to the same institution for additional study. Graduation is usually assumed to be the goal of the stopout, but it will occur "sometime" rather than "on time."
> *Dropout:* One who leaves the institution and does not return for additional study at any time.

In their discussion of factors relating to retention and attrition, Lenning, Beal, and Sauer indicate that academic factors represent the strongest predictors of retention, but the correlation may be no more than .50. The main factors predicting retention may be the level of students' previous academic attainments and their educational aspirations. For example, both high school GPA and classwork correlate with productivity and appear to be the best predictors of persistence and attrition. In addition, most studies show a strong relationship between persistence and entrance examination scores. Further relationships between poor study habits and persistence, along with other variables, have been reflected in the literature.

Ramist (1981, p. 2), in a review of the literature on retention and attrition, estimates that the overall graduation and dropout rates of entrants to a representative cross section of four-year colleges are as follows:

Graduation within four years after entry	
From original college of entry	35–40%
From different college	10–29%
Total from any college	45–60%
Graduation five years after entry (any college)	10–15%
Graduation six or more years after entry (any college)	10–15%
Total graduation (any college)	65–90%
Dropouts who never receive degrees	10–35%

Reflecting on the available evidence, Ramist states that almost three quarters of the students who complete their sophomore year without interruption complete all four years without interruption.

After reviewing operational, motivational, and demographic factors relating to attrition, one finds that the relationships are not very clear and the results of studies somewhat contradictory. Therefore, each individual institution interested in addressing the issue of retention must compile a relevant data base that reflects its own unique situation. Every effort should be made to regularize the gathering and analysis of this type of information, with the objective of evaluating factors that appear to impinge on the progress of students toward their degree objective. Although the self-report mechanisms used to solicit information from students have inherent drawbacks, the reasons that they give for dropping out are noteworthy. A review of the available research indicates that the most frequently cited reasons for dropping out of school are those of an academic nature

—namely, poor grades, boredom with courses, change in career goals, and inability to take desired courses or programs. The second most frequently cited reason is financial difficulty. It is this area that needs further clarification if retention programs involving student aid policy and personnel are to be effective.

Students indicating financial difficulty as a major factor in dropping out are most often minorities, women with poor high school records, early dropouts, and temporary dropouts. Ramist indicates that counselors rate this category much lower in importance than students do. Students might, of course, report financial difficulties because such difficulties are less threatening to them and are "socially acceptable." If that is so, the student aid officer can find an opportunity to contribute to the retention of students.

Beal and Noel (1980) have compiled and analyzed information about campus efforts for improving student retention in higher education. What appears striking in their survey is the modest position that financial aid seems to play in current efforts to improve retention. The survey did show that inadequate financial aid was the most important factor related to attrition in four-year private schools, while adequate financial aid was identified as positively related to retention.

In their summary report, Beal and Noel list the most important factors influencing student retention, as perceived by college officials at 858 colleges responding to their survey. The top negative factors were ranked as follows:

1. Inadequate academic advising.
2. Inadequate curricular offerings.
3. Conflict between class schedules and jobs.
4. Inadequate financial aid.
5. Inadequate counseling support systems.

The top positive factors were:

1. Caring attitude of faculty and staff.
2. High quality of teaching.
3. Adequate financial aid.

4.   Student involvement in campus life.
5.   High quality of advising.

   Retention strategies carry a price tag, and many institutions are not willing or able to apply them under current fiscal realities. The dilemma, therefore, is one where current fiscal constraints preclude the implementation of retention strategies because of their cost. This, in turn, inhibits the implementation of the very programs and strategies that would enhance one of the major revenue-generating options available to most institutions—namely, the increased retention of already enrolled students.
   Since financial aid is a relatively influential factor in the persistence of students, it is appropriate to focus on how student aid can be utilized in a more constructive manner. Astin (1975a, 1975b) has concluded that the source and amount of financial aid can be important factors in students' ability to complete college. Several of his general conclusions are as follows:

1.   Receiving support from parents for college expenses generally enhances students' ability to complete college.
2.   Students who are married when they enter college persist better if their spouses provide major support for their college costs.
3.   Scholarships or grants are associated with small increases in student persistence rates.
4.   Loans are associated with decreased persistence among men in all income groups.
5.   Participation in federal work-study programs seems to enhance student persistence, particularly among students from middle-income families, women, and blacks.
6.   Reliance on savings or other assets decreases the student's chances of finishing college.

   Astin's findings suggest that, as the cost of postsecondary education increases, students will question the value of encumbering themselves or their parents with excessive debt levels.

The question of what is a reasonable and manageable level of debt for students needs much closer scrutiny. Jensen (1981) suggests that the increasing loan obligation included in the aid package as the amounts of awards increase might hamper persistence, even though the availability of such loans may initially increase access. Similarly, Astin and Cross (1979) found that large loans seemed to reduce the persistence of minority students; however, if the loan was part of an aid package that included a large grant, it did not have the same effect. Apparently, traditional student loan programs must be rethought in light of contemporary social and economic realities. Long-forgotten concepts, such as a national student loan bank and repayment based on a certain percent of income, should be allowed to resurface as a basis for future consideration.

Policies for Improving Retention

Institutions must decide whether they will, as a matter of policy, attempt to meet the demonstrated financial need of all students. Since inadequate financial aid is a major factor in attrition, while adequate financial aid is a significant retention factor, the policy of committing an institution to meet full financial need is profoundly critical. Such a policy should encourage increased retention rates. However, since impending shortfalls in federal and state student aid programs will require institutions to make up the difference, each institution should carefully consider the implementation of such a policy decision. In this area of policy review and implementation, most student aid personnel seem inadequate; nonetheless, they must find the opportunity and the means to participate in the process.

If such policy decisions are to be carried out, institutionally administered funds may have to be redeployed. Shortfalls in financial aid may mean that previously unquestioned practices of offering no-need scholarships must be reassessed. These scholarships could require a work component or could be entirely utilized as a complement to the existing student employment program. Such a switch in emphasis might well enhance the retention rate, since student work programs seem to have a positive impact on persistence. Grants also appear to increase students' chances of completing college, but the effects are generally smaller than for work programs.

It seems clear, then, that most institutions would benefit from offering on-campus work opportunities to all students, whether need is a factor or not. Because an effective on-campus student employment program meets both financial aid and manpower needs, the institution would have much to gain, as opposed to giving away funds under a no-need scholarship program. When one considers that persistence also seems related to student employment, a closer look at this particular resource is warranted.

A review of available supporting documents in the student work area brought to the surface a rather lengthy memo—dated December 21, 1970—from Warren Trautman, who was then chief of the Work-Study Branch of the Division of Student Financial Aid in the U.S. Office of Education. In this memo Trautman provides an extended argument for the value of student work programs. Supporting evidence, representing scholarly research rather than opinion, also encourages the utilization of student work options as a means not only of meeting student's financial need but of increasing retention as well. Interestingly, Astin (1975a) showed that whether the job is in an academic or nonacademic sector does not make any appreciable difference, nor does the degree of relevance to the student's course work or career plans. Even job satisfaction is not a major factor. Students improve their chances of finishing college even if they dislike their on-campus job. The only qualification concerning student employment's positive effect is the number of hours worked; these should be limited to not more than twenty hours per week. These findings are of special relevance, since in many cases institutions have been unable to clearly define the role of student employment or have not recognized the multiplicity of roles a student employment program plays in the life of an institution. This is an area that student aid administrators should take the initiative to investigate in depth. It seems clear that student employment programs could use more attention from the financial aid community if such a resource is to be of maximum benefit to both the institution and to its students.

While the ability to assume and hold part-time employment seems to be a positive factor in persistence, it is by no means the only one. There is every indication that if additional ways can be found to involve students more in the life and environment of the institutions, their chances of staying in college are improved. This assertion is based on a theoretical approach developed by Spady (1970) and since validated in a number of studies of the dropout process. According to Spady, both the academic and the social systems of the university are important frameworks in which the dropout process must be examined. In college the student's personal and academic attributes are exposed to the influences, expectations, and demands of faculty, administration, and peers. The interaction that results provides the student with an opportunity to assimilate into the academic and social systems of the college. This assimilation process, if successful, should also improve retention. Of special relevance is the role of institutional work programs as an appropriate vehicle for promoting the assimilation process.

In another paper Spady (1971) contends that the decision to leave a particular social system is the result of a complex social process that includes, among other variables, family and previous educational background, academic potential, friendship support, and social integration. His model has three important implications: First, intellectual and cultural growth is greatest for students with strong intellectual orientations. Second, although much of a student's intellectual growth undoubtedly takes place in the formal curriculum, outside contacts with faculty members and others seem to be very important. Third, attitudes toward learning appear to be more important than the quality and amount of previous academic-intellectual experience.

The findings of a recent study by Pascarella and Terenzini (1979) support the importance of informal contacts with faculty outside the classroom in fostering student social and academic integration and, therefore, the likelihood that students will stay in college. What emerges is a clearer understanding of the need to heighten the level of social and academic integration of our students into our institutions. The challenge is how best to do this when resources are limited and when faculty retrenchment leaves little time for individualized instruction. Available mechanisms might include admissions, freshman orientation, counseling, academic advisement, extracurricular activities, housing, and student services. However, research by Astin seems to indicate that the reason students give most frequently for leaving college is directly related to the institution's academic program. Specifically, this reason is students' boredom with courses. This finding should be communicated to financial aid staff, who are seldom part of the classroom establishment. Obviously, financial aid personnel have an undefined role in addressing the issues of poor teaching, uninteresting courses, and superfluous requirements, all of which lead to unfulfilled expectations. If student boredom could be reduced or minimized, many students who become dropouts might well remain in college. Again, it is important to note that the most frequent reasons cited by Astin for dropping out for both men and women are as follows: boredom with classes, financial difficulties, dissatisfaction with requirements or regulations, and change in career goals. The challenge for all financial aid administrators is essentially to see that they indeed are educators and that they can and should affect educational policy.

Cope and Hannah (1975) summarize their findings on "the causes and consequences of dropping out, stopping out, and transferring" as follows:

1. The withdrawal rate is high, has been high for the fifty years of attrition research, and seems to change little over time.
2. Since most talented students persist in their studies toward degrees, there is little attrition among the most promising entrants, at least in terms of degrees earned.
3. Men and women discontinue, stop out, transfer, and so on, in approximately equal proportions, but for different reasons: men more often because of matters related to competence, adequacy, and identity searching; women more often because of intellectual-aesthetic and social dimensions, including dating and marriage.

4. Colleges typically know little about the reasons for withdrawal, the process of withdrawal, or the actual proportion of students leaving their campuses.
5. The rate of college degree completion varies considerably among different colleges and universities. The prestigious private universities experience little attrition over four years, while some of the less prestigious private colleges, the state colleges, and the community colleges have most of their students withdraw prior to completion of any degree.
6. The primary factor in "holding power" is the student's identification with the college. Colleges are more likely to retain the student who chooses the institution because of its clear image, values, and program, and knows this is what he or she wants.
7. Most quantitative research (such as admissions data) is without value in either predicting withdrawal or understanding the reasons for discontinuance.
8. It seems clear that there is no dropout personality, only individual personalities interacting with different campus environments at various times in their mutual and changing lives.

For those who drop out of higher education entirely (40–50 percent of all freshmen), the cost can be high. Leaving often involves a substantial cost to the student in lost earnings potential and immediate out-of-pocket costs, which may include the repayment of an educational loan. The institution also loses, since it expends substantial sums of money to recruit students and invests time, energy, and financial resources in teaching, counseling, record maintenance, housing, and other functions. Of more direct concern to the present discussion are the monetary commitments our institutions make in the form of vastly expanded student aid programs. Both state and federal student aid programs have grown tremendously over the years. The spirit of accountability will, I believe, lead to a closer examination of the cost-effectiveness of publicly supported student aid programs—an examination that goes beyond the limited objective of enrolling eligible students and progresses toward attrition and retention issues.

For those of us who have a specific interest in student financial aid programs and the financing of educational costs, it seems appropriate to mention the tentative conclusion reached by Cope and Hannah (1975), that financing college is not a major problem in persistence, although it may be a barrier to starting college. Lack of money seems to be a socially acceptable reason to discontinue attending school, regardless of actual financial position. Family income has been an important variable in many studies of attrition, and a number of these studies have found family incomes unrelated to persistence. Jencks and Riesman (1968), for instance, concluded that "dropping out is probably not related to parental income [but] is related in some cases to parental parsimony." Parental parsimony is an especially relevant issue at high-cost institutions, where even the most concerted efforts of a student to make up an expected parental contribution will leave that student far short of meeting institutional costs. Cope and Hannah believe that the motivational climate of the family contributes far more to the student's commitment to finish college than the actual financing of education does. Many of the claims of dropping out because of financing could easily be claims of dropping out because of lack of commitment.

According to Cope and Hannah, personal commitment to an academic or occupational goal is the single most important determinant of persistence in college. It follows that the "fit" between student and college (the presence of it or lack of it) accounts for most of the persistence and for most of the transferring, stopping out, and dropping out. It seems logical that the lower dropout ratio at private colleges is the partial result of students' selecting colleges with values that are similar to their own. Variations in dropout rates among institutions are substantial, ranging from 10 percent at some highly selective liberal arts colleges to 80 percent at less selective state colleges. The dropout rate among community college students is apparently considerably higher than the average rates at four-year colleges.

All institutions should consider whether their recruitment policies result in the enrollment of students who do not "fit." In the process of enticing students—whether by means of need-based grants regardless of academic ability or interest, no-need scholarships, so-called flexible standards, or other activities of dubious merit—they may be sowing the seeds of attrition and retention problems that they are unwilling or unable to cope with.

Conclusion

The implications of the findings reported in this chapter for institutional policy seem obvious. If in the process of allocating scarce institutional resources, evidence is available that will provide guidance in the most effective use of limited resources, how can institutions persist in offering ineffective no-need scholarships? Why do institutions persist in emphasizing loan programs when such aid seems to be the least effective in enabling students to complete their degree objectives? Clearly, the positive impact of student employment programs, especially on students from middle-income families, indicates that such programs should be prudently encouraged for all students, as opposed to giving funds away on the basis of academic or athletic abilities.

In light of the institutional concern about decreasing enrollments, student aid officers should become more knowledgeable about both attrition and retention. For many of us this will allow a viable alternative in meeting our enrollment goals; for others it will provide an opportunity for much-needed institutional self-study of goals and policies. Assuming that this concern will directly assist the individual student in his or her intellectual, personal, and social development, one must be cautiously optimistic that all of us will be in a stronger position to face the demands of the future. By whatever yardstick one uses, if an institution of higher education is not special, marketable, attractive, and academically sound, students will neither enroll nor persist in significant numbers.

If student financial aid is to play a more central role in assuring students the completion of their educational objectives, administrators of such programs must broaden their perspectives beyond that of the latest regulations published in the *Fed-*

eral Register. Likewise, institutions must wean themselves from dependence on federal and state largess and see to it that available resources are prudently and effectively utilized. This will require a combined effort of administrative officers who previously may not have seen any need or desire to work in tandem; namely, admissions, student aid, fiscal, fund-raising, and student services personnel. The challenge of coordinating and utilizing institutional resources in the most effective and efficient manner will require painful decisions at all levels of institutional commitment.

A student financial aid policy that is aimed simply at enticing students to enroll must be rethought. Since students who successfully complete the first two years of a four-year program are likely also to complete the entire program, institutions must make every effort to enhance the educational experience offered to students during this most important period. The payoff in increased retention will, however, make such efforts worthwhile.

Efforts to match and fit our students with educational offerings that maintain educational standards and integrity while at the same time meeting the personal and educational needs of our students will strain the creativity of all involved. Students are recruited to our institutions for many reasons. One of these reasons is budgetary. As a result of our efforts, many students who enroll are predisposed to persistence problems and represent a target for enhancing their persistence.

Action programs must be tailored to each campus, since the variety of our institutions precludes any set of standard programs that will enhance persistence. Strategies to increase retention must involve administrative and educational areas that have historically gone their separate ways. Marketing and recruitment efforts in particular must be carefully reviewed. Student aid programs should be carefully and skillfully communicated, since students with the best information will best utilize available programs.

Another source of potential enhancement of retention efforts is the area of student services. Many institutions already have special services available for students experiencing academic difficulty. It is recommended that student financial aid personnel be enlisted to complement the advising and counseling efforts of such programs. The importance of getting students off to a good start academically cannot be overstated. The aid officer's role does not end at the time the student accepts his or her financial aid offer. In fact, this should be only another step in the ongoing relationship the student has with the aid office.

Retention-oriented student aid personnel must rethink the role of student employment. Student work programs should consist of more than the authorization of an amount of dollars students may earn. Thoughtful and competent student work supervisors need to be indoctrinated into the philosophy behind the concept of a student employment program. The entire student work program should be upgraded to reflect the importance of this activity.

Under this set of recommendations, a symbiotic relationship clearly begins to develop between student aid programs and the various sectors of the institution. As federal and state support declines, student aid officers will need to cooperate in the fund-raising efforts of the institution. Who is better equipped than the aid officer to articulate the need for private support of programs previously funded by federal and state appropriations? Student aid officers must also become a part of the total budgetary process. They must make their institution aware of the cost and benefits of increased retention. If the various sectors then agree that the goals of increasing retention and reducing attrition are important, a plan of action can be put in place. Such a plan should include a detailed list of responsibilities, goals, and methods of evaluation. It is up to the aid administrator to develop the organizational skills necessary to ensure that student aid programs will be sufficiently integrated in the total institutional strategy. The goal of increasing retention is one that all who are interested in sustaining a strong educational system have a vested interest in pursuing. If student aid personnel aspire to become educators as well as functional staff members, they will see to it that they are an integral part of any retention effort.

Bibliographical Note

Although the studies by Cope and Hannah (1975) and by Astin (1975a, 1975b) are becoming quite dated, they remain unmatched in scope and importance to this field. It is hoped that a large-scale investigation of student aid and retention will be initiated soon by these or other qualified researchers.

For a grasp of the overall picture, I recommend the monumental final report of the Carnegie Council on Policy Studies in Higher Education (1980), entitled *Three Thousand Futures: The Next Twenty Years for Higher Education.* In addition, the books by Beal and Noel (1980), Lenning, Beal, and Sauer (1980), and Ramist (1981) contain ample bibliographies that thoroughly review the issue of attrition and retention.

Articles by Bates (1973) regarding coordination of campus employment with financial aid awards and by McKenzie (1981) on student employment and persistence are especially relevant to any discussion of retention. Finally, I would like to mention my article in the *College Board Review* (Wenc, 1977). Preparation of that manuscript led eventually to this more comprehensive treatment of the subject.

16

Legal Aspects of
Administering Aid Programs

Bruce M. Richardson

"Forewarned is forearmed" summarizes the purpose of this chapter. The discussion presented is intended to forewarn the reader of the quantum leap in the frequency of litigation. It is also intended to forearm financial aid and academic administrators by identifying areas of legal sensitivity. This general introduction to financial aid legal issues can assist in the prevention of legal problems. It also may be useful to the aid officer and academic administrator in working with legal counsel as specific problems arise.

Because of the breadth of the subject, the limitations of space, and the fact that the law is not uniform nationwide, this chapter cannot be exhaustive. Realizing that federal district and circuit courts are not uniform in their interpretation of federal law and that state law often varies between states, financial aid personnel and academic administrators should consult institutional legal counsel prior to acting on a matter involving a legal issue.

Generally, the legal considerations discussed herein vary depending on the type of aid, whether in the nature of a gift, a loan, or for work; the source of the aid, whether private, institutional, or public; and the nature of the financial aid administrator, whether a private individual or entity or a public official or entity. These background variables dictate the nature of the legal issue when the institution accepts the aid, administers the aid, attempts to collect overdue loans and overpayments, and terminates aid. Accordingly, this chapter is organized into sections that deal with these stages of student aid: acceptance, administration, collection, and termination of financial aid. A final section addresses liability of financial aid personnel.

Accepting the Aid

When student financial aid is offered to an institution, two questions should be asked: (1) *Can* the institution accept the aid? (2) *Should* the institution accept the aid? The answer to the first question is usually a legal one. The answer to the second question is one of policy, with legal factors to be considered.

Most institutions, when presented with the prospect of accepting state or federally funded financial aid, have accepted the aid and agreed to abide by the prescribed eligibility standards. Indeed, colleges and universities have sued state or federal authorities that have turned down their requests for publicly funded financial aid (see, for example, *St. George's University School of Medicine* v. *Bell,* 514 F. Supp. 205 (D.D.C. 1981); *Board of Trustees of Leland Stanford Junior University* v. *Cory,* 79 Cal. App. 3d 661, 145 Cal. Rptr. 136 (1978); *Commonwealth, Penn. Higher Education Assistance Agency* v. *Abington Memorial Hospital,* 478 Pa. 514, 387 A.2d 440 (1978)). The decision to accept the aid, however, should be made only after careful examination of the obligations that the institution thereby incurs.

The cost to the institution to participate in the major federal student financial aid programs authorized under Title IV of the Higher Education Act of 1965 and its amendments has increased over the years. As chronicled in federal statutes and regulations, institutions and programs must fulfill an increasing number of requirements in order to continue receiving federal funds. Most institutions have determined that the benefits accruing from the aid outweigh the burdens placed on the institution. Although this will likely be the position of most institutions in the future, the decision should be made with the understanding of what it means in terms of institutional cost.

In addition to federal aid, student financial aid may come from state sources. Typically, state statutes authorizing the aid contain conditions for institutional eligibility as well as conditions under which the aid may be disbursed. These also should be carefully considered in determining whether the institution can participate in the aid program and whether it should participate.

Legal issues are more commonly posed by the offer of privately funded financial aid. Gifts and bequests from individuals or gifts from private entities for financial aid purposes typically include conditions which should be reviewed to determine whether the institution can or should administer them. The most troublesome conditions are those that limit eligibility to some immutable characteristic of the financial aid recipient, such as race, national origin, or sex.

The following sources of law must be examined to determine whether the financial aid can be accepted by the institution.

Federal Constitutional Requirements. Public institutions must consider whether the equal protection clause of the Fourteenth Amendment of the United States Constitution permits the institution to accept and administer the aid. Public institutions (because their activities are considered "state action") are generally governed by the proscription against denying persons "the equal protection of the laws." Distinguishing between people on the basis of race, alienage, or national origin is so disfavored that, in order to legally justify treating people differently on such bases, a public entity must demonstrate that the different treatment is "necessary to accomplish a compelling state interest." The required justification is usually very difficult to meet: first, the difference in treatment must further a "compelling state interest"; second, the particular means employed must be "necessary" to accomplish the compelling state interest. Because of this high standard of justification, legal counsel and courts have generally concluded that such restricted aid may not be accepted or administered. Under particular circumstances, however, a court might conclude that a compelling state interest in achieving a diverse student body or in overcoming the effects of past discrimination justifies the restrictive means employed (see, generally, *Regents of the University of California* v. *Bakke,* 438 U.S. 265, 98 S. Ct. 2733, 57 L. Ed. 2d 750 (1978)).

Beyond the "suspect" classifications of race, alienage, and national origin, the Fourteenth Amendment's equal protection clause generally requires that differences in treatment based on any other classification (for example, state residency, income, scholastic achievement) must be justified as rationally related to achieving a legitimate state objective. Since the rational basis standard is more easily met, such restrictions do not cause the legal difficulty encountered with the "suspect" classifications.

The activities of a private institution are generally not considered state action, even when the institution receives substantial public financial assistance; therefore, the requirements of the equal protection clause do not apply to such institutions. The equal protection clause, however, may operate to invalidate discriminatory restrictions in financial aid which involve governmental officers and agencies in their administration or enforcement. For example, the involvement of governmental officers or agencies as trustees of a charitable trust would constitute "state action" and therefore, under the equal protection clause, would invalidate a discriminatory restriction (see *Commonwealth of Pennsylvania* v. *Board of Directors,* 353 U.S. 230, 77 S. Ct. 806, 1 L. Ed. 2d 792 reh. denied 353 U.S. 989 (1957), and *Commonwealth of Pennsylvania* v. *Brown,* 392 F.2d 120 (3d Cir.) cert. denied 391 U.S. 921 (1968), commonly known as the *Girard College* cases; *Bank of Delaware* v. *Buckson,* 255 A.2d 710 (Del. Ch. 1969); see also Annotation, "Validity and Effect of Gift for Charitable Purposes Which Excludes Otherwise Qualified Beneficiaries Because of Their Race or Religion," 25 A.L.R.3d 736 (1969)).

Federal Statutory Requirements. Public and private institutions must determine whether federal statutory requirements permit the acceptance and administration of restricted financial aid. By accepting federal funds, an institution, public or private, becomes subject to four federal acts that prohibit discrimination.

1. Title VI of the Civil Rights Act of 1964, 42 U.S.C. secs. 2000d through 2000d-4 (with regulations in 34 C.F.R. Part 100), prohibits discrimination on the basis of race, color, or national origin in any program or activity receiving federal financial assistance. Institutions receiving such assistance may not, on the basis of race, color, or national origin, treat people differently in awards, disbursements, or any other matter related to financial aid. (See 34 C.F.R. sec. 100.3(b)(1)-(4) for a listing of specific prohibitions.) The Title VI regulations, however, do allow race, color, and national origin to be considered if an institution is attempting to overcome the effects of past discrimination (34 C.F.R. sec. 100.3(b)(6)(i)) or of nondiscriminatory conditions that resulted in limited participation of persons of a particular race, color, or national origin (34 C.F.R. sec. 100.3(b)(6)(ii)) or to make the benefits of a program more widely available to persons of a particular race, color, or national origin who are underrepresented in the program or not being served by the program (34 C.F.R. sec. 100.5(h)(i); see also "Policy Interpretation," 44 Fed. Reg. 58509-58511 (Oct. 10, 1979)).

2. Title IX of the Education Amendments of 1972, 20 U.S.C. secs. 1681-1683 (with regulations in 34 C.F.R. Part 106), prohibits discrimination on the basis of sex in any program or activity receiving federal financial assistance. The Title IX regulations prohibit treating people differently on the basis of sex in the provision of financial aid (34 C.F.R. sec. 106.37 (a)). The scope of proscribed involvement is suggested in the following regulation, which requires that a recipient institution "shall not":

(2) through solicitation, listing, approval, provision of facilities or other services, assist any foun-

dation, trust, agency, organization, or person which provides assistance to any of such recipient's students in a manner which discriminates on the basis of sex; or

(3) apply any rule, or assist in application of any rule, concerning eligibility for such assistance which treats persons of one sex differently from persons of the other sex with regard to marital or parental status" [34 C.F.R. sec. 106.37(a)].

Two exceptions to the general proscription against sex-restricted aid are allowed: (1) aid established by domestic or foreign wills, trusts, bequests, or similar legal instruments or by acts of a foreign government; and (2) athletic financial aid. However, these exceptions must be administered in such a way that no discrimination results. Sex-restricted aid established by legal instruments may be awarded only if the selection is carried out without regard to sex and the qualified applicant happens to be of the sex permitted by the restriction. Thus, although no blanket proscription against administering sex-restricted aid exists, such aid may not in fact be able to be used. With regard to athletic scholarships, the regulations provide that reasonable opportunity must exist for financial aid for each sex "in proportion to the number of students of each sex participating in interscholastic or intercollegiate athletics" (34 C.F.R. 106.37(b) and (c)).

3. Section 504 of the Rehabilitation Act of 1973, 29 U.S.C. sec. 794 (with regulations in 34 C.F.R. Part 104), prohibits discrimination on the basis of handicap. The federal regulations implementing Section 504 prohibit discriminating on the basis of handicap against qualified handicapped persons in the provision of financial aid (34 C.F.R. sec. 104.46(a)(i)). An institution may be permitted to administer aid established by legal instruments that discriminates on the basis of handicap as long as the overall effect of the institution's award of financial assistance is not discriminatory on the basis of handicap (34 C.F.R. sec. 104.46(a)(2)).

4. The Age Discrimination Act of 1975, 42 U.S.C. secs. 6101-6107 (with regulations in 45 C.F.R. Part 90), prohibits

discrimination on the basis of age in any program or activity receiving federal financial assistance. Although the federal regulations that implement this law are less specific than those already considered, age may not be used as a basis on which to grant or deny financial aid. The regulations, however, do recite some narrow exceptions to this rule (see 45 C.F.R. secs. 90.14 and 90.15) but place on the recipient institution the burden of proving that the age distinction falls within one of these exceptions.

State Constitutional Requirements. The institution must determine whether state constitutional proscriptions prevent acceptance of the aid. The requirements of the state's constitution should be examined to determine the legality of a public institution's accepting restricted aid. Although sex restrictions may pass federal constitutional requirements, the standard of review under a state constitution's equal rights amendment or the state's decisional law may be more strict. Such requirements may impose the same test of the necessity to accomplish a compelling state interest or some intermediate test in order to justify acceptance or administration of such restricted financial aid by a public institution.

A state's constitutional proscription against discrimination may also affect the administration and enforcement of a private institution's charitable trusts which discriminate on a state-proscribed basis. The institution's legal counsel should be consulted to determine the impact, if any, of the state's constitutional requirements on the institution's privately funded financial aid.

State Statutory Requirements. State statutory requirements may have an impact on the decision whether to accept or administer restricted financial aid. The propriety of discrimination on the basis of race, color, national origin, sex, handicap, and age as well as other bases may be addressed in state statutes and regulations. These requirements should be examined to determine whether differential treatment required by the financial aid restriction would be legally appropriate.

Institutional Rules and Policies. The institution's governing rules and policies should be consulted for any proscriptions concerning the acceptance and administration of restricted financial aid. An institution must comply with its own rules and policies reposed in its charter, articles of incorporation, or trust provisions. In addition, an institution's governing board may create its own "law" in the form of bylaws, rules, or statements of policy. These should also be examined to determine whether restricted financial aid may be accepted and administered by the institution.

In addition to restrictions that relate to the immutable characteristics of the recipient, the institution should examine any other terms or conditions that may affect the aid. For example, the eligibility qualifications may be so restricted that the burden of administering the aid outweighs its potential benefit to the institution. Or requirements to invest the gifted funds in a particular manner or to administer the aid in unusually complex ways may dictate a decision not to accept the aid.

Obviously, if the opportunity exists, donors should be encouraged to reduce, if not remove, aid restrictions. Donors, however, may not be willing to do so. If the restrictions cannot be removed, the donor should be encouraged to state in the legal instrument the donor's general charitable intent in giving the aid to the institution. Such a statement may be helpful if subsequent developments dictate the need to remove the restrictions by way of the doctrine of *cy pres,* discussed later.

Administering the Aid

Student Eligibility for Financial Aid. The legality of the bases for determining eligibility for financial aid may be challenged in the courts. The reported decisions have followed the contours of the law discussed in the previous section. Public instrumentalities that select recipients on the basis of citizenship, thereby excluding aliens, have been questioned or struck down by the courts (*Nyquist* v. *Mauclet,* 432 U.S. 1, 97 S. Ct. 2120, 53 L. Ed. 2d 63 (1977), affirming 406 F. Supp. 1233 (W.D.N.Y. 1976); note, however, that Congress can prescribe United States citizenship as a prerequisite for the receipt of federal financial aid). The courts also have questioned or prohibited public instrumentalities that select recipients on the basis of minority status, thereby excluding nonminorities (*Flanagan* v. *President and Directors of Georgetown College,* 417 F. Supp. 377 (D.D.C. 1976); but compare this result with that reached in *Bakke,* supra). Standards used to determine eligibility which do not involve a "suspect classification" have been upheld if rationally related to a legitimate state objective. In *O'Brien* v. *Weinberger,* 453 F. Supp. 85 (D. Minn. 1978), the BEOG standard of "independent student" was upheld. In *Wayne State University* v. *Cleland,* 590 F.2d 627 (6th Cir. 1978), VA regulations designating students as part time were upheld. In *Carbonaro* v. *Reeher,* 392 F. Supp. 753 (E.D. Pa. 1975), the state aid standard of "satisfactory character" was upheld.

In addition to the eligibility standards prescribed by the source of the aid are external standards prescribed by such voluntary intercollegiate associations as the National Collegiate Athletic Association (NCAA). Thus, in *Begley* v. *Corporation of Mercer University,* 367 F. Supp. 908 (E.D. Tenn. 1973), the court sustained the action of the institution in denying an athletic grant-in-aid to a student who did not meet the predicted grade point average prescribed by NCAA rules. In *Wiley* v. *NCAA,* 612 F.2d 473 (10th Cir. 1979), cert. denied 446 U.S. 943 (1980), the court addressed an NCAA rule limiting the amount of financial aid that may be awarded to an athlete. The aid recipient argued that, for purposes of the rule as it then existed, the Basic Educational Opportunity Grant should not be included in the calculation of aid given. Without deciding the issue, the court dismissed the case for lack of a substantial federal question.

Equal Credit Opportunity Act. In awarding financial aid in the form of loans, the institution must also comply with the federal Equal Credit Opportunity Act, 15 U.S.C. secs. 1691–1691f (with regulations in 12 C.F.R. Part 202). In part, the act's regulations require an institution to respond within thirty days to an application for aid; to give reasons for aid denial, if so requested; and to maintain records for a period of twenty-five months after eligibility notification. Failure to comply may result in assessment of actual damages against any institution and punitive damages against nongovernmental institutions.

Contracting for Off-Campus Employment. The contract with off-campus entities for employment of financial aid recipients, either under the federal College Work-Study program or some other aid employment program, should be reviewed by legal counsel. The off-campus agreement should adequately address such issues as liability for workers' compensation coverage in case of injury to the student-worker, responsibility for personal injury or property damage arising out of the negligent acts or omissions of the student-employee, salary payment arrangements, financial aid limit of eligibility, and such miscellaneous considerations as what to do in case of strike or other work stoppage (see Appendix B to College Work-Study regulations in 34 C.F.R. Part 675). Addressing these matters in advance can avoid legal problems later on.

Aid Recipients' Rights of Privacy. State and federal laws protecting personal information maintained in financial aid records should be understood and followed by financial aid personnel. In addition to a general state constitutional right of privacy that may exist (see, for example, *Porten* v. *University of San Francisco,* 64 Cal. App. 3d 825, 134 Cal. Rptr. 839 (1976)), state and federal statutes address data subjects' rights to personal access to records, accuracy of records, and restriction of third-party access to records containing nonpublic information. The 1974 federal Family Educational Rights and Privacy Act, 20 U.S.C. sec. 1232g (with regulations in 34 C.F.R. Part 99), applicable to institutions that receive federal funds, provides that an institution may not permit access to student records or student record information without the prior written consent of the student. Exceptions to this requirement include disclosures "in connection with a student's application for, or receipt of, financial aid" (20 U.S.C. sec. 1232g(b)(1)(D); see also 34 C.F.R. sec. 99.31 (a)(4)). Despite this exception, aid application documents should contain a signed permission statement authorizing the institution to disclose pertinent information in connection with the collection of loans, including disclosure to credit bureau organizations. Since state laws may impose even more restrictive conditions, they should be consulted to ensure compliance with all privacy requirements.

Changes in Laws Governing Federal Aid Programs. Although tracing the development of an institution's obligations under the federal Title IV financial aid programs is not appropriate for purposes of this overview, such an analysis would be appropriate to determine an institution's obligations in any particular year. Generally, a statute or regulation speaks prospectively, as of its effective date. Thus, unless a contrary legislative intent is expressed, a change in the law does not apply retroactively, affecting previous agreements, disbursements, or understandings. The law seeks to be fair, giving effect to the expectations of institutions and aid recipients that received funds under the law as it then existed. When the law changes, with corresponding changes in the terms and conditions under which the aid is administered, future funds are governed by the changed law.

Thus, an institution's obligation under a Title IV program, when changes are made in the law, depends on the effective date of the statutory requirements, the requirements of the statutes, the limits on the authority of the federal office or department to promulgate rules implementing the statutory requirements, the effective date of the final rules, the requirements of the final rules, and whether the final rules were adopted in compliance with the federal Administrative Procedure Act.

Administering Charitable Trusts. Donations for financial aid purposes to an institution usually create a special kind of trust, called a "charitable trust." Even though such trusts may not comply with all the formal trust requirements, courts generally enforce and protect them (*In re Estate of McClain*, 435 Pa. 408, 257 A.2d 245 (1969); *In re Estate of Hall*, 193 So. 2d 587 (Miss. 1967)). By accepting a donation, the institution becomes a trustee with duties to care for and manage the property of the trust, to comply with the conditions of the trust, and to carry out the charitable intent of the donor. The duties of the trustee typically include the duty to invest the trust funds and to make such investments as a prudent man would make in similar circumstances. In some states, statutes prescribe the kinds of investments that a public institution can make of its trust assets. The institution-trustee should exercise care to avoid breaching its duties as a trustee by complying with the state statutory requirements and with the terms and conditions of the trust and by fulfilling its duty to invest the trust funds prudently.

If it becomes impossible, impractical, or illegal to carry out the exact purpose of a charitable trust, the doctrine of *cy pres* (an excerpt from the Norman French phrase *cy pres comme possible,* meaning "so nearly as may be") is available in many states to permit a court to save the trust from failure and allow it to be used for a similar charitable purpose. The doctrine is a rule of liberal construction which a court may employ to give effect to the trust's charitable purpose provided the trust was originally valid and that general charitable intent of the donor is found. The institution has no authority to make a *cy pres* application on its own, without approval of the court. (See, generally, 15 Am. Jur. 2d, Charities Sec. 157 et seq., and Annotations at 68 A.L.R.3d 997 and 1049 (1976).) Exemplary of the cases in which this doctrine has been applied are *Wilbur* v. *University of Vermont,* 129 Vt. 33, 270 A.2d 889 (1970), where *cy pres* was invoked to eliminate a financial aid trust restriction on the numbers of students who could be admitted to the College of Arts and Sciences; and *Howard Savings Inst. of Newark* v. *Peep,* 34 N.J. 494, 170 A.2d 39 (1961), where *cy pres* was applied to eliminate a religion restriction in a trust, thereby enabling Amherst College to accept the scholarship loan fund.

Collecting the Aid

Overawards, awards given by mistake or procured by misrepresentation, awards given to a recipient who then becomes ineligible, and overdue student loans involve the institution in collecting the aid.

Nonloan Financial Aid. The legal problems involved in collecting nonloan financial aid are reduced when the terms and conditions of the aid clearly specify the conditions of eligibility and are clearly communicated to the student, and the student agrees to receive the aid subject to the terms and conditions. The treatment of overawards in the federal Title IV campus-based programs is outlined in the federal regulations governing the particular program. To collect other nonloan financial aid, the institution should seek agreement with the recipient to repay the amount. Failing that, the institution may employ the institutional-based remedies of offset and withdrawal of services and the judicial remedies available in the state in which the institution is located. These remedies may include actions for fraud in the inducement, breach of contract, or "money had and received."

Loan Documents. Additional considerations are involved in successfully collecting student loans. Since repayment is contemplated when the aid is awarded, the institution can employ "an ounce of prevention," which will increase the likelihood of successfully collecting the money. Of primary importance is the drafting of a promissory note. The note should be written in clear and precise language that explains the repayment schedule; the amount and commencement of interest; penalties for delinquent payments; the borrower's obligation to keep the institution informed of any change in address; what constitutes default under the note; and the rights of the institution in collecting the note—including the dissemination of delinquency information to credit bureaus, the use of institutional remedies of offset and withholding of services, the right to accelerate the note, reimbursement of collection costs to the institution, the right to assign the note for collection purposes to a collection agency, and the inclusion of a guarantor who will repay the note on default of the borrower. Although NDSL loans are now exempt, the institution should be certain to employ disclosure documents that comply with the federal truth-in-lending law (15 U.S.C. secs. 1601-1666j; 12 C.F.R. Part 226).

Skip Tracing, Accord and Satisfaction, and Statute of Limitations. Well-informed loan collection personnel are as important as well-considered loan documents. Such personnel should be familiar with available skip-tracing services—especially the service provided by the federal Internal Revenue Service for National Direct Student Loan accounts, although legal limitations attach to such information (26 U.S.C. secs. 6103(m)(4), 7213). When genuine disputes arise, loan collection personnel also should be aware that "accord and satisfaction" may be implied if they accept a check marked "paid in full" and that a finding of "accord and satisfaction" may extinguish any future obligation. The meaning and operation of the state's statute of limitations for written contracts are also important to understand. As each installment becomes delinquent, a statutorily prescribed period during which a lawsuit may be commenced begins to run for that installment. The period of time may be extended for various prescribed reasons, such as while the borrower is out of state or is fraudulently concealing his or her whereabouts. Also, the period may begin anew after a partial payment or written acknowledgment of indebtedness. The expiration of the limitations period does not prevent the institution from suing the borrower unless the borrower raises it as a defense. If the borrower does raise it, and if the defense is granted by the court, then the institution cannot use the court in collecting the debt.

Judgment. Once judgment is obtained in a court of competent jurisdiction, the judgment supersedes the promissory note as the embodiment of the borrower's legal obligation. Thus, the applicable rate of interest on the unpaid balance of the obligation is at the legal rate prescribed by statute and not at the usually more favorable rate prescribed in the promissory note. Similarly, any deferment or cancellation provisions are superseded in the judgment, and the statutorily prescribed time within which the institution may employ judicial process to collect a judgment is considerably longer than for a written contract. The institution and the borrower should, therefore, look to the judgment and the state statutes that regulate its status.

Offset and Withholding of Services. If the expiration of the statute of limitations results in the institution's not being able to employ judicial process in collecting the loan, the institution still may employ its own means of collection (see *Spas v. Wharton,* 106 Misc. 2d 180, 431 N.Y.S.2d 638 (Sup. Ct. 1980)). If the institution owes the borrower money, such as the payment of salary, the educational loan may be offset against the amount the institution owes the borrower; however, the institution may not offset an amount greater than the amount that would be available by way of garnishment under judicial process. Some public institutions have state statutes providing for offset against excess state income tax withholding. Before a public institution may employ an offset against a debt owed the borrower, the institution must first give the borrower prior notice of its intention to offset and provide an opportunity for a hearing. Although private institutions do not need to provide such "due process," they should follow their own rules and procedures concerning offset.

In addition to offset, an institution may withhold services, including the furnishing of official transcripts, from a delinquent borrower. As with offset, public institutions must give notice to the borrower that the services requested are being withheld because of the delinquency and give the borrower an opportunity for a hearing. Private institutions should, likewise, follow whatever procedures have been adopted concerning withholding of services. Despite the student rights of access to educational records under the Family Educational Rights and Privacy Act, institutions may deny the delinquent borrower an official transcript of grades until the delinquency is paid (*Spas* v. *Wharton,* supra; *Girardier* v. *Webster College,* 421 F. Supp. 45, 48 (E.D. Mo. 1976, 563 F.2d 1267, 1276) (8th Cir. 1977)).

Bankruptcy. Delinquent borrowers may seek removal of personal liability for repayment of an educational loan by filing either a Chapter 7 or a Chapter 13 bankruptcy. A Chapter 7 bankruptcy liquidates a debtor's nonexempt assets, pays what can be paid to creditors, and releases the debtor from all dischargeable debts. A Chapter 13 bankruptcy, available to those with a regular income, allows a debtor to keep assets and seeks confirmation of a repayment plan under which creditor will be paid an approved percentage of the debt, with the unpaid remainder of the debt discharged after completion of the plan.

When an institution receives the "Order for Meeting of Creditors . . ." in a Chapter 7 bankruptcy, it must cease all collection activities. What it does next, however, depends on whether its legal counsel determines that the educational loan exception is self-executing or requires a court hearing to except it from discharge. The Bankruptcy Reform Act of 1978, 11

U.S.C. secs. 101 et seq., added Section 523(a)(8), which excepts from discharge educational loans that first became due and payable within five years from the date of the borrower's filing the petition in bankruptcy. An exception to the five-year nondischargeability rule exists if the debtor can demonstrate that not discharging the debt will impose an "undue hardship on the debtor's dependents." The position that the educational loan exception is self-executing is based on the Senate's statement "This provision is intended to be self-executing and the lender or institution is not required to file a complaint to determine the nondischargeability of any student loan" (S. Rep. No. 95-989, 95th Cong. 2d Sess., reprinted in (1978) U.S. Code Cong. and Ad. News 5787, 5865). If the institution's counsel determines that this statement reflects the law, the institution need not file a complaint but should await receipt of the notice of discharge (see *In re Mendoza,* 16 B.R. [Bankruptcy Reporter] 990, 992 (S. Cal. 1982)). Since the notice of discharge announces the release of the debtor from all dischargeable debts, the institution may proceed with the collection of the nondischargeable loan. To successfully assert the "undue hardship" exception, the debtor must file a complaint, participate with the institution in a court hearing, and obtain a favorable decision by the court that the undue hardship exists. If the institution's legal counsel determines that the educational loan exception is not self-executing, the institution will have to direct legal counsel to file and serve a summons and complaint to determine dischargeability of the educational loan and participate in an adversary hearing resulting in a court determination of dischargeability.

A Chapter 13 bankruptcy also begins with an "Order for Meeting of Creditors," which requires the institution to cease all collection efforts. Since the educational loan exception does not apply to a Chapter 13 bankruptcy, the institution as an unsecured creditor must decide whether to object to confirmation of the plan, which frequently proposes a very small repayment, or to go along with the plan. The institution should in all cases file a Proof of Claim in order to participate in whatever distribution occurs. The decision whether to object to confirmation of the plan will rest, in part, on legal counsel's evaluation of the likelihood of obtaining a better plan in light of the state of the law in the particular jurisdiction (compare, for example, *In re Terry*, 630 F.2d 634 (8th Cir. 1980), with *In re Goeb*, 675 F.2d 1386 (9th Cir. 1982); see also *Deans* v. *O'Donnell*, 692 F.2d 968 (4th Cir. 1982)). The institution is required to cease all collection efforts, including those against guarantors, as long as the debtor is following the approved repayment plan. Once the plan is completed, and completion can take as long as three years, the debtor is discharged of all remaining debt liability.

Once the discharge has occurred, either under Chapter 7 or Chapter 13, a public institution may not continue to withhold services (*Handsome* v. *Rutgers University*, 445 F. Supp. 1362 (D.N.J. 1978). A private institution, however, may continue to withhold services (*Girardier* v. *Webster College*, supra). After a Chapter 7 or 13 discharge, a guarantor of the debt is liable to the amount of guarantee for any amount left unpaid by the discharge.

Terminating the Aid

Terminating Student Eligibility. Whether a legal problem will arise in terminating a student's financial aid eligibility largely depends on when and under what circumstances the decision to terminate is made. If the student is receiving aid that must be renewed each year and the student is found to be ineligible as a result of that review, the risk of legal difficulty is slight. At most, the student would be entitled, under the provisions of the Family Educational Rights and Privacy Act, to review all records maintained by the institution concerning eligibility. If, however, the student's aid is terminated at times other than the regular eligibility review or is terminated because of student misconduct or is terminated in the face of an agreement with the student to continue such aid, legal problems will likely arise. Often the destruction of expectations of continued financial support is challenged with claims of denial of due process or breach of contract.

The attempts by federal and state governments in the

1970s to terminate aid for student disruption were largely met with failure in the courts. Courts found that the financial aid termination process failed to afford the financial aid recipient an adequate notice or a hearing or otherwise violated the student's due process before the statutory entitlement could be withdrawn (see *Corr* v. *Mattheis,* 407 F. Supp. 847 (D.R.I. 1976), and *Green* v. *Dumke,* 480 F.2d 624 (9th Cir. 1973); but note *Barker* v. *Hardway,* 283 F. Supp. 228, 239 (S.D. W. Va. 1968)). The courts also held that the statutes under which aid was terminated were constitutionally defective (see, for example, *Corporation of Haverford College* v. *Reeher,* 329 F. Supp. 1196, 333 F. Supp. 450 (E.D. Pa. 1971), and *Undergraduate Student Association* v. *Peltason,* 367 F. Supp. 1055 (N.D. Ill. 1973)).

Public institutions and state and federal governments should terminate aid only after prior notice to the aid recipient and an opportunity for hearing. For example, in *Devine* v. *Cleland,* 616 F.2d 1080 (9th Cir. 1980), the Veterans Administration was required to provide a thirty-day prior written notice to veterans whose educational benefits were to be terminated because of a college's alleged poor record-keeping practices; to afford each recipient an "in-person interview with a VA representative"; and to permit recipients to inspect their files and to submit written evidence contesting facts contained in the files. Private institutions should carefully comply with the terms and conditions of the contract between the student and the institution and provide whatever process is reasonably due before terminating a student's financial aid.

The termination of financial aid to athletes is exemplary of these general rules. A public institution that terminates an athletic grant-in-aid must give the athlete prior notice of the termination and an opportunity for a hearing (*Marcum* v. *Dahl,* 658 F.2d 731 (10th Cir. 1981)). Rules of intercollegiate associations may also contain procedural safeguards that must be followed before an athletic scholarship may be revoked. Thus, in *Rutledge* v. *Arizona Board of Regents,* 660 F.2d 1345 (9th Cir. 1981), affirmed by U.S. Sup. Ct., 51 U.S.L.W. 4356 (U.S. Apr. 4, 1983), the court of appeals noted that, under the constitution and bylaws of the National Collegiate Athletic Association, an athletic scholarship could be revoked only "for good cause." A court also may find that a contractual relationship exists between the institution and the athlete (see, for example, *Gulf South Conference* v. *Boyd,* 369 So. 2d 553, 558 (Ala. 1979)) and that aid termination must comply with the terms and conditions of the contract (*Taylor* v. *Wake Forest University,* 16 N.C. App. 117, 191 S.E.2d 379 (Ct. App. N.C.), cert. denied 192 S.E.2d 197 (Sup. Ct. 1972)).

Terminating Institutional Eligibility. As with the termination of student eligibility, so the federal government cannot terminate an institution's eligibility for federal financial aid funds without affording the institution, whether public or private, due process of law (*Devine* v. *Cleland,* supra). Prior notice and an opportunity for a hearing are constitutionally required even if the regulations do not provide for it. Federal aid termination safeguards are important for institutions that participate in the federal campus-based financial aid programs as well as those that do not so participate but whose students receive the aid. (See *Bob Jones University* v. *Johnson,* 396 F. Supp. 597 (D.S.C. 1974), affirmed 529 F.2d 514 (4th Cir. 1975), in which only VA educational benefits were involved; and *Grove City College* v. *Harris,* 500 F. Supp. 253 (W.D. Pa. 1980), reversed 687 F.2d 684 (3d Cir. 1982), petition for certiorari granted 51 U.S.L.W. 3611 (U.S. Feb. 22, 1983) (No. 82-792), in which BEOG eligibility was involved.)

Liability of Financial Aid Personnel

Occasionally, financial aid personnel and academic administrators are personally named in lawsuits that arise out of the performance of their duties. The fact that a lawsuit has been instituted should not be cause for undue concern. It is relatively simple to initiate litigation. It is much more difficult, however, to prosecute a lawsuit to a successful conclusion. A few general comments concerning this process should be of some aid and comfort to those who may be named in litigation.

Lawsuits may be instituted by any number of allegedly

aggrieved parties, including unsuccessful aid applicants, aid recipients whose aid has been terminated, and delinquent borrowers who decide to take the offensive and sue the creditor. The basis for a lawsuit may include such diverse causes of action as alleged breach of contract (for example, breach of a work-study agreement with an off-campus entity or breach of an alleged contract to provide student financial aid), alleged commission of a civil wrong (such as invasion of privacy or defamation), or alleged violation of a constitutional or statutory requirement (such as failure to administer public funds in the prescribed manner or denial of civil rights in the termination of financial aid). In most instances the educational institution, usually the most important defendant, will be named in the complaint in addition to the financial aid officer. Occasionally, only the financial aid officer is named. In either instance the officer should not despair as long as the alleged wrongdoing arose within the scope of the officer's employment with the educational institution. Whether the institution is public or private, provision is usually made for legal defense and indemnification of its personnel who are sued for acts or omissions arising in the scope of employment. The legal defense and payment of any adverse judgment may be provided through insurance or by the institution itself. In either case the protection should be available to relieve employees from the anxiety of litigation that may arise from their employment.

Generally, an employee is deemed to be acting within the scope of employment even though the employee is negligent; that is, the employee does something that an ordinarily prudent person would not do or fails to do something that an ordinarily prudent person would do. An employee, however, would likely not be acting within the scope of employment if the employee is guilty of intentional wrongdoing; for example, the employee is guilty of fraud, corruption, or actual malice. In order to enjoy the defense of the institution's legal counsel and the payment by the institution of any adverse judgment, the employee ordinarily is required to cooperate in good faith in the defense of the lawsuit.

Although a lawsuit must be filed with the court before it

can be served, it does not begin until a summons (usually a one-page document hailing the defendant on whom it is served into court) and a complaint (a multipage document that states the causes of action and pleads for relief) are served on the defendant. State law dictates how the summons and complaint may be served. Generally, service can be accomplished by personal delivery or by mail. If by mail, state law usually provides that an acknowledgment of service be returned by the addressee. As soon as the summons and complaint are received, the appropriate institutional officer should be notified, so that legal counsel can be involved as soon as possible. Since time is critical, the summons and complaint should be immediately forwarded to counsel with a request for defense and a statement of precisely how (by mail or by personal delivery) and when the summons and complaint were received. It would be appropriate to consult with legal counsel to determine how the service by mail should be acknowledged. Counsel should also be informed of the institution's contact person, to whom questions and requests for further documentation may be directed. Legal counsel will then prepare, file with the court, and have served on the plaintiff an answer to the complaint, which will appropriately deny the complaint's allegations and include any affirmative defenses to the complaint.

Under the direction of legal counsel, the financial aid officer may be requested to compile a complete chronology of events and to include letters, contracts, and other pertinent documents that detail the development of the facts surrounding plaintiff's allegations. Counsel may also request a list of witnesses, with a summary of what each witness can testify to in defending the lawsuit. Involvement of counsel may be necessary for these materials to receive the protection of the attorney-client privilege and the exclusion of the attorney's work product from attempts by opposing counsel to obtain copies of such compilations. Thereafter, financial aid personnel should work cooperatively with institution's counsel in defending the lawsuit.

The fear of personal liability is generally unfounded for the financial aid administrator who in good faith seeks to perform his or her responsibilities. Whatever small risk of personal liability exists can be reduced if the administrator avoids legal problems altogether through knowledgeable and prudent financial aid administration, immediately contacts legal counsel when served with a summons and complaint, and cooperates with counsel in the defense of the litigation.

Conclusion

Since legislative bodies will continue to enact statutes and courts will continue to publish opinions, financial aid personnel and academic administrators should consult institutional counsel to obtain the most recent and pertinent points and authorities governing an institution's financial aid operations. The timely involvement of institutional legal counsel in financial aid issues can be of great assistance to the success of the program. Counsel should be utilized not only in a curative posture, to advocate the institution's position once a legal problem arises, but also in a preventive posture, to furnish advice to financial aid personnel so as to avoid the problem altogether. Institutional counsel can work with financial aid personnel to provide advice on the state and federal law applicable to the particular institution and its unique circumstances. Counsel can provide a "legal audit" of financial aid procedures and documents to ensure compliance with the law and to place the institution in the best possible position to successfully accomplish its objectives in the financial aid programs. Of course, advice of counsel should be followed even when contrary to the conclusions expressed in this chapter. This chapter, however, should be helpful in making the relationship between financial aid personnel and legal counsel more productive.

Bibliographical Note

In the late 1960s and the early 1970s, the reported decisions in state and federal court cases involving colleges and universities focused primarily on student rights in the context of campus turmoil; in the late 1970s, they focused on employee issues in the context of civil rights. Despite these emphases, student financial aid issues have been addressed by the courts with increasing frequency. A search through West Publishing Company's *General Digest* and *Decennial Digests,* available in many law libraries under the heading of "Colleges and Universities," will provide reference to many of these cases. Also available in many law libraries are helpful summaries, called "Annotations," of different aspects of student financial aid law. These summaries are published in the Lawyers Cooperative Publishing Company's and Bancroft-Whitney Company's *American Law Report* (A.L.R.) series. A search through the "Colleges and Universities" and "Charities" sections of the index to ALR will identify the pertinent annotations.

Although few scholarly articles directly addressing legal issues in student financial aid have appeared in the law reviews and educational law journals, one can find the articles that have been published or will be published by searching the *Index to Legal Periodicals* under "Colleges and Universities." The principal source of articles on this and related topics is the National Association of College and University Attorneys' *Journal of College and University Law,* issued quarterly and edited by the West Virginia University College of Law. Other sources include the *School Law Journal,* published semiannually by the National Organization on Legal Problems of Education (NOLPE), and the *Journal of Law and Education,* published quarterly by the Jefferson Law Book Company.

A major source of information concerning the legal issues involved in the collection of National Defense and Direct Student Loan accounts has been and continues to be the lectures and program materials of the "Student Loan Collection Workshops," jointly sponsored by the National Association of College and University Business Officers and the National Association of Student Financial Aid Administrators.

A few texts briefly address financial aid legal issues. *The Colleges and the Courts* (Chambers, 1972) includes materials on student financial aid, principally cases involving charitable trusts. (Earlier editions published in 1964 and 1967 also are available; editions published in 1936, 1941, 1946, and 1952 have long been out of print.) Likewise, *College and University Law* (Alexander and Solomon, 1972) includes materials on charitable trusts and *cy pres*. *The Law of Higher Education* (Kaplin, 1978) and *The Law of Higher Education 1980* (Kaplin, 1980) address the subject more comprehensively. *The Yearbook of Higher Education Law* (published annually by NOLPE) includes a section summarizing the year's court decisions concerning student financial aid.

Kaplin's texts and Edwards and Nordin's (1979) *Higher Education and the Law* suggest the scope and the depth of legal issues in postsecondary education through the last two decades. Such comprehensive legal summaries will likely continue to be published, with greater attention given to issues in student financial aid. No text or summary, however, including this one, can substitute for the advice of an institution's legal counsel.

17

Overview, Synthesis, and Additional Perspectives

Robert H. Fenske
Robert P. Huff

Our purpose in this chapter is to review the salient points contained in the preceding sixteen chapters and to add a dimension of integration and synthesis that could not be developed in the separately authored chapters. In a collected work such as this, the authors of the individual chapters work under the disadvantage of focusing on a discrete topic without knowledge of the way in which the other fifteen topics are being developed. After the completion of the manuscript, the editors have the opportunity of pulling together the main threads of ideas and topics running through the preceding material.

Obviously, in a single chapter we are able to include only a sampling of the important points contained in sixteen previous chapters. An important criterion for selection of the points to include was how well each could be synthesized into an overview that has a logical underlying structure. We hope that this particular criterion did not seem to our authors to result in arbitrary or capricious selection.

As indicated in the Preface, we have oriented this book toward providing a basic information resource for the field. Beyond this, our efforts at review and synthesis in preparation for this chapter also resulted in identification of highlights and recurrent themes that seemed to produce some new, or at least different, perspectives on important problems and prospects for student aid. Our efforts will be well rewarded if these perspectives serve as a starting point for the interpretive and critical analyses of important topics that now need to be undertaken by scholars and researchers in the field.

Importance of Student Aid to the Institution

Student financial aid provides a large proportion of the tuition and fees that support the operating budgets of nearly all colleges and universities today, both public and private. Over half of all students in higher education today rely on one or more forms of financial aid at some time during their academic career. The crucial role of student financial aid in higher education today is a quite recent phenomenon. For this reason, policy makers and institutional administrators are just beginning to realize how important student aid is to their institution and its students.

Most student aid funds originate from public sources, principally the federal government but also (to a much lesser extent) state governments. Accountability measures for the public funds have engendered a complicated maze of regulations and requirements. Consequently, there is so much technical detail and emphasis on mechanics that it is easy to lose sight of the nature and purpose of student financial aid. In this book we have tried not only to cover the practical aspects of student financial aid but also to review the purposes for which the aid was provided by the funding sources.

The three principal sources (federal, state, and institutional/private) are not formally coordinated to any great extent, but their impact on institution and student is closely interrelated.

Changes in funding level of any source, especially the predominant federal one, affect the other sources significantly. Any major reduction of funding would lower enrollments almost immediately. To illustrate some of the impacts, it may be useful to envision the unlikely scenario of a sudden withdrawal of all student aid funds. The operating budgets of both public and private institutions would be hard put to replace the nearly seventeen billion dollars of student aid which finds its way into the operating funds and auxiliary services, such as dormitories and bookstores, of the institutions. For the large number of private colleges that depend almost entirely on tuition income for the operating budget, the results of sudden withdrawal of student aid might be serious, if not fatal. Public institutions would find that they must go to hard-pressed legislatures for large increases to their budget. The parents of the majority of students who receive student financial aid would find that they must borrow extra money, take second jobs, or find some other way to take up the slack. Many students who would find their aid withdrawn must either drop out of college to earn the missing funds or borrow from relatives, work more hours during school, or locate other sources. Other students could continue their education only by transferring to lower-cost institutions. In any case, those who would be able to continue in school would probably find their academic performance seriously affected by the financial strain.

In this hypothetical scenario of a sudden withdrawal of all student financial aid, recent studies suggest that there would be a differential impact according to socioeconomic levels and other background characteristics of students. Minority and economically disadvantaged students would be affected the most seriously and, in a large majority of cases, would be among the students forced to drop out of college or unable to enter college because of a lack of finances. Even for students from these backgrounds who could find enough financial resources to consider college, the range of choice would be severely restricted. Most minority and disadvantaged students would be channeled into the lowest-cost institutions—namely, the urban commuter two-year colleges.

While the above scenario may be useful to illustrate the significant impacts of student aid, the possibility of any sudden, or even protracted, demise of student aid is extremely remote. Federal, state, and institutional/private aid programs have long been seen as effective instruments of important social and economic policies. Student aid may well be reduced in scope during periods of economic recession and/or political conservatism, and new and different forms may emerge. But student aid, whether funded from private and institutional sources or from federal or state governments, is here to stay.

Sources of Student Aid

The three principal funding sources (institutional/private, state, and federal) developed differently over time and for essentially different purposes. Institutions began supporting students with special funds early in the history of higher education in this country. The emphasis was on helping poor but talented students. At first, since the colleges were nearly all of a religious orientation, the students who were assisted also had to be demonstrably pious and morally upright. As institutions and society became more pluralistic, the institutions sought deliberately to use the donated scholarships to vary the student mix and also to attract specialized talents to the student body, such as in the arts and athletics.

Institutional and private student financial aid sources remain a valuable and substantial supplement to the federal and state programs. In the academic year 1980-81, these funds amounted to over three billion dollars from a wide variety of sources both within and outside the institutions. In the large majority of individual cases, the student recipients are also able to demonstrate great financial need. Institutions use their own funds or funds granted to them by private individuals or corporations to accomplish very specific purposes, such as meeting enrollment goals of a certain type of student (including racial and ethnic minorities), successfully competing on a national basis for highly talented students, and providing stability of student recruitment efforts over a long period of time. The distribution of available institutional/private student aid funds varies greatly among institutions of higher education. Some highly prestigious and selective institutions are richly endowed with such funds. In many other institutions, such funds are negligible.

Early in this century, a few states set up student financial aid programs to increase the attraction of academically talented students to the states' institutions. After World War II, more states set up programs, and most of the states with aid programs assisted private colleges and universities by providing state scholarships that students with high academic ability, but perhaps not financially able to attend higher-priced institutions, could use to attend the private colleges and institutions of the state. In the 1960s and the 1970s, the emphasis of the state programs turned toward widening access to colleges and universities, both public and private, to graduates of the states' high schools. The new grant (rather than scholarship) programs were based on financial need and did not require high levels of academic ability.

By comparison with the level of expenditures by the federal government in student financial aid, the role of state programs is relatively modest. Even though the advent of the state student aid programs predated the federal efforts by many decades, the current ratio of expenditures is approximately 12 to 1 in favor of the federal government. Nonetheless, the state effort is quite substantial, amounting to nearly one billion dollars in academic year 1982-83, most of which at the present time is awarded almost entirely on the basis of financial need.

Involvement in student aid is by no means equalized across the fifty states. In 1980-81 well over half of the state dollars awarded in financial aid were provided by only five states (New York, Pennsylvania, Illinois, California, and New Jersey). A large number of states established programs primarily in response to the State Student Incentive Grant (SSIG) program established by the federal government in the Education Amendments of 1972. This program offered matching federal funds to states for student financial aid. The program was successful in that it encouraged the establishment of student aid programs in a large number of states that had not previously established them. Within a few years after the SSIG program, all fifty states and all eligible territories had established a student aid program.

Typically, states operate both loan programs and grant programs in addition to a small number of traditional scholarship programs. As might be expected, the fifty states developed a wide variety of programs tailored to their individual needs. Nevertheless, there are considerable similarities in that many states have adopted similar systems of evaluating student financial need, and also have a tendency to establish programs that assist private colleges through the student aid programs. In 1982-83, 56 percent of the state-funded award dollars went to students enrolled at private colleges.

The federal government has moved from using student aid to serve specific purposes, such as providing higher education opportunity to a relatively small number of academically able but financially poor students, to using student aid to enact broad national policies, such as wide access to higher education and maintenance of a choice of institutions by the students. Prior to the Higher Education Act of 1965, federal student financial aid programs were seen as temporary remedies for prevailing social conditions. For example, the small student loan and employment program operated during the 1930s by the National Youth Administration was intended to enable college students to remain in college during the period of economic recovery from the depths of the Depression. Similarly, a student loan program in the 1940s was intended to enable certain students to begin college during World War II. The GI Bill was definitely student financial assistance; however, it was specifically intended to apply to a specific group of persons, mainly veterans of World War II. Even the National Defense Education Act (NDEA) of 1958 was not seen as a permanent program, but was intended primarily to close the apparent gap in science and military preparedness between the United States and the Soviet Union.

Earlier, the President's Commission on Higher Education (the Truman Commission) of 1946 had proposed an ongoing national program of grants and loans to provide all students "who are able to benefit from higher education" with equal opportunity to attend a college or university. But not until the Higher Education Act of 1965 were permanently established grant and loan programs developed to ensure access, especially for racial and ethnic minorities and the economically disadvantaged. The College Scholarship Service had developed the concept of an interinstitutional system of standardized individual need analysis in 1954. The programs specified in Title IV of the Higher Education Act of 1965 utilized this concept rather than allowing the institutions complete freedom to select the recipients of the aid funds. For the first time, also, the federal government began to develop fairly detailed regulations and requirements for the supervision of funds disbursed to students.

The Basic Educational Opportunity Grant (BEOG) program, created under the 1972 Education Amendments, was established to create a national foundation for all other student aid programs. The grants (later called Pell Grants) were intended to entitle all students to access to higher education. Applicants who were admissible to the colleges of their choice qualified for these grants solely on the basis of their financial need, with colleges having little or no part in selecting the recipients. Under the same amendments, earlier federal programs were recast and expanded.

In dollar volume and number of recipients, the primary programs by 1980 became the Pell Grants and the Guaranteed Student Loan (GSL) programs. The growth rate was especially rapid after the Education Amendments of 1978. Whereas the initial program under the NDEA (the National Defense Student Loan program) expended only about $9.5 million during the academic year 1958-59, by the academic year 1980-81 the federal programs administered by the Department of Education (and these do not include such high-volume programs as veterans benefits and Social Security benefits) provided nearly $12 billion in direct student aid to about 4.5 million students. Originally, only about 1,100 colleges and universities decided to participate in the initial National Defense Student Loan program in 1958. By 1981-82 about 6,700 institutions participated in one or more of the federal programs administered by the Department of Education. This number includes about 3,300 proprietary colleges, most of which offer career-related programs. Clearly, the federal government has not only enabled large numbers of students to have access to the college of their choice but also has indirectly but significantly aided institutions, since much of the operating budget is derived from tuition and fees provided by students' financial aid. Beginning in 1980 a more conservative administration and Congress tightened the financial need requirements for recipients. Nonetheless, the funding levels of the federal programs and the large numbers of students served remain extremely significant.

The Delivery System

In public programs of any type, questions and criticisms often arise concerning the means by which the resources are delivered to recipients. The various state and federal welfare programs are often prime targets of such criticism; student financial aid programs have also not been immune. Questions involve efficiency, equity, effectiveness, and sound fiduciary practices. Because student aid programs are diverse, uncoordinated, and subject to constant change by political action, the delivery system is under constant strain.

To operate efficiently, the delivery system must synchronize determination of eligibility for aid with a student's educational plans. Notification and delivery of awards must also coincide with financial requirements for tuition, purchase of books, and room-and-board contract payments. In the case of the federal programs, lack of synchronization of program schedules with the academic year calendar has been a persistent problem. The appropriation process of Congress moves at its own pace, which only coincidentally accords with timely delivery of aid to students trying to select a college and register for classes. Even after the huge sums are appropriated, the ponderous regulatory machinery of the administrative branch of the federal government must be set in motion. Program regulations are developed through a complex process involving studies, hearings, consultation, legal testing, and, finally, approval. The result is a complex web of detailed "regs" necessary to maintain effective oversight and control of the billions of dollars involved. The funds are administered by thousands of student aid professionals in 6,700 different institutions and delivered to millions of students. Perhaps the most remarkable aspect of the delivery system is not that it creaks and groans at times but that it works at all. Even more remarkable is that it even works smoothly a good portion of the time.

The overall student aid delivery system can be divided into three main parts: (1) information dissemination and the application process; (2) financial need determination; and (3) packaging, disbursement, and control.

Informing Students About Aid. The student aid delivery system recognizes a subtle, but important, shift in the relationship between student and college. Prior to 1972 the student was regarded as one who attended a college or university as a matter of privilege extended by the institution. By 1972, and as expressed in the Education Amendments of that year, the student was recognized as a client or consumer of the educational process, with certain rightful expectations. In other words, the student was recognized as having consumer rights, which needed to be protected by law and regulation. The billions of dollars expended by the federal government and by the states were seen as purchasing access and choice of college on behalf of students.

Part of the new attitude involves assurance that the students who most need the student aid funds receive accurate and timely information about the availability of those funds and detailed instruction on how to apply for them. Special problems in effective dissemination and communication occur with racial and ethnic minority and also economically disadvantaged students. Typically, these students do not have the family history and support system to be knowledgeable about the process of obtaining funds to attend college. Also typically, students from such families are usually the first in the family to consider attending college. In addition to these special cases, the "consumer protection" attitude was extended toward all students in postsecondary education. The 1972 amendments created special programs targeted toward minority students, and a number of important studies were undertaken to determine the most effective way to disseminate information about the application process. A prime example of the new attitude toward the relationship between student (consumer) and institution (provider of educational services) was contained in the 1976 amendments. Specifically, the amendments required institutions disbursing Title IV funds to provide students with basic information about student assistance, student retention, and, when available, student completion rates at that institution.

Whatever laws and regulations are enacted, the fact remains that the main burden of providing financial information to students rests on the individual financial aid officer at the postsecondary institutions. He or she is not only burdened with administering the programs but also must actively communicate with prospective applicants. The aforementioned studies indicated that the decision process about attending college begins somewhat earlier in the high school and even junior high school career than was earlier assumed. These findings clearly pointed to the necessity for the college financial aid administrator to go to the schools to work directly with counselors, teachers, and student groups. The college student aid administrator is also required to know about the latest communication technologies, including effective publications, audio and visual aids, and a wide variety of information techniques. An effective communication and information dissemination effort will result in applications for aid initiated by all students who are eligible and need such aid. The application process involves the aid administrator with three potential sources for information about an applicant. These are the application form filled out by the student and his or her family, records from other institutional offices and the applicant's high school, and one or more need assessment forms.

Need Analysis. Of all the steps in the delivery system, the most sensitive by far is the need assessment process. The uniform methodology along with the GSL and Pell Grant eligibility systems are the three most widely used need analysis systems approved by the federal government. Two national service organizations, the American College Testing Program and the College

Scholarship Service, evaluate the needs according to the two systems. The Pennsylvania Higher Education Assistance Agency has also been authorized to provide need analysis under the two systems. In addition, many of the state student aid programs have their own need analysis systems. Adding to the complexity, many institutional and privately funded programs have need analysis requirements that are different from either the states' or the federal government's.

Need analysis has been largely based on practical considerations rather than social and economic theory. Despite the emphasis on practicality, considerably deeper issues are, of course, involved. Analysis of financial need is a way of determining who needs assistance in obtaining access to the system of higher education, which, in turn, largely determines who gets ahead in society, who is allowed to keep pace, and who falls by the wayside. Institutional and private student aid systems historically made this determination of need largely on a case-by-case, individual basis. However, when states and then the federal government stepped into the picture, full classes of people were affected. Basically, the calculation is simple and straightforward: cost of education minus the financial resources of the student and his or her family equals need for financial assistance. Determination of each of the three elements of the equation is, of course, considerably more complex.

One of the difficulties in determining the ability of the student and his or her family to pay lies in the concept of current and/or liquid assets available for college costs. Early in the development of need analysis, it was decided that families would not be required to borrow against real estate, business or farm assets, and retirement income. In other words, the family would not be required to mortgage its present and future economic security in order to meet college costs. Potential inequities are readily apparent. The family that continually carries large debt obligations and maintains a relatively small flow of liquid current assets would not be required to contribute as much as the family that purposely built up a relatively large store of current funds, sometimes specifically for the purpose of sending children to college. All other factors being equal, the second family's contribution required to meet college costs would be larger than the first.

The element of college cost is also a variable. Assuming an equal parental contribution, the student who chooses to go to a high-cost private institution would probably demonstrate financial need. A second student with the same level of parental contribution might elect to attend a local public two-year college with negligible or even no tuition. Need analysis for the second student would likely show little or no eligibility for financial assistance.

The concept of the "independent" student is another facet of need analysis. Obviously, not all students are financially dependent on their parents. Sometimes such independence is a matter of choice—for example, in the case of students who do not wish for psychological, economic, or emotional reasons to remain dependent on their parents. Others may have no choice in the matter—for example, students whose parents refuse financially to support them or whose parents have died or are no longer accessible to the student for financial support. Since students rarely have sufficient income and/or savings to provide a substantial contribution toward their college costs, they typically are eligible for maximum financial assistance. The potential for abuse of a system striving toward equity is obvious. By meeting the technical requirements for "independence" (the primary one being not declared on the parental income tax as a dependent for at least one calendar year), students are able to receive considerable sums of student financial assistance. Unscrupulous students may choose to meet the requirements solely as a deliberate strategy (perhaps in collusion with equally unscrupulous parents) to receive public student aid funds as an alternative to otherwise available parental contributions.

Packaging, Disbursement, and Control. The development of the uniform methodology in 1975 was a major step in standardizing the entire need analysis process. Because of the diversity of student needs, institutional costs, and the resources of each student's family, the tendency toward overall standardization results inevitably in reduced flexibility in awarding student aid to some individuals. Flexibility can be maintained by tailoring financial aid to individual needs in the process of packaging.

The process involves determining the proper mix of differing kinds of resources to be made available to meet students' financial needs at various times during their college career. The different kinds of resources include direct grant assistance, as in the Pell Grants or state-funded grants; loans from federal, state, or institutional sources; specially targeted grant or scholarship programs (for example, those intended for nurses or engineers); campus employment or other part-time work; and, finally, a variety of institutional or private funds and tuition waivers that might be available to "fill out" remaining critical financial need.

Efforts that students make to meet college costs by using their own present and future financial resources (termed "self-help") are differentiated in packaging from parental contributions and aid from other persons or agencies. Self-help is viewed as current earnings, savings from past earnings, or loans against future earnings. There has long been great support throughout society for the concept of self-help in obtaining a college education. The concept is consistent with the so-called Puritan ethic and other frequently espoused American ideals of sacrifice and hard work. The appropriate mix of self-help and other financial assistance (including scholarships, grants, fellowships, gifts from relatives and parental contributions, and so forth) is typically a decision made by the institution, usually in consultation with the financial aid officer. This process is one in which the counseling function of the aid officer comes into play. The administrator is required to make a determination of the potential impact of certain types of self-help on the decision to enter college and the ability of the student to succeed in the educational program. For example, a heavy component of employment in the financial aid package might be detrimental to a student whose prior academic achievement and tested ability indicate that maximum scholastic effort would be needed to succeed in the educational program. A large loan component might prove similarly detrimental. Some students required by determination of the financial aid package to borrow large sums of money might react by leaving school early, or shifting from a longer-term academic program (such as in one of the traditional professions) to a shorter-term program with prospects of more immediate employment.

In general, it might be stated that packaging involves the

"art" of student financial aid administration. Certainly, the process involves a high degree of sensitivity toward the applicant's individual circumstances, as well as an intimate knowledge of college costs and the demands of academic programs.

The final important element of the delivery system involves the fiduciary responsibilities of the aid officer toward the funds donated by public or private sources. This function is maintained by parallel systems of control—one internal, the other external. The internal system of control consists of various checks and balances, including budgeting, accounting, and auditing functions. A basic principle of the internal control system is that no office can both authorize payments and disburse funds to students. The external control system consists of a variety of program reviews and audits by external agencies. The external control system comes into play when funds are provided by state and federal government programs. Although they are highly technical and seemingly mechanical processes, disbursement and control represent the "moment of truth" for both the student and the institution in the delivery system. When conducted effectively and efficiently, disbursement and control are also important in a larger sense, for they maintain public confidence in the tax-funded programs of student financial assistance.

The Aid Office in the Institutional Setting

The campus student aid delivery system comprises staff and facilities housed in an office or a set of offices. These are institutional resources committed to communicating with applicants and delivering advisory and other assistance, as well as actual monetary aid to students. The institution's perception of, and status accorded to, these functions can be inferred to some extent by the quantity of resources (staff, budget, and facilities) and physical location on campus. But a more telling indicator is where the student aid office is placed in the organizational structure of the institution. This placement suggests much about the institution's philosophy concerning the purpose of student aid (for example, as a source of financial support for the institution or to assist students in their educational growth) and the status accorded this function relative to other institutional activities.

Status of Student Aid in the Institution. The status of any function derives from recognition of its importance to the organization. In that sense, status is usually earned, but status attainment is not an automatic, immutable process. Those identified with a newly important function can actively promote its recognition. Status attainment within the institutional organization is not only influenced by those striving to be recognized; it is also dependent on the receptivity to such recognition by central administrators who are responsible for determining administrative reporting relationships.

Student aid is rapidly gaining recognition commensurate with its importance in the institution. The significance of the amount of funds involved is in itself enough to move student aid toward a status level consistent with actual importance. Sometimes a crisis will accelerate the process of status attainment: on many a college campus, student aid receives immediate high-level attention when eligibility for state or federal aid funds is in danger of being rescinded. Quick action by central administration is the usual response to such a threat. The vice president or dean responsible for the area sees to it that the staff and resources are quickly provided to reinstate the institution in the good graces of the funding agencies and other donors.

On any campus, student aid will be well served if it has a sympathetic and knowledgeable sponsor in the upper echelon of the central administration. In most institutions the aid director reports to a dean or vice president, and where this administrator is located in the organization chart (academic, business, or student service areas) will obviously influence the philosophical and operational orientation of the office. Location in the organizational structure is important; however, it is even more important that the administrator to whom the aid director reports be supportive of the aid office and successfully advocate allocation of sufficient resources. This is likely to be the case if the administrator-advocate is keenly aware of student aid's growing importance to the institution. It is also helpful if he or she is aware that student aid influences virtually every other important function on campus.

There is no standard solution to the problem of correct placement in the organizational structure of the institution. The history and current philosophy of the institution, the myriad relationships the aid office has with other offices in the institution, the personality of the aid administrator, and the resources allocated by central administration to the aid function are all important factors that are unique to each institution.

Staffing and Administration of the Aid Office. Aside from the fortunately rare occurrence of crises, the normal pattern of growth in organizational recognition and status attainment of student aid has been orderly and evolutionary. Delivery system processes now involve large numbers of student contacts, paper forms, data entries into computer systems, and dollars to be awarded or loaned. As the volume of these transactions increased rapidly over the last twenty years, a more or less commensurate growth occurred in aid office staff, space, and budget. Because the aid function was "the new kid on the block," recognition and resources seemed, at least to the aid officer, to lag too far behind the actual operational needs. During this growth period, the aid office was, in every budgeting cycle, competing against long-established functions with entrenched staffs and patterns of influence. In contrast with the budget for teaching staff positions, which can grow rapidly because it is tied directly by formula or ratio to the number of enrollees, the budget for support services in an institution of higher education typically grows in small increments. Over the past twenty years, and particularly during the last decade, small annual budgeting increases lagged far behind the skyrocketing growth in work load of the aid office.

After a period of trial and error in the 1960s, staffing formulas were developed and implemented on many campuses by the mid-1970s. Initial formulas based solely on enrollment figures often proved inadequate in institutions with high proportions of students applying for student aid. Other formulas that were based primarily on dollars awarded or loaned underestimated staff needs because it was found that unsuccessful applicants took at least as much processing time as those who were awarded aid. The key impetus for appropriate and workable staffing formulas was a specific regulation in the federal Educational Opportunity Grant program of 1965 that institutions demonstrate adequate capability to administer this and other programs in order to continue eligibility for funding.

Currently, the formulas that seem to work best, not only for compliance with federal regulations on staffing adequacy but also for operative efficiency in actual practice, are those based on a combination of institutional enrollment, total aid dollars awarded, and number of applications received. Of these variables, the key factor seems to be the number of applications received, since it is the one that is subject to the most rapid fluctuations due to changes in program funding levels and application requirements mandated by the funding agencies.

In addition to the regular full-time administrative and supporting staff in the aid office, another important source of help for the large and growing work load is the use of student peer counselors. Experience has shown that peer counselors can contribute greatly if they are well trained, supervised, and evaluated.

The tone of the entire aid operation is set by the administrators assigned to the office, especially the director. Currently, aid administrators come from a wide variety of experiential backgrounds and levels of academic preparation. The majority of student aid practitioners do not have graduate degrees. Their training has been largely in-service, through the widespread network of a wide variety of training opportunities. These have been funded by various federal programs and other sources and are offered through national, regional, and state professional associations; service organizations such as the American College Testing Program and the College Scholarship Service; consulting firms; and others.

Organization of the Office. The aid office not only is located in the vertical or hierarchical structure; it also interacts daily in a complex horizontal structure of other institutional offices and functions. Typically, this would include, at a minimum, the admissions office, the registrar, the counseling bureau, the bursar's office, and the veterans' affairs office.

One of the newer approaches to organizing an institutional student aid office would acknowledge the continuing importance of these interactions and focus primarily on a network function. This approach would bypass the historical argument of counseling/student services versus a fiscal emphasis. This dichotomy has led many an office either to turn its operational emphasis and staffing patterns toward one emphasis or another or, alternatively, to attempt fully to incorporate both functions. The newer networking approach would acknowledge that the typical aid office is not in an either/or situation. Effective student aid is involved with efficient stewardship of money when it grants awards to the most needy, scholarships to the most deserving, and loans to those likely to repay them. The aid office is also involved with counseling students on budgeting, housing costs, and other matters that affect both personal and educational growth. In addition, academic matters such as admissibility, matriculation, satisfactory progress, continued full-time enrollment, or discontinuance are almost always involved in packaging and awarding of student aid.

The networking approach would not attempt to fully carry out any of these functions; rather, it would focus on communicating aid availability to prospective applicants and assisting the student directly in the application process. Beyond that, all other needs of a student applicant would be handled by referral to other appropriate offices on campus, with the aid office standing ready to act as broker for any of these services needed. By this is meant that the aid office would have accurate knowledge of the other services and try to ensure that the student receive efficient and effective service from these offices.

Evaluating Effectiveness and Efficiency. A number of external and internal constituencies require evaluation of the institutional aid office. Donors of funds, especially state and federal governmental programs, mandate evaluation measures as a condition of acceptance of the public funds. Private donors such as foundations or corporations will generally require at least a report on the use of the aid funds. The institution itself will typically conduct periodic reviews of the aid office, just as is done for any of the functional offices, particularly those that handle significant sums of money.

Institutions must consider whether an evaluation is measuring a program's efficiency or its effectiveness, because the two concepts are inherently different. Effectiveness refers to a goal or set of goals external to the program itself. Effective programs are those that approach or achieve the social policies that they were established to achieve. An example of evaluating effectiveness in an institutional aid program is measuring the extent to which a target population of potential students are identified and reached with information about the institution's aid programs. A further stage of such evaluation would determine how many of those who received information actually applied for aid. The donor or donors of funds to the aid program may also have highly specific goals regarding the recipients of the funds and the impact of the aid on the students' decision to enroll, choice of program, and persistence in those programs. For example, a large foundation or federal program may provide funds for the express purpose of increasing the number of Hispanic graduates in engineering. Evaluation of the effectiveness of the institution's aid program would begin by establishing base-line data on the number of such graduates prior to donation of the funds. Numbers of potential students in the appropriate population would be determined, and attainable goals would be established. Procedures specific to the program are then set up and put into operation. A schedule for the aid program cycle would begin when aid information is communicated to potential applicants and would continue through at least one of the four- or five-year time periods required for normal progression through the engineering baccalaureate program. Effectiveness is measured in this simplified example by the increase in the number of Hispanic students who graduate from the institution's engineering programs over an appropriate period of time. The social policy goals of the aid fund donors would be attained if they judge that the increase in number of Hispanic engineering graduates justifies the funds expended.

Evaluation of efficiency is quite different, since the focus is on the process rather than the attainment of goals. The questions asked in the evaluation of efficiency pertain to costs of internal operations in terms of time, money, and energy. Using the same simplified example above of an aid fund intended to increase the number of Hispanic engineering graduates, evaluation of efficiency would focus on how well the internal resources of the aid office are utilized in the various procedures and operations of the aid office. Attainment of desired levels of efficiency is measured in such quantitative terms as the cost of mailing informational material to prospective applicants by one method versus another, the staff time committed to group counseling compared with individual counseling, and the amount of computer programming needed to track academic persistence of the target group of aid recipients versus that needed for other students receiving aid.

Effectiveness and efficiency are interrelated and complementary: the more efficient an aid office, the better chance it has to be effective in attaining program goals. Conversely, the clearer the program goals are, the easier it is to achieve high levels of efficiency, since operational processes can be determined more quickly and with less ambivalence.

Institutional aid offices are more process oriented than goal oriented; consequently, most of the evaluation activities center on questions of efficiency and control. The various program reviews and audits applied to aid offices can and should be used to continually improve future management practices in addition to summarizing the efficiency of past operations.

Utilizing Student Aid for Institutional Purposes

The aid office has many constituencies. The donors of aid funds have a legitimate basis for assuming that the aid office should serve the goals for which the funds were appropriated by legislative bodies or donated by private individuals or organizations. Aid officers often cite service to students as the highest priority of the office. But the clearest and least ambiguous allegiance of the aid office is to the institution of which it is a part. Due to the growing importance of student aid to institutional vitality, the aid office can be invaluable in helping the institution attain important goals. Conversely, no college or university will long tolerate an aid office that operates in contradiction to institutional goals, regardless of how much the office may be pressured to do so by other constituencies, such as students or donors.

Not all institutional goals are proactive. Some—for example, the perpetuation of a favorable public image or the avoidance of litigation—are passive and self-protective. The aid office deals in granting or denying monetary awards to students; therefore, it is a particularly frequent object of lawsuits, because the basis of most civil suits is loss of an actual or anticipated sum of money or tangible benefit, such as opportunity to enroll in and complete a higher education program. In this area the aid office can help realize institutional goals by taking preventive action designed to avoid lawsuits. All delivery system procedures must, to the greatest extent possible, affect aid applicants and recipients in an objective and equitable manner. The legal requirements of donors (federal and state agency regulations, conditions of private donors contractually agreed to by the institution, and so forth) must be complied with continually. The aid officer should ask the institution's general counsel to keep him or her apprised of areas that are particularly vulnerable and susceptible to lawsuits. If the aid officer is doubtful about the legality of conditions or regulations imposed by any donor, he should check such legality with the institution's counsel *before* accepting or administering the funds. "Forewarned is forearmed" is also a good motto for the aid officer in terms of personal liability. Prevention of legal problems is a valid, even though passive, goal of the aid officer and, by extension, of the institution.

Planning and Research. The aid officer should consider goals at two levels in planning and research activities. The first level relates to goals of the institution; the second, to those of the aid office itself. These two sets of goals are not identical, but they must always be consistent and compatible. In formative research for planning purposes or summative research for reporting on operations, the frame of reference is the set of goals of the institution.

Much of the data gathering and analysis engaged in by the

aid office is a part of the normal evaluation and review procedures required by state and federal agencies, private donors, and higher echelons of the institution itself. These reports can often be used for purposes beyond the necessity of furnishing a single agency or administrator's office with summary data. The same data can often be used directly, or in slightly altered form, to describe and promote office activities with others. For example, reports describing the number of successful and unsuccessful applicants of differing characteristics can communicate useful information of direct interest to many academic, business, and student services offices in the institution, particularly if the data show trend lines pertaining to enrollments.

In addition to generating required reports, the aid office can anticipate information needs of the institution by projecting trends or by simulating the impact of impending changes in funding levels or student groups targeted by public agencies. New computing equipment and data analysis techniques have greatly expanded the capabilities for such research and planning on the part of aid offices by reducing the time, cost, and expertise levels formerly required. Data are easily, quickly, and economically assembled, analyzed, and reported by computers that are accessible to student aid staff with only minimal programming skills.

Marketing, Admissions, and Retention. It is generally acknowledged that students are the lifeblood of the institution. Helping to get them and keep them are the most vital contributions to be made by the student aid office.

In recognition of the increasing competition among institutions for enrollees, the process of locating potential students and convincing them to come to the campus and matriculate is called marketing. Many of the same theories and strategies used in the business world are being adopted for use in recruiting students. In this context, student aid is used as an inducement in the same way that automobile manufacturers use cash rebates to recruit customers and the military services use promises of travel and training to recruit enlistees. For institutions to whom a successful marketing campaign is a matter of survival, it is a moot point that use of student aid as a competitive edge in recruiting may somewhat distort the intent of donors. For example, when Congress and state legislatures established student aid programs, they were often more concerned with providing access to needy students than influencing choice of college.

Privately donated and other funds over which the institution has discretionary control provide a more useful competitive edge in marketing than the publicly funded programs available equally to all applicants. An exception to this rule is that students attracted to high-cost institutions are eligible for larger amounts of aid, since need is calculated on college costs as well as ability of the student and his family to pay. However, even though students can receive more publicly funded aid if they attend high-cost colleges, the increased aid will typically cover only a portion of the higher costs.

Colleges with large amounts of aid from their own sources would seem to have a considerable advantage over colleges that must rely almost entirely on the public aid funds available to students at all colleges. Nonetheless, colleges with little aid funds under their own control can and do compete successfully with colleges that have large private funds. They compete with aggressive, imaginative strategies that promise maximum use of public aid funds and attractive packaging of available aid. These strategies require maximum attention to individual counseling of student aid applicants as a central part of the total student recruitment effort. The necessity for close coordination of efforts among admissions, business, academic, and student aid offices is manifest in a marketing campaign requiring intense individualization of recruiting activities.

Successful marketing begins with realistic enrollment goals, coordination of effort across many offices and functions of the college, open and ethical communication with potential applicants on the actual amounts of aid that will be available to them not only in their freshman year but also through their college career, and continued attention to matching student interests and abilities with the academic and social environment of the campus.

The pressure placed on student aid officers to use financial aid as a strong inducement for students to enroll has too often resulted in a flawed success. That is, effective student aid-based recruitment campaigns that focus almost exclusively on meeting enrollment goals often result in serious attrition problems later. A valid case can be made that institutions with only slight or moderate problems in maintaining sufficient enrollment would be better off concentrating more on retention of enrolled students than on recruiting new enrollees, especially if the recruitment efforts pay little attention to a felicitous matching of students to the campus environment. Simple economics show that it is much more cost-effective to retain students already on campus than to recruit new students in the intensively competitive arena outside the campus.

Obviously, it is advantageous to a college to use student aid to selectively recruit students who are likely to persist to graduation. Student aid can also be effectively used in combating unacceptably high attrition rates. As is the case in packaging for successful recruitment, a highly individualized approach is best in using student aid in retention efforts. For example, students from certain socioeconomic or ethnic backgrounds are especially resistant to assuming large amounts of loans. Their concern over future indebtedness can be met by providing other forms of student aid, such as grants or employment. Packaging of aid for continuing students (or repackaging for those already receiving aid) should include on-campus employment for many, or even most, students. On-campus jobs evidently include elements of social networking that foster persistence, in addition to the obvious benefit of providing more funds to meet college costs.

As is the case for successful recruitment campaigns, retention strategies should involve coordinated efforts of many offices and functions across campus. Effective use of student aid in prevention of attrition can occur if teachers, counselors, and even students inform the aid office of students known to them who have financial problems, whether long term or emergency, that may result in their dropping out. Often the aid office can find funds, even on short notice, to ameliorate the problem and encourage the student to persist to graduation.

Additional Perspectives

Professionalism. It seems unlikely that the training of aid administrators will shift from the current emphasis on in-service training to that of preservice professional preparation and traditional certification by attainment of advanced degrees. However, in an academic institution, much significance is naturally given to the attainment of conferred degrees. These degrees are used in and of themselves to help determine status or level of administrative responsibility. In the case of student aid, few administrators in the field have doctoral degrees. In the academic setting, this fact would seem to be a self-limiting factor in personal status attainment, and also in status accorded to the centralized aid office within the organizational structure. This is a fact of academic life, regardless of the actual and growing importance of student aid to the continued vitality of the institution. Many student aid practitioners would like to see the area in which they work recognized not only as a clearly important institutional function but also as a professional field. In-service training, while clearly effective from an operational standpoint, cannot substitute for the academic credibility that would be provided by attainment of graduate degrees.

The roots of the current dilemma lie partly in circumstance and partly in policies established early in the recent growth period of student aid, particularly in the early and mid-1960s. The large new programs, especially at the federal level, created instant need for administrative offices in the institutions and did not allow time for prior preparation of staff for these offices. In other words, urgent staffing needs preceded training programs, and persons were hastily recruited from other functions in the institution and from a variety of sources outside the institution. These rather sudden needs arose during a period when qualified administrators were in short supply throughout higher education and the demand for them in well-established fields was great. In particular, administrators who were not only experienced but had the ultimate credential of a doctoral degree could typically choose from a variety of high-status positions. The new field of student aid had little chance to attract such persons, at least initially. In response to the urgent need for in-service education of those who did staff the aid offices, a vast network of training opportunities rapidly developed. By the early 1970s, when an abortive attempt was made within the na-tional professional association to institute a system of credential-ing, in-service education was already entrenched as the principal means for administrators to acquire the necessary preparation to operate effectively in the field.

In-service, in preference to preservice, professional prepa-ration seems to be "locked in" for a number of reasons. The majority of student aid professionals who do not possess one or more graduate degrees may feel that degree requirements may not only be unnecessarily threatening to their status in the pro-fession but perhaps unnecessary for practical reasons as well. They can justifiably point to their record of success in the field as prima facie evidence that a graduate degree may be irrelevant. At the same time, the relatively small proportion of student aid professionals who do possess a doctorate, or at least a master's degree, often occupy leadership positions in the field and in the professional associations. They are unlikely to urge that gradu-ate degrees become the norm rather than the exception, since they would consequently lose their relatively high status. Final-ly, a number of practical reasons also militate against the devel-opment of preservice professional preparation. There is not now, nor is there likely to be, any overall authority to mandate the switch from emphasis on in-service to preservice prepara-tion; it would not be possible for present administrators to leave their present positions long enough to attain graduate de-grees; and, finally, specific academic programs to provide the appropriate professional preparation simply do not exist in suf-ficient numbers to meet any significant level of demand. The manifest excellence of the in-service training and materials now available probably also contributes to the lack of demand for any alternative.

Policy Analysis. Student aid directly affects the number and characteristics of students on campus, and also the financial resources for the educational and supportive programs to serve them. Therefore, practically all areas of the institution are influenced by the amount and type of student aid. This presents problems of where to begin in conducting research that can influence policy making in the institution. A useful approach is to divide study and planning areas into primary and secondary categories or, alternatively, areas that are directly or indirectly affected by student aid. This division will vary somewhat according to the unique characteristics of each campus, but some basic dividing points suggest themselves rather readily. For example, a good place to start is with the relationship between number of students enrolled and financial resources directly derived from those numbers; that is, administrators may want first to determine the proportion of the operating budget provided by student tuition and fees, and the percentage of that figure derived from various external and internal sources of student aid. Expressed as a per-student dollar average, this amount can serve as a useful unit of analysis for many important studies, projections, and planning efforts.

We do not mean to suggest, however, that the influences of student aid can be determined and utilized in a simplistic and straightforward manner. Consider, for example, the matter of determining direct and indirect effects of student aid. Budget planning is a good candidate for an area primarily affected by student aid, since budgets will be determined partly by aid-derived tuition and fees. Similarly, planning for student services needs, such as housing units and number of counselors, is directly affected by enrollment growth or decline related to the enrollment-inducing and attrition-reducing influence of student aid. Conversely, areas such as plant maintenance, public relations, and adult evening programs seem to be only indirectly affected by undergraduate student aid. But the extremes of direct and indirect influence leave large, important areas in between, especially those areas related to the academic program. It is typically not at all apparent to most academic administrators, for example, how direct the influence of student aid may be on staffing the educational program. Obviously, the number of faculty position "lines" is largely dependent on the number of students to be taught in some reasonable student-teacher ratio. And the number of enrolled students to be taught can be seen as related to the availability of student aid. But consider a few of the significant subtleties of the matter. Different types of student aid attract different types of students. For example, grants categorically targeted toward disadvantaged students will bring on campus many students who have considerable need for remedial and developmental support programs. At the other extreme, scholarships reserved for the most academically gifted students will attract students on campus with completely different teaching and academic support needs from those of the categorical grants just mentioned. Recent studies have shown that there is considerable variance among different types of academic programs in regard to the proportion of students in the programs who receive student financial aid. For example, some of the humanities and liberal arts areas attract fewer aid recipients than areas such as criminal justice, education, and social work. The impact of an institution-wide program, such as Pell Grants, does not fall at all evenly across the array of academic programs on campus. The academic administrator must also gauge the permanency of the impact of student aid when he or she considers hiring tenure-track staff. A budgetary and political nightmare would be created for the academic administrator who hired a large number of young, tenured staff for a program largely supported under a student aid program from which funding was suddenly withdrawn.

As institutions increasingly realize that student aid is vital, the aid office can more easily become a part of the policy-making process by effectively reporting on the dollars and students involved in the aid office functions in the recent past, the present, and the future. This information can directly influence decision making by central administration, and the aid office, perhaps in collaboration with the office of institutional research, is in an ideal position to gather, analyze, and report such vital data. Although it is true that the expertise, experience, and traditions of data analysis have generally been lacking in student aid offices, the period of financial stringency we are now entering creates an open door for the aid office to enter the institutional decision-making process in a highly significant, perhaps indispensable, role.

18

Future Directions
of Student Aid

Lawrence E. Gladieux

Student financial aid has become "the very lifeblood of most institutions," declares one leader of American higher education
(Atwell, 1981, p. 69). Those responsible for the management
and health of colleges and universities are paying attention to
student assistance as never before. After two decades of spectacular growth, the sharp leveling off and possibility of significant contraction of student aid in the early 1980s have brought
home its importance to the postsecondary enterprise.

What lies ahead for student aid? Much will depend on the
course of larger events in national life and politics, the performance of the economy, election returns, and outcomes of the
perennial debate in both Washington and the state capitals over
taxes, spending, and the responsibilities of government. Such a
host of imponderables is enough to daunt any would-be fore-
caster. This chapter, however, will try to identify the forces
likely to be at work and the issues and indicators to keep an eye
on in the coming decade.

A search for clues about the future must always begin with the past. Previous chapters of this volume have sketched the historical roots of student aid, including the earliest private and institutional efforts and the much later evolution of public (federal and state) programs. This chapter will begin by briefly assessing the role of government in financing student aid over the past two decades, the philosophical underpinnings of such public support, and the dollar growth of aid during this period. The chapter next turns to the period of transition, consolidation, and reexamination that student aid has recently entered—the intensified competition for scarce public dollars and the questions being pressed by taxpayers and policy makers about the value and efficiency of the programs. Against this background the chapter speculates on what are likely to be some of the major directions and challenges ahead, taking into account shifting economic and demographic forces as well as the variable of public attitudes and perceptions. A closing section summarizes implications for campus administrators.

Two Decades of Expansion

Democratization of college opportunities can be traced through two centuries of American history, from the land-grant college movement and the establishment of state universities to the GI Bill experience, the explosion of enrollments following World War II, and the rapid expansion of community college systems. Major phases in the growth of American higher education have served to broaden access and extend educational opportunity to new groups in the society. It is in the past two decades, however, that the concept and ideal of "equal opportunity" have taken on a particular urgency and a central place in public policy for higher education. And its principal expression has been the stunning growth in programs to help students and their families meet the costs of college attendance.

The burgeoning of federal student assistance in such a relatively short period of time is especially remarkable when viewed against the backdrop of previous controversy on the issue. Proposals for scholarships to undergraduates, whether based on financial need or academic merit, generated heated debate during the Eisenhower and Kennedy years. Resistance to giving students a "free ride" doomed one such proposal after another in Congress.

Something happened in the mid-1960s. Whether it was the national mood triggered by the Kennedy assassination and legacy, the impact of the civil rights movement, the legislative arm-twisting of LBJ, or all of the above, the 89th Congress of 1965–66 presided over the broadest sweep of social legislation in modern times. And along with the breakthroughs in civil rights came large-scale aid to education, including the Higher Education Act of 1965. The act embodied for the first time an explicit federal commitment to equalizing college opportunities for needy students through grants and through programs such as Talent Search designed to facilitate access for the college-able poor. Colleges and universities, if they wanted to participate in the new Educational Opportunity Grant program, were required to make "vigorous efforts" to identify and recruit students of "exceptional financial need." The closely related College Work-Study and Upward Bound programs were ushered in as part of the War on Poverty legislation.

Detailed legislative history is not in order here. The point is that a new dynamic began to shape the federal role in higher education. Earlier federal initiatives that directly or indirectly helped support higher education were prompted by various national concerns—fostering a strong democratic citizenry, sponsoring research in the national interest, meeting perceived manpower shortages in the economy, compensating those who had served the country in wartime, promoting international understanding, exploring outer space, and so on. Military preparedness, of course, was the explicit rationale for the post-*Sputnik* National Defense Education Act of 1958, designed to strengthen American education in science, mathematics, foreign languages, and other critical areas. The 1960s highlighted another imperative—removing barriers to opportunity, assuring that an individual's chances of advancement through education are not limited by one's economic origins. Making good on this traditional American promise was the goal; aid to needy students was to be the major federal instrument for its implementation.

The rest of the scenario is broadly familiar to observers

of higher education. Congress expanded the commitment to student aid in 1972, authorizing Basic Educational Opportunity Grants (now called Pell Grants), intended as a floor or foundation under other forms of aid. Congress also aimed to promote a partnership with the states in supporting needy students through the State Student Incentive Grant program.

Several states long preceded the federal government in providing direct aid to students, in the form of both loans and grants or scholarships. It was the federal stimulus following the 1972 legislation, however, that prompted the balance of the states to launch need-based grant programs of their own. During the same period, an increasing number of states also responded to federal incentives to help generate credit financing for students under the terms of the Guaranteed Student Loan program. (See Chapter Three on the development of state programs.)

By the mid-1970s, then, a battery of aid programs was in place designed to equalize opportunity for higher education, programs generally targeted (especially the federal ones) on low-income students. But pressure had begun to mount for broadening the base of eligibility—for some kind of response to a perceived "middle-income squeeze" in financing college costs. Proposals for college tuition tax credits built a head of steam in Congress in 1978. To reduce the pressure, the Carter administration went along with a legislative package, the Middle Income Student Assistance Act, to liberalize eligibility for basic grants and open subsidized, guaranteed loans to any student regardless of income or need.

The dynamics of expansion and liberalization carried through the Education Amendments of 1980. In that legislation Congress adopted new, more liberal provisions of need analysis to govern the need-tested aid programs while shielding the now open-ended Guaranteed Student Loan program from major proposals to curb eligibility, reduce subsidies, or otherwise control the suddenly ballooning costs of this form of aid.

Thus, the current decade began with student aid on a dramatic growth curve, the federal government spending upward of $7 billion on its principal loan, grant, and work-study programs (excluding Social Security and veterans' educational benefits) and the states investing another billion dollars-plus. And bold new federal legislation was on the books.

At the same time, a new administration took office, aggressively determined to shrink the role of government in domestic affairs.

Deceleration and Reappraisal

To paraphrase Mark Twain, reports of the death of student aid were greatly exaggerated in the aftermath of the November 1980 elections. Public and congressional reaction to proposals by the Reagan administration has at least held in abeyance any notion of wholesale abandonment of national commitments and programs in this area. Legislators of both parties have gotten the message from students, parents, and school officials all over the country about how disruptive the Reagan cuts would be.

Still, as highlighted by Table 1 and Figure 1, the era of dramatic increases in student aid has clearly passed. The fiscal mood and circumstances of the early 1980s spell at least short-run austerity. At the federal level, declining revenues and staggering deficits exert enormous downward pressure on domestic spending. The outlook in the states varies widely, but economic recession has severely constrained most state budgets as well. Roughly level funding of student aid, which would amount to a loss in real terms as college costs continue to rise, may be the best one can hope for in the early part of the current decade.

Student aid in the new era faces changing political as well as fiscal realities. In a sense student aid is paying the price of explosive growth: sudden vulnerability. Now encompassing a multibillion-dollar set of programs, student aid has come to rank with food stamps and Social Security as a "big ticket" item in the national budget. Student aid is no longer an invisible issue; it is now highly politicized. Not only the appropriation levels but the philosophy, rules, and details of student aid are being scrutinized in the political process as never before.

Table 1. Student Assistance: State and Federal Costs and Total Aid Available to Students, 1964–1983, Selected Years[a] (in billions of dollars).

	1964	1970	1974	1976	1978	1980	1981	1982	1983[f]
State Funds									
Scholarships and Grants[b]	n/a	.2	.4	.5	.7	.8	.8	.9	1.0
Federal Costs of Major Programs									
Pell 1 Grants	—	—	.5	1.0	1.6	2.4	2.4	2.4	2.4
Campus-Based/State Incentive Programs[c]	.1	.5	.8	1.0	1.1	1.3	1.2	1.1	1.1
Guaranteed Student Loans[d]	—	.1	.4	.4	.7	1.6	2.6	3.1	2.5
Subtotal for Dept. of ED Programs	.1	.6	1.7	2.4	3.4	5.3	6.2	6.6	6.0
Social Security	—	.4	.8	1.1	1.4	1.7	2.0	1.4	.8
Veterans	.1	.8	3.2	5.5	2.8	1.9	1.9	1.6	1.2
TOTAL	.2	1.8	5.7	9.0	7.6	8.9	10.1	9.6	8.0
Aid Available to Students[e]									
Loans	.1	1.0	1.6	2.1	2.7	5.8	7.7	7.1	7.2
Grants and Work	.1	.6	1.4	2.2	3.1	4.4	4.4	4.3	4.4
Social Security and Veterans's Benefits	.1	1.2	4.0	6.6	4.2	3.6	3.9	3.0	2.0
TOTAL	.3	2.8	7.0	10.9	10.0	13.8	16.0	14.4	13.6

[a]Costs shown in the table are for fiscal years; figures on aid available to students are adjusted as appropriate to reflect academic years.

[b]Data from National Association of State Scholarship and Grant Programs, annual surveys. Does not include small state expenditures for work-study and direct loans.

[c]The campus-based federal student aid programs are Supplemental Educational Opportunity Grants (SEOG), National Direct Student Loans (NDSL), and College Work-Study (CWS). The federal matching portion of the State Student Incentive Grant (SSIG) program is also included in this line.

[d]Figures for Guaranteed Student Loans (GSL) represent federal costs for in-school interest subsidies, special allowance payments, default-related claims, and administrative expenses. These GSL expenditures support an annual loan volume that grew from $800 million in 1970 to $2 billion in 1978 and over $7 billion in 1981.

[e]Available aid includes federal funding for all programs (except GSL), GSL (and parental/auxiliary) loan volume, institutional matching funds in Work-Study and NDSL, new loans made from NDSL revolving funds, and state funds for grant and scholarship assistance. It does not include other institutional and private aid; such aid amounted perhaps to another $2 billion in 1982; but nonfederal, nonstate sources of aid are extremely diverse, and data on them are spotty.

[f]Figures for 1983 are estimated at time of writing.

Source: College Entrance Examination Board, Washington office.

Figure 1. Total Aid Available to Students for Selected Years, 1970–1983[a]
(in billions of dollars).

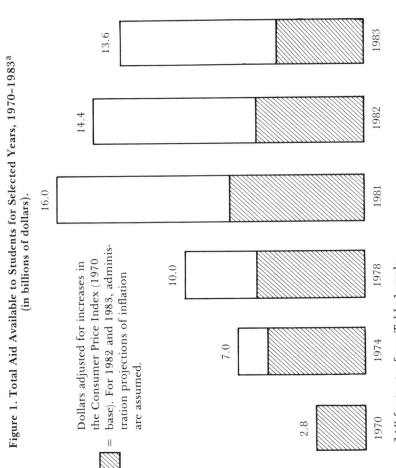

Dollars adjusted for increases in the Consumer Price Index (1970 = base). For 1982 and 1983, administration projections of inflation are assumed.

[a]All footnotes from Table 1 apply.

The questions and challenges to student aid have become a familiar litany:

- Has there been too much expansion? Too much money in the system?
- Has financial aid made college attendance too easy—too attractive a life alternative, especially for ambivalent or marginally motivated students?
- Have parents been "let off the hook," too readily relieved of their traditional responsibility for paying the college expenses of their children?
- Is student aid subsidizing student life-styles, indirectly financing consumer expenditures beyond legitimate educational outlays?
- Why are there such "excessive default rates" in the loan program?
- What about fraud and abuse—falsification of data on application forms, student loan profiteering, students (and families) manipulating the system to qualify for aid under self-supporting definitions?
- And what about reports of schools cheating both students and taxpayers through incompetent administration, outright fraud, or a combination of the two?

(For a discussion of some of these questions of efficiency, see Chapter Twelve.)

Critics point to a further inefficiency: Too many recipients of student aid do not maintain satisfactory progress in their academic programs and ultimately fall short of completing their degrees. The president of Harvard, in fact, has asserted that "much of the value the government seeks by providing [aid] will be lost on young men and women who fail their courses or leave college prematurely" (Bok, 1982, p. 6).

Few would deny that there is room for tightening up the allocation and administration of student aid dollars. Ideally, reform and retrenchment would weed out of the programs only the undeserving among students and institutions. Realistically, the process and the results are unlikely to be so tidy. Budgetary contraction, combined with heavier government regulation to squeeze inefficiencies out of the system, is likely to have more profound effects. At stake in the period ahead is continued progress toward equal educational opportunity, influencing whether and where great numbers of people decide to attend college. At stake, too, is the investment in human capital required to meet the needs of the nation's economy and defense; for the level of educational support will affect the numbers, quality of training, and skills of those who enter the work force in the next decade.

A Question of Values

Support for student aid, indeed for the higher education enterprise, will rest as always on fundamental value judgments about the benefits of education beyond high school. These judgments are not emblazoned in governmental statutes but are a composite of myriad perceptions and decisions of citizens, taxpayers, voters, politicians, and policy makers.

One might easily take a pessimistic view—that higher education will lose out badly in the sharp competition for public attention and resources during the current decade. Demography alone—declining numbers in the eighteen- to twenty-four-year-old traditional college-age bracket—will to some extent undercut the case for college and university support and student aid in the 1980s and early 1990s. During the same period, lower schools will begin laying claim to increased support because they will be absorbing the "echo" of the postwar baby boom, the children recently born to those who came of age in the 1960s and now approach middle age.

Then, too, the American public is not as enamored of higher education as it seemed to be at one time. On the heels of higher education's golden age of growth and prosperity in the 1960s, the past decade spawned a measure of skepticism about the worth of higher learning. If a degree was once a sure ticket to preferred status and economic security, problems of unemployment and underemployment of college graduates and Ph.D.s beginning in the early 1970s jolted traditional assumptions about the return on investment in higher learning. Had higher education been oversold and overbuilt? Were there "too many people" going to college? A new questioning crept into public dialogue on higher education. Books were written about "the great training robbery" (Berg, 1970), "the case against college" (Bird, 1975), and "the overeducated American" (Freeman, 1976).

Such skepticism notwithstanding, postsecondary schooling has continued to claim a major share of the nation's resources. There is no doubt that the connection between the labor market and higher education has weakened since the 1960s; job prospects for the highly educated are not nearly as buoyant as they were fifteen years ago. Yet for great numbers of the young, the campus experience remains a "rite of passage"; and for people of many ages, higher learning continues to hold the promise of self-improvement and greater opportunity, or at least is viewed as a "best bet" in a constantly changing society and economy.

Economists and policy researchers have long debated the benefits of higher education and have attempted to quantify "rates of return" on investment in it. Some argue that the gains are primarily personal and not shared by society in general. At an extreme, conservative economist Milton Friedman has maintained that alleged social gains, or "external benefits," from higher education are always "vague and general," cannot be measured, and therefore should not be presumed to exist (1968, p. 110). Few analysts—or anyone else—seem willing to discount so sweepingly the monetary and nonmonetary values of higher education, to society or to the individual. Many of the benefits may defy quantification, but there seems an abiding and substantial public confidence in American higher education—despite the jolts and doubts of recent times. And this general confidence undergirds personal and governmental decisions to invest in the enterprise. As one observer notes, higher education will hardly be spared "the joys of squabbling over shares of a fixed or slowly growing pie in what promises to be a contentious decade" (Breneman, 1981, p. 18). But neither is higher education likely to sink out of sight in the nation's scheme of priorities. In the words of the Carnegie Council on Policy Studies in Higher Education (1980, p. 97), "We do not anticipate a fast or slow fade-out for American higher education. We expect it to continue to move forward in response to both national and individual aspirations."

In fact, as we approach the mid-1980s, emerging economic and technological conditions seem to be refocusing attention on the link between education and the nation's productivity—and thus the importance of investing in people through education. Such a trend—should it prove more than momentarily fashionable—could reshape student aid policies and patterns in the years ahead.

Reopening the "Human Capital" Agenda

Educational shortfalls in math, science, and engineering are increasingly coming to light, and the growing national concern on this score recalls the post-*Sputnik* mood of a quarter century ago: "Nobody can build a high-quality economy with low-quality components, and the human component in the American economy is not being raised in quality fast enough. . . . After the *Sputnik* shock in the 1950s, the United States embarked on a successful major program to upgrade human skills. A similar effort will be necessary in the 1980s, even though education and training are now out of fashion" (Thurow, 1982, p. 31).

Today we are constantly reminded that the country is shifting from a manufacturing-based to an information- and service-oriented economy. Rapidly emerging "high technologies" appear to be the cutting edge of the economic future—developments like robotics, lasers, genetic engineering, fiber optics, not to mention computers and their constantly expanding applications in banking, insurance, health care, and communications as well as in the home. The international competition in these areas is intense. Will American industry be able to draw on an adequate pool of highly trained workers in this decade and the next to maintain its technological edge?

The manpower projections are worrisome. While overall

unemployment has persisted at near-record levels in the early 1980s, there are particular labor shortages—from machinists to engineering Ph.D.s, computer professionals, and specialists in various applied fields. Moreover, shortages of technical and scientific personnel seem likely to grow more acute as one looks down the pipeline. There will be fewer college graduates overall as the age group shrinks in the next ten years, and there appear to be severe gaps in the quality and quantity of math and science education in the secondary schools. Too few of the best students are taking challenging courses in these fields, and too few competent teachers are available to teach them. A lag in scientific and mathematical literacy among the young will likely translate into a prolonged undersupply of the highly skilled manpower needed in the new technological era.

Meanwhile, the educational systems of other developed countries may be better geared to the challenge; Japan, for example, now annually produces twice the number of electronics engineers per capita as the United States, and the gap is widening. The National Science Foundation forecasts a nearly 50 percent shortage of industrial engineers in this country in the current decade (Choate and Epstein, 1982).

When business and policy leaders talk about the need for "reindustrialization" of America and the importance of increased "capital formation," investment in physical plant and equipment typically comes to mind. But there seems to be a growing recognition that investment in human capital is equally important, that what goes on in the schools and universities and what comes out of them will have a great deal to do with the long-run success of economic recovery and the country's ability to compete in the world economy.

Student Aid and the Manpower Issue. The human capital theme has been sounded frequently in the reaction to proposed cutbacks in federal student aid. Don't dismantle the programs, it is argued, just when the need for developing our human resources is so clearly evident. The major federal student aid programs, however, are general in scope and purpose, not tailored to manpower projections or targeted on students with particular career goals.

Might current student aid programs be recast or new ones devised in response to perceived manpower problems? Manpower forecasting is a notoriously tricky business. Surpluses and shortages come and go, and often the problems that policies are designed to address have changed or disappeared by the time the policies are implemented. Federal policy in the 1960s, for example, fed the overproduction of some types of Ph.D.s, and loan forgiveness policies for students going into teaching persisted long after schoolteachers were in substantial oversupply. Likewise, many states have kept various categorical student aid programs on the books well after their original purposes have become obsolete. History tells us that manpower planning tends not to work very well, either in centrally controlled countries or in pluralistic, mixed governmental systems such as our own.

There will nonetheless be strong impulses in the period ahead to try to mesh educational financing policies more explicitly with the emerging needs of the economy. Congress already has before it an outpouring of proposals along these lines (American Society for Training and Development, 1982). Prospective legislation bearing titles like the "National Engineering and Science Manpower Act," "National Science and Technology Revitalization Act," or "Pre-College Math and Science Education Act" reflects the growing public spotlight on such issues. One proposal would establish special, low-interest loans to college students preparing to be elementary and secondary math and science teachers. Others would retrain teachers and foster computer literacy, or provide faculty fellowships in math, science, and engineering. Congressional sponsors of such measures hardly expect quick enactment, since the prevailing mood in Washington weighs against almost any new spending initiatives in the human resources field. But congressional worries about the "high-tech knowledge gap," as headlined by the *Washington Post*, are on the rise.

A sort of "market philosophy" characterized the thrust of most federal student aid in the 1970s. The idea was to ensure individual opportunity in higher education by putting purchasing power in the hands of needy students and letting them make their own choices in the postsecondary "marketplace." The

1980s may witness a partial return to more categorical approaches and selective subsidies. And concerns about quality and excellence will probably revive the notion of competitive, merit-based award policies. These questions will at least be in the air as Congress debates the future of the aid programs.

Also likely to attract more legislative attention in the period ahead is the issue of graduate student finance. Federal support of higher education in the 1950s and 1960s was heavily concentrated at the graduate level; during the past decade, however, the trend reversed, and the vast bulk of student aid dollars flowed to the undergraduate sector. In the 1980s the pendulum may swing again. Two factors will put increased focus on graduate and professional education: first, the aging of university faculties and the need to ensure an adequate flow of young scientists and scholars into the academic ranks of the major research institutions; and second, the manpower needs of industry as technological change demands more workers with training at the most advanced levels.

State governments will probably be worrying about some of the same questions of human capital investment and manpower planning, perhaps especially so if the national administration continues to try to shift such responsibilities as much as possible to the state level and Congress takes no independent action. Economic disparities among the states seem to be widening, especially between some of the resource-rich Sun Belt states and those in the Frost Belt more vulnerable to recession in the manufacturing and housing industries. Many of the states hit hardest economically seem to be in a race to attract rapid-growth high-technology and service industries as a basis for recovery, and policy makers in such states are beginning to pay greater attention to the role of higher education in supplying the necessary labor force for the economy of the future. (For a discussion of the link between higher education and regional economic renewal, see Hoy, 1982.)

While few states appear willing to try to make up for recent losses in federal student support, state student aid strategies are likely to be reviewed in the coming years with an eye toward manpower concerns. New state initiatives can be expected in the area of work-study and cooperative education, merit-based scholarships, and business–higher education partnerships designed to channel students into applied technical fields and other areas of need.

A Larger Corporate Role in Student Support. Corporations invest substantial sums in education and training of their employees, by some estimates over $30 billion a year. Most of this expenditure is for in-house, specific job-related skills development. Some of it supports joint ventures with nearby colleges and universities. In addition, to fill gaps in traditional academic curricula, companies are creating a variety of formal courses of their own, some of which are now recommended by the American Council on Education as suitable for academic credit; and a few companies have established full degree-granting postsecondary programs. In fact, one of the variables in the fortunes of traditional higher education in coming years could be the extent to which such corporate educational offerings compete for enrollments; increasing numbers of vocationally oriented students may view tuition-free, industry-based education, associated with a paying job, as an attractive alternative to the campus.

One thing seems certain: Accelerating technological change combined with demographic trends—a gradually aging work force and a shrinking pool of prospective young employees, the latter disproportionately black, Hispanic, and disadvantaged —will greatly increase training and retraining requirements of industry in the next decade. Time will tell how and where these needs are met. By and large, the corporate sector would prefer not to have to take on educational tasks traditionally expected of the schools and colleges, especially not remediation in basic competencies.

The years ahead will likely see greater use of company tuition assistance plans. The vast majority of large companies offer tuition benefits, sometimes negotiated by unions, to help workers enroll in college and university courses, and most of these benefits are exempt from federal income taxes paid by the employee. (Legislation now pending in Congress would reauthorize and extend the coverage of this tax exemption to spouses and dependents of employees.) Nonetheless, the rate of employee participation in these plans, at least until recently, has tended to be very low—less than 5 percent, according to analysis by the National Institute of Work and Learning. Here is an area of underutilized potential for student support, since employees rarely use the amount of money earmarked in corporate budgets for such benefits.

In addition to employee education plans, corporations support colleges and universities in a variety of other ways, as documented annually by the Council for Financial Aid to Education. Despite an overall decline in corporate earnings, contributions to education appear to have increased in response to recent federal funding cutbacks. Dow Chemical Company, for example, has doubled its aid to education programs in 1982, including a large chunk for college scholarships. Many firms are concentrating their support at the graduate level, with particular attention to engineering, the hard sciences, and computer studies. Some business leaders are beginning to worry that industry has been "eating its own seed corn" by hiring away top students and faculty in key fields, depleting the university ranks and raising a question about who will be left to teach tomorrow's graduates. Some companies are likely to step up their contributions in the form of liberal fellowship aid for graduate students going into teaching and research.

In short, there appears to be much fertile ground for higher education and industry to collaborate in addressing the "human capital" agenda in the coming decade. Diverse forms of student support will emerge as business looks to recruit the trained talent it needs and the campuses try to respond. The Commission on Higher Education and the Economy of New England (1982), for example, urges industries, especially in the high-technology fields, to form consortia to finance "work scholarship" contracts. Under such contracts companies would jointly finance loans for college and university students they might wish eventually to employ, the loan becoming a work scholarship and forgiven when and if the student graduates and is hired by a participating company. Student loan forgiveness, as in the form of the cancelable loans advocated by Beloit College, could be adopted as a general recruiting practice. Companies that recruit graduates who have accumulated substantial debts in the course of their education might agree to help with repayment obligations. Companies also might consider a pre-recruitment approach practiced in England, where businesses take on top-rated students as summer interns, then in return pay their tuition during the school year. These and other ideas bear exploration by campus and corporate representatives in the period ahead.

Military Needs and Postsecondary Financing. The military establishment has its own human capital agenda and strategies. Like business and industry, the military services (especially the Army) are worried about the quality and quantity of prospective manpower and must contend with some of the same demographic variables affecting the youth cohort in the population. The growing complexity of technology, as in industry, appears to increase training and skill requirements of military personnel. (Horror stories have become commonplace about semiliterate soldiers and sailors at a loss to operate and maintain sophisticated weaponry.)

The goals and incentives adopted by the armed forces for recruitment and retention in the coming years will have major implications for postsecondary education. On the one hand, the military and higher education will compete as they both try to draw from the declining number of young people. On the other hand, the military is a major source of direct and indirect support for students in higher education—through ROTC scholarships and in-service benefits (the military branches contract with colleges for training on campus and make available limited tuition aid for enlistees wishing to pursue college courses on their own) and through postservice benefits (the GI Bill and the more recent Veterans Education Assistance Program, or VEAP).

As the youth pool shrinks in the 1980s, pressure will inevitably mount from some quarters in the military for reinstating the draft as the only viable solution to the military manpower problem. In what promises to be a sharp debate, opponents of conscription will advance various measures for sustaining the all-volunteer policy, including augmented military pay and benefits. Revival of the GI Bill and its extensive education benefits is one approach already under review. Other education-related inducements might include loan forgiveness; legislation pending in Congress would cancel college loan repayment obligations of enlistees.

VEAP, which replaced the GI Bill in 1976, was widely judged a failure in its original form—a program under which the government matched contributions by the participating service-man to a fund providing at best modest postservice education benefits. To shore up the program, the Army and the Navy have added substantial bonuses, or "kickers," for selected recruits who score well on the armed forces qualification test and agree to enlist for training in certain skill areas. The Army version of the new VEAP can provide—to a limited number of servicemen —over $20,000 in college benefits for three to four years of mili-tary service. And this incentive has reportedly been successful in attracting high-quality enlistees. Whether such attractive benefits should be extended to military recruits across the board is the question Congress will have to answer as it con-tinues to look at proposals to revive the old-style GI Bill.

Despite the general popularity of the idea, several factors will work against passage of a new GI Bill. One is its multibillion-dollar expense, dwarfing what is now spent on VEAP. In addi-tion, there is disagreement about a new GI Bill's potential effec-tiveness in addressing military staffing needs. Some observers argue that a new GI Bill could actually worsen manpower prob-lems by reducing retention of servicemen, who would have in-centives to leave the military and use their accumulated benefits to attend college. The military branches are divided on the issue. The Army is the strongest supporter of a GI Bill approach; the Air Force would rather spend the money in other ways to upgrade its personnel.

College Benefits in Return for National Service? One con-ceivable way around the prohibitive expense of a new GI Bill would be to tap part or all of the monies now spent on the civil-ian federal student aid programs, perhaps converting them into a comprehensive plan that would make college tuition benefits conditional on a period of military or other service to the coun-try. Such a linkage has been discussed actively in some military and other circles in recent years. Advocates of this youth service plan say that, in addition to aiding military recruitment, it would foster a greater sense of the obligations of citizenship among young people and promote a variety of other national interests. The government would offer college assistance in return for specified periods of active and reserve duty in the military *or* service in civilian community and volunteer agencies (schools, hospitals, nursing homes, libraries, recreation facilities, and the like) where help is needed.

Those concerned with the military's recruitment problems have increasingly come to view Pell Grants and other federal student aid as undue competition. A report of the Atlantic Council observes: "We have today a system that in effect offers more to those who do not serve their country than those who do. Under the Veterans Education Assistance Program . . . government expenditures are less than $90 million annually. In comparison, federal aid to college students . . . is estimated at . . . $7.0 billion for [fiscal year] 1982. In effect, we have a GI Bill without the GI" (Working Group on Military Service, 1982, p. 37). Military representatives will continue to press this point of view, calling into question the appropriateness of having a "GI Bill without the GI." And they may be bolstered by those who support the concept of comprehensive national youth service. The idea of tying student aid to a service obligation may not be an idea whose time will come right away, but it is likely to attract growing attention and debate in the 1980s.

Filling the Gap: Who Will Pay?

However student aid fits into the human capital agenda and however it may be reconfigured to meet perceived needs of the economy and the military, the likelihood remains, at least in the short run, that there will be less help overall for students and their families to pay college expenses than there was in the expansionary years of the 1970s. As always, the question is how the burden of paying for higher education will be shared among taxpayers, through governmental policies that maintain low (subsidized) tuition and provide aid to students; parents, through past savings, current income, and obligations on future income (loans); students, through savings and self-help (loans, summer and part-time work); colleges and universities themselves, through earnings on their endowments; and businesses, charitable organizations, alumni, and private donors, through gifts and grants.

The last category, private gifts and grants, covers only a small fraction of the costs of higher education. Even combined with earnings on college endowments, private donations amount to less than 10 percent of the income of institutions of higher education. President Reagan has "jawboned" the private sector to step in and do more as the federal government cuts back, and there is certainly potential for increased corporate effort, as noted earlier. Neither philanthropy nor investments by industry in its own best interest, however, are likely to be of sufficient magnitude to "fill the gap" as government aid shrinks in the years ahead. At most, private support will inch up as a share of general higher education revenue and as a source of aid for students in particular. Private foundations are besieged by requests for funding in areas running the gamut of social and human services. Moreover, giving to higher education from whatever source—corporations, foundations, churches, community agencies, and the full range of nonprofit groups as well as alumni—can scarcely be expected to rise dramatically as long as the economy remains in recession or manages only sluggish recovery.

The cost burden borne by students and families will, of course, depend a great deal on tuition levels set by private college and university officials on one hand and by state authorities for public institutions on the other. Success in bringing general inflation under control would certainly make a difference, but odds are that the college tuition squeeze will continue unabated and may intensify.

"Prices" in higher education on average have tracked the Consumer Price Index fairly closely, at least until recently. In the early 1980s, tuition rates seem to be running somewhat ahead of general inflation, especially as hard-pressed states look for additional revenue by boosting student charges in the public colleges. More and more state systems are developing formu-

las for indexing fees to instructional expenses; the years ahead
will likely see differential charges for lower- and upper-division
undergraduates and for graduate students, and possibly variable
rates depending on individual program costs. More controversial
is the proposal to tie what the student pays to the earnings potential of graduates in the field in which the student is enrolled;
for example, engineering students might pay a surcharge based
on the assumption that they will be making considerably higher
salaries than liberal arts graduates.

The overall trend in the states will be toward charging
students an increasing percentage of the costs of their education. Likewise, more community college systems will find that
they must resort to charging tuition for the first time or will
hike their currently nominal charges. And independent institutions will probably be forced to continue raising tuition despite
their fears that they might "price themselves out of the market." No significant narrowing of the public-private "tuition
gap" seems in store.

How will families and individuals cope with what will
likely be higher prices and less aid in the 1980s? The bedrock of
the need-based student aid tradition since the 1950s has been
the assumption that parents have the primary obligation, to the
limit of their ability, to pay for their offspring's education. This
expectation of parental responsibility and sacrifice will have to
be reinforced in the period ahead. Though systematic data do
not exist to document the phenomenon, it seems clear that families on average plan and save less for college than they did, say,
twenty years ago. Many influences have been at work—changing
life-styles and consumer aspirations, competing claims on the
discretionary income of families, and—not least—the easier availability of student assistance, especially subsidized loans in recent years. Renewed pressure will be directed at parents to fulfill their customary responsibility in financing higher education.

This said, it must also be acknowledged that, for growing
numbers of students enrolled in postsecondary education, the
assumption of parental support is untenable, impractical, or
questionable. The full-time, dependent student of "college age"
(eighteen to twenty-two) has become less and less typical of

college-going patterns and will become still less so in the 1980s. More adults, of course, are returning to higher education for a "second chance" or retraining and mid-career change. At the same time, more young people are tending to stretch out their education, enrolling part time, "stopping out," or alternating periods of work and education. No one argues that the parental obligation should last indefinitely, but where to draw the line will be perhaps the most vexing issue of student aid policy in this decade. Should the determination be keyed automatically to such factors as the student's age and marital status? In what measure does the parental obligation extend to graduate and professional education?

Undoubtedly, some well-off students have established self-supporting status under government rules by artificially claiming that they are financially independent of their parents, thereby increasing the aid they might receive. Such abuse will continue to generate controversy, and the issue will be how to screen out students who manipulate the system without unfairly treating those who can only be viewed as free-standing adults, for whom an expectation of parental support would be awkward at best.

However much parents may be induced to save and sacrifice more for their children's education in the years ahead, it is clear that students themselves, whether treated as dependent or self-supporting, will have to be more resourceful. In response to federal cutbacks, campus aid offices are getting the message to students about ways to economize, to "do more with less." Campus life-styles may become a bit more Spartan. More important, we will likely see an accelerating trend toward mixing patterns of work and postsecondary study—more students opting for part-time enrollment combined with full- or part-time employment.

Many campuses are already dealing with the complexities of constructing expense budgets, conducting need analysis, and designing consistent award policies for largely nontraditional student bodies—students who are older, often attending less than full time, and typically coping with work and family responsibilities while in school. Many more campuses will be facing such complexities in the 1980s. They may find it relatively easy, for example, to tell a twenty-year-old undergraduate to live by a standard expense budget; but how can they make judgments about and impose expectations on older students who come from a variety of life situations and are accustomed to different standards of living?

More nontraditional students will also mean that institutions will increasingly have to deal with questions involving the interaction between student aid and other major benefit programs—welfare, food stamps, vocational rehabilitation, Social Security, and manpower training. And already difficult issues in the treatment of part-time students will become more pressing. As Froomkin (1978, p. 30) observes, "Should a student who attends a postsecondary institution part time and, for any reason, has a minimal income, be helped? . . . Is it equitable to require students with above minimal, but still low, incomes to pay tuition and fees out of this pittance? Most thinking about the adequacy of student aid has been dominated by the needs of full-time students and by the urge to facilitate their access. Whether the treatment of part-time students is equitable has not been considered."

One thing is clear. There will not be enough money to go all the way around in the coming years. "Trade-offs" between part-time and full-time, independent and dependent, graduate and undergraduate, older and younger students will make the business of student aid administration even more complicated—and more highly charged with issues of social equity—than it has been in the past.

The Loan Scramble. In an age of Visa, MasterCard, massive consumer credit, and "creative financing," it is perhaps not surprising that loans have been the primary focus of efforts and plans to fill the gap for students and parents. Compared to twenty-five years ago, credit financing of college costs is commonly accepted today, a trend greatly augmented by the pervasive availability of Guaranteed Student Loans (GSL) in the period following passage of the Middle Income Student Assistance Act of 1978. Increasingly, postsecondary education has come to be looked on as another consumer item to be "financed"—stretched out and paid for from the student's and/or parents' future earnings.

As soon as the specter of federal retrenchment loomed in 1981, the search was on among colleges, state authorities, and other partners in the student aid process for loan alternatives that might make up for prospective losses in federal support. Independent institutions in many states have pushed for state legislation to raise new capital for student loans through the sale of tax-exempt bonds. And some colleges have been exploring the feasibility of sponsoring new loan programs of their own. Foundations, corporations, pension funds, insurance companies, and a variety of other sources are also being plumbed for possible help in financing, guaranteeing, subsidizing, and providing secondary markets for college loans. Hope, too, has been placed in the relatively new federal program entitled Parental Loans for Undergraduate Students (PLUS), a less subsidized supplement to GSL, designed to help parents with cash-flow problems. (Graduate and independent students later became eligible to receive aid under this program.)

In the face of contraction and uncertainty regarding federal aid policies, it is only prudent that states and institutions begin to design realistic options to ensure the availability of loans on reasonable terms for students and parents. One danger of an increasingly decentralized approach to loan financing, however, is a proliferation of terms and conditions that could become hopelessly confusing to students and parents as well as lenders, aid administrators, and the secondary markets that trade in loan paper. Existing loan arrangements, developed largely within the overall structure of federal legislation, are complicated enough. (The GSL program has at least fostered a measure of standardization over the years.)

Moreover, a continuing surge toward credit financing of college expenses runs the risk of saddling students with excessive debt burdens after they graduate. Will today's student borrowers be able to manage their repayment obligations? Levels of indebtedness for many students are already extremely high. With prospects of federal retrenchment, the worry has been that loan money might run short. But the reverse could become more worrisome—that too much loan money is available, that student borrowers may be taking on obligations they will not be able to handle in later years. Defaults have always been an issue in student loan programs; the problem could become much worse down the road if present trends continue. Some observers believe that existing systems for servicing and collecting student loans are already nearing the point of saturation.

Another problem should not be overlooked. Disproportionate reliance on loan financing may not serve the financial needs of students and prospective students at the lower end of the economic scale—especially those from minority groups, who may be wary of borrowing. In the scramble for alternative funding, many of the plans and ideas that have surfaced tend to be tailored for students and families in the middle- and upper-income ranges or to be designed for the better-endowed institutions. But schemes that address the cash-flow problems of families and institutions do not necessarily strengthen the safety net for those with the greatest need.

All the above concerns as well as the persistent pressure in Washington to curb the mounting expense of the GSL program (roughly $3 billion in 1982, compared to less than $700 million in 1978) could redirect attention to long-standing proposals for fundamentally recasting the entire framework of student loan financing. Wide-ranging reforms have been suggested and advanced for a number of years, including creation of a national student loan bank that would streamline and centralize the process of raising capital for student loans and presumably do it more cheaply by eclipsing the network of incentives and allowances that are extended to participating lenders under the present GSL structure. In one scheme persistently promoted by Boston University president John Silber, the federal government would create a "Tuition Advance Fund" from which students could draw advances to be repaid through payroll deductions after they graduate, the repayment percentage climbing as income increased. Such schemes will be debated in the 1980s, and their appeal may grow in proportion to the confusion and fragmentation that may result from the current scramble for loan alternatives among states and institutions. More likely, however, the national loan bank and other overarching reform plans will remain more theoretical than practical possibilities in the coming years.

Tuition Tax Credits? Another response to the college cost squeeze in the 1980s will be a further round of proposals for tuition tax relief. For twenty years or more, bills have been introduced and reintroduced in Congress to promote college tax credits in one form or another, and the popularity of the idea has crested periodically. Pressure for their enactment, in fact, helped produce the original Guaranteed Student Loan program in 1965; that program was devised by the Johnson administration and incorporated in the Higher Education Act as a way to help defuse the tax credit movement in Congress. Thirteen years later the Middle Income Student Assistance Act was triggered by the same pressure.

More recently President Reagan has followed through on his campaign promise to support legislation for tuition tax credits—but only for elementary and secondary schooling expenses, not the costs of higher education. The coverage was so limited only because the administration wanted to moderate the proposal's several-billion-dollar estimated expense in potential revenue that would be lost to the United States Treasury. If elementary/secondary tax credits ever do win passage, however, it is a good bet that postsecondary education will be covered as well or will not be far behind.

The continuing debate over tuition tax credits will be heated, and it will be dominated by the constitutional and policy issues that come into play—primarily regarding elementary and secondary education, although the potential repercussions for higher education are also substantial. Watered down as any tax credit bill is likely to be if finally enacted, the legislation would not amount to much help for individual students and families, but the large "tax expenditure" incurred in the aggregate would undoubtedly cut into future funding of direct federal student aid. Tax credits, furthermore, tend to help the advantaged who pay taxes, not the disadvantaged who have little or no tax liability—and thus not poor families or self-supporting students as a rule. The national higher education associations have consistently opposed tax credits over the years as inequitable, unsound from the standpoint of tax policy, and likely to draw resources away from other forms of federal support for higher education.

The big price tag on tuition tax credits limits chances of their enactment when federal deficit projections are running higher than ever. But the tax credit idea can never be counted out, especially as long as a national administration is in office that firmly believes it is better to adjust the tax system than support direct-spending programs to address social goals.

Tax-Sheltered Savings Plans? Tax credits for current college expenses are not the only type of tax advantage that might be extended to students and their families. In fact, a number of tax provisions already exist that can be used to help save and pay for higher education, and these are receiving increasing attention. From personal finance counselors and newspaper columnists, the message—beamed particularly at parents in the middle- and upper-income ranges—is to start saving for college early and to do so in ways that save on taxes. The idea is to shift income or assets to a child or to borrow and put the proceeds in a child's name, taking advantage of the fact that the child almost always will pay taxes at a lower rate than the parent. A number of specific schemes, such as Crown loans and Clifford trusts, have become popular. (Some methods have been the subject of litigation and may ultimately be ruled illegal under the federal tax code.)

Proposals are also being floated in Congress to create new tax incentives to encourage saving for college, and such proposals could become an alternative (though equally or more expensive) to the more traditional tuition tax credit concept. One idea is the Individual Education Account (IEA), modeled on the tax-exempt Individual Retirement Account (IRA) for retirement purposes. Parents could put aside a certain amount of their income each year tax free for the purpose of saving for their children's higher education. In a similar vein, the use of IRA funds could simply be extended to include paying for college costs of family members.

The matter of tax policy has rarely been considered in

discussions of who pays and who should pay for higher education. Yet tax expenditures of the federal government (as well as some states) indirectly affect how the burden of paying for higher education is distributed; they seem likely to become a still larger factor in the current decade.

Full Circle: The Issue of Equity

In the final analysis, the fundamental question comes down to this: Who is going to be served by student financial aid in an era of retrenchment? A changing mix of manpower, economic, technological, and military goals, plus new agendas focusing on educational quality and excellence, will influence student aid policies in this and the next decade. And, overall, students and families will likely have to shoulder a larger share of the costs of higher education by one means or another. But who will get the aid that continues to be generated from public and private sources? On the heels of rapid growth and the broadening of eligibility to a much larger base of the population in the late 1970s, who will be squeezed out in the process of tightening down? Can we sustain the momentum of the past two decades toward an educational system based on wide access and freedom of choice for students? Can programs and policies be made more efficient? Can they be made to serve newly important goals without abandoning or dimming the prospect of equal opportunity for all groups in the society?

More concretely, in an old phrase from political science, it is a matter of who gets what, where, and how—and such issues become all the more fractious in a period of contraction. The government's commitment is shrinking. Will subsidies continue for those who could afford to invest in higher education on their own without the government's help, or will the programs be refocused and the available help concentrated on those who "but for such aid" would not be able to attend higher education or might be barred from enrolling in the program or institution of their choice?

Students from all types of circumstances and backgrounds have been and will be affected by the scaling back of student aid. Some observers suggest that recent cutbacks amount to a repeal of the Middle Income Assistance Act, that the harshest impact will be on middle-income students and parents in the period ahead. In fact, the greater hazard of policy in the 1980s is likely to be a squeeze on students and families in the lower economic range, those operating on the thinnest margin. Cutbacks not just in student aid but in the spectrum of income maintenance and other social programs have fallen disproportionately on the poor. And within the student aid portion of the national budget, grant aid, targeted traditionally on the neediest, has stabilized or declined; and the trend toward loan financing translates broadly into a shift of subsidies from the less well off to those in higher income brackets. If tax credits should be enacted, budget trade-offs would work further to the disadvantage of the poor.

There are other straws in the wind. Many private institutions, as well as some of the more selective public campuses, appear to have slackened in their efforts or are simply finding it more difficult to attract and enroll minority and low-income students. Some independent schools are beginning to rethink their policies—especially in light of federal cutbacks—of accepting students regardless of their ability to pay. Admission practices at such institutions have perhaps never been totally "need blind," but the intent for many years has been to try to admit students as much as possible without regard to their need for financial aid. This commitment may be eroding. Meanwhile, there are indications that some students may be gearing down their educational aspirations and choices to fit real or feared financial constraints. Community colleges in many parts of the country seem to be absorbing new enrollments from this type of shift. If fairer access to higher education is one way to lessen class differences in our society, a restratification of enrollment along economic lines would be a real step backward.

Student aid cannot be all things to all people, and it certainly cannot provide something for everybody in the conditions of austerity that so far dominate the 1980s. Competing claims and priorities will have to be shaken down. The challenge will be to strike a balance that does not compromise the democratic imperative of advancement toward equal educational opportunity.

A Note on Delivery Systems and Technology

No matter what goals are adopted for student aid in the 1980s, the dollars will be of little use if systems are not operating properly for delivering the aid to students in a timely fashion. In fact, delay and confusion in getting aid to students may be as harmful to the process of student access and choice as budget cuts themselves.

The National Task Force on Student Aid Problems (the Keppel Commission) examined the delivery system exhaustively in the mid-1970s and urged that the system be governed by a voluntary coalition of students, postsecondary institutions, state and private agencies, and the federal government. The Keppel Commission further recommended a common "methodology" for need analysis, a common application form, and a common calendar for the entire annual cycle of student aid. Some years later we are far from realizing the lofty vision of the commission's report (National Task Force on Student Aid Problems, 1975).

Efforts to simplify and coordinate the system are blocked in part by the sheer diversity and number of programs and aid sources that have been created piecemeal over the past quarter century. The maze of forms, deadlines, family contribution schedules, rules, and regulations makes it possible for one party, not infrequently the federal government, to stall the system and impede chances for timely and effective coordination. And the result, so evident recently, can be to leave students and institutions waiting for a painfully long time to learn how programs will actually operate in a given year. Part of the problem, too, is that the mechanics and technology of delivering aid have not fundamentally changed in twenty-five years. The system is still massively based on paperwork—endless pieces of paper filled in by students, parents, and administrators and carried in different directions across the country by hand or by the postal service. The effects of delay and disjointedness might well be alleviated if the cumbersome paper-based process were replaced by a system based on rapid electronic communications, with the potential to link all the major components of the financial aid delivery system. Such technology, of course, would not dispel the problems that stem from controversy over funding and control of governmental programs, but it could greatly simplify procedures and reduce the time required to adjust the system in response to political decisions.

The technology now exists for substantially unifying and streamlining the nuts and bolts of student aid administration. The question in the 1980s is whether we can find the will and the wisdom to harness available technology to serve students, families, and the objectives of public policy more effectively. Some states and institutions are already using it to great advantage to speed the processing and packaging of aid.

A Note to Campus Administrators

As always, the many different strands of student financial aid policy will be brought together and woven into practice on each campus. Here is where public and institutional goals are melded and implemented in patterns of support for students. The foregoing pages—one observer's peerings into a cloudy future—have suggested a number of implications for campus planners and administrators. A few closing reflections follow.

A first point needs to be addressed to senior administrators: The critical importance of recruiting the best possible people to run the student aid programs on campus cannot be overemphasized. The administration of student aid will intersect with every phase of institutional management in the 1980s: planning, budgeting, financial management, development, alumni and public relations, admissions, student services. The student aid function extends well beyond the mechanistic implementation of programs; on most campuses it goes to the heart of institutional finance, enrollment prospects, and the character of the student body.

With declining resources every institution will need to review its goals in student aid. In the years of massive growth, many campus aid offices became accustomed to being able to serve a wide spectrum and proportion of students on campus—something for everyone or almost everyone. Now choices and trade-offs must be weighed more carefully when award and packaging policies are devised. There are many ways of rationing scarce funds, but some arbitrary and expedient solutions may not be equitable. For example, when aid application deadlines are moved forward (as they have been at some institutions), disproportionate numbers of disadvantaged and minority students tend to be screened out.

Fundamentally, each institution must choose what mix of students it wishes to have on campus. If social and economic diversity continues to be viewed as important, this value must be reflected in outreach, counseling, and targeted aid policies. Much is at stake here for the future of affirmative action in higher education. Some institutions appear to be in retreat from such commitments of the past decade, less willing to take risks on prospective students from educationally and economically disadvantaged backgrounds. Institutions should bear in mind, however, one of the few certainties about this decade and the next: minorities, blacks, and especially Hispanics will make up an increasing percentage of younger people in the population. Nationally, though especially in the Sun Belt, the dwindling supply of high school graduates will consist more and more of students from minority backgrounds. Colleges looking primarily for young, white, middle-class, full-time students to fill their classes will be casting in a smaller and smaller pool. Generalizations are hazardous, since each institution will face a different set of market factors in the 1980s—as suggested by the title of the Carnegie Council report *Three Thousand Futures* (Carnegie Council on Policy Studies in Higher Education, 1980). One can say with some assurance, however, that the vast majority of institutions will have to address the needs of various nontraditional, minority, and older adult students if they are to remain vital in this decade.

Once institutional sights have been broadly established for the future, the task in student aid becomes twofold: to make better use of existing resources and to search widely for new ones. Efficiency and creativity will both be important. Institutions will need to:

- Reinstill the expectation among parents that the responsibility to finance college costs rests in the first instance with them, student aid coming only after they have fully contributed to the extent of their ability. Careful counseling and need analysis can yield potential savings by increasing parental contributions.

- Encourage students to tighten their belts in reasonable ways —to "do more with less."
- Clarify and reinforce student self-help expectations and policies in the packaging of aid.
- Foster flexible and multiple work-study options. Students will need latitude in combining part-time jobs and enrollment and in alternating periods of work and education.
- Secure adequate and, if necessary, new resources of loan financing but take care to set prudent limits on student indebtedness. College finance must not become strictly a credit transaction. Overindebtedness of graduates will aggravate collection and default problems and will not enhance alumni relations in years hence.
- Develop stronger ties with business and industry and explore the potential of company employees' educational benefits, corporate contributions to scholarship and fellowship funds, the concept of loan forgiveness for graduates hired by companies, and other forms of corporate help for students.
- Make student aid a prominent theme of capital campaigns and general fund raising. The private sector has an obligation to contribute to the investment in human capital through education, and publicity about government cutbacks strengthens the argument that the private sector needs to do more.
- Step up "public relations" on behalf of student aid, countering some of the negativism of recent years and getting the word to the public about the success stories and good things that result from student assistance.

The above checklist is not exhaustive, but if student aid became "the very lifeblood" of higher education in the 1970s, these are some of the things that institutions will need to think about to keep it flowing in the 1980s and beyond.

Bibliographical Note

Breneman (1981) has insightfully analyzed economic factors that will bear on higher education in the 1980s. With an eye toward helping institutional administrators plan ahead, he reviews the outlook for inflation, demographic trends, and changes in the labor market. See also Breneman (1982) on the enrollment crisis facing different sectors of higher education.

Three Thousand Futures, the last report of the Carnegie Council on Policy Studies in Higher Education (1980) under the leadership of Clark Kerr, evaluates prospects for higher education over the next twenty years. It presents enrollment projections and analyses—nationally and by region and sector; and it probes nearly every phase of the academic enterprise, making recommendations for institutional as well as government policy. Analyses of student aid are updated from earlier Carnegie reports.

Froomkin (1978) reassesses federal policy—in light of the potential demand for higher education and the fiscal, economic, and demographic forces likely to be important in the subsequent decade—and presents alternative and unconventional models for future public policy.

In an article in *Change Magazine,* I examined the passage and outcomes of the 1980 congressional reauthorization of the Higher Education Act and forecast some of the issues—such as costs, priorities, and the proper targeting of federal assistance for higher education—that are likely to be revisited throughout the 1980s in national debates over student aid programs and policies (see Gladieux, 1980).

Hauptman (1982) prepared a report for the Washington Office of the College Board to guide states, educational institutions, and others trying to develop alternative student loan programs to help make up for reductions in federal aid.

A Selective Guide
to the Literature

Robert H. Fenske
Louis C. Attinasi, Jr.
Richard A. Voorhees

The publications in student financial aid included in this bibliography were culled from a wide-ranging review of several hundred journal articles, research reports, monographs, and books. They were selected for inclusion according to one or more of the following criteria: significance to the field, relevance to the purpose of this book, and representativeness of certain genre in the literature—for example, reports of statewide surveys of aid recipients or analyses of federal student aid policies.

Seventeen of the preceding eighteen chapters conclude with a bibliographical note, the purpose of which is to guide the interested reader toward the key sources of further information on the topic of the chapter. Obviously, the chapter authors in aggregate have already made a substantial contribution to the goals of this bibliography. We have filled in sources in certain areas not covered by any of the authors; and occasionally— when the work's scope and/or significance seemed to warrant further treatment or when the chapter author reviewed only part of a comprehensive work—we have extended their reviews. Together, the end-of-chapter bibliographical notes and this bibliography provide an up-to-date overview of the significant literature in student financial aid.

A substantial portion of that literature is published by four organizations: the National Association of Student Financial Aid Administrators (NASFAA), the College Entrance Examination Board (especially the board's Washington, D.C., office), the American College Testing Program, and the American Council on Education. In addition, Jossey-Bass Inc., Publishers, has contributed several significant works on student aid, including an important report of the Carnegie Council on Policy Studies in Higher Education and two quarterly sourcebooks. Many other interesting and valuable works, however, are not disseminated through the usual general channels for cataloguing publications (channels such as the Educational Resources Information Center (ERIC), the *Education Index,* and *Dissertation Abstracts International*). Consequently, they are largely unavailable to the general readership of scholars and other professionals. The literature on student aid in Illinois is illustrative of the problem.

Beginning in 1969, triennial surveys of recipients of financial aid from the Illinois State Scholarship Commission (ISSC) were conducted to evaluate the effectiveness of the commission's programs. These surveys were duly distributed to similar agencies in other states. Certain findings of the surveys were presented as research papers at professional meetings and published as journal articles. In addition, the annual reports of the commission contain a wealth of statistical information, and for over ten years the commission published the annual surveys of the National Association of State Scholarship and Grant Programs. Special studies of the impact of ISSC programs were conducted by Illinois legislative commissions, the statewide coordinating agency, and research scholars at Illinois universities. All

this information on student aid in Illinois is clearly of interest
within the state; however, the findings of the studies also reveal
much of interest to other states for normative and comparative
purposes, as well as to scholars researching certain aspects of
student aid. Despite the potential interest in and value of the information, it is difficult to obtain and assemble for review because of the lack of adequate networking and the failure to
insert the reports into cataloguing services such as ERIC. One
would have to know personally of the variety of resources on
Illinois state student aid in order to obtain a comprehensive
overview. The same is true of other states, and the problem is
multiplied many times over at the institutional level across the
country, where further reports and studies might also be of importance. As student aid "comes of age" as a profession, it is
hoped that researchers and policy analysts in the field will share
their findings routinely and conscientiously. The *Journal of Student Financial Aid* and other publication programs of NASFAA
have made considerable strides toward the sharing of valuable
information that marks a mature profession.

General Works

The three annotated bibliographies currently available on
student aid were consulted during the preparation of this chapter and found most useful:

American College Testing Program. *An Annotated Bibliography
in Student Financial Aid, 1960–1973.* Iowa City: American
College Testing Program, 1974. This collection is organized
into five sections: broad financial aid areas; scholarships, fellowships, grants, awards, and gifts; student loans and loan
funds; cooperative education; and student employment. It
has largely historical significance for researchers and scholars
because it mainly considers sources published during the
1960s and does not contain the more voluminous literature
published later.

Davis, J. S., and Van Dusen, W. D. *Guide to the Literature of
Student Financial Aid.* New York: College Entrance Exami-

nation Board, 1978. Intended as a comprehensive overview of literature published in the 1970s in the area of financial aid, this collection is organized into seven parts: sources of program information; the history, philosophy, and purpose of aid; financial aid administration management and problems; financial aid administration as a profession; federal and state issues and problems in student aid; financial aid and financing postsecondary education; and research on financial aid. Generally, a section or subsection is preceded by a description of its theme and the content of the included items. This bibliographical collection is well organized and is a valuable resource for readers wishing to investigate the available literature from 1970 through 1976, a time when increased attention was paid to financial aid by the academic community. NASFAA plans to publish an updated version of this bibliography in 1983.

Illinois State Scholarship Commission. *Annotated Bibliography of Student Financial Aid.* Deerfield: Illinois State Scholarship Commission, 1981. This compilation updates the two bibliographies just noted by covering selected entries from 1975 through 1980. It is organized into ten sections: history, philosophy, and purpose of financial aid; general information about financial aid programs; student financial aid counseling; legal aspects of the financial aid profession; administration and management of the financial aid office; scholarships, grants, awards, and gifts; student employment and work programs; student loan and loan funds; financial aid annual reports and program information; and research in the financial aid profession. The purpose of this guide was to provide administrators with general information about the literature on student aid, but it is also of considerable benefit to researchers and scholars. Compilation and publication of this bibliography were funded by the State Student Financial Aid Program of the Office of Student Financial Assistance, U.S. Department of Education.

Only four general treatments of student aid were published prior to the present book. Because they do not fit into any of the sections that comprise the balance of this bibliography, they are reviewed here.

Binder, S. (Ed.). *New Directions for Student Services: Responding to Changes in Financial Aid Programs,* no. 12. San Francisco: Jossey-Bass, 1980. The main theme of this collected work is that changes in student aid programs will continue to occur. The initial chapter reviews the development of financial assistance programs, emphasizing in particular the implications of recent changes in federal policy. Subsequent chapters include descriptions of programs designed to respond, at the institutional level, to changes brought about by legislation and regulation, and of a model for research on the effects of student aid.

College Entrance Examination Board. *Perspectives on Financial Aid.* New York: College Entrance Examination Board, 1975. This resource book for financial aid administrators includes papers devoted to historical sketches of federal, state, and institutional involvement in student assistance and to fairly comprehensive descriptions of the aid programs operating at each of these levels in the mid-1970s. The role and functions of the aid administrator as well as the organization and operation of the aid office are also considered. Much of the content of this volume, particularly the descriptions of the specific aid programs, is out of date, but it remains useful for its historical perspective on student aid and for the valuable insights of leaders in the field in the mid-1970s.

Henry, J. B. (Ed.). *New Directions for Institutional Research: The Impact of Student Financial Aid on Institutions,* no. 25. San Francisco: Jossey-Bass, 1980. Among the topics considered in this sourcebook are the effects of enrollment changes on student aid policies and programs, student aid as a variable in institutional planning and research, student aid and the market-model approach to recruitment, the impact of student aid on individual student achievement and adjustment to campus life, and the potential future impact of aid on institutions. This publication is especially timely in view of the pressing need to address the issues surrounding the impact of financial aid funds and their delivery on students, postsecondary institutions, and society in general. The volume not only addresses such issues but also suggests practical steps for effectively administering aid programs.

Keene, R., Adams, F. C., and King, J. E. (Eds.). *Money, Marbles, or Chalk: Student Financial Support in Higher Education.* Carbondale: Southern Illinois University Press, 1975. The most comprehensive treatment of student aid to date, this book considers student financial aid as an emerging profession in the area of higher education administration. Included are papers on the history and development of student financial assistance (Part I), the programs and problems of student support (Part II), the organization and administration of financial aid (Part III), the training and functioning of student aid professionals (Part IV), and the future of financial aid (Part V). The editors conclude the volume with recommendations in two areas: student financial support (they recommend and predict a deemphasis on grants in favor of student self-help) and professionalism (they believe that increased formal academic training is needed). Much of the book's relevance has been minimized by the passage of time; its strength remains in its historical discussions.

The presentation of the remaining sources in this bibliography parallels the thematic, four-part organization of this book: (1) the background, development, and current dimensions of financial aid; (2) the financial aid delivery system; (3) ensuring the aid program's effectiveness; (4) utilizing student aid for institutional purposes. Within each of the sections, the works are listed alphabetically.

Part One:
Development, Scope, and Purposes of Student Aid

The four chapters in Part One (Chapters One through Four) cite many of the important sources in this area and also annotate a number of the most significant works. Chapter Two in particular provides a much-needed single, comprehensive listing of the key documents on federal student aid programs. Following are descriptions of valuable additional publications on the purposes, policies, and dimensions of federal, state, and institutional programs.

Astin, A. W. *Minorities in American Higher Education: Recent Trends, Current Prospects, and Recommendations.* San Francisco: Jossey-Bass, 1982. Higher education has responded to the needs of minorities through open admissions, recruitment, financial aid, and the establishment of ethnic studies programs. Because of federal and state budget cuts, Astin speculates that many of these efforts will be either eliminated or reduced. He provides summaries of data collected to evaluate minority access and attainment and the factors that influence the college attendance and academic success of minorities—specifically, blacks, Chicanos, Puerto Ricans, and American Indians. Included are data concerning financial aid awarded to minorities and the impact of various types of aid on minority persistence.

Astin concludes by recommending that inequity in higher education be confronted and eliminated. Specific recommendations include the replacement of normative measures in assessing student ability, increased articulation with secondary schools, revitalization of the community college transfer function, and expansion of basic skills programs. Astin also recommends that policy makers expand their traditional concept of equality of opportunity and assess the quality and resources of the institution attended by minority students. In addressing financial aid, he recommends that aid packages emphasize grants rather than loans and that work-study aid be limited to less than half-time employment on campus.

Atelsek, F. J., and Gomberg, I. L. *Estimated Number of Student Aid Recipients, 1976-1977.* Higher Education Panel Report, No. 36. Washington, D.C.: American Council on Education, 1977. This report—the third survey of student aid programs and recipients undertaken by the Higher Education Panel of the American Council on Education—summarizes the results of surveys of a stratified sample of public and private two-year colleges, four-colleges, and universities. Participation in five federal assistance programs (BEOG, SEOG, NDSL, CWS, and GSL) is reported by institutional type and student characteristics; summaries of average aid by source and institutional type are also provided. These reports should be of considerable interest to institutional decision makers who want to know whether their federal aid programs—particularly, the discretionary campus-based aid programs—are distributing similar amounts and types of assistance as programs at other, comparable institutions. At this writing, the panel plans to publish an updated survey of recipients of federally funded aid programs.

Breneman, D. W., and Finn, C. E., Jr. (Eds.). *Public Policy and Private Higher Education.* Washington, D.C.: Brookings Institution, 1978. This book is the most scholarly and insightful work available on the politics and economics of private higher education. Following an overview of the recent history of public-private issues and of policy options for the future, the chapters consider, in turn, statistics on the financing of private higher education; the current and future demand for private higher education; federal policy in the areas of educational law making, student aid and tax matters; state policy, covering political relationships and financing options; and the college president's view of private higher education. Most germane to this bibliography is Chapter 5, "Federal Options for Student Aid," which assesses the present role of the federal government in financing students in private institutions. The distortion in federal programs resulting from attempts to minimize perceived harm to the private sector is pointed out, and reforms of federal policies are proposed. Chapters 7 and 8 consider aspects of student aid at the state level, especially as it represents an alternative to direct aid to the private institution. Among the editors' general recommendations in the concluding chapter are suggestions for reforming the present student grant and loan programs.

Carnegie Council on Policy Studies in Higher Education. *Next Steps for the 1980s in Student Financial Aid: A Fourth Al-*

ternative. San Francisco: Jossey-Bass, 1979. In this important report, the Carnegie Council discusses the current system of student aid (including need analysis, student aid packaging, and the impact of aid on enrollments and institutions) and considers specific opportunities for change (such as strengthening the need-based system, improving the student loan system, and enhancing program coordination). Most important, however, is the council's proposed alternative to the revision of the Higher Education Act. In lieu of (1) simply extending the then existing legislation with little change, (2) expanding the "middle-income thrust" of the legislation, or (3) supplementing (or even substituting) a program of cost-of-education tax credits, the council recommends a major overhaul of the existing system to make the programs, within present financial confines, more equitable in their impact and more sound in their administration. Specifically, the council's proposal calls for (1) no increase in the total amount spent on student aid by the federal government; (2) a redistribution of funds in the direction of what the council considers the greater needs; (3) a better coordination of federal and state programs, with greater incentives for increased state expenditures; and (4) changes that will contribute to the integrity, simplicity, and flexibility of the overall program. Only the first component of this alternative has been realized in the years since the report was published.

College Entrance Examination Board, Washington Office. *The Guaranteed Student Loan Program: Options for Controlling Federal Costs While Preserving Needed Credit for College.* Washington, D.C.: College Entrance Examination Board, Washington Office, 1981. This report examines the causes of the escalating costs of the Guaranteed Student Loan program prior to its "capping" in 1982. Two major policy questions are explored in the report: (1) Which students, if any, should be eligible for the in-school interest subsidy? (2) How much should students or their families be eligible to borrow at below market rates of interest? To reduce the amount of subsidy and to bar the well off from borrowing under the program, the Reagan administration has considered eliminating the in-school interest subsidy, restricting eligibility to the amount of a borrower's demonstrated financial need, and charging a market rate of interest for the parent loan option. These actions, however, may drastically curtail student loans for the needy and drive up administrative costs. After outlining the strengths and weaknesses of alternative cost-cutting strategies, the authors opt for an index of need that determines both borrower eligibility and permissible loan amounts. Together with modest increases in interest rates, elimination of some of the current provisions that allow students in specified circumstances to defer repayment of their loans, and modification in the special allowance formula that governs the rate of return to lenders, the index offers the most direct and reasonable way to control program costs and reduce excessive borrowing.

Franklin, P. *Beyond Student Financial Aid: Issues and Options for Strengthening Support Service Programs Under Title IV of the Higher Education Act.* New York: College Entrance Examination Board, 1980. Franklin argues that student financial aid is not enough to equalize opportunity for postsecondary education; federal support service programs, Talent Search, Upward Bound, and Special Services for Disadvantaged Students (known as the "Trio" programs), as well as the more recent Educational Information Centers, are critical to the achievement of this goal. The heart of this publication is Chapter 3, which assesses issues and options that span the Title IV support service programs. These involve (1) level of authorization, (2) interprogram overlap and duplication, (3) interprogram integration and/or coordination, and (4) student eligibility. The final chapter contains program-by-program recommendations intended to help clarify the purpose and scope of Trio programs and enhance their respective operations. This publication is an illuminating discussion of the policy options for the "other" provision of Title IV.

Gladieux, L. E., and Hansen, J. S. *The Federal Government, the States and Higher Education: Issues for the 1980s.* New York: College Entrance Examination Board, 1981. This report explores the implications of federal financing of higher education for the states. The discussion centers on direct student assistance, where federal activity has increased most rapidly and where recent developments pose important policy questions for many states. Specifically, the explosive growth of the Basic Educational Opportunity Grants (now called Pell Grants) has tended to give the federal government increasing influence over the entire network of aid systems, including state and institutional programs. This has forced states into the role of supplementing federal aid programs. Various state responses to the increased federal role in student assistance are examined. Also considered are the implications of the recent mixed signals from Washington about federal loan programs for the future of state loan agencies and the increasing threat to federal student aid posed by overzealous state monitoring. In their concluding discussion, the authors argue that colleges and states are likely to be faced with a continued pattern of decentralized, fragmented support at the federal level. (For information on the growth of state student aid programs from 1969 through 1980, see Fenske and Boyd, 1981, reviewed in the Bibliographical Note in Chapter Three.)

Gladieux, L. E., and Wolanin, T. R. *Congress and the Colleges: The National Politics of Higher Education.* Lexington, Mass.: Lexington Books, 1976. In an attempt to address a serious deficiency in the literature on federal policy making for postsecondary education, the authors describe the genesis, enactment, and consequences of the Education Amendments of 1976. They regard these amendments primarily as omnibus or "grab bag" legislation, broadening and elaborating the federal role in an area (including student aid) where there was already a consensus on government's legitimate involvement. The book is at the same time an intellectual history, a chronicle of social and political events, and a case study of federal policy making. As such, it effectively addresses several different audiences: citizens with an interest in American government and politics; students and teachers, who are directly affected by the legislation; and those, including college and university administrators, with a professional interest in the substance of federal higher education policy.

Green, K. C. *Access and Opportunity: Government Support for Minority Participation in Higher Education.* Washington, D.C.: American Association for Higher Education, 1982. This research report traces the history of federal and state involvement in financing equal educational opportunity and offers an assessment of the success of these efforts. The postwar redirection of the federal role from passive consumer of educational services to active sponsor of educational policy initiatives is examined. State efforts in promoting equality of opportunity for disadvantaged citizens are also reviewed. Throughout the development of financial support from both levels of government, minority groups have often been the implicit, if not specific, beneficiaries of the programs designed to assist the economically disadvantaged. Green, however, makes a strong argument that equality of opportunity is not synonymous with equal education. For example, incentives supplied by the federal government have been responsible for much of the increase in minority enrollment in public colleges. Yet, as the report notes, minority enrollments are greatest in those public institutions with the fewest resources, the two-year colleges; the underrepresentation of minorities in four-year institutions continues. Therefore, although federal expenditures for programs specifically directed at minorities generally have had positive impacts (particularly student financial aid), other tactics may now be required if equality of education is to be achieved.

Green analyzes current programs, such as Title III (Support to Developing Institutions), and discusses the implications of various federal policy options. In an era of declining resources, he urges greater cooperation and planning among federal agencies, state officials, and institutional representatives. This tactic may deliver the most promise for equal opportunity, since, as the report notes, money is not in itself a panacea.

Hansen, J. S. *The State Student Incentive Grant Program: An Assessment of the Record and Options for the Future.* New

York: College Entrance Examination Board, 1979. This report examines the partnership between state and federal government in the smallest of the Title IV grant programs, the State Student Incentive Grant (SSIG) program. It traces the history of the SSIG program, enumerates the requirements that states must meet to participate in it, and examines three aspects of the program that limit its effectiveness: (1) its "closed-ended" matching provision, which limits the expansion of state dollars by specifying a limit for federal contributions; (2) the use of a fixed base year, instead of a "rolling" base year, for determining the matching funds a state can receive; and (3) the enrollment-dependent state allocation formula, which treats all states alike regardless of their varying commitments to student aid. Most states contribute directly to student grants under the SSIG program, but a few rely on the alternative matching concept—in the form of state funds appropriated to postsecondary institutions for state grants or of institutional funds contributed to the state to satisfy their matching requirements. The report concludes by suggesting options to decision makers.

Hauptman, A. *Financing Student Loans: The Search for Alternatives in the Face of Federal Contraction.* Washington, D.C.: College Entrance Examination Board, Washington Office, 1982. Student loans are seen as alternatives for states, educational institutions, and others seeking to make up for recent and anticipated reductions in federal grant aid. Educational institutions might consider expanding federal loan availability, reducing the cost of borrowing, and/or establishing private loan programs. Other alternatives are corporate involvement, tax-exempt financing, establishment of secondary markets, and the implementation of savings plans and tax incentives linked to loans for college. The author speculates on the success of these alternatives, identifies possible pitfalls, and suggests variations that might be helpful. This paper is important and timely reading for the financial aid community because, as federal assistance contracts, state, institutional, and private loan programs will become increasingly important components of student financial aid.

Hauptman, A., and Rice, L. D. *Student Grant Assistance in New York State*. New York: College Entrance Examination Board, 1980. New York spends nearly one third of a billion dollars on student aid, a level of effort unmatched by other states. This report discusses the state's lack of coordination with the federal Basic Educational Opportunity Grant program. For example, a student with maximum need may receive a maximum BEOG and a state need-based Tuition Assistance Program (TAP) grant. The result is that students have 70 to 80 percent of their need met by grants alone. For students of moderate means, a family's contribution is calculated twice and the student's award is reduced in both programs. Several alternatives are suggested, including making the state grant a flat grant, limiting grants to a percentage of cost, and calculating BEOG grants as a portion of the student's available resources in determining a corresponding TAP grant. This report demonstrates that state and federal programs of student assistance are interdependent and that state policy, or lack of it, can affect the entire complexion of higher education in a state with many private and public institutions. In New York the state university system and community colleges can charge a relatively higher tuition amount because the amount of TAP assistance will increase along with these changes. The combined availability of both grant sources has narrowed the tuition gap between the public and private sectors.

National Association of Student Financial Aid Administrators. *Student Financial Aid: An Investment in America's Future*. Washington, D.C.: National Association of Student Financial Aid Administrators, 1982. This document answers questions frequently raised by students, parents, and others on the nature, distribution, and use of financial aid and examines the costs and actual benefits of student aid expenditures. The authors conclude that student financial aid is beneficial because (1) it helps parents and students pay for postsecondary educational expenses, (2) it has greatly expanded educational opportunities to millions of Americans, and (3) it has had a positive effect on the institution's ability to enroll and retain students.

Essentially, this report was designed to mobilize support for student aid in the ongoing congressional debates during the early Reagan administration.

Nelson, S. C. *Community Colleges and Their Share of Student Financial Assistance.* Washington, D.C.: College Entrance Examination Board, Washington Office, 1980. In this report Nelson examines two conflicting concerns often voiced about community college participation in student aid programs: underutilization and overawarding. Institutional packaging of aid—combined with entitlement aid, such as veterans' benefits—can result in substantially higher awards. Other factors, however, limit the community colleges' share of available assistance dollars. In all but nine states, for example, state aid is awarded only to full-time students. As a result, a substantial segment of the community college clientele is underfunded. The major contribution of this report is its recognition that the need of community college students for financial assistance must be determined. Policy can be altered, but to do so requires clear definitions; and, as the report notes, more complete data are needed on the state of community college financial aid.

Stampen, J. O. *Student Aid and Public Higher Education: A Progress Report.* Washington, D.C.: American Association of State Colleges and Universities, 1983. In this first report of a national study of student financial assistance, data are presented on the distribution of student aid among varied groups of over 12,000 recipients at 226 public colleges and universities during 1981–82. The principal finding is that student aid programs do what they were intended to do—that is, distribute dollars to students who would otherwise have difficulty financing a college education. By making higher education affordable to those least able to pay, these programs promote vertical equity. Stampen also reports the following additional findings: (1) In 1981–82 recipients of aid from need-based programs included about 31 percent of the total head-count enrollment. (2) Seventy percent of the 1981–82 recipients received need-based aid from at least one federal, state, or institutional program; 27 percent received aid not determined by need, largely Guaranteed Student Loans. (3) Lower-income students received the greater part of their aid in the form of grants; higher-income students received theirs in the form of loan assistance. (4) On the whole, need-based aid did not increase proportionately with college costs; variance in aid levels was related to family income.

The information in this report should be useful to all who are concerned with the financing of higher education: lawmakers, federal and state officials, college officials, and student aid officers. The creation of a data base on student aid recipients in public higher education represents an important new resource for policy makers in the area of student assistance.

Van Dusen, W. D. *The Coming Crisis in Student Aid: Report of the 1978 Aspen Institute Conference on Student Aid Policy.* New York: Aspen Institute for Humanistic Studies, 1979. At the conference whose proceedings are reported here, the participants—many of them influential leaders in student aid—raised questions concerning "The Public Commitment to Student Aid," "Funding the Commitment," "Operating the System," and "The Governance of Student Aid." Although the conference is already five years old, the questions about the optimum rate of participation in postsecondary education, the distribution of financial aid to induce and maintain that level, and the most effective mechanism for delivering financial support are still valid.

Part Two:
Delivering Aid to Students on Campus

The literature on the delivery of financial aid is uneven in coverage. For example, while numerous sources review the philosophy and practice of need assessment and budget construction, few publications examine the concept of aid packaging. The bibliographical notes appended to the chapters in Part Two (Chapters Five through Eight) adequately describe most of the important how-to guides to institutional delivery of financial aid and, in some instances, indicate philosophical treatments and research studies of the subject. The following annotations are intended to supplement and enhance the contents of those essays.

American College Testing Program. *Handbook for Financial Aid Administrators.* Iowa City: American College Testing Program, 1981. This handbook, updated annually, provides an invaluable source of topical information for financial aid administrators. It reviews the guidelines for the uniform methodology developed by the National Task Force on Student Aid Problems (see National Task Force in this section). This review is updated each year to reflect any changes adopted by the National Student Aid Coalition. The handbook provides formulas and tables to be used in assessing a family's ability to contribute to educational expenses and to estimate student educational expenses. It also provides sample cases and takes the reader, step by step, through the calculation process. Finally, it explains the services provided by ACT and the various documents used by ACT in calculating and reporting student and family financial data. CSS publishes a similar guide (see College Scholarship Service, 1982, in this section).

Barnes, G. *An Economist's View of the Uniform Methodology.* Iowa City: American College Testing Program, 1977. The author argues that the uniform methodology (the need analysis model used by ACT and CSS) is inequitable and cumbersome to administer because its measure of parents' ability to pay includes the actual income of parents adjusted for nondiscretionary expenditures *and* an income supplement from wealth. For example, in its present form, the uniform methodology favors parents who are homeowners, well educated, widowed or divorced, and who own wealth in forms other than stocks, bonds, bank accounts, or real estate. Barnes proposes an alternative model of need analysis—the annuity income approach. Annuity income is the constant income that parents would receive each year (for all years remaining in their expected life spans) if they sold all their wealth today and bought an annuity. Any measure of ability to pay, Barnes contends, should be based on the assumption that parents will consume their wealth over their lifetimes. In his view, the annuity income approach is superior to the uniform methodology because it is easier to administer, since it does not require data on both actual income and the market value of wealth; it is more stable, since annuity income is inherently less volatile than actual income; and, most important, it is more equitable, since it treats all forms of wealth the same.

Caliendo, N., and Curtice, J. K. "Title IX: A Guide for Financial Aid Administrators." *Journal of Student Financial Aid,* 1977, 7 (1), 32-43. The guide discussed and presented here is to be used by aid administrators for self-assessment to determine compliance with Title IX of the Education Amendments of 1972, which is intended to halt discrimination on the basis of sex in federally supported programs and institutions. Each of the guide's six sections deals with a topic addressed in the Title IX regulations: publications and informational brochures, application procedures and policies, need analysis format, aid programs, evaluation and compliance with Title IX regulations, and resolution of noncompliance. An additional section provides guidelines on how to use institutional data to determine proportions and ratios of aid to recipients. The guide in its entirety is appended to the article.

College Entrance Examination Board, Washington Office. *Income Maintenance Programs and College Opportunity.* Washington, D.C.: College Entrance Examination Board, Washington Office, 1982. This report examines the impact of the 1981 Omnibus Reconciliation Act on students receiving support from seven sources: Social Security, Aid to Families with Dependent Children (AFDC), Medicaid, food stamps, public housing assistance, the Comprehensive Education and Training Act (CETA), and vocational rehabilitation aid. Before passage of the Omnibus Act, states had the option of providing AFDC support for all students between the ages of eighteen and twenty-one in regular attendance at postsecondary institutions. All but eleven states elected to exercise this option. The Omnibus Act, however, eliminated payments on behalf of these students, and it is unlikely that states can continue such payments solely from state funds. The report also examines the phasing out of Social Security benefits for students and shows how, for students with remaining eligibility, the expected contribution students must make from Social Security payments will escalate. Although the findings reported here may have only temporary validity, given that other, perhaps more substantial, budgetary reductions are contemplated, it does provide a valuable benchmark for financial aid administrators in calculating available student budgets. It also demonstrates the impact of new federal policies that shift decision-making burdens to the individual states. A chart is provided which summarizes the information provided in the body of the report.

College Scholarship Service. *Making It Count: A Report on a Project to Provide Better Financial Aid Information to Students.* New York: College Entrance Examination Board, 1977. On the basis of an eighteen-month study undertaken to determine the extent of the information gap among financial aid offices and students, the authors of this report conclude that financial aid offices do a poor job of communicating basic information to students. Therefore, the authors present criteria for ensuring that the messages of the financial aid office are not lost on its audience. They found, for example, that many prospective students are interested in ascertaining the long-range total costs of college attendance; slightly fewer are interested in specific, short-range cost breakdowns. The report specifies the elements of an ideal communication flow and proposes guidelines for providing students with up-to-date information on their statuses.

College Scholarship Service. *CSS Need Analysis: Theory and Computation Procedures.* New York: College Entrance Examination Board, 1982. This comprehensive description of the College Scholarship Service's need analysis system is updated periodically as changes occur within the system. The authors discuss the computational procedures used in determining student need, the principles and practice of student financial aid administration, and the history and theory of need analysis. Detailed steps for handling the CSS Financial Aid Form are also provided. This book's counterpart is the ACT *Handbook for Financial Aid Administrators* (see American College Testing Program in this section).

Collins, J. S., Maguire, J. J., and Turner, R. M. "Unmet Need: How the Gap Is Filled." *Journal of Student Financial Aid,* 1979, *9* (2), 4-15. This article describes a study undertaken at Boston College to determine how undergraduate students with unmet need (80 percent of those sampled were underfunded by an average of $1,400) finance their cost of attendance. The researchers found that students coped with the financial shortfall by increased parental contributions, working and earning more, and borrowing more under the Guaranteed Student Loan program. The authors speculate that these attempts to compensate for unmet need may be outstripped by an inflationary economy. Therefore, they recommend that greater resources, such as an expanded Basic Educational Opportunity Grant program, be implemented in response to an ever-increasing need gap.

Heisel, M., and Hensley, M. R. "The Independent Student Dilemma: An Approach Toward Equity Packaging." *Journal of Student Financial Aid,* 1977, 7 (3), 41-46. The central premise of this article is that students who willfully attain independent status in order to take advantage of greater financial aid should have to resort to loans and employment to finance their education. According to the authors, nonrepayable aid should substitute for the contribution that parents from economically deprived backgrounds often cannot give their children and should be targeted on that group. The article describes a legislative effort in California that sharply circumscribes the eligibility of independent students for state-funded grants. With few exceptions, independent students who wish to qualify for state grants must furnish parental income information.

McCormick, J. L. *State Allocation Formulas for Campus-Based Federal Student Aid Programs: A Descriptive Study.* Iowa City: American College Testing Program, 1978. How effective are existing state allotment formulas (specifically, those for the National Direct Student Loan, the Supplemental Educational Opportunity Grant, and the College Work-Study programs) in providing an equitable distribution of federal student aid dollars? After analyzing these formulas and the resulting allocations to the states, McCormick concludes that the size of the allocation made to a state is unrelated to the total funds required by a state. The computation producing the total funds to be allocated is not related to that producing the total funds required. He calls for reform of the present state allotment formulas in the direction of a more equitable allocation system. This study should be of particular interest to policy makers, given the increasing importance of campus-based aid to the overall student support program and, simultaneously, the general lack of research on the method of distribution of such aid.

National Association of College and University Business Officers. *Management of Student Aid*. Washington, D.C.: National Association of College and University Business Officers, 1979. Intended for all decision makers on matters concerning student aid, this manual serves three purposes: (1) helping senior officers (presidents and deans) understand the effects of student financial aid on their institutions; (2) explaining the financial aid process; and (3) encouraging and promoting institutional self-regulation of financial aid operations. Although such topics as planning and acquiring financial aid resources are touched on, the emphasis of the publication is on the disbursement and control functions of the financial aid office. Its discussion of the management of these functions, which includes numerous charts and sample forms and letters, is the most comprehensive treatment of the topic available.

National Task Force on Student Aid Problems. *Draft Final Report*. Brookdale, Calif.: National Task Force on Student Aid Problems, 1975. The National Task Force on Student Aid Problems, a voluntary association established in the mid-1970s by the College Entrance Examination Board and other organizations, examined the complex problems inherent in need analysis and in integrating the packaging of student financial aid from among various types, sources, processes, and purposes. This report discusses the need to provide the various types of aid available to students in a sequence likely to be most helpful to them, the burden of completing numerous—and often redundant—application forms, and other associated issues involved in the awarding process. A prototypical form for collecting student and family financial data is included. Also discussed are the management and staff training needs of the financial aid office. This report is an excellent source of information and presents the management issues of financial aid in a straightforward, thoughtful manner. Of particular significance is the conceptual framework used to analyze the state of student financial aid. The widespread participation of experts in financial aid assures the completeness of the topic of packaging and makes this report an excellent resource for the financial aid office.

Olivas, M. A. *Financial Aid: Access and Packaging Policies for Disadvantaged Students.* Palo Alto, Calif.: Institute for Research on Educational Finance and Governance, Stanford University, 1981. The first study ever conducted to analyze Hispanic student financial awards, this report provides valuable information on effective ways to package aid for these students and to conduct research in this area. The use of confidential records of a national Hispanic counseling program permitted exceptional detail and accuracy. The study describes the composition of awards, including the proportion of reimbursable aid, family contributions, and student "quality" indexes (GPA, test scores). A major finding is that Hispanic students rely overwhelmingly on governmental, not institutional, funding and that nearly three quarters receive only one kind of aid. The paper concludes with models for aid awards based on public policy objectives and with descriptions of several packaging policies recommended for use by aid administrators.

Petersen, L., and others. "Student Peer Counseling in Financial Aid." *Journal of Student Financial Aid,* 1978, *8* (3), 35–42.

This article examines the issues inherent in establishing a peer counseling program—issues such as the institution's individual needs, remuneration for peer counselors, and selection procedures—and argues for constant evaluation of the program. If such a program is to benefit an institution, the authors emphasize, it must receive sufficient resources and administrative support.

Part Three:
Ensuring Effectiveness in Administering Aid Programs

The four chapters in this part of the book (Chapters Nine through Twelve) deal with the organizational, functional, and technological components of an effective program. There is very little useful literature on professional development in the field. It almost seems that the topic has been avoided since the abortive moves toward certification in the early 1970s and the continued lack of development of formal (degree) graduate programs in the field. In contrast, management of financial aid has received much more attention from authoritative sources and prominent organizations like the American Council on Education. In fact, the main thrust of training development by NASFAA has been in management. This review highlights the main sources and also covers representative works not cited by the chapter authors.

Brossman, W. "On the Administration of Student Financial Aid." *Community College Review,* 1976, *4,* 6-14. In the day-to-day administration of student aid funds, the community college aid office faces numerous problems—among them, the lack of district matching funds, adequate support staff, and advance commitments from state or federal sources from year to year. Some community colleges still do not participate in available programs designed for needy students; others have experienced such growth in their financial aid programs that they find themselves without sufficient staff to administer them. Community colleges are urged to examine their student financial aid operations in order to maximize acquisition of federal and state student assistance dollars and to use these funds most effectively. The author makes no specific recommendations on improving acquisition and use of funds. Rather, he calls for revision of federal and state programs in order to remove provisions that are biased against community college students. A helpful step would be to shift the forms of the BEOG (Pell Grant) program from assistance for instructional costs to assistance for other costs, such as subsistence and commuting. Another would be to eliminate the one-half cost limitation on BEOG awards in order to make community college students eligible for larger grants.

Brouder, K. *The College Cost Book, 1982-83.* New York: College Entrance Examination Board, 1982. This annual publication, initiated in 1980, incorporates and replaces the earlier series *Student Expenses at Postsecondary Institutions.* Nationwide analyses of student expenses and lists of student expenses at individual postsecondary institutions, updated annually, are provided. Information collected from participating institutions includes tuition and fees, resident room and board, cost of private housing, commuter expenses, and additional out-of-state tuition. This information is organized by state. Valuable intrainstitutional cost comparisons that would be of considerable interest to parents, students, counselors, and financial aid personnel are included. These data can be used for normative purposes in constructing model student college expense budgets.

Chaney, K., and others. "Model Preservice Financial Aid Training Module for School Counselors." *Journal of Student Financial Aid,* 1979, *9* (1), 39-44. This article describes the development of a preservice module on financial aid for students in a graduate program in high school counseling. According to the authors, such a module is needed because the financial aid area is virtually overlooked in the training of high school counselors and because in-service training does not provide a basic level of understanding. Among problems encountered in the course of developing the module were the issues of content (how much detail), terminology (how much jargon), module length (the counseling curriculum is already over-crowded), and timing (when it should be introduced in the graduate program). The final product consisted of three com-ponents: (1) a thirty-minute videotape providing background information on the topic of financial aid, (2) a printed sum-mary of the uniform methodology, and (3) a list of potential policy-related questions that can be used to structure a panel discussion on financial aid. This article brings to the attention of the financial aid community the general neglect of the training of high school counselors in the increasingly impor-tant area of student financial assistance for college.

El-Khawas, E. *Management of Student Aid: A Guide for Presi-dents.* Washington, D.C.: American Council on Education, 1979. Prepared for use by presidents, trustees, and other se-nior administrators of colleges and universities, this volume is designed (1) to help these administrators understand the ef-fects of student aid on their institutions, (2) to review major policies and control points in the financial aid process, and (3) to promote effective campus management of student aid. While this guide provides a quick review of principles, deci-sions, and responsibilities in financial aid management, its main value lies in its consideration of the possible implica-tions of aid for institutional concerns: enrollment, financial stability, and institutional mission. It also offers a checklist of major questions to be used as a basis for initiating top-management reviews of all financial aid programs.

El-Khawas, E. (Ed.). *Special Policy Issues in Management of Student Aid.* Washington, D.C.: American Council on Educa-tion, 1980. Supplementing the editor's *Management of Stu-dent Aid: A Guide for Presidents,* this document offers more detailed information and guidance in areas where policy deci-sions and strong management are especially important. The first paper considers the award process, stressing the need for policy judgment in developing expense budgets and aid pack-ages. The second paper deals with administrative monitoring of the use of institutionally funded student aid. The final paper offers guidance regarding the effective management of student loans.

Farmer, J., and others. *A Guide to the Design of Student Financial Aid Systems.* Washington, D.C.: Systems Research, 1978. A primer on student financial aid systems, this guide identifies the characteristics of these systems in conjunction with the major goals of student financial aid operations. The framework developed here can be used to evaluate student financial aid systems and to classify major data processing designs. The link between financial aid systems and other institutional systems, including intersystem communication and data-base integration, is discussed. This guide is intended both for financial aid administrators, in specifying needs and weighing data processing alternatives, and for information system specialists, who must communicate design characteristics to student financial aid staff and identify the strengths and weaknesses of alternative data processing systems.

Ferguson, J. L. "College Presidents and Financial Aid Officers." *College Board Review,* 1981, *121,* 3-24. This article reports the results of a survey examining the extent of the student aid officer's influence on institutional policy. The author compared the aid officer's impression of the degree of influence required to perform his or her job with the president's perception of how much influence the aid officer has. Institutions with aid officers identified as influential were examined closely to determine the characteristics of management and operation that persuade the administration to allow the director of financial aid such influence. The results of the survey indicate that the aid officer is consulted on a broad range of issues but, most frequently, in the areas of requesting or administering federal student financial aid. The extent of the influence of the aid officer was found to be positively related to proximity to the president in the organizational hierarchy; having frequent meetings with the president; being tenured; and belonging to an institution that is privately affiliated, has a high dependency on tuition income and federal aid, and is experiencing enrollment gains. Unfortunately, the author does not say how the sampling was conducted, what types of institutions were sampled, and what percentage of those sampled responded. Consequently, the generalizability of the results remains in doubt.

Miller, S., Dellefield, W., and Musso, T. *A Guide to Selected Financial Aid Management Practices*. Washington, D.C.: United States Department of Education, 1980. Four areas of practice warranting improved and/or more consistent administration are identified: (1) the role of the aid office in the institutional hierarchy, (2) development and dissemination of information sources for students, (3) financial aid counseling for special student populations, and (4) financial aid packaging. Financial aid offices are encouraged to retain or improve their positions in the institutional hierarchy by keeping policies and procedures closer in line with the overall mission of the institution. Aid offices are also urged to use a combination of approaches (written materials, radio-TV spots, seminars, and posters) for disseminating aid information to students. To ascertain what information to include, a survey of an institution's prospective and enrolled students should be conducted. Among recommendations for dealing with special student populations are that institutional aid applications, need analysis material, and counseling sessions be used to identify special students; a counseling program be developed to address the needs of special students; and a close relationship with the donors of funds to special aid programs be maintained. Although financial aid packaging is largely a local phenomenon, certain factors should always be taken into consideration. These are discretionary aid resources, educational cost, demographic characteristics of the student body, and institutional characteristics (length of academic programs, structure of the academic year, aid office traits). Special features of this publication are descriptions of widely used financial aid manuals, a detailed listing of aid sources for special student populations, and a model of a student financial aid publication.

Moore, D. R. "Certification of Financial Aid Professionals." *Journal of Student Financial Aid,* 1975, *5* (3), 15-20. This article lists competencies required of all financial aid professionals—especially directors and assistant directors. For all professionals the competencies may be grouped under three headings: "counseling and interpersonal relationships," "knowledge of the field," and "organizational and administrative ability." For directors and assistant directors, an additional set of competencies, gathered under the heading "continuing and professional growth," is specified. The author argues for competency-based testing and certification of staff members by the aid director, and of aid directors by a national certifying committee subsequent to a review by a regional or state certifying committee. Competent financial aid personnel are viewed as safeguarding aid programs and ensuring the success of the profession. Although the certification of financial professionals is currently a moot point, this article is useful for its delineation of financial aid staff competencies.

National Association of Student Financial Aid Administrators. *Characteristics and Attitudes of the Financial Aid Administrator: A Report on the 1977 Survey of the Profession.* Washington, D.C.: National Association of Student Financial Aid Administrators, 1978. In a 1977 survey of its membership, NSFAA gathered data on (1) background characteristics, (2) salary levels, (3) attitudes and opinions, (4) office characteristics, (5) external contacts, (6) professional development, and (7) research activities. It found that the typical aid administrator was a male Caucasian, thirty-eight years of age, and employed full time. He was the holder of a master's degree and had six or more years of experience in financial aid. Only one out of ten administrators was a member of a minority subpopulation. The report includes numerous tables depicting cross-tabulations of variables; each table is accompanied by a narrative highlighting its findings. Although now somewhat dated, this is the most recent survey of the financial aid community and underscores some of its critical needs.

Parish, H. C. "Professional Associations—Genesis and Development." In R. Keene, F. C. Adams, and J. E. King (Eds.),

Money, Marbles, or Chalk: Student Financial Support in Higher Education. Carbondale: Southern Illinois University Press, 1975. The professionalization of student aid administration is traced from the establishment of the College Scholarship Service in 1954 through the development of regional associations to the emergence of the National Association of Student Financial Aid Administrators in the early 1970s. The origin of professional development as a response to the many needs of the student aid officer of the mid-1960s is described, as are the parallel growths of federal involvement in student aid and professional student aid associations. This paper is a brief but comprehensive account of the first fifteen years of student aid professional associationism.

Pennell, K. "Computerized Financial Aid Operations: Points to Consider Before Committing to Increased Utilization of Computer Systems." *Journal of Student Financial Aid,* 1981, *11* (1), 4–9. Based on the author's own experiences at the University of Oklahoma, this article discusses the issues to be considered prior to institutional purchase of a software system for financial aid operations. The issues are organized under three themes: "Analysis Before Implementation" (evaluation of current operation, need analysis, long-range plan for implementation), "Implementation" (sufficient time for implementation, personnel preparation), and "Public Relations" (relationship with the institutional computer operation, dissemination of information to the public).

Pernal, M. "Efficiency and Accountability: A Computer-Assisted Financial Aid Operation for the Small College." *Journal of Student Financial Aid,* 1977, 7 (3), 47–55. The thesis of this article is that the small institution with limited student aid resources and staff can still design and implement an effective computer-assisted program. A computer-assisted financial aid system currently in operation at Eastern Connecticut College is described from the point of development (Phase One) through the collection and reporting of data (Phase Six). The following benefits of the program are cited: (1) The activities of the aid professional can be altered to permit more contact with students and more time for coordinating the aid operation with related administrative areas. (2) The students receive more accurate and timely information about their package and have more contact with aid officers. (3) Clerical staff are freed from the endless filling out of forms, allowing them to devote time to other areas where professional attention is important. The article is particularly useful because of the detail with which it describes implementation of the computer-assisted program.

Van Dusen, W. D., and O'Hearne, J. J. *A Design for a Model College Financial Aid Office.* (3rd ed.) New York: College Entrance Examination Board, 1980. Intended as a compendium of "the general philosophical considerations" that should inform a student-oriented aid office, this guidebook describes the ideal office—both its internal organization and its external relationships with other institutional units and with off-campus agencies. Often cited and in its third revision, this publication presents a comprehensive model for a student financial aid office. Its consideration of some common problems (such as document control and student consumerism) confronting aid administrators is informative and timely.

Part Four:
Importance of Aid in Meeting Student Needs
and Institutional Goals

Of the four parts in this book, we found the literature "thinnest" in this final section, which includes research and planning, marketing, retention, legal implications, and the future of student aid. A great deal of research has been done, and the findings have been reported widely; however, much of this research has not found its way into the systematic repositories from which it can be retrieved for review. Literature on planning for changes in student aid at the institutional level is almost nonexistent. In the area of institutional marketing, most of the writing has been for the general business field; admissions personnel in charge of marketing have had to make the necessary interpolation. Admissions and student aid have often functioned independently of one another. Consequently, the literature on potential linkages between the two in institutional marketing efforts is sparse. Curiously, student aid is also absent from consideration in retention efforts, even though the correlation seems intuitively obvious. Rather than include the hortatory literature on "mobilizing the campus" for retention (with little or no inclusion of student aid in the effort), we include only relevant research findings. Litigation in student aid is relatively new, and we found nothing beyond the sources included by the chapter author in his Bibliographical Note. Finally, there have evidently been few attempts to divine the future of student aid, and this fact is reflected in the paucity of such works in the following selections.

American College Testing Program. *Postsecondary Undergraduate Student Financial Aid Resources and Need Study Based on the 1975-76 Academic Year.* Iowa City: American College Testing Program, 1977. Commissioned by the State of Louisiana Board of Regents, this study was designed to provide a data base for evaluating the current status of financial aid resources within the state and the estimated need for these resources. Data were obtained from governmental and other agencies that administered aid programs, from financial aid officers who packaged aid programs for students, from high schools, from the census, and from applications for Basic Educational Opportunity Grants. Independent analyses were made of resources available to meet the financial need of applicants at Louisiana postsecondary institutions and of all potentially eligible Louisiana postsecondary students. The results of the study indicate that the state has sufficient resources to accommodate the needy students who actually apply for aid. However, when *total* potentially enrolled needy students are considered, there is a general deficit of aid resources to meet the need. This study is typical of those dealing with state resource and need analyses and of commissioned research performed by ACT.

Astin, A. W. *The Impact of Student Financial Aid Programs on Student Choice.* Los Angeles: Higher Education Research Institute, 1978. With data from a large-scale longitudinal study,

Astin attempted to determine how students' institutional choices are affected by (1) student characteristics, (2) characteristics of the students' higher education environment, (3) state and federal financial aid programs, and (4) student aid packages offered by institutions. He found that state and federal aid programs do have an effect on student choice, but the impact is limited by several conditions—namely, differences in student ability and aspirations, institutional admissions policies, and the type of higher education system in the student's home state. For example, although students living in states with strong aid programs are more likely to choose high-cost and selective institutions, this relationship occurs only among higher-ability students. Similarly, the tendency of students in such states to pick a college in their home state is confined to individuals in the higher ability ranges.

Astin, H. S., and Cross, K. P. *Student Financial Aid and Persistence in College.* Los Angeles: Higher Education Research Institute, 1979. Longitudinal data were analyzed to determine the impact of financial aid on student persistence. The data were obtained from 40,515 students who entered college as first-time freshmen in fall 1975. These students were followed up in fall 1977 in order to study their progress in college and find out whether financial aid had affected their persistence. To identify the significant predictors of persistence and withdrawal, each of eleven major subpopulations were analyzed separately. These groups were low- and high-income whites, white men and women, all blacks as well as blacks in predominantly black and mostly white institutions, Puerto Ricans, American Indians, Chicanos, and Asian Americans. Four sets of predictor variables were used: (1) personal and background characteristics; (2) environmental and institutional features; (3) financial aid variables; and (4) attitudes, values, and experiences while in college. Some variables served as predictors for all the subgroups, others for just one. The most common predictors included high school achievement, as measured by grades and SAT scores, and the student's type of high school curriculum (college preparatory or vocational).

With respect to financial aid variables, loans, especially large ones, negatively predicted staying in school. However, if the loan was part of an aid package that included a large grant, it did not have the same effect. Women with outright grants were more likely than other women aid recipients to persist, as were blacks awarded college work-study money. In general, loans predicted withdrawal, especially when they were large or given in combination with college work-study funds. The study has important implications for students, parents, and high schools, for colleges and universities, and also for the state and federal governments.

College Entrance Examination Board, Washington Office. *Student Aid and the Urban Poor.* New York: Ford Foundation, 1981. This report focuses on the mechanics by which students apply for and receive benefits—the delivery system of financial aid and, in particular, the obstacles it presents to urban low-income students. The study's findings are based largely on the experiences of counselors, students, and parents at the Washington, D.C., Educational Opportunity Center. The authors describe problems facing the urban poor in applying for student aid: multiple forms, varying deadlines, confusing language, lack of aid program continuity, special family circumstances, and inadequate counseling. Recommended changes in the system to meet their needs include (1) streamlining the application process, (2) improving communications to students, (3) personalizing the system, and (4) changing existing laws to make student aid programs work more effectively for the urban poor. Examples of the last recommendation include a student aid set-aside for the federal Trio programs, and new federal or state prohibitions against counting student aid as family income when determining a family's eligibility for public assistance. The intent of this study is to help the Department of Education and other agencies in the continuing task of making the financial aid process simpler, more intelligible, and more equitable. This is an important goal, given the long-standing commitment of higher education to equal educational opportunity.

Hearn, J. C. *Equity and Efficiency in the Basic Grants Program: The Case of the "Prior-Year" Proposal.* ACT Research Report, No. 81. Iowa City: American College Testing Program, 1981. Eligibility for Basic Educational Opportunity Grants (now Pell Grants) is determined on the basis of federal income tax data from the calendar year immediately preceding the academic year for which a student applies for aid. This report examines the impact of utilizing income information that is a year older than is now the practice. The use of older data would, presumably, speed the Pell application process because students would not need to wait to apply for assistance until January of the year they seek admittance. This report contrasts eligibility calculations produced under the standard system with those that would be produced under the hypothetical "prior-year" system. The author found that the use of prior-year data would produce wide fluctuations in student eligibility and concludes that one-year-old data predict need more accurately than two-year-old data. This study is an excellent example of research that may be modeled to project the feasibility, or appropriateness, of various policy options.

Holmes, R. B., and Petersen, L. B. "A Survey of Undergraduate Student Assistance in the State of Michigan." *Journal of Student Financial Aid,* 1980, *10* (1), 18–28. This article presents a comprehensive picture of types of aid available, unmet need, numbers of needy undergraduates without aid, and total administrative expenses associated with undergraduate programs in Michigan from the 1974–75 through the 1976–77 academic years. The results show an increase in both the amount of undergraduate aid available in this three-year period and in unmet need. Contrasts in the percentage of federal need-based aid available to the private and public sectors are also noted. This article illustrates what states might do to determine the financial needs of their undergraduate college students and the costs associated with meeting their needs. As more states conduct these types of studies, interstate comparisons can be made available to guide the efforts of institutional, state, and federal policy makers.

Jensen, E. L. "Student Financial Aid and Persistence in College." *Journal of Higher Education,* 1981, *52* (3), 280-294. This study is intended to determine whether receipt of financial aid enhances persistence, whether denial of financial aid decreases persistence, and whether the amount of financial aid received is positively related to persistence. The results show that student financial assistance makes a small contribution to the persistence of students who receive it in their first year; that denial of financial assistance to students who perceive need results in a slight decrease in their persistence; and that the amount of aid received per semester has a negative but statistically insignificant effect on persistence. Jensen's research is limited to the study of the effects of a student's total aid award. Because no consideration is given to the particular effects of individual aid programs or aid packages, the usefulness of the findings is restricted. Still, the study models an effective research design for examining the link between financial aid and persistence.

Martin, D. *1981-82: A Year in Review.* NASFAA Special Report, No. 4. Washington, D.C.: National Association of Student Financial Aid Administrators, 1982. Events in Washington affecting the financial aid community, particularly the membership of NASFAA, are chronicled. The "Student Aid Calendar of Events" provides a detailed listing of significant federal actions on student support during the period July 29, 1981, to June 30, 1982. This report is a convenient guide to recent federal activity in the area of financial aid.

Pantages, T. J., and Creedon, C. F. "Studies of College Attrition: 1950-1975." *Review of Educational Research,* 1978, *48,* (1), 57-72. This article examines research on student persistence and summarizes findings of studies covering a twenty-five-year span. The authors also summarize the equivocal and sometimes contradictory results of research on financial aid and attrition. They note the inconsistent definitions of persistence. Most previous studies fail to make distinctions among students who leave an individual institution and enroll elsewhere, reenroll at the same institution at a later date, or leave postsecondary education permanently. Researchers are urged to make distinction between permanent and temporary dropout. Regarding the relationship between financial aid and persistence, the review indicates that only the awarding of scholarships and grants has been found to increase persistence and that loans and work-study programs apparently do not increase persistence. Interpretations of such correlational studies are difficult because of the variability in college costs and financial aid resources of each college.

Smith, M. K. (Ed.). *Profiles of State Student Financial Aid Programs.* (2 vols.) Denver: Education Commission of the States; Boulder, Colo.: National Center for Higher Education Management Systems, 1980. These documents display selected information in the form of charts, tables, and graphs about (1) the State Student Incentive Grant program and other state-level financial assistance programs; (2) the primary state agency or organization responsible for administering these programs; and (3) the general state characteristics relating to student financial aid, including college-age population, postsecondary education enrollments, and characteristics of applicants for and recipients of state student aid monies. A profile containing this information is developed for each of the fifty states. In the aggregate, these profiles represent an information base that can be built on and used to study the SSIG program and other state student support programs within the context in which they operate. This is a valuable resource tool for individuals interested in state-level assistance, particularly from a cross-state perspective.

References

Note: An asterisk preceding an item indicates that the item is discussed in the Selective Guide to the Literature (SG). The specific location (that is, SG, General Works; SG, Part One; SG, Part Two; SG, Part Three; or SG, Part Four) appears in parentheses at the end of the item.

Adams, F. C., and Stephens, C. W. *College and University Student Work Program: Implications and Implementations.* Carbondale: Southern Illinois University Press, 1970.

Alexander, K., and Solomon, E. S. *College and University Law.* Charlottesville, Va.: Michie, 1972.

*American College Testing Program. *An Annotated Bibliography in Student Financial Aid, 1960-1973.* Iowa City: American College Testing Program, 1974. (SG, General Works)

*American College Testing Program. *Postsecondary Undergraduate Student Financial Aid Resources and Need Study Based on the 1975-76 Academic Year.* Iowa City: American College Testing Program, 1977. (SG, Part Four)

*American College Testing Program. *Handbook for Financial Aid Administrators.* Iowa City: American College Testing Program, 1981. (SG, Part Two)

American Society for Training and Development. *Proposed Legislation Relating to Job Education and Training.* Washington, D.C.: American Society for Training and Development, 1982.

Anderson, S. B., and Associates. *Encyclopedia of Educational Evaluation: Concepts and Techniques for Evaluating Education and Training Programs.* San Francisco: Jossey-Bass, 1975.

Anderson, T. F., and Zelditch, M., Jr. *A Basic Course in Statistics.* New York: Holt, Rinehart and Winston, 1968.

Anton, K. P., and others. "Staffing Patterns in Financial Aid Offices: An Overview of the NASFAA National Survey." *Journal of Student Financial Aid,* 1981, *11* (2), 9–20.

Astin, A. W. *Financial Aid and Student Persistence.* Los Angeles: Higher Education Research Institute, 1975a.

Astin, A. W. *Preventing Students from Dropping Out.* San Francisco: Jossey-Bass, 1975b.

*Astin, A. W. *The Impact of Student Financial Aid Programs on Student Choice.* Los Angeles: Higher Education Research Institute, 1978. (SG, Part Four)

*Astin, A. W. *Minorities in American Higher Education: Recent Trends, Current Prospects, and Recommendations.* San Francisco: Jossey-Bass, 1982. (SG, Part One)

*Astin, H. S., and Cross, K. P. *Student Financial Aid and Persistence in College.* Los Angeles: Higher Education Research Institute, 1979. (SG, Part Four)

*Atelsek, F. J., and Gomberg, I. L. *Estimated Number of Student Aid Recipients, 1976-1977.* Higher Education Panel Report, No. 36. Washington, D.C.: American Council on Education, 1977. (SG, Part One)

Atwell, R. H. "What Academic Administrators Should Know About Financial Aid." In R. Atwell and M. Green (Eds.), *New Directions for Higher Education: Academic Leaders as Managers,* no. 36. San Francisco: Jossey-Bass, 1981.

*Barnes, G. *An Economist's View of the Uniform Methodology.* Iowa City: American College Testing Program, 1977. (SG, Part Two)

Barnes, J. S., and Keene, R. "A Comparison of the Initial Academic Achievement of Freshman Award Winners Who Work and Those Who Do Not Work." *Journal of Student Financial Aid,* 1974, *4* (3), 25–29.

Bates, G. "Utilization of On-Campus Employment in a Student Aid Program." *Journal of Student Financial Aid,* 1973, *3* (1), 32-38.

Beal, P. E., and Noel, L. *What Works in Student Retention.* Iowa City: American College Testing Program; Boulder, Colo.: National Center for Higher Education Management Sytems, 1980.

Berg, I. Education and Jobs: *The Great Training Robbery.* New York: Praeger, 1970.

Binder, S. "The Application of Open System Theory to Student Financial Aid Administration." In S. Binder (Ed.), *New Directions for Student Services: Responding to Changes in Financial Aid Programs,* no. 12. San Francisco: Jossey-Bass, 1980a.

*Binder, S. (Ed.). *New Directions for Student Services: Responding to Changes in Financial Aid Programs,* no. 12. San Francisco: Jossey-Bass, 1980b. (SG, General Works)

Bird, C. *The Case Against College.* New York: McKay, 1975.

Blum, W. J., and Klaven, H., Jr. "The Anatomy of Justice in Taxation." In *The Great Ideas Today.* Chicago: Encyclopaedia Britannica, 1973.

Bok, D. C. *The President's Report.* Cambridge, Mass.: Harvard University Press, 1982.

Bowie, N. E. *Toward a New Theory of Distributive Justice.* Cambridge, Mass.: Harvard University Press, 1971.

Boyd, H. *Marketing Research: Text and Cases.* (5th ed.) Homewood, Ill.: Irwin, 1981.

Boyd, J. D. "History of State Involvement in Financial Aid." In *Perspectives on Financial Aid.* New York: College Entrance Examination Board, 1975.

Boyd, J.D., and others. *The Illinois State Scholarship Commission Monetary Award Program: A Longitudinal Analysis, 1968-1980.* Deerfield: Illinois State Scholarship Commission, 1981.

Breneman, D. W. "Higher Education and the Economy." *Educational Record,* 1981, *62* (2), 18-21.

Breneman, D. W. *The Coming Enrollment Crisis: What Every Trustee Must Know.* Washington, D.C.: Association of Governing Boards of Colleges and Universities, 1982.

*Breneman, D. W., and Finn, C. E., Jr. (Eds.). *Public Policy and Private Higher Education.* Washington, D.C.: Brookings Institution, 1978. (SG, Part One)

*Brossman, W. "On the Administration of Student Financial Aid." *Community College Review,* 1976, *4,* 6-14. (SG, Part Three)

*Brouder, K. *The College Cost Book, 1982-83.* New York: College Entrance Examination Board, 1982. (SG, Part Three)

Brubacher, J. S., and Rudy, W. *Higher Education in Transition.* New York: Harper & Row, 1976.

*Caliendo, N., and Curtice, J. K. "Title IX: A Guide for Financial Aid Administrators." *Journal of Student Financial Aid,* 1977, 7 (1), 32-43. (SG, Part Two)

California State Scholarship and Loan Commission. *Student Resources Survey.* Sacramento: California State Scholarship and Loan Commission, 1973.

California State University. *Budget Formulas and Standards Manual.* Long Beach: California State University, 1982.

California State University and Colleges System. *Audit of Financial Aid Programs: Trustees Audit Team Report.* Long Beach: California State University and Colleges System, 1972.

California State University and Colleges System. *Manual of Financial Aid Policies and Procedures.* Long Beach: California State University and Colleges System, 1975.

California State University and Colleges System. *Budget Formulas and Standards Manual.* Long Beach: California State University and Colleges System, 1981.

Carnegie Commission on Higher Education. *The Capitol and the Campus: State Responsibility for Postsecondary Education.* New York: McGraw-Hill, 1971.

Carnegie Commission on Higher Education. *Higher Education: Who Pays? Who Benefits? Who Should Pay?* New York: McGraw-Hill, 1973.

Carnegie Council on Policy Studies in Higher Education. *The States and Private Higher Education: Problems and Policies in a New Era.* San Francisco: Jossey-Bass, 1977.

*Carnegie Council on Policy Studies in Higher Education. *Next Steps for the 1980s in Student Financial Aid: A Fourth Alternative.* San Francisco: Jossey-Bass, 1979. (SG, Part One)

Carnegie Council on Policy Studies in Higher Education. *Three Thousand Futures: The Next Twenty Years for Higher Education.* San Francisco: Jossey-Bass, 1980.

Carnegie Foundation for the Advancement of Teaching. *The States and Higher Education: A Proud Past and a Vital Future.* San Francisco: Jossey-Bass, 1976.

Cartter, A. M. *New Approaches to Student Financial Aid.* New York: College Entrance Examination Board, 1971.

Case, J. P., and Finello, J. V. *The Uniform Methodology: Past, Present, and Future.* New York: College Entrance Examination Board, 1980.

Center for Helping Organizations Improve Choice in Education. *A Guide to Choice.* Syracuse, N.Y.: Center for Helping Organizations Improve Choice in Education, Syracuse University, 1978.

Chambers, M. M. *The Colleges and the Courts.* Danville, Ill.: Interstate, 1972.

*Chaney, K., and others. "Model Preservice Financial Aid Training Module for School Counselors." *Journal of Student Financial Aid,* 1979, *9* (1), 39–44. (SG, Part Three)

Chapman, D. W. (Ed.). *Improving College Information for Prospective Students.* Washington, D.C.: Council for Advancement and Support of Education, 1980.

Choate, P., and Epstein, N. "Workers of the Future, Retool." *Washington Post,* May 9, 1982, sec. D, pp. 1, 5.

Clark, R. B. *A Handbook for Use in the Preparation of Student Expense Budgets.* (Rev. ed.) Washington, D.C.: National Association of Student Financial Aid Administrators, 1983.

Coalition of Independent College and University Students. *Financial Aid Peer Counseling Manual.* Washington, D.C.: Coalition of Independent College and University Students, 1980.

College Entrance Examination Board. *Student Financing of Higher Education in Washington.* Palo Alto, Calif.: College Entrance Examination Board, Western Regional Office, 1972.

*College Entrance Examination Board. *Perspectives on Financial Aid.* New York: College Entrance Examination Board, 1975a. (SG, General Works)

College Entrance Examination Board. *A Survey of Plans for Education and Careers: A View of What the Iowa High School Senior Class of 1975 Plans to Do Following Graduation and Why.* Evanston, Ill.: College Entrance Examination Board, Midwest Regional Office, 1975b.

*College Entrance Examination Board, Washington Office. *The Guaranteed Student Loan Program: Options for Controlling Federal Costs While Preserving Needed Credit for College.* Washington, D.C.: College Entrance Examination Board, Washington Office, 1981. (SG, Part One)

*College Entrance Examination Board, Washington Office. *Student Aid and the Urban Poor.* New York: Ford Foundation, 1981b. (SG, Part Four)

*College Entrance Examination Board, Washington Office. *Income Maintenance Programs and College Opportunity.* Washington, D.C.: College Entrance Examination Board, Washington Office, 1982. (SG, Part Two)

College Entrance Examination Board and American Association of Collegiate Registrars and Admissions Officers. *Undergraduate Admissions: The Realities of Institutional Policies, Practices, and Procedures.* New York: College Entrance Examination Board, 1980.

*College Scholarship Service. *Making It Count: A Report on a Project to Provide Better Financial Aid Information to Students.* New York: College Entrance Examination Board, 1977. (SG, Part Two)

College Scholarship Service. *The College Cost Book, 1982–83.* New York: College Entrance Examination Board, 1982a.

*College Scholarship Service. *CSS Need Analysis: Theory and Computation Procedures.* New York: College Entrance Examination Board, 1982b. (SG, Part Two)

*Collins, J. S., Maguire, J. J., and Turner, R. M. "Unmet Need: How the Gap Is Filled." *Journal of Student Financial Aid,* 1979, *9* (2), 4-15. (SG, Part Two)

Commission on Higher Education and the Economy of New England. *A Threat to Excellence.* Preliminary Report. Wellesley, Mass.: New England Board of Higher Education, 1982.

Coopers and Lybrand, Inc. *Higher Education Management Letter.* Boston: Coopers and Lybrand, Fall 1981.

Cope, R. G., and Hannah, W. *Revolving College Doors: The Causes and Consequences of Dropping Out, Stopping Out, and Transferring.* New York: Wiley, 1975.

Cravens, D., and others. *Marketing Decision Making Concepts and Strategy.* (Rev. ed.) Homewood, Ill.: Irwin, 1980.

Cunningham, J. J. "The Peer Counselor: A Possible Solution to Two Problems in Financial Aid Administration." *Journal of Student Financial Aid,* 1981, *11* (1), 22-24.

*Davis, J. S., and Van Dusen, W. D. *Guide to the Literature of Student Financial Aid.* New York: College Entrance Examination Board, 1978. (SG, General Works)

Dejarnett, R. P. "The Organization of Student Support Programs in Institutions of Higher Learning." In R. Keene, F. C. Adams, and J. E. King (Eds.), *Money, Marbles, or Chalk: Student Financial Support in Higher Education.* Carbondale: Southern Illinois University Press, 1975.

Delaney, F. H., and others. "A Taxonomy of Objectives for the Training of Financial Aid Administrators." *Journal of Student Financial Aid,* 1974, *4* (3), 5-12.

De los Santos, A. G., and others. "Mexican-American/Chicano Students in Institutions of Higher Education: Access, Attrition and Achievement." Unpublished paper. Austin: Office for Advanced Research in Hispanic Education, University of Texas, 1980.

Dent, R., and others. *Oregon Student Resources Survey.* Salem, Ore.: Education Coordinating Council, 1973.

Dickmeyer, N., Wessels, J., and Coldren, S. *Institutionally Funded Student Financial Aid.* Washington, D.C.: American Council on Education, 1981.

Doermann, H. "The Future Market for College Education." In *A Role for Marketing in College Admission: Papers Presented at the Colloquium on College Admissions, May 16-18, 1976, at the Abbey on Lake Geneva, Fontana, Wisconsin.* New York: College Entrance Examination Board, 1976.

Edwards, C. T. "Disbursement of Financial Aid Funds: An Alternate Approach." *Journal of Student Financial Aid,* 1978, *8* (2), 12-18.

Edwards, H. T., and Nordin, V. *Higher Education and the Law.* Cambridge, Mass.: Harvard University Press, 1979.

El-Khawas, E. H. *Better Information for Student Choice: Report of a National Task Force.* Washington, D.C.: American Association for Higher Education, 1977.

*El-Khawas, E. *Management of Student Aid: A Guide for Presidents.* Washington, D.C.: American Council on Education, 1979. (SG, Part Three)

*El-Khawas, E. (Ed.). *Special Policy Issues in Management of Student Aid.* Washington, D.C.: American Council on Education, 1980. (SG, Part Three)

*Farmer, J., and others. *A Guide to the Design of Student Financial Aid Systems.* Washington, D.C.: Systems Research, 1978. (SG, Part Three)

Federal Interagency Committee on Education. *Toward a Federal Strategy for Protection of the Consumer of Education.* Washington, D.C.: U.S. Department of Health, Education and Welfare, 1975.

Feingold, S. N., and Feingold, M. *Scholarships, Fellowships and Loans.* Vol. 7. Arlington, Mass.: Bellman, 1982.

Fenske, R. H. *Final Report: Assessment of Training Needs for Arizona Student Financial Aid Practitioners.* Phoenix: Arizona Commission for Postsecondary Education, 1979.

Fenske, R. H. "Current Trends." In U. Delworth, G. R. Hanson, and Associates, *Student Services: A Handbook for the Profession.* San Francisco: Jossey-Bass, 1980a.

Fenske, R. H. "Setting Institutional Goals and Objectives." In P. Jedamus, M. W. Peterson, and Associates, *Improving Academic Management: A Handbook of Planning and Institutional Research.* San Francisco: Jossey-Bass, 1980b.

Fenske, R. H. *Renewing and Developing the Partnership: Federal/State/Campus Cooperation in Student Financial Aid.* Iowa City: American College Testing Program, 1981.

Fenske, R. H., and Boyd, J. D. *State Need-Based College Scholarship and Grant Programs: A Study of Their Development, 1969-1980.* New York: College Entrance Examination Board, 1981.

Fenske, R. H., Boyd, J. D., and Maxey, E. J. "State Financial Aid to Students: A Trend Analysis of Access and Choice of Public or Private Colleges." *College and University,* 1979, *54* (2), 139-155.

Fenske, R. H., and Parker, J. D. "A Model for Institutional Policy Analysis: The Case of Student Financial Aid." Paper presented at the annual forum of the Association for Institutional Research, Minneapolis, May 1981.

*Ferguson, J. L. "College Presidents and Financial Aid Officers." *College Board Review,* 1981, *121,* 3-24. (SG, Part Three)

Fife, J. D. *The College Student Grant Study.* University Park, Pa.: Center for the Study of Higher Education, 1975.

Fox, D. J. *The Research Process in Education.* New York: Holt, Rinehart and Winston, 1969.

*Franklin, P. *Beyond Student Financial Aid: Issues and Options for Strengthening Support Service Programs Under Title IV of the Higher Education Act.* New York: College Entrance Examination Board, 1980. (SG, Part One)

Frantz, T. "Backgrounds of Student Personnel Workers." *Journal of College Student Personnel,* 1969, *10* (3), 193-196.

Freeman, R. B. *The Overeducated American.* New York: Academic Press, 1976.

Friedman, M. "The Higher Schooling in America." *Public Interest,* 1968, *11,* 108-112.

Froomkin, J. *Needed: A New Federal Policy for Higher Education.* Washington, D.C.: Institute for Educational Leadership, George Washington University, 1978.

Gaston, M. "A Study of the Effects of College-Imposed Work-Study Programs on Grade-Point Averages of Selected Students at Western Washington State College." *Journal of Student Financial Aid,* 1973, *3* (1), 19-26.

Giddens, T. R. "The Origins of State Scholarship Programs: 1647-1913." *College and University,* 1970, *46* (1), 37-45.

Gladieux, L. E. "What Has Congress Wrought?" *Change Magazine,* 1980, *12* (7), 25-31.

*Gladieux, L. E., and Hansen, J. S. *The Federal Government, the States and Higher Education: Issues for the 1980s.* New York: College Entrance Examination Board, 1981. (SG, Part One)

*Gladieux, L. E., and Wolanin, T. R. *Congress and the Colleges: The National Politics of Higher Education.* Lexington, Mass.: Lexington Books, 1976. (SG, Part One)

Godzicki, R. J. "A History of Financial Aids in the United States." In R. Keene, F. C. Adams, and J. E. King (Eds.),

Money, Marbles, or Chalk: Student Financial Support in Higher Education. Carbondale: Southern Illinois University Press, 1975.

*Green, K. C. *Access and Opportunity: Government Support for Minority Participation in Higher Education.* Washington, D.C.: American Association for Higher Education, 1982. (SG, Part One)

*Hansen, J. S. *The State Student Incentive Grant Program: An Assessment of the Record and Options for the Future.* New York: College Entrance Examination Board, 1979. (SG, Part One)

Hansen, W. L., and Feeney, S. *New Directions in State Loan Programs for Postsecondary Students: Problems and Policy Alternatives.* New York: College Entrance Examination Board, 1977.

Hartshorn, D. *Do You Need a Computer?* Washington, D.C.: National Association of Student Financial Aid Administrators, 1981.

*Hauptman, A. *Financing Student Loans: The Search for Alternatives in the Face of Federal Contraction.* Washington, D.C.: College Entrance Examination Board, Washington Office, 1982. (SG, Part One)

*Hauptman, A., and Rice, L. D. *Student Grant Assistance in New York State.* New York: College Entrance Examination Board, 1980. (SG, Part One)

*Hearn, J. C. *Equity and Efficiency in the Basic Grants Program: The Case of the "Prior-Year" Proposal.* ACT Research Report, No. 81. Iowa City: American College Testing Program, 1981. (SG, Part Four)

*Heisel, M., and Hensley, M. R. "The Independent Student Dilemma: An Approach Toward Equity Packaging." *Journal of Student Financial Aid,* 1977, 7 (3), 41-46. (SG, Part Two)

*Henry, J. B. (Ed.). *New Directions for Institutional Research: The Impact of Student Financial Aid on Institutions,* no. 25. San Francisco: Jossey-Bass, 1980. (SG, General Works)

*Holmes, R. B., and Petersen, L. B. "A Survey of Undergraduate Student Assistance in the State of Michigan." *Journal of Student Financial Aid,* 1980, *10* (1), 18-28. (SG, Part Four)

House Committee on Education and Labor. *Education Amendments of 1980: Report No. 96-52.* Washington, D.C.: U.S. Government Printing Office, 1979.

Hoy, J. C. "The Future of New England's Knowledge-Intensive Economy." *Educational Record,* 1982, *63* (1), 33-36.

Huff, R. P. "No Need Scholarships: What 859 Colleges Said About Granting Money to Students Without Regard to Financial Need." *College Board Review,* 1975, *95,* 13-15.

Huff, R. P. "A Proposal for the Funding of Financial Aid Training in California." Unpublished paper prepared for State Steering Committee on Training, Stanford, Calif., 1981.

Human Resources Network. *How to Get Money for Education.* Radnor, Pa.: Chilton Books, 1975.

Ihlanfeldt, W. "A Management Approach to the Buyer's Market." *Liberal Education,* 1975, *41* (2), 133-148.

Ihlanfeldt, W. *Achieving Optimal Enrollments and Tuition Revenues: A Guide to Modern Methods of Market Research, Student Recruitment, and Institutional Pricing.* San Francisco: Jossey-Bass, 1980a.

Ihlanfeldt, W. *Marketing in College Admissions: A Broadening Perspective.* New York: College Entrance Examination Board, 1980b.

*Illinois State Scholarship Commission. *Annotated Bibliography of Student Financial Aid.* Deerfield: Illinois State Scholarship Commission, 1981. (SG, General Works)

Jencks, C., and Riesman, D. *The Academic Revolution.* New York: Doubleday, 1968.

*Jensen, E. L. "Student Financial Aid and Persistence in College." *Journal of Higher Education,* 1981, *52* (3), 280-294. (SG, Part Four)

Johnson, J. L. "The Guaranteed Student Loan Program: A Survey of State-Level Administration." *Journal of Student Financial Aid,* 1981, *11* (3), 9-15.

Kaplin, W. A. *The Law of Higher Education: Legal Implications of Administrative Decision Making.* San Francisco: Jossey-Bass, 1978.

Kaplin, W. A. *The Law of Higher Education 1980.* San Francisco: Jossey-Bass, 1980.

Kauffman, J. "View from the Top." Paper presented at annual meeting of the National Association of Student Financial Aid Administrators, Dearborn, Mich., July 1982.

*Keene, R., Adams, F. C., and King, J. E. (Eds.). *Money, Marbles, or Chalk: Student Financial Support in Higher Education.* Carbondale: Southern Illinois University Press, 1975. (SG, General Works)

Koontz, H., and others. *Essentials of Management.* (3rd ed.) New York: McGraw-Hill, 1982.

Korn, B. P. *Statistical Concepts for the Social Sciences.* Cambridge, Mass.: Winthrop, 1975.

Kotler, P. *Marketing for Nonprofit Organizations.* Englewood Cliffs, N.J.: Prentice-Hall, 1975.

Kotler, P. *Marketing Management: Analysis, Planning and Control.* (3rd ed.) Englewood Cliffs, N.J.: Prentice-Hall, 1976.

Kurtz, D. *Professional Selling.* (3rd ed.) Plano, Texas: Business Publications, 1982.

Lenning, O. T., Beal, P. E., and Sauer, K. *Retention and Attrition: Evidence for Action and Research.* Boulder, Colo.: National Center for Higher Education Management Systems, 1980.

Lenning, O. T., and Cooper, E. M. *Guidebook for Colleges and Universities: Presenting Information to Prospective Students.* Boulder, Colo.: National Center for Higher Education Management Systems, 1978.

Levine, M. "Corporate Education and Training." Unpublished paper prepared for National Commission on Student Financial Assistance, Washington, D.C., 1982.

McCarthy, J. *Basic Marketing: A Managerial Approach.* (7th ed.) Homewood, Ill.: Irwin, 1981.

*McCormick, J. L. *State Allocation Formulas for Campus-Based Federal Student Aid Programs: A Descriptive Study.* Iowa City: American College Testing Program, 1978. (SG, Part Two)

McKenzie, D. "Student Employment and Persistence." *Journal of Student Financial Aid,* 1981, *11* (2), 38–42.

*Martin, D. *1981–82: A Year in Review.* NASFAA Special Report, No. 4. Washington, D.C.: National Association of Student Financial Aid Administrators, 1982. (SG, Part Four)

Marx, K. *Critique of the Gotha Programme.* Moscow: Progress Publications, 1971. (Originally published 1891.)

Meade, R. C. "The Development and Significance of State Scholarship Programs." *Journal of Student Financial Aid,* 1972, *2* (1), 41-46.

Meigs, W. B., Larsen, E. T., and Meigs, R. F. *Principles of Auditing.* Homewood, Ill.: Irwin, 1977.

Miller, L. "Computer Assisted Financial Aid and Disbursement and Loan Collection." *Journal of Student Financial Aid,* 1975, *5* (3), 27-34.

*Miller, S., Dellefield, W., and Musso, T. *A Guide to Selected Financial Aid Management Practices.* Washington, D.C.: United States Department of Education, 1980. (SG, Part Three)

Moon, R. G. "History of Institutional Financial Aid in the United States." In *Perspectives on Financial Aid.* New York: College Entrance Examination Board, 1975.

*Moore, D. R. "Certification of Financial Aid Professionals." *Journal of Student Financial Aid,* 1975, *5* (3), 15-20. (SG, Part Three)

Morris, T. "A Report on the Financial Aid Internship Program at the California State College, Fullerton." *Journal of Student Financial Aid,* 1972, *2* (1), 35-40.

Musgrave, R. A., and Musgrave, P. B. *Public Finance in Theory and Practice.* (3rd ed.) New York: McGraw-Hill, 1980.

*National Association of College and University Business Officers. *Management of Student Aid.* Washington, D.C.: National Association of College and University Business Officers, 1979. (SG, Part Two)

National Association of College and University Business Officers. *Managing Student Financial Aid: Techniques for Business and Fiscal Officers.* The Business Officer's Guide to Student Aid, monograph 1. Washington, D.C.: U.S. Department of Education, Office of Student Financial Assistance/ Student Financial Assistance Training Program, 1981.

National Association of State Scholarship and Grant Programs. *Thirteenth Annual Survey.* Harrisburg, Pa.: National Association of State Scholarship and Grant Programs, 1981.

*National Association of Student Financial Aid Administrators. *Characteristics and Attitudes of the Financial Aid Adminis-

trator: A Report on the 1977 Survey of the Profession. Washington, D.C.: National Association of Student Financial Aid Administrators, 1978a. (SG, Part Three)

National Association of Student Financial Aid Administrators. *Training Modules: Professional Development Phase, Management Planning Phase, Need Analysis Phase, Awarding Phase, Record Maintenance Phase, Student Relations Phase.* Washington, D.C.: National Association of Student Financial Aid Administrators, 1978b.

National Association of Student Financial Aid Administrators. *Financial Aid Support Staff Training Guide.* Washington, D.C.: National Association of Student Financial Aid Administrators, 1979.

National Association of Student Financial Aid Administrators. *1979 SSFATP Summaries and 1980 SSFATP Summaries.* Washington, D.C.: National Association of Student Financial Aid Administrators, 1980.

National Association of Student Financial Aid Administrators. *Fundamental Financial Aid Self-Learning Guide.* Washington, D.C.: National Association of Student Financial Aid Administrators, 1981.

National Association of Student Financial Aid Administrators. *Guide for the Development of a Policies and Procedures Manual.* Washington, D.C.: National Association of Student Financial Aid Administrators, 1982a.

National Association of Student Financial Aid Administrators. *Institutional Guide for Financial Aid Self-Evaluation.* (5th ed.) Washington, D.C.: National Association of Student Financial Aid Administrators, 1982b.

*National Association of Student Financial Aid Administrators. *Student Financial Aid: An Investment in America's Future.* Washington, D.C.: National Association of Student Financial Aid Administrators, 1982c. (SG, Part One)

National Association of Student Financial Aid Administrators. *A Guide to Evaluating and Acquiring Financial Aid Software.* Washington, D.C.: National Association of Student Financial Aid Administrators, 1983.

National Center for Education Statistics. *Part-Time Financial*

Aid Counselors in Institutions of Higher Education. Washington, D.C.: National Center for Education Statistics, 1977.

National Commission on the Financing of Postsecondary Education. *Financing Postsecondary Education in the United States.* Washington, D.C.: U.S. Government Printing Office, 1973.

*National Task Force on Student Aid Problems. *Draft Final Report.* Brookdale, Calif.: National Task Force on Student Aid Problems, 1975. (SG, Part Two)

Nelson, J. E. "Research That I Can or Should Do." Paper presented at annual meeting of College Entrance Examination Board, New York, Oct. 1978.

*Nelson, S. C. *Community Colleges and Their Share of Student Financial Assistance.* Washington, D.C.: College Entrance Examination Board, Washington Office, 1980. (SG, Part One)

New Jersey Commission on Financing Postsecondary Education. *The Needs and Resources of Undergraduate Students in Postsecondary Education in the State of New Jersey, 1974-75.* Princeton: New Jersey Commission on Financing Postsecondary Education, 1976.

O'Hearne, J. "Financial Aid Office Management." *Journal of Student Financial Aid,* 1973, *3* (2), 27-33.

*Olivas, M. A. *Financial Aid: Access and Packaging Policies for Disadvantaged Students.* Palo Alto, Calif.: Institute for Research on Educational Finance and Governance, Stanford University, 1981. (SG, Part Two)

*Pantages, T. J., and Creedon, C. F. "Studies of College Attrition: 1950-1975." *Review of Educational Research,* 1978, *48* (1), 57-72. (SG, Part Four)

*Parish, H. C. "Professional Associations—Genesis and Development." In R. Keene, F. C. Adams, and J. E. King (Eds.), *Money, Marbles, or Chalk: Student Financial Support in Higher Education.* Carbondale: Southern Illinois University Press, 1975. (SG, Part Three)

Pascarella, E. T., and Terenzini, P. T. "Student-Faculty Informal Contact and College Persistence: A Further Investigation." *Journal of Educational Research,* 1979, *72* (4), 214–218.

*Pennell, K. "Computerized Financial Aid Operations: Points to Consider Before Committing to Increased Utilization of Computer Systems." *Journal of Student Financial Aid,* 1981, *11* (1), 4–9. (SG, Part Three)

Pennsylvania Higher Education Assistance Agency. *Student Resources Survey No. 2.* Harrisburg: Pennsylvania Higher Education Assistance Agency, 1976a.

Pennsylvania Higher Education Assistance Agency. *A Survey of Plans for Education and Careers of Pennsylvania High School Seniors, Fall, 1975.* Harrisburg: Pennsylvania Higher Education Assistance Agency, 1976b.

*Pernal, M. "Efficiency and Accountability: A Computer-Assisted Financial Aid Operation for the Small College." *Journal of Student Financial Aid,* 1977, 7 (3), 47–55. (SG, Part Three)

Petersen, L., and Holmes, R. B. "Statewide Financial Aid Administrators Training—Phase One." *Journal of Student Financial Aid,* 1980, *10* (3), 22–32.

Petersen, L., Tatum, J., and Winegar, M. "Michigan Student Financial Aid Office Salary and Staffing Patterns." *Journal of Student Financial Aid,* 1977, 7 (1), 5–16.

*Petersen, L., and others. "Student Peer Counseling in Financial Aid." *Journal of Student Financial Aid,* 1978, *8* (3), 35–42. (SG, Part Two)

Phillips, J. P. *Preliminary Report of DHEW/USOE Task Force on Management of Student Assistance Programs.* Washington, D.C.: U.S. Government Printing Office, 1973.

Potter, D. A., and Sidar, A. G., Jr. *No Need/Merit Awards.* New York: College Entrance Examination Board, 1978.

President's Commission on Higher Education. *Higher Education for American Democracy.* (6 vols.) Washington, D.C.: U.S. Government Printing Office, 1947.

Proia, N. C., and Di Gaspari, V. *Barron's Handbook of American College Financial Aid.* (3rd ed.) Woodbury, N.Y.: Barron's Educational Series, 1978.

Rackham, H. (Trans.) *Aristotle's Nicomachean Ethics.* Cambridge, Mass.: Harvard University Press, 1968.

Ramist, L. *College Student Attrition and Retention.* New York: College Entrance Examination Board, 1981.

Rawls, J. *A Theory of Justice.* Cambridge, Mass.: Harvard University Press, 1971.

Reilley, R., and Cauthern, I. "The Literature of College Student Personnel—A Sample." *Journal of College Student Personnel,* 1976, *17* (5), 363-367.

Rescher, N. *Distributive Justice: A Constructive Critique of the Utilitarian Theory of Distribution.* Indianapolis: Bobbs-Merrill, 1966.

Robinson, M. "Staffing of Student Financial Aid Offices: Review of a Formula Budgeting Approach." Unpublished paper, Long Beach, Calif., May 1981.

Rudley, S. *Financial Aid Peer Counseling Manual.* Washington, D.C.: Coalition of Independent College and University Students, 1980.

Rudolph, F. *The American College and University.* New York: Knopf, 1962.

Russo, J. "Off-Campus College Work-Study: An Alternative Approach." *Journal of Student Financial Aid,* 1972, *2* (2), 13-18.

Sandage, C. *Advertising Theory and Practice.* (10th ed.) Homewood, Ill.: Irwin, 1979.

Sanford, T. R. "Financial Aid Fallout." *College Board Review,* 1981, *121,* 9, 25.

Scott, R. A. "Beleaguered Yeomen: Comments on the Condition of Collegiate Middle-Managers." *College and University,* 1979, *54* (2), 89-95.

*Smith, M. K. (Ed.). *Profiles of State Student Financial Aid Programs.* (2 vols.) Denver: Education Commission of the States; Boulder, Colo.: National Center for Higher Education Management Systems, 1980. (SG, Part Four)

Smith, R. E. "The Training of Financial Aid Administrators." *Journal of College Student Personnel,* 1964, *6* (2), 90-94.

Spady, W. G. "Dropouts from Higher Education: An Interdisciplinary Review and Synthesis." *Interchange,* 1970, *1* (1), 64-85.

Spady, W. G. "Dropouts from Higher Education: Toward an Empirical Model." *Interchange,* 1971, *2* (3), 38-62.

*Stampen, J. O. *Student Aid and Public Higher Education: A Progress Report.* Washington, D.C.: American Association of State Colleges and Universities, 1983. (SG, Part One)

Stark, J. S. *Inside Information: A Handbook on Better Information for Student Choice.* Washington, D.C.: American Association for Higher Education, 1978.

State of California, Office of Governor. *Governor's Task Force Study on Higher Education: Student Financial Aid.* Sacramento: State of California, Office of Governor, May 1971.

Stegura, D., and Olsen, L. "Students Counsel Students in Financial Aid Offices." *College Board Review,* 1978, *106,* 17-23.

Student Financial Assistance Study Group. *Report to the Secretary: Recommendations for Improved Management of the Federal Student Aid Programs.* Washington, D.C.: U.S. Department of Health, Education and Welfare, 1977.

Tarpey, O., and others. *A Preface to Marketing Management.* Plano, Texas: Business Publications, 1979.

Thurow, L. "America in the 1980s: Thurow's Third Way." *The Economist,* 1982, *282,* 29-32.

Tombaugh, R. L., and Heinrich, K. R. *Final Report: Research on Part-Time Campus Student Financial Aid Personnel.* Washington, D.C.: Educational Methods, 1977.

Trautman, W. T. "Who Should Work?" Memo to Directors of Student Financial Aid. Washington, D.C.: Bureau of Higher Education, U.S. Office of Education, 1970.

Trewatha, R., and Newport, M. *Management: Functions and Behavior.* Dallas: Business Publications, 1979.

United States Department of Education. *Audit Guide: Campus-Based Student Financial Aid Programs.* Washington, D.C.: U.S. Department of Education, 1980a.

United States Department of Education. *Reaching Students: Student Views on Communication About Financial Aid.*

Final Report of the Third Student-Commissioner Conference on Financial Aid and Access to Postsecondary Education. Washington, D.C.: U.S. Department of Education, 1980b.

United States Department of Education. *Audit Guide: Pell Grants.* Washington, D.C.: U.S. Department of Education, 1981a.

United States Department of Education. *Federal Student Financial Aid Handbook.* Washington, D.C.: U.S. Department of Education, 1981b.

United States Office of Education. *Educational Opportunity Grant Manual.* Washington, D.C.: U.S. Office of Education, 1966.

*Van Dusen, W. D. *The Coming Crisis in Student Aid: Report of the 1978 Aspen Institute Conference on Student Aid Policy.* New York: Aspen Institute for Humanistic Studies, 1979. (SG, Part One)

Van Dusen, W. D. "The Handyperson's Guide to Student Aid Research." In S. Binder (Ed.), *New Directions for Student Services: Responding to Changes in Financial Aid Programs,* no. 12. San Francisco: Jossey-Bass, 1980.

Van Dusen, W. D., Higginbotham, H. F., and Jacobson, E. C. *The CSS Guide to Implementing Financial Aid Data Processing Systems.* New York: College Entrance Examination Board, 1980.

*Van Dusen, W. D., and O'Hearne, J. J. *A Design for a Model College Financial Aid Office.* (3rd ed.) New York: College Entrance Examination Board, 1980. (Originally published 1968; 2nd ed., 1973.) (SG, Part Three)

Wedemeyer, R. H. "Computerizing Student Financial Aid." *Journal of Student Financial Aid,* 1978, *8* (1), 23-28.

Wenc, L. M. "The Role of Financial Aid in Attrition and Retention." *College Board Review,* 1977, *104,* 17-21.

Wilson, J. *Federal Campus-Based Student Aid: A Study of the Recipients and of the Possible Effects of Proposed Budgetary Changes.* Phoenix: Arizona Commission on Postsecondary Education, 1981.

Windham, D. M. *Education, Equality, and Income Distribution: A Study of Public Higher Education.* Lexington, Mass.: Heath, 1970.

Working Group on Military Service. *Toward a Consensus on Military Service.* Washington, D.C.: Atlantic Council of the United States, 1982.

Index

179, 183, 189; eligibility for, 40, 44; in federal program, 3, 29, 44, 45, 48, 52, 377, 402; and marketing, 314; and need analysis, 128, 133, 137; and office organization, 243, 247, 249; and packaging, 167; problems with, 40-41, 49; and staffing, 201, 203, 205-207; and state programs, 62-66; and trends, 422, 423, 424, 425
Gulf South Conference v. *Boyd*, 365

Handsome v. *Rutgers University*, 363
Hannah, W., 340-341, 342, 346, 477
Hansen, J. S., 70, 444-445, 446-447, 479, 480
Hansen, W. L., 63, 480
Hartman, R. W., 26
Hartshorn, D., 228-229, 230, 236, 480
Harvard University: and attrition, 407; financial aid office at, 222; first scholarship fund at, ix, 78
Hauptman, A., 71, 433, 447-448, 480
Haverford College, in legal case, 364
Hawaii: aid program in, 59; guaranteed loans in, 65; index of effort in, 72
Health Professions Educational Assistance Act of 1963, 11
Health Professions Student Loan Program, 189
Hearn, J. C., 468, 480
Heinrich, K. R., 208, 488
Heisel, M., 454, 480
Henning, G. E., xviii, 282, 307-329
Henry, J. B., 26, 439-440, 480
Hensley, M. R., 454, 480
Higginbotham, H. F., 257, 276, 277, 280, 489
Higher Education Act of 1965: in bibliography, 443, 444; in federal program, x, 2, 376, 377, 401, 425; legal aspects of, 348-349, 357, 358-359; provisions of, 11-12, 29, 33, 35, 39; Title IV of, 11, 51-53, 62, 120, 152, 153, 160-162, 183, 184, 187, 240, 249, 272, 380

Higher Education Assistance Foundation, and guaranteed loans, 65
Higher Education Facilities Act of 1963, 11
Hispanic students, aid to, 17-18, 456
Hollerith, H., 275
Holmes, R. B., 211, 215, 468, 480, 486
Horizontal equity, in need analysis, 126, 132, 134
House Committee on Education and Labor, ix-x, 12, 51, 481
Howard Savings Inst. of Newark v. *Peep*, 358
Hoy, J. C., 413, 481
Huff, R. P., xiii-xix, 3-4, 77-93, 192-193, 212, 237-257, 283-284, 371-398, 481
Human capital: agenda for, 410-418; corporate role in, 414-416; and manpower issue, 411-414; and military needs, 416-417; and national service, 417-418
Human Resources Network, 89, 93, 481

Idaho: aid program in, 59, 74; index of effort in, 72
Ihlanfeldt, W., 315, 318, 329, 481
Illinois: administrators surveyed in, 310; aid program in, 57, 58, 59, 73, 74, 375; early aid program in, 6, 9; grants in, 69, 70; index of effort in, 72; information dissemination in, 102; legal case in, 364; literature on student aid in, 436-437
Illinois State Scholarship Commission (ISSC), 17, 76, 308, 310, 436-437, 438, 481
In re Estate of Hall, 357
In re Estate of McClain, 357
In re Goeb, 363
In re Mendoza, 362
In re Terry, 363
Income supplement, in need analysis, 133-134
Indiana: administrators surveyed in, 310; aid program in, 59; grants in, 70, index of effort in, 72
Indiana University, and staff training, 213

Individual Education Account (IEA), 426
Individual Retirement Accounts (IRA), 129-130, 426
Inflation, impact of, 23
Information dissemination: analysis of, 99-115; with awards, 111-112; background on, 99-100; bibliography for, 122-123, 453; to enrolled students, 110-111; to families of students, 113-114; to high school counselors, 114-115, 458-459; legislative amendments on, 104-106; and marketing, 107-108; overview of, 379-380; publications for, 108-109, 110; research findings on, 100-104; to students, 106-114
Institutional aid: amount of, 77, 374; defined, 77; employment as, 78, 88-89; flexibility of, 80, 314; and marketing, 393; redeployment of, for retention, 337-338; from restricted funds, 81-87; sources and uses of, 80-89, 374-375; for tuition and fees increases, 87-88; unrestricted funds for, 87-89
Institutional mission: analysis of student aid in relation to, 281-370; background on, 281-284; bibliography for, 464-470; and evaluation, 261-262, 279; and financial aid office, 225, 235; and marketing, 307-329; and packaging, 163-164; and research, 285-306; and retention, 330-346; student aid used for, 390-394; trends in, 430-432
Institutional studies office, and financial aid research, 292-293, 295
Institutions: acceptance of aid by, 348-354; dilemma of, 331; eligibility of, legal aspects of, 365; and federal programs, 30, 46-47; guidelines for, 431-432; packaging policy of, 153-154, 164-166; preservation of, and state aid, 24; private, 247-248, 350, 428, 442; records of, for disbursements, 187-189; rules and policies of,

353-354; and state programs, 74-75; student aid importance to, 372-374
Internal Revenue Service, 129, 131, 359
Iowa: administrators surveyed in, 310; aid program in, 59; grants in, 70; index of effort in, 72; information dissemination in, 102-103

Jacobson, E. C., 257, 276, 277, 280, 489
Japan: electronics engineers in, 411
Javits, J., 69, 70
Jefferson Law Book Company, 369
Jencks, C., 342, 481
Jensen, E. L., 337, 469, 481
Johnson, J. L., 64, 76, 481
Johnson administration, 2, 29, 33, 401, 425
Johnstone, D. B., xviii, 192-193, 237-257
Jossey-Bass Inc., Publishers, 26, 436

Kansas: aid program in, 59; grants in, 70; index of effort in, 72
Kaplin, W. A., 370, 481
Kauffman, J., 293, 482
Keene, R., 88, 93, 440, 472, 482
Kennedy administration, 401
Kentucky: administrators surveyed in, 310; aid program in, 59; index of effort in, 72; information dissemination in, 112
Keppel, F., 62, 155
Keppel Committee. See National Task Force on Student Aid Problems
Kerr, C., 433
King, J. E., 440, 482
Klaven, H., Jr., 148, 473
Koldus, J., 279-280
Koontz, H., 226, 236, 482
Korn, B. P., 300, 482
Kotler, P., 307, 328, 482
Kramer, M., 25
Kurtz, D., 329, 482

Land-Grant College Act of 1862, 7, 10, 13
Lange, M. L., xvii, 192, 221-236

and federal programs, x, 38, 42, 402, 422, 425, 428; and staffing, 199

Midwest Association of Student Financial Aid Administrators, and staff training, 213

Military needs, and human capital, 416-417

Miller, L., 173, 483

Miller, S., 236, 461, 483

Minnesota: administrators surveyed in, 310; aid program in, 59; grants in, 70; index of effort in, 72; legal case in, 355

Minority students: in bibliography, 441, 456; impact of aid on, 15-21; issues of, 20-21; kinds of institutions attended by, 18-19; as late applicants, 161; and loans, 424; participation rates of, 16-18; persistence by, 19

Mississippi: aid program in, 59; index of effort in, 72; legal case in, 357

Missouri: administrators surveyed in, 310; aid program in, 59; grants in, 70; index of effort in, 72; legal case in, 361

Montana: aid program in, 59; index of effort in, 72

Moon, R. G., 7, 25, 483

Moore, D. R., 462, 483

Moore, J. W., xvii, 2-3, 27-54

Morrill Act, 7, 10, 13

Morris, T., 209-210, 483

Mowlson, A., ix, 78

Musgrave, P. B., 148, 483

Musgrave, R. A., 148, 483

Musso, T., 236, 461, 483

National Association of College and University Attorneys, 369

National Association of College and University Business Officers (NACUBO), 483; and disbursement, 174, 180-181, 183, 185; and legal issues, 369; management system of, 262-263, 455; and office relationships, 256; and packaging, 157-159; and staff training, 213

National Association of State Schol-

arship and Grant Programs (NASSGP), 3, 59n, 60, 68, 71, 74n, 76, 405n, 436, 483

National Association of State Universities and Land-Grant Colleges, 71

National Association of Student Financial Aid Administrators (NASFAA), xv, 3, 483-484; commissions of, 218; Committee on Institutional Management Services of, 233; and disbursement, 174, 185, 187, 188, 189-190; and evaluation, 264-265, 280; and information dissemination, 112; and legal issues, 369; and management, 263, 457; and office organization, 225, 236; and packaging, 157, 160-162, 168; as publisher, 436, 437, 438, 448-449, 469; and research, 287; and staffing, 206, 213, 214, 215, 216, 217, 218, 219-220, 462, 463; Title IV Committee of, 160-162

National Center for Education Statistics, 208, 484-485

National Center for Higher Education Management Systems, 122

National Collegiate Athletic Association (NCAA), and legal cases, 355, 364-365

National Commission on the Financing of Postsecondary Education, 10, 485

National Defense Act of 1916, 10

National Defense Education Act of 1958 (Public Law 85-864): and federal programs, x, 10, 28-29, 30, 44, 48, 376, 377, 401; and financial aid offices, 221, 240; Title II of, 31

National Defense Student Loan. *See* National Direct Student Loan

National Direct Student Loan (NDSL): amounts from, 404-406; analysis of, 31-33; in bibliography, 442, 455; and defaults, 32-33, 49-50, 267, 268, 359, 369; and disbursement, 177-178, 188, 189; eligibility for, 31; establishment of, 29; and evalua-